The Muslim Brotherhood

The Muslim Brotherhood is one of the most influential Islamist organisations in the world today. Based in Egypt, its network includes branches in many countries of the Near and Middle East. Although the organisation has been linked to political violence in the past, it now proposes a politically moderate ideology.

This book provides an in-depth analysis of the Muslim Brotherhood during the years of al-Hudaybi's leadership, and how he sought to steer the organisation away from the radical wing, inspired by Sayyid Qutb, into the more moderate Islamist organisation it is today. It is his legacy which eventually fostered the development of non-violent political ideas.

During the years of persecution, 1954 to 1971, radical and moderate Islamist ideas emerged within the Brotherhood's midst. Sayyid Qutb's ideas inspired a radical wing evolved which subsequently fed into radical Islamist networks as we know them today. Yet, it was during the same period that al-Hudaybi and his followers proposed a moderate political interpretation, which was adopted by the Brotherhood and which forms its ideological basis today.

Barbara H.E. Zollner is presently a Lecturer in Islamic Studies at Birkbeck College. She is also engaged as a BRISMES Network Coordinator on Faith, Society and Politics.

Routledge Studies in Political Islam

The Flourishing of Islamic Reformism in Iran
Political Islamic groups in Iran (1941–61)
Seyed Mohammad Ali Taghavi

The Political Thought of Sayyid Qutb
The theory of Jahiliyyah
Sayed Khatab

The Power of Sovereignty
The political and ideological philosophy of Sayyid Qutb
Sayed Khatab

Islam and Political Reform in Saudi Arabia
The quest for political change and reform
Mansoor Jassem Alshamsi

Democracy in Islam
Sayed Khatab and Gray D. Bouma

The Muslim Brotherhood
Hasan al-Hudaybi and ideology
Barbara H.E. Zollner

The Muslim Brotherhood

Hasan al-Hudaybi and ideology

Barbara H. E. Zollner

LONDON AND NEW YORK

First published 2009
by Routledge
2 Park Square, Milton Park, Abingdon, Oxon, OX14 4RN

Simultaneously published in the USA and Canada
by Routledge
711 Third Avenue, New York, NY 10017

Routledge is an imprint of the Taylor & Francis Group, an informa business

First issued in paperback 2011

Typeset in by
Exeter Premedia Services, India.

British Library Cataloguing in Publication Data
A catalogue record for this book is available from the British Library

Library of Congress Cataloging in Publication Data
A catalog record for this book has been requested

ISBN10: 0-415-43557-9 (hbk)
ISBN10: 0-415-66417-9 (pbk)
ISBN10: 0-203-88843-X (ebk)

ISBN 13: 978-0-415-43557-4 (hbk)
ISBN 13: 978-0-415-66417-2 (pbk)
ISBN 13: 978-0-203-88843-8 (ebk)

In memory of my father, Alfred Zollner.

Contents

Acknowledgements

The core of this book was initially submitted as a PhD thesis in Near and Middle East Studies at the School of Oriental and African Studies, University of London. I remember my time as student there with fondness and enthusiasm, but also one of great challenges and hard work. My supervisor, Dr Kate Zebiri, helped me on this journey and deserves to be mentioned first. I also want to thank fellow students and colleagues, some of whom became life-long friends. Amongst them are Dr Judith Fox, Dr Richard Fox and Dr Paul Tremlett. During the writing process I had the opprotunity to go on fieldwork. My time in Egypt would not have been as successful if Brother Dr Kamal El-Helbawi had not helped to arrange meetings and interviews.

After submitting the thesis, I had some time for more research and to rethink some of my arguments. It was during this time that Dr Ahmad Achtar, my former colleague at Birkbeck College and one of my closest friends, helped me with his amazing knowledge of books and sources. I thank him and his wife, Dr Nouha Khalifa, for the many coffees and chats. In the same vein, I want to mention Dr Reza Hajatpour, who has been an amazing friend for the past 20 years. I would not have started studying Islamic Studies if it had not been for him. Special thanks also to Anne Corkery for reading through drafts again and again; I probably would not have been able to meet deadlines if it were not for her accuracy and support. My thanks also to Professor Gwen Griffith-Dickson for being a mentor, colleague and friend. I hope we will work on many good projects in the future. Above all, I must thank Stefanie Lang, who listened to me, helped me to organise myself and urged me on whenever I was about to give up.

Introduction

Hasan Isma'il al-Hudaybi led the Society of the Muslim Brotherhood during a time of crisis and dissolution. Succeeding Hasan al-Banna', who was the founder and first leader of the organisation, al-Hudaybi was to be its head for more than twenty years. During his leadership he faced severe criticism from fellow Brothers. Following the Revolution of July 1952, he was pitted against the antagonism of 'Abd al-Nasir, who became increasingly influential in the council of leading Free Officers. 'Abd al-Nasir's determination to thwart the cause of the Brotherhood and its influence on society was part of his path to absolute rule.

Considering the significance of al-Hudaybi's years as leader of the Muslim Brotherhood, it is surprising that there is little scholarly work on the subject. When taking into account that his moderate ideas continue to have a strong influence on the policy and attitude of today's Muslim Brotherhood, e.g. his conciliatory position towards the state system and his refutation of radical ideas, the fact that so little attention is paid to his writing is even more startling. Certainly, there has been interest in the Muslim Brotherhood. There are quite extensive studies available on Hasan al-Banna': the founder and first leader of the Muslim Brotherhood has been described as a model figure of Islamic campaigning; others depict him as the originator of threatening political activism in the name of Islam. There has been even more interest in the ideas of Sayyid Qutb; some see him as the ideologue of Islamist radicalism, whose concepts trained extremist groups; others describe him as a victim of state persecution who developed a theology of liberation in reaction to his maltreatment. No doubt, it is important to examine the work of these thinkers in order to understand currents of Islamist ideology and Islamist movements. Whatever the verdict on al-Banna' and Qutb, it is a fact that certain ideas of the two thinkers have been incorporated into the modern-day Muslim Brotherhood. However, this focus has led to an incorrect perception that the Islamic movement is necessarily radical in its thinking and/or militant in its deeds, an assumption which has, in recent years, been questioned by a number of scholars, among them John L. Esposito, Fred Halliday, François Burgat, and Gudrun Krämer.[1] The following study of Egypt's Muslim Brotherhood under the leadership of Hasan al-Hudaybi will form an addition to these theses, addressing and reassessing the viewpoint that political Islam is a monolithic block, all in all disposed towards violent means.

There are reasons why al-Hudaybi is hardly mentioned in the literature on the Muslim Brotherhood. The first that comes to mind is the observation that Islamist movements are, by definition, seen as fundamentally radical, anti-democratic and anti-Western. This reasoning questions any distinction between moderate Islamism and its radical counterpart. The argument goes that both have the objective of establishing an Islamic state system, that they both aim to replace existing secular governance and that they therefore differ only in the degree of their methods, but not in principle. This book, however, clearly joins the scholarly circle on political Islam, which identifies arguments such as these as neo-Orientalist. As Esposito shows, this approach to political Islam is based on what he terms 'secular fundamentalism'.

The external view of political Islam is focused primarily on radical thought, and this may be due to the creation, on the part of power politics, of a fear of Islam as a religion, which is different, strange and seemingly in opposition to Western thought. Alternatively, it may be because radical or even militant groups are constantly appearing in the media by reason of their actions. In fact, militant Islamists actually seek such publicity. While radical thought and militant action make it necessary to study extremist groups, the focus on terrorism in the name of Islam marginalises moderate Islamists. It also makes it difficult to explain the differences between radical and moderate Islamism. In effect, the scholarly focus on radical or militant groups reinforces the generally negative public perception of Islam in the West.

A further reason why al-Hudaybi in particular has not been studied by Western scholars has to do with the internal affairs of the Brotherhood. It is astonishing that his name is not mentioned much by the writers of the Muslim Brotherhood itself. There is no simple explanation for this. One reason may be that members particularly stress their sympathies for al-Banna', depicting him as an ideal leader who died for his activist convictions. However, as many Brothers endured imprisonment, hard labour and even torture inside 'Abd al-Nasir's prisons and camps, their personal histories have resulted in a dearth of discourse on Hasan al-Hudaybi. Thus, there is a tendency to remember al-Hudaybi's period of leadership as a time of near defeat and destruction. Still, the experiences of the persecuted are caught in the ambiguous relationship between forgetting and reappraisal. Many personal accounts of the time have been published since the mid 1970s,[2] narrating stories of torture and stressing steadfastness of faith. Only a few of the books written by Muslim Brothers take a broader approach, which includes discussion of a crisis within the organisation and of al-Hudaybi's part therein. Those authors who do tackle this issue not only reveal the society's weak position vis-à-vis 'Abd al-Nasir, but also expose signs of disintegration within the Muslim Brotherhood.[3] This has led to differing attitudes towards al-Hudaybi, with most portraying him as an incompetent leader lacking the charismatic personality of his predecessor, al-Banna'. In particular, he was accused of not commanding the authority to bring together the different wings of the Muslim Brotherhood or to adopt a strong position in relation to the authoritarian state system. In the latter view lies an ambiguity, for it would appear to show al-Hudaybi not just as a failure, but also as a victim of the political situation. Finally, these accounts reveal an ideological gap which opened at the beginning of the period of persecution in 1954. To a certain extent, Sayyid Qutb filled this gap. During his imprisonment he developed a radical approach, rejecting the then state system as illegitimate and 'un-Islamic'. In developing a revolutionary concept and explaining thereby the reasons underlying the persecution, he turned the condition of victimisation into one of pride. Thus, he gave many imprisoned Muslim Brothers, particularly young members, an ideology that they could hold on to.

It has to be said that al-Hudaybi did not react decisively to the situation of internal crisis and dissolution. Indeed, to a certain extent his indecisiveness triggered this situation. This was especially obvious during the period of persecution (1954–71), when he omitted to provide any guidelines to help in overcoming the feeling hopelessness ushered in by 'Abd al-Nasir's mass imprisonments. His reaction to the radical ideas which flourished in the prisons and camps among certain, especially young, members came fairly late. Even then, his scholarly and juridical argumentation did not have the same sweeping effect as Sayyid Qutb's writings. In 1969, al-Hudaybi proposed a moderate concept in his writing *Du'at la Qudat (Preachers not Judges)*.[4] This writing, which was secretly distributed among fellow Brothers, is considered the first substantial refutation of Sayyid Qutb's ideas.[5] Qutb, who was hanged in 1966, was by then considered to be a martyr, his thoughts already having a considerable influence. This does not mean that the majority of Muslim Brothers did not pursue a moderate approach, but the lack of guidelines left them voiceless and reinforced the perception of al-Hudaybi as a weak leader.

Nevertheless, al-Hudayb'is moderate thought had an impact on his fellow Muslim Brothers. After the general amnesty of 1971, al-Hudaybi played a major part in the re-establishment of the organisation. Although he died in 1973, his moderate and conciliatory ideas continued to be relevant. The fact that close companions such as Muhammad Hamid Abu Nasr, 'Umar al-Tilmisani and Muhammad Mashhur, who died recently, succeeded him as leaders shows the continuance of his thought. Furthermore, his son Ma'mun al-Hudaybi has played a major role in his capacity as the Brotherhood's secretary and spokesman. Another reason why his thinking became important lies in the changed attitude towards the Muslim Brotherhood since Anwar al-Sadat's presidency. Al-Sadat, who succeeded 'Abd al-Nasir, released the imprisoned Brothers and offered the organisation a half-legal though not officially recognised status. A period of reorganisation (1971–77) followed, during which the government lifted the censorship of books written by Muslim Brothers. Many memoirs of formerly imprisoned members were published, such as Zaynab al-Ghazali's account or al-Hudaybi's book *Du'at la Qudat (Preachers not Judges)*. Dealing with the past, these books did not merely preserve the memory of the cruelties of 'Abd al-Nasir's persecution. Al-Sadat followed his own agenda when he allowed these publications to fill the market; this was a deliberate political stratagem, implying a change of direction and aimed at distancing the new government from the old. The posthumous publication of al-Hudaybi's writings was not merely aimed at providing ideological guidance to the Muslim Brothers; they were distributed because of their statements against radical thought, and were thus used to address a new and rising problem, namely the establishment of Islamist groups, which began to fight actively against the political system in the early 1970s. In these terms, *Du'at la Qudat* remains an important critique of radical thought.

Hasan al-Hudaybi's main aim was to change society, i.e. Egyptian society, which, in his view, was not aware of the political nature of Islamic belief. Thus, real change could only be brought about through creating awareness and by tackling the issue of Islamic identity (as opposed to a Western perception). Only through developing a sense of Islamic consciousness could the ultimate goal of the establishment of an Islamic society be reached. Given this approach, al-Hudaybi refuted revolutionary overthrow, instead preaching gradual development from within. A major point was therefore education and social engagement, as well as participation in the political system, appealing by means of mission (*da'wa*) to the consciousness of the individual believer.

This path of his is now followed by today's Muslim Brotherhood, which endeavours to be recognised as a political party and which influences political decision making by infiltrating the political participatory structures (parliament, administration, non-governmental organisations). This study of the Muslim Brotherhood from the 1950s until the early 1970s, therefore, is not only a piece of research into the modern political history of Egypt and an analysis of a religious ideology, but has also a relationship to current politics.

Structure of the book

The study has three main objectives. First, to present a historical discussion focusing on Hasan al-Hudaybi's years as leader of the Muslim Brotherhood. Second, to show that the ideas of Sayyid Qutb have to be understood with reference to the context of their development. In spite of the fact that his ideas had an impact on the radicalisation of Islamists, the leadership of the Brotherhood, under Hasan al-Hudaybi as its Murshid, took steps to counter a turn towards extremism among the ranks of the organisation. The third objective is to present a detailed interpretative analysis of *Du'at la Qudat*. It is this work which builds the theological basis of the Muslim Brotherhood's ideology since the late 1960s. These overall aims are reflected in the structure of the book.

Chapter 1 presents a description and analysis of the history of the Brotherhood during its most challenging period, from the death of al-Banna' to the short-lived time of cooperation with the revolutionary regime and the years of persecution under 'Abd al-Nasser. Section 1.1 questions the commonly held idea that the Brotherhood's first leader, Hasan al-Banna', had unquestioned authority and control over the movement. In section 1.2 al-Hudaybi's struggle to secure his leadership of the organisation is described. Section 1.3 addresses the Brotherhood's relationship with the Revolutionary Command Council (RCC), which took power in Egypt following the Revolution of 1952. The historical analysis thus investigates al-Hudaybi's role in the initial period of cooperation and his part in the gradual corrosion of that relationship with the state and asks questions with regard to his responsibility for the ensuing time of persecution. Section 1.4 looks at the years of persecution, focusing on the internal networks which linked the imprisoned members of the Brotherhood and enabled scattered cells to communicate with each other. This section also examines the reformation of the Brotherhood and demonstrates how al-Hudaybi and his followers in the Guidance Council regained their authority and how their policies were implemented in the strategies of the Brotherhood from 1971 onwards.

Chapter 2 discusses the dispute within the Muslim Brotherhood during the time of persecution. Section 2.1 engages with Sayyid Qutb's development of ideas, questioning commonly held perceptions such as, for example, that Qutb's work can be reduced to radical thought and that he was the initiator or radical Islamist theology. Section 2.2 examines the content of Qutb's propagandist work *Milestones* and its impact on so-called 'Qutbists', who selectively used ideas implicit in this text to support their radical world-view. The discussion focuses on concepts such as *hakimiyyat Allah* (absolute sovereignty of God) and *jahiliyya* (state of ignorance), which were used to call for *takfir* (charge of apostasy). This line of thought sought to legitimise violent actions against the state, which was regarded as having infringed upon divine power. While Qutb's work had an impact on radical Islamists, he also continued to be admired by politically moderate, mainstream Muslims. This requires us to rethink the relationship between his work and the interpretations of those he inspired.

Chapter 3 presents a critical analysis of the book *Preachers not Judges*. The main aim of this chapter is to explain the use of Muslim theological and juridical arguments which present a refutation of radical thought. Section 3.1 attempts to determine whether the text of *Preachers not Judges* was indeed written by Hasan al-Hudaybi. There is reasonable evidence to suggest that the book may in fact has been written by a circle of trusted companions. Yet, the completed work was distributed in his name and it therefore needs to be assumed that it had his editorial approval. Section 3.2 deals with the most essential question in the refutation of radical ideologies and the concept of *takfir*: the definition of a Muslim and *kafir*, believer and apostate. *Preachers not Judges* presents a minimal definition, and thus one which calls for tolerance. Further, the book returns to classical interpretations, such as that of sin, and considers mitigating circumstances which can be brought forward in defence of a Muslim who has not complied with the rigid definitions of belief. Section 3.3 looks into the issue of defining shari'a law. Whereas the more radical interpreters tend to describe shari'a as a set code of divine law, the book *Preachers not Judges* takes issue with this narrow interpretation, arguing that there is still room within it for decision making. This interpretation thus also allows for legislative changes and legislative input. Section 3.4 analyses notions of an Islamic state as proposed in *Preachers not Judges*. It is striking that the depiction largely follows a classical interpretation of the state, thus reiterating medieval concepts of the caliphate, the function of the leader and his responsibility towards God. The book thus implicitly argues for the re-establishment of the caliphate under the rule of a single authority.

Section 3.5 presents the discussion on whether obedience is mandatory in order to avoid *fitna* (discord) within the community of believers or whether it is the duty of Muslims to take opposition to or even militant action against any form of governance perceived to be un-Islamic. The book permits violent opposition only as an absolutely final resort. Further, it attempts to find some balance in that it calls generally for obedience to the state, but also emphasises the need for appropriate, non-violent opposition.

Primary sources

As already indicated, the interpretative analysis of *Du'at la Qudat* shows that al-Hudaybi's response to the radical thought of his time refers not only to the Qur'an and Sunna, but draws arguments particularly from classical Islamic theology and jurisprudence. It is therefore necessary to describe his stance with reference to secondary sources on these subjects. Since the focus of the book is on the interpretative analysis of *Du'at la Qudat*, it has been impossible to provide a literary review of the large amount of relevant secondary literature.

Regarding the historical account of the Muslim Brotherhood during the years 1951 to 1971, some remarks on the sources are necessary. The majority of primary literature, especially about this period and about al-Hudaybi, is in Arabic, published in Egypt. Many of the sources are written either by members of the Muslim Brotherhood or by people affiliated to the movement. Additionally, other documents, like newspaper articles, governmenl statements and orders, have been consulted. As secondary, scholarly literature, the work of Richard Mitchell, Gilles Kepel as well as Olivier Carré and Gérard Michaud has been of greatest assistance.[6] In particular, Mitchell's scholarly work on the Society of the Muslim Brothers is essential reading for any student interested in the organisation.

Regarding the study of Hasan al-Hudaybi's life, a few further remarks are in order, to show the difficulties encountered when dealing with the source material. There are only a few biographical accounts of Hasan Isma'il al-Hudaybi. These are relatively sparse on information and/or partly tendentious. Additionally, all primary sources and biographical descriptions are in Arabic and, as such, not easily accessible to Western scholars following modern trends in Islam. There are two main biographies: of these, 'Abd Rabbih's *Hasan al-Hudaybi* is the less useful.[7] It is a very tendentious, in parts almost hagiographical, account of al-Hudaybi's life which contains little accurate information and a great, uncritical accumulation of hearsay about the second leader of the Brotherhood, without providing references. Additionally, 'Abd Rabbih's work contains some incorrect details. It is also surprising that parts of this biography match an account by Sayyid Ahmad, who compiled al-Hudaybi's speeches and articles and edited them into a book entitled *al-Islam wa al-Da'iyya* (Islam and Mission).[8] As Sayyid Ahmad's collection was edited in 1977, thus preceding 'Abd Rabbih's book (first published in 1987), it is likely that the latter copied the text, which is not uncommon and is not necessarily considered plagiarism in the Islamic scholarly tradition. The most reliable biographical source is *Hasan al-Hudaybi. Al-imam al-mumtahan* by Jabir

Rizq, who was a member of the Muslim Brotherhood and therefore had first-hand information. The major part of this work consists of a collection of interviews and comments by leading Brothers and other people with whom al-Hudaybi dealt, as well as extracts from shorter writings by the *Murshid*,[9] such as speeches and letters. Still, the compilation has the disadvantage that precise references and dates for sources used are only partially given.

It has to be noted, though, that the scholarly work on the period before the time of persecution, e.g. the research done by Mitchell, draws its information mainly from newspapers and magazines. Here lies the problem; it has to be considered that these sources often reflect a non-independent point of view – this is particularly the case after May/June 1954, when the press was purged and severe censorship was introduced. Moreover, the commentators and journalists may not have had the necessary insight, as internal Brotherhood matters as well as government actions were (presumably) kept secret. Additionally, a change of attitude towards the Muslim Brotherhood should be noted. Articles written shortly before and especially after the assassination attempt on 'Abd al-Nasir in 1954, which refer back to the relations between the Revolutionary Command Council and the Society maintain a very propagandistic tone, accusing the *Ikhwan* of a double game. There may be documents maintained in archives which have not yet been considered. Although these sources will chiefly match the government view, there may be some surprises waiting as Egyptian archives start to release files relating to this time.

There are a number of sources written by members of the Muslim Brotherhood that deal with the time of persecution. Particular attention should be drawn to the works of 'Abd al-Halim, 'Abd al-Khaliq, Shadi, al-Sisi, Ramadan, 'Abd Majid and Ra'if.[10] An extensive scholarly analysis of this 'prison literature' is still awaited. The above-mentioned stress on alternative primary sources, i.e. sources written by members of the Muslim Brotherhood, was deliberate. Generally, the same precautions as in dealing with governmentl or journalistic sources have to be considered and applied – one has to be aware that these accounts present a specific point of view and were written for a certain purpose. Second, the accounts of members of the Muslim Brotherhood writing about this period sometimes contain discrepancies, which makes the analysis difficult. Therefore, specifically in relation to these primary sources, which are mostly memoirs, one must ask which author is able to provide trustworthy and insightful information.

In making these remarks on the use of primary sources I want to draw attention to some fundamental considerations. The intention has been to provide an alternative point of view, tending away from an official version of the history of events, i.e. the version drawn up by the government side of the period, which was then picked up unquestioningly by scholars using government documents and state-censored media sources.[11] By consulting these kinds of primary sources I do not claim to be rewriting the Egyptian history of time; rather, the historical study presented should be seen as an addition to and extension of scholarly work on the movement of the Muslim Brotherhood. The intention is to draw attention to history as it is commonly seen or experienced within the organisation itself.

Therefore, the research does not claim to givprovidee an objective, historical insight; the latter is a project which this author is generally doubtful of.

The aim in providing a historical account is to create a basis for discussion of the theoretical texts. They reflect a theological dispute about the fundamentals of Islamic belief, a dispute that cannot be comprehended outside its historical context, i.e. the political situation in Egypt during this period and the position of the Society of the Muslim Brotherhood.

1 The Muslim Brotherhood during the years 1949–73

1.1 The Brotherhood in disarray: the legacy of Hasan al-Banna'

Hasan al-Banna', who was the founder and first General Guide (*Murshid al-'Amm*) of the Society of the Muslim Brothers (*Jama'at al-Ikhwan al-Muslimin*), is seen by his followers as an example of the combination of religious conviction with moral courage and public engagement. Not only in the past, but even today, followers of the Brotherhood portray his leadership as charismatic and appealing to the masses of believers; they describe his ideology as exemplifying Islamic ideals.[1]

In contrast, Hasan Isma'il al-Hudaybi, who succeeded al-Banna' as *Murshid*, is a much more controversial figure. There are some brothers who put forward rather negative views on his period as leader. Al-Hudaybi's policies in the early 1950s were described as disastrous for the future of the Brotherhood; he was accused of weakness, of failing to unify the organisation in its opposition to the political system and of letting down the Brotherhood in its efforts to contain 'Abd al-Nasir's despotic exertions. Others depict al-Hudaybi's style of taking charge of the Brotherhood as autocratic, not permitting the building of democratic structures.[2] These and other comments about al-Hudaybi's ability resulted in downplaying of his contribution to the history of the Muslim Brotherhood. However, since the late 1990s one can trace instances of reconciling al-Hudaybi's reputation as one of the most important leaders of the first generation. In the same vein, there is a growing recognition that he and his vision of the organisation paved the way for the ideological profile of today's Society of the Muslim Brotherhood.[3] This can be seen in the fact that official statements of the Muslim Brotherhood clearly emphasise non-violence, with an occasional reference to *Du'at la Qudat* (*Preachers not Judges*).[4] Additional evidence for al-Hudaybi's legacy is the fact that successive leaders, such as 'Umar al-Tilmisani, Mustafa al-Mashhur and his son Ma'mun al-Hudaybi, were trusted companions of al-Hudaybi during his prison years.[5] The influence of al-Hudaybi on the subsequent leadership can be measured by the fact that the current *Murshid*, Muhammad Mahdi Akif, also refers to Hasan al-Hudaybi as a major influence on his thinking.[6] Similarly, the now General Secretary Mahmoud Ezzat said that Hasan al-Hudaybi encouraged his followers to read Qutb, but that the Brotherhood 'should follow the rules mentioned in the research "*Preachers not Judges*"'.[7]

The success of the founder, al-Banna', seems to be so pertinent that it was the measure by which his successor Hasan al-Hudaybi was assessed. Not only for this reason is it necessary to engage, albeit briefly, with Hasan al-Banna's legacy. However, it is not the intention here to present a comprehensive history of the rise of the Muslim Brotherhood under al-Banna', since the topic is beyond the scope of this book and because it has already been done elsewhere in greater detail. What is left to be done here is to focus on the historical circumstances of the late 1940s and to ask what impact this context had on the leadership of al-Banna's successor. Considering that the government issued an order of dissolution in December 1948 and that al-Banna' was murdered, it is fair to ask whether the latter's policies were indeed successful. To put it bluntly: did al-Banna', despite his success in building up the Brotherhood and its significance as a political mass movement, fail in the end? Was he really the ultimate example of a leader, or was he the root of a crisis which befell the Brotherhood by 1949? Were political circumstances such that the organisation was made a scapegoat for the failures of an ill-functioning political system? Was the Brotherhood becoming too powerful, too much a competitor for power? Or was the Brotherhood an organisational giant which lacked internal command and structure? These and other questions set the tone for the Brotherhood's prospects after al-Banna'.

The Society of the Muslim Brothers, generally referred to as the Muslim Brotherhood, was established in 1928.[8] Founded by Hasan al-Banna', the organisation developed rapidly from a local circle in Isma'iliyya to an Islamist mass opposition movement.[9] The growth of the Society during the 1930s and up to the late 1940s is remarkable. Although it is difficult to give exact figures, the organisation had an estimated number of 1,700–2,000 branches in 1948, with about 1 million followers and sympathisers in Egypt alone.[10]

Without going into much detail about the various social, economic and political factors contributing to the Brotherhood's evolution from a group which was mainly concerned with educational reform into a religious–political movement, it needs to be emphasised that the failure of the liberal political system contributed much to the Society's ideological and organisational growth.[11] The political system of a constitutional monarchy, which Marsot has described as 'Egypt's liberal experiment', was introduced with that country's declaration of independence on 28 February 1922. During the three decades that followed, national politics was marked by an ongoing internal battle which eventually paved the way for the coup d'etat of 1952. The reasons for the failure of the political system, a failure which became obvious during the course the Second World War and its aftermath, are manifold and are interlinked with the political world scene. To a great extent, however, Egypt's constitutional monarchy was torn apart by competition between the political forces, namely the king, the British, the parliamentary political parties and the growing power of non-governmental opposition movements, among them the Muslim Brotherhood.[12]

At least nominally, the British Empire ended its protectorate over Egypt in 1922 and released the country to independence.[13] Yet, Egypt remained under the spell of Britain, which secured its interests through the influence of the High

Commissioner and the presence of large quantities of troops. Although the Anglo-British treaty of 1936 restricted the number of troops during peace time, their presence in the Suez Canal Zone remained a thorn in the side of many Egyptians.[14] The endorsement of the Anglo-Egyptian treaty must be seen in connection with the growing possibility of war with Nazi Germany; Great Britain was keen to secure its relations with Egypt as a future ally and as a place of strategic importance. Nevertheless, the treaty was seen by nationalist Egyptians as a warrant for continuous control over Egypt. Anti-British sentiments were on the rise in Egypt when the confrontation between Jewish settlers and Muslim natives in Palestine, a land under British mandate, escalated.[15] The first Palestinian uprising in 1936 became a widely supported cause among Egyptian nationalists as well as Muslim Brothers.[16] With the beginning of the Second World War, feelings against Britain rose to a peak, not only because Egypt was unwillingly becoming a theatre of war, but because Britain now actively demanded power over national politics.[17] Consequently, the constitutional monarchy, its parliamentary system and the idea of an elected government became an empty shell. The inability of the king and the government to withstand British intervention led to widespread disillusionment with the democratic movement and the parliamentary system. Foreign intrusion into national politics was thus a contributory factor in undermining the authority of the state system.

Even after the war, Egypt's democratic system was unable to recover. Traumatised by the legacy of British intervention, a malfunctioning administration and governance were unable to implement effective policies to address the most pressing social and economic problems. As the political system fell apart, non-governmental opposition movements grew in popularity. Among them were the Muslim Brotherhood, and also nationalist right- and internationalist left-wing movements, some of which were close to political parties. Similarly to the Brotherhood, many of these movements had their own youth organisations, but were also running scout groups and even guerrilla forces.[18]

While the political system showed signs of disintegration, the Muslim Brotherhood grew under Hasan al-Banna's leadership to become a non-governmental force and an opposition with immense influence. The Brotherhood's official line regarding party politics was rather negative. Labelling it as '*hizbiyya*', which could be translated as the rule of party politics, al-Banna' argued that the existing parliamentary democracy merely followed party interests rather than the demands of the people and the guidelines of Islam.[19] Despite the official rhetoric, political influence was exerted on a number of levels. It is well known that al-Banna' twice stood for election, once in 1942, when he withdrew his candidacy after reaching an agreement with the Wafd, and once in 1945, when he was defeated.[20] Real political influence was, however, played out behind the scenes. Under al-Banna's guidance, the organisation gradually built up contacts with notables and party representatives. The Society had broad support among individuals, mainly from the middle class, and was successful in building an effective network.[21] The sympathies of the middle class secured considerable financial funds and opened the doors to a political network which reached both the political top level as well as the working masses. Hence, while leading Brothers negotiated with the government they also called on their supporters to express their political protest. Through mass demonstration, organised rallies and meetings, the Brotherhood evolved into a political pressure movement. As it competed successfully for the backing of the general public, the organisation became increasingly feared by the official parties, the government and the British. Through a flood of leaflets and articles in various Brotherhood-owned magazines, the organisation clearly targeted the opinion of the wider publics.

While the Brotherhood's critique of the government grew bolder, the parliamentary system was unable to reassert itself. This was particularly the case after the Second World War. In the chaotic state of affairs which was marked by domestic instability, minority government and the rule of martial law, the Muslim Brotherhood clashed increasingly with the political powers.[22] Lacking popular support, constantly changing governments eventually turned to repressive methods which far exceeded the legal framework.

Like a snowball effect, political violence accelerated violence. Ultimately, it is thus impossible to place blame for the collapse of political stability on a particular actor or factor. However, there can be no doubt that the Brotherhood started to use its paramilitary force against the Egyptian government in this situation of unrest.

The Secret Unit and violence

Like other political movements of the time, the Brotherhood had its own paramilitary unit, which was known as the Secret Unit (*al-Jihaz al-Sirri*) or the Special Organisation (*al-Nizam al-Khass*).[23] The beginnings of the combat unit go back to the year 1936, when the Brotherhood sent volunteers and arms to Palestine in support of the uprising. From then on, the organisation ran camps, where volunteers were instructed in guerilla warfare. The Brotherhood's youth, sports, rover and scouts divisions furnished the unit with potential recruits. They were then trained and prepared ideologically, mentally and physically.[24] The established camps were the location of exercises, and a number of veterans returning from Palestinian combat were responsible for instruction, logistics and eventually for the command of the recruits.

The chosen clique of members kept their affiliation to the Secret Unit covert; even fellow Brothers knew nothing of its members. Internally, the unit was structured around cells which operated almost independently, fighters not knowing about the activities of other clandestine cells. The vertical chain of command was short and had a tight hierarchical structure. Members gave their oath of obedience to the commander of the group; the commander reported to the Head of the Secret Unit, who took orders only from the *Murshid,* Hasan al-Banna'.[25] The first Head of the Secret Unit (*Ra'is al-Nizam al-Khass*) was Salih al-'Ashmawi. An indication for al-'Ashmawi's personal influence within the Brotherhood and the growing influence of the paramilitary unit within the wider movement is that he was nominated the Deputy (*Wakil*) of the Brotherhood in 1947. The command of the Secret Unit was then passed on to 'Abd al-Rahman al-Sanadi. Maintaining close relations with al-'Ashmawi, but less so with al-Banna', al-Sanadi transformed the Secret Unit into an autonomous combat unit which acted without directions from the organisation's administration and leadership.[26]

It would be wrong to assume that the Egyptian government did not know about the existence of the Secret Unit. On the contrary, it was aware of training camps run by the Brotherhood and in fact tolerated its activities, at least throughout the years of the Second World War and for as long as fighters were engaged in the Palestinian conflict and the Israeli–Palestinian war.[27] However, in the environment of increasing political chaos after 1945, the Secret Unit was not just a paramilitary group which was used outside Egypt. It now became the Brotherhood's spearhead through which the organisation tried to push its agenda on the national scene.

In the year of 1948, the struggle between the Brotherhood and the then ruling Sa'adi government, under Prime Minister al-Nuqrashi, accelerated into a state of near-persistent violence. Mitchell's scholarly work on the history of the Brotherhood provides a comprehensive picture of the increasingly anarchic situation, during which the Brotherhood and its Secret Unit became known for their terror activity.[28] Without recapitulating details, there is no doubt that the Brotherhood was linked to a number of assassination attempts, to the incitement of terror and to growing anti-Jewish violence. The exposure of weapon arsenals at a training camp on the hills of the eastern fringes of Cairo and at the estate of Muhammad al-Farghali, who was the leader of the Brotherhood's contingent in Palestine, furthered suspicion that the organisation was preparing to overthrow the government by force. When incriminating documents were detected in a Jeep, the Sa'adi government under al-Nuqrashi saw sufficient evidence to press for the dissolution of the Society of the Muslim Brothers.[29] The government announced the Brotherhood's dissolution in the decree of 8 December 1948.[30] The order contained the government's account of events and described the Brotherhood as a terrorist organisation. The document refers to the training camps as places for terrorist instruction. The Brotherhood was accused of responsibility for the deaths and injury of a number of individuals and was charged with intending to overthrow the political system.

The dissolution of the Muslim Brotherhood and the imprisonment of a large number of members, either in connection with the acts of violence or as a result of the dissolution order, followed. The adoption of a hard line against the Brotherhood was indeed an immense blow and threatened the very existence of the organisation.[31] However, the repressive measures of the government neither prevented terror nor calmed the situation. On the contrary, three weeks after the order of dissolution, Prime Minister al-Nuqrashi was assassinated, on 28 December 1948.[32] The Sa'adi leader 'Abd al-Hadi succeeded al-Nuqrashi as prime minister. He was determined to spell the end of the Brotherhood. Since a state of martial law had been declared, Brothers were summoned to military trials rather than to criminal or civil courts. Facing harsh punishments in the event of conviction, a large number of Brothers faced charges of conspiracy, illegal possession of weapons and membership in a terrorist organisation.

Knowing that this could be the end of the Society, al-Banna' aimed to find some form of settlement with the government. He made several official statements in which he condemned the escalation of violence and the assassination of al-Nuqrashi.[33] Arguing that the incidents were not instigated centrally, but rather the regrettable acts of individual Brothers, al-Banna' tried to distance himself from the events of recent months. He argued that Brothers who incited terror and engaged in terrorist activities had no orders to do so and, in fact, misunderstood the aims of the organisation. With regard to the Secret Unit, he stated that it was not the aim of the special branch to conspire against the state or to overthrow the political system. On the contrary, the Brotherhood's armed group was trained so that it was prepared for the defence of national interests. Al-Banna' argued that he was acting in agreement with the government; the unit was to provide troops which would eventually serve in the Palestine war. Yet, his efforts were not successful. On 12 February 1949, al-Banna' was killed.[34] The murder was probably instigated by the government as a means of retaliation and in order to put an end to the influence of the organisation.

Analysing the events, it must be said that the Brotherhood's Secret Unit was indeed engaged in terrorist activities. Al-Banna's argument that the paramilitary group was merely preparing for combat in Palestine does not stand up to scrutiny. The *Murshid*'s statements in this regard attempted to downplay the situation in order to open the possibility of negotiation with the government over the Brotherhood's future. That the Secret Unit was initially set up for warfare in Palestine is true. However, arguing that violence was committed only by individual members of the Brotherhood or of the Secret Unit does obscure the actual question of responsibility. There can be no doubt that the Secret Unit, with the knowledge of al-Banna', provided the Muslim Brotherhood with a devoted force willing to fight against the Egyptian political system. Although it was the Brotherhood's official position that it was not promoting a terrorist organisation, it is a matter of fact that violent acts were planned and carried out by the Secret Unit.[35] However, whether al-Banna' ordered the Secret Unit to engage in terrorist activities remains unclear. Considering that the influence of 'Abd al-Rahman al-Sanadi and Salih al-'Ashmawi in the Brotherhood was growing steadily, there is a question as to whether al-Banna' really retained control over the Secret Unit.[36] Critically, Salah Shadi, who was the Head of the Brotherhood's Police Forces (*Ra'is Tanzim Dhabat al-Bulis*), remarked that the Secret Unit under al-Sanadi's leadership gradually evolved into an autonomous faction which exceeded al-Banna's control.[37] Indeed, this assessment lends some credibility to al-Banna's later denial that the Brotherhood as an organisation was involved in planning to overthrow the political system, while he obviously conceded apologetically that some of its members were involved in terrorist activities. This should not detract from al-Banna's responsibility; as a leader he was ultimately accountable.

The issue of whether al-Banna' was indeed in control of the Secret Unit has wider implications. If the *Murshid* was not commanding the Brotherhood's spearhead, was he at least in control of the organisation at large? The picture given by most accounts, not only those of Brothers but also by scholars writing about the

Brotherhood, is that al-Banna's charisma carried the organisation, whose members where unequivocally united behind him. However, this picture is far from reality. It was during the crucial period of 1947 to 1948, the years during which the conflict with the Egyptian government became most obvious, that inner organisational disputes and conflicts came to the fore.[38]

The inner organisational dissent blew up on a number of occasions. Two incidences stand out and should be mentioned here to illustrate that the internal unity of the Brotherhood was in jeopardy and that al-Banna's leadership was by no means unquestioned. The first episode was in connection with an internal inquiry against the Secretary General of the Muslim Brotherhood, 'Abd al-Hakim 'Abidin, who happened also to be al-Banna's brother-in-law. A first inquiry was initiated in 1945 upon complaints that 'Abidin had abused his position to his personal advantage. In early 1947 the Guidance Council decided upon the dismissal of 'Abidin, largely following the advice of an internal committee appointed for the investigation of the case.[39] Not pleased with the outcome, al-Banna' intervened, with the result that all allegations were dropped. The incident did, however, leave some marks. One of al-Banna's oldest companions, Ibrahim Hasan, decided to leave the organisation in protest. Only a few months later, another comrade of the early days was to leave the Brotherhood. 'Abd al-Rahman al-Sukkari was a founding member of the Brotherhood and, in his position of Deputy, he was the second in line after al-Banna'. Unhappy about the Brotherhood's official line towards party politics, and particularly its antagonism towards the Wafd party, al-Sukkari finally permitted his reservations about al-Banna's policies to come to the fore. Under pressure from al-Banna', the Consultative Assembly then agreed with al-Banna' to exclude his old friend from the Brotherhood. The successor to al-Sukkari as Deputy was the aforementioned Salih al-'Ashmawi, the leader of the Secret Unit.

A number of implications are tied to these examples of inner organisational dissent. First, the general assumption that al-Banna's leadership was characterised by unequivocal harmony is not sustainable. Although al-Banna' managed to hold internal factions together, playing a cunning political game and (at times) resorting to repressive means, internal frictions became apparent during a time when the Brotherhood was clashing increasingly with the government. It was under these circumstances of internal weakness that Salih al-'Ashmawi, and with him the Secret Unit, won a dominant position within the Brotherhood. While developing into the Brotherhood's vanguard, the Secret Unit also gradually escaped from al-Banna's control and formed a largely independently acting group.[40] If we take into account that al-Banna' was nevertheless the *Murshid*, one can only agree with Carré and Michaud's evaluation, which stresses that al-Banna' either was duplicitous, i.e. publicly refuting violence while commanding the Secret Unit to engage in terrorist actions, or must have been incapable of managing the Special Branch.[41]

The fact that al-Banna' had to contend with inner opposition and may not have had full control of the Secret Unit is a reason for reassessing Hasan al-Hudaybi's beginnings as the second *Murshid*. Certainly, the existing inner organisational discontent brings into question the general assumption that dissent only evolved during al-Hudaybi's time. The Muslim Brotherhood was overshadowed by inner organisational crisis; the Secret Unit became an uncontrollable terrorist faction, even though it still operated under the umbrella of the movement. Last, but not least, the Brotherhood had to deal with the government's dissolution order and the imprisonment of its members. Al-Banna may have been celebrated as a charismatic figure by the general fellowship. In fact, he is still commemorated as such. However, it is a fact that his leadership was not undisputed during his lifetime, nor was it without faults. Since he was not able to bring order and calm to the organisation and since it is obvious that the was not able to control the Secret Unit, one can say that al-Banna' left behind an organisation in disarray.

1.2 The struggle for new leadership: al-Hudaybi and his competitors

Hasan al-Banna's assassination, the dissolution order, the public shaming of the Brotherhood in a number of military trials, the persecution and torture of members, left the organisation in a deep crisis. In this situation, the survival of the idea of this political–religious movement was at stake. Under the circumstances, it was less important and, in fact, impossible to organise the election of a new *Murshid*. While the organisation had to operate in secrecy, it was kept alive by the circle of leaders and their network.

For two years, from December 1948 to mid 1951, the Muslim Brotherhood survived in an environment of tactical retreat and secrecy. Key administrative members were behind bars.[42] A number of accounts written by Muslim Brothers speak about the difficulty of upholding the organisation.[43] Nevertheless, the established network of personal relations saved the Brotherhood from disappearing into public oblivion. Political and personal relations spun in the 1940s were vital for the continuation of the Society underground.[44] The complex set of connections, both between individual brothers and with influential public personalities enabled the organisation to cope with the pressure of the official ban, albeit functioning at a lower level. Accounts by Muslim Brothers recalling the period agree that the leading circle included 'Abd al-Hakim 'Abidin, 'Abd al-Rahman al-Banna', Shaykh Hasan al-Baquri and Mustafa Mu'min.[45] One name which frequently stands out as the figurehead is that of Salih al-'Ashmawi, the Deputy and the former Head of the Secret Unit. However, without an officially designated *Murshid*, the future of the Society was indeed under threat.

According to the Brotherhood's constitution, the new *Murshid* had to be elected by ballot of the General Assembly. Furthermore, the Assembly needed to be attended by no fewer than 80 per cent of its members on the day of election.[46] Considering the circumstances, it was hardly possible to call such a meeting. Moreover, the most likely candidates for nomination, namely members of the leading circle, were well aware that a public contest would put even more strain on the organisation. Since Salih al-'Ashmawi, 'Abd al-Hakim 'Abidin, 'Abd al-Rahman al-Banna', Shaykh Hasan al-Baquri and Mustafa Mu'min signified different ideological positions within the Brotherhood, an open debate would have exposed the intended public appearance of a unified and coherent organisation as not being genuine.[47] In fact, the internal rift was already deep, as the dispute between Salih al-ʿAshmawi and Mustafa Muʾmin shows. While Salih al-ʿAshmawi represented the military and ideologically radical wing of the Brotherhood, Mustafa Muʾmin stood for a more democratic distribution of power and was ideologically close to the Wafd. As will be shown below, it was during the crucial 'Jeep case' trial of 1950 that the difference between the two factions came to the fore, with the result that the Guidance Council sided with al-ʿAshmawi and opted to expel Muʾmin. The affair also showed that, despite internal challenges, al-ʿAshmawi, with the Guidance Council on his side, had the leadership of the organisation firmly in his hands. Nevertheless, under the pressures of the dissolution and persecution, it was not possible to hold elections for a new *Murshid* in the immediate future.

In his capacity of Deputy Leader of the Muslim Brotherhood Salih al-ʿAshmawi seemed the most probable successor to the vacant post of the *Murshid*. In accordance with the Brotherhood's constitution, he was, in the absence of an elected *Murshid*, the top figure. Because he had been the Head of the Secret Unit and because he was friendly with his successor al-Sanadi, he had the advantage of being connected to a strongly organised underground network. With the potential force of weapons behind him, an increase in his power would have meant that the organisation had clearly chosen the radical and military option, which inevitably would have led to further clashes with the political system. Other figures of the inner circle had profiles which spoke for their candidacy. All had had a devoted relationship to al-Bannaʾ, were members of the Guidance Council and, beyond that, held influential positions in the organisation's administration. ʿAbd al-Hakim ʿAbidin was al-Bannaʾs brother-in-law and the Brotherhood's Secretary-General (al-Sikritir al-ʿAmm). ʿAbd al-Rahman al-Bannaʾ was Hasan al-Bannaʾs brother. Shaykh Hasan al-Baquri was a respected cleric trained in Islamic jurisprudence and a prominent member of the Guidance Council (*Maktab al-Irshad*). Lastly, Mustafa Muʾmin was the leader of the Brotherhood's student organisation. As indicated, the choice of one contestant over the other would have had immediate implications for the future outlook of the organisation. Apart from the ideological considerations which were inevitably attached to the choice, the inner organisational unity was at stake. If Salih al-ʿAshmawi were to succeed to the post, there would be an immediate risk of the Brotherhood falling apart into factions. The continuity of the Brotherhood as a political mass organisation, as opposed to a terrorist and secretive elite, depended much on the improvement of its public image. A vote for Salih al-ʿAshmawi would have jeopardised the aim of reconciling with the state and thus bringing the organisation back into legality. Instead, it would have meant a clear decision for underground operation of the Brotherhood. This, however, did not match the objectives of the other contestants, or the interests of the wider membership. Facing this dilemma, the movement accepted al-ʿAshmawi's power for the time being, while the other contenders kept him in check. In the mean time, the issue of designating a new *Murshid* was put to rest.

The most immediate concern, then, was not the election of a new leadership, but focus on the legalisation of the organisation. However, the lifting of the dissolution order was no longer merely a political and governmental decision, but also depended on the outcome of the trials pending against the Brotherhood and its jailed members.[48] Of primary significance were the tribunals dealing with the assassination of Prime Minister al-Nuqrashi, and the so-called 'Jeep case', which dealt with the discovery of incriminating documents and arms linked to activities of the Secret Unit. The discovery was also seen to be linked to an -arsenal of weapons which was discovered on Muhammad al-Farghali's property. Central for the outcome of the trials was to convince the courts that the Brotherhood, as an organisation, was not responsible for acts of violence and that it was not preparing to overthrow the state system. As long as the country was under martial law, the cases had to be heard by a military court. Emergency law also gave the government the right to appoint the lawyers for the defence.

The al-Nuqrashi trial was the first major hearing to go ahead. The aim of the prosecution case was to prove that al-Banna' was responsible for the assassination. The question of accountability was a central aspect of the court case, since, if his responsibility could be proved, there would be sufficient grounds for the dissolution order. While it was established that the young assassin was member of the Secret Unit, the judge concluded that a ruling against the organisation as a whole could not be justified. Accomplices who had been incriminated by the defendant during police interviews had been killed, and thus could not be heard. The trial ended on 25 April 1950 and the court sentenced the Prime Minister's killer to death, but did not pass a verdict on the liability of the entire organisation.

Without a verdict on the issue of whether the Muslim Brotherhood constituted a terrorist organisation, the focus then shifted to the 'Jeep case'. The prosecution presented the documents and weapons found in the vehicle as evidence of terrorist activities. The defence drew its argument from al-Banna's speeches and statements and rejected the accusations on all counts. Regarding the use of violence, the Brotherhood's lawyers argued that the organisation could not be held liable for the acts of individual members, who 'misunderstood their training'.[49] They argued that the organisation's Special Branch had no objectives and no directives to target the state system or to plan the overthrow the government. While maintaining that the organisation was not impairing state security, the Brotherhood's lawyers set out to undermine the integrity of the prosecution. Pointing out that confessions had been extorted, they questioned the fairness of the examination of the case. The defence also submitted documents to the court which evidenced that the British, American and French embassies had demanded the dissolution of the Muslim Brotherhood. The credibility of the Sa'adi government in instigating a politically motivated lawsuit having been thus challenged, the outcome of the trial was still a startling sensation. The presiding judges announced the verdict on 17 March 1951. They concluded "a criminal conspiracy to overthrow the form of government, on the basis of the evidence and investigation, to be without foundation".[50] The outcome meant a total victory for the Brotherhood, which absolved them from for any accusations of being a terrorist organisation.

The success of the Brotherhood in these two most important trials was key to the organisation's objective of restoring its public reputation and re-establishing its influence. Nevertheless, it was the political networking behind the scenes which really saved the organisation. While prospects of winning the court cases had been low at the beginning of the first trial, with the Sa'adi government under 'Abd al-Hadi in power, circumstances changed when the Wafd replaced the Sa'adi government in July 1949. Calling upon its connections with Egypt's political establishment, al-'Ashmawi deployed Mustafa Mu'min to network and to negotiate with the Wafd under Husayn Sirri. The brief alliance between the Wafd and the Society had mutual advantages; while the Brotherhood's reasons were to influence politics and jurisdiction, the Wafd needed a partner in its campaign against the Sa'adi party. The Brotherhood's efforts paid immediate dividends: in the course of the first hearings, a joint legal representation of the Wafd and the Brotherhood replaced the original Sa'adi defence lawyers. By the time 'Jeep' trial commenced in December 1950, the political context had changed entirely. The Wafd ended the state of emergency, thus permitting the trial to go before a civil court and allowing the Brotherhood to choose its own defence.

The temporary good relations between the Wafd and the Brotherhood were thus crucial in winning the court cases and hence a big step towards rehabilitation. Although the organisation was dented by the trials and the order of dissolution, the leading Brothers managed to guide it through the immediate crisis. Having fought off the legal allegations, the Muslim Brotherhood could now turn to its next big aims, namely, returning to legality and electing a new leader. The first of the two objectives was taken up immediately. On 1 May 1951 martial law came to an end. Shortly after, the Guidance Council came together for a meeting and announced that the Society was still in existence. Two weeks later, on 17 May, the Consultative Assembly held its first summit. Although the order of dissolution was still officially in place, it was no longer of any real consequence. Back on course, the Brotherhood regained its financial assets and property, including the headquarters in Cairo. Also, the circle of leading members now turned to the still unresolved issue: the nomination of a new *Murshid*.

The nomination of Hasan al-Hudaybi

Without clear leadership and facing persecution by the state, the Brotherhood found itself in a desperate situation which threatened the existence of the organisation. It was hence of prime importance to use all possible channels to restore the reputation of the Muslim Brotherhood and to defend it against the accusation of being a threat to Egypt's political system. However, members of the leading circle were encumbered by the stigma of violence and internal crisis. Thus, the candidate for the post could not be one of the well-known figures, but had to be recruited externally. As part of the strategy for public rehabilitation, the ideal nominee had to be publicly recognised and well connected to the network of political power. Yet, the group of who were in charge during the interim period had no intention of giving up their influence. The choice was indeed difficult, but a satisfactory decision was essential for the continued existence of the organisation.

Hasan al-Hudaybi was approached in 1950. A first meeting between him and leaders of the Brotherhood was initiated by Munir al-Dilla, a member of the Brotherhood who was particularly well connected to the Egyptian upper class of wealthy landowners of Upper Egypt. Although it is unclear whether the purpose of these meetings was related to the search of a new *Murshid*, it became clear during the course of the year 1951 that the leading circle was searching for a compromise candidate. The ideal was to find a well-respected public figure, but one who lacked influence within the Brotherhood, since the interim leaders of the organisation had no intention of giving up their power and control.

The nomination of al-Hudaybi was therefore a pragmatic decision. As a formerly high-ranking representative of the judiciary, his influence in state institutions as well as his contacts with relevant persons was useful.[51] As al-Hudaybi's brother-in-law was the chief of the royal household, he also had links to the palace.[52] Struggling to overcome the order of dissolution of December 1948 and to become legalised again, the Muslim Brotherhood desperately needed a figurehead with a 'clean slate' in order to improve its reputation and adjust itself so as to fall into line with the political system. His connections and personal profile made him appear to be a candidate with great potential. Added to this, the fact that the election of one of the major contenders would exacerbate a latent conflict within the organisation made him the perfect candidate.[53] Seeking a figurehead behind whom the existing leaders could continue to act, as opposed to a strong leader from within, the leadership chose al-Hudaybi. In Shadi's words, the leaders took the position that

> It is enough for us, if you are the symbol around which we gather. It is then up to the Brothers to carry the burdens.
>
> (Shadi, in: Rizq (1991) 47).

The statement demonstrated a certain attitude. Al-Hudaybi was seen as a temporary solution and compromise.[54]

Eventually, the circle which included Salih al-ʿAshmawi, ʿAbd al-Hakim ʿAbidin, ʿAbd al-Rahman al-Banna' and Shaykh Hasan al-Baquri proposed to al-Hudaybi his nomination for the leadership. It appears that he refused the offer initially, only reconsidering his negative response some months later. In October 1951, it was finalised that al-Hudaybi should become the new *Murshid*.[55] Until his official 'election' through the General Assembly, his nomination was kept secret. It must be noted that his nomination was not in accordance with the constitution of the Muslim Brotherhood. The rules dictated that the leader must have been a member of the Consultative Assembly for at least five years and that he must be elected from among the members of the Assembly. The constitution also demanded that no fewer than 80 per cent of its members should be present in the Assembly meeting on the day of election.[56] For the vote to be valid, a 75 per cent majority in favour of the candidate was needed. Al-Hudaybi, of course, was not a member of the Assembly, nor did he receive the necessary majority of the quorum. The Assembly was not attended by the obligatory number.[57] As his nomination had been determined by the de facto leaders of the Brotherhood during the meeting in Munir al-Dilla's home, the Assembly's role in the election process was reduced to approving a foregone decision. The only duty which remained was to administer the oath of allegiance (*bai'a*) to the new *Murshid*.

Hasan al-Hudaybi: introductory biographical notes

Before commencing with the historical context, it is useful to digress and give a short biographical profile of Hasan Isma'il al-Hudaybi before his time as *Murshid al-'Amm*.

Hasan Isma'il al-Hudaybi was born in December 1891 in 'Arab al-Suwaliha.[58] His family was of poor, working-class origin. Al-Hudaybi had four sisters and three brothers, of whom he was the eldest. As was common in those days, his education began at the village school (*kuttab*), where he was taught to read and recite the Qur'an. It was the wish of al-Hudaybi's father that his eldest son should have the opportunity to receive an education in theology and become a cleric. Therefore, the young Hasan was sent to an Azhar primary school. Only a year later, he transferred to a government primary school. Mitchell cites an interview in which al-Hudaybi stated that it was his own decision to opt for a secular education.[59] Having finished his primary education, he went on to attend a government secondary school, from which he graduated in 1911. The same year he commenced his studies at the School of Law and four years later he received his licence to practice. It is worth noting the non-religious, secular nature of al-Hudaybi's education.[60]

It was during al-Hudaybi's time at school that the Egyptian national independence movement reached its peak. A wide section of society, and foremost among them students, actively demonstrated their enthusiastic support of Mustafa Kamil. Strikes at schools and universities were a frequent way of showing opposition to the British presence.[61] Rizq mentions that al-Hudaybi was at the forefront of the action; he even indicates that he was a member of a secret congregation founded by Muhammad Farid Khalifa and Mustafa Kamil.[62] Rizq states that al-Hudaybi was even threatened with a year's suspension from the School of Law because of his brave devotion to the cause. Rizq's enthusiastic account was clearly intended to depict al-Hudaybi as an upcoming national hero who was politically involved during his student years. However, one needs to be extremely careful in drawing such conclusions. In fact, Rizq is the only source to make such assertions. In other words, the accuracy of Rizq's information is questionable. If we see al-Hudaybi in the context of his career and his personality, it is more than likely that he was not extraordinarily politically engaged.[63] Like many others of his generation, he may have demonstrated nationalist leanings, but to say that he was a front runner is certainly an overstatement.

Al-Hudaybi began his working life in the year of his graduation, in 1915. He completed his legal clerkship in the offices of Kamil Husain and Hafiz Ramadan, a leader of the National Party (*Hizb al-Umma*).[64] In 1918, he attempted to run his own law practice, which he opened in Shibin al-Qanatir. When his business did not take off, he moved to Sauhaj. Work in this major city in Upper Egypt was more promising. However, after a few years he was offered promotion to a judge-ship. In 1925 he received his first appointment in Qana'. However, as a junior judge he frequently had to move from one city and post to another, moving to Naj' Hamadi, to al-Mansura, thereafter to Minya and later to Asyut and Zaqaziq. In each of these towns he worked for only a brief period. Finally, he was offered an appointment at the judicial office in Giza. Gradually climbing the career ladder, al-Hudaybi worked his way to the top of the juridical system. By the end of the 1940s, he was one of the highest-ranking representatives of the Egyptian judi-ciary. As judge of the Egyptian High Court, he was the Director of the Department of Public Prosecution; he also headed the Juridical Supervisory Authority and was an Advisor to the Chamber of Appeal.[65]

While there is some verifiable information about his career, not much is known about his early contact with the Brotherhood or the nature of his relations with Hasan al-Banna'. What knowledge we have is conveyed only by a few personal statements on the subject, which are published by Rizq.[66] Unfortunately, the scar-city of sources leaves us with just a few glimpses of his association with the Brotherhood before he entered its limelight as the *Murshid*.

According to his own statement, Hasan al-Hudaybi was aware of the existence of the Society of the Muslim Brotherhood from the late 1930s onwards. While he first met al-Banna' only much later, he mentions that his first encounter with the Brotherhood was at a socialengagement.[67] Al-Hudaybi recalls that he listened to a public speech given by al-Banna' in February 1945; this encounter was to precipi-tate a major change in his life.[68] Some time later, al-Hudaybi and al-Banna' were introduced to each other.[69] A friendship grew between them and al-Hudaybi was to assist the latter as a personal advisor. In this way, al-Hudaybi was introduced to the internal affairs of the Brotherhood, albeit in an unofficial capacity. Whether he had joined the organisation by this time is not clear. Certainly, members of the higher ranks close to al-Banna' came to know him; beyond this circle he was not otherwise known as an associate.[70] There were reasons why al-Hudaybi's affilia-tion with the Muslim Brotherhood was kept secret, as Ahmad correctly points out. For one, al-Hudaybi, himself wanted to work in secrecy, while al-Banna' needed some close affiliates to remain invisible. Most importantly, Egyptian law banned members of the judiciary from membership in organisations considered to be of a political nature.[71] When al-Hudaybi decided to accept the invitation to become the Brotherhood's leader his life merged with the future of the organisation. The nomi-nation was officially announced on 19 October 1951, coming as a surprise to many members. Soon afterwards al-Hudaybi resigned from his position as a judge.[72]

Change of direction

Within a short time it became apparent that the new *Murshid*, al-Hudaybi, intended to pursue his role of leader in much more than a symbolic way. Even upon the vote for him as leader, he made clear that his acceptance of the position was dependent on a number of conditions. He demanded that certain key positions in the administration of the Muslim Brotherhood be delegated to candidates of his choice. Following this, 'Abd al-Qadir 'Auda was announced as Deputy (*Wakil*). Six months later, the new position of Vice-Leader (*Na'ib al-Murshid al-'Amm*) was created; the *Na'ib* ranked higher than the position of *Wakil*. The new post was to be occupied by Muhammad Khamis Humayda.[73] Second, and perhaps most important, al-Hudaybi insisted that the Secret Unit, the Brotherhood's military (i.e. terrorist) branch, be dissolved.[74] How serious al-Hudaybi was about this second condition is demonstrated by the fact that he announced his intention to resign when, four months after he entered office, the Secret Unit was still in existence, A crisis was averted only when it was decided to establish a special committee with responsibility for its dissolution.

Al-Hudaybi's insistence on these demands made enemies for him within the organisation. Of course, his interference in the internal administration was not without risk. Some influential members, among them certainly al-'Ashmawi, saw this 'interference' on the part of a relative newcomer as a personal affront.[75] This even more so since the former Deputy Leader drew much of his support from members of the Secret Unit. But this cannot be the only reason. One can also argue that al-Hudaybi's stance broke an administrative and structural continuum. He insisted on change during a period in which the organisation was in dire need of internal stability. While the challenge of dissolution was still fresh in the memory of Brothers, many believed that secret networks and personal relations were the safeguard for the organisation's survival. Further, the strong personal bonds among those affiliated with the Secret Unit ensured that al-Hudaybi's efforts to dissolve it would meet with failure. Even though al-Hudaybi was now the *Murshid*, the Secret Unit was supported by a well-organised hierarchical structure which acted relatively independently of the main branch of the Brotherhood.[76] In summary, al-Hudaybi's plan to abandon terrorist activity led to conflict with advocates and members of the Special Unit, in particular with Salih al-'Ashmawi and 'Abd al-Rahman al-Sanadi.[77]

The political setting of the early 1950s greatly contributed to al-Hudaybi's inability to consolidate his power as leader within the organisation. As mentioned before, the organisation needed a leader who was able to reach out to political actors. While it was crucial to manoeuvre strategically, many members were suspicious of politics, given the recent experience of dissolution and persecution. In this situation, al-Hudaybi tried to maintain and use his contacts, particularly his connection to the royal household. In spite of voices opposing the monarchy, he accepted invitations to an audience with the king.[78] This step further aggravated opposition on the part of fellow Brothers. Salih al-'Ashmawi and Muhammad al-Ghazali spearheaded the opposition; they found support among some of the younger members, especially the students. Arguing against al-Hudaybi's opening up to the elite, they maintained that such contacts would compromise the independence of the organisation. Apart from that, several of the Brothers viewed the relationship as an insult, openly criticising the king's lifestyle.

The debate between al-Hudaybi and his opponents revealed yet another issue, namely attitudes towards the political system of the liberal era. Maintaining close contact with officials while rejecting the party system, al-Hudaybi was attempting to hover between the palace and party representatives, on the one hand, and his own organisation on the other. Since he saw the Brotherhood as the true representatives of the people, he considered himself a spokesperson for all Muslims. As such, he felt himself to be in a privileged position and wished to be consulted about current government affairs.[79] This attitude met with suspicion among secular and liberal politicians. In summary, while he gambled with the political actors in the collapsing state system, he simultaneously claimed to be independennt of those same institutions and even refuted their legitimacy. As a result, he ended up being criticised from all sides.

The crisis within the Brotherhood's ranks became obvious when the question of Egypt's relationship with Britain flared up again in 1951.[80] The context was the then Prime Minister al-Nahhas's termination of the Anglo-Egyptian Treaty of 1936 and the Sudan Convention of 1899; both agreements had secured Britain's interests in the region. Al-Nahhas's move to declare Sudan part of Egypt inflamed the national cause against Britain, most of whose troops were stationed in the north-eastern Delta and the Suez area. Al-Hudaybi criticised the Prime Minister's decision and preached restraint, thus inadvertently adopting a stance in support of the British presence.[81] Opposing the *Murshid*'s point of view again was Salih al-'Ashmawi, who called on fellow Brothers to summon up resistance to the foreign troops. When British soldiers intervened on 25 January 1952 to storm the headquarters of the Egyptian resistance fighters in Isma'iliyya, anti-British sentiments were reaching an explosive level. The following day, the centre of Cairo was plundered and set alight. The date 26 January became know as 'Black Saturday'. It is unclear whether the burning of central Cairo was planned and initiated by members of the Brotherhood. There is sufficient evidence, however, to suggest that Muslim Brothers were involved in the riots and the destruction of shops, which they saw as 'idols of Westernisation'.[82] Al-Hudaybi, however, denied any organised participation.[83] Whatever the case, the *Murshid* denied any organised involvement. With certain parallels to the arguments put forward by al-Banna' after the assassination of al-Nuqrashi, his successor had to now stand up in defence of the Brotherhood. As before, there was the question of responsibility. Considering that al-Hudaybi intended to dissolve the Secret Unit and steer the Brotherhood on a clear course, we can assume that he did not give any orders which would have encouraged members of the Brotherhood to participate in the riots. However, Brothers were involved, which shows that they were not under his command., al-Hudaybi's defensive in public reaction demonstrated his weak position and indicated the presence of internal disaffection.

In conclusion, it can be said that the hope which had been nurtured with al-Hudaybi's nomination soon faded. Admittedly, al-Hudaybi had to face great challenges at the beginning of his leadership. However, in the way in which he approached these, hemiscalculated his influence and power. As a consequence it became apparent fairly early on during his time as the *Murshid* that he had difficulties in overcoming internal and external the suspicions and in winning a wide basis of support.

1.3 The Brotherhood and the Revolution: cooperation, contention, clash

A few days after the Free Officers took power on 23 July 1952, al-Hudaybi declared the Muslim Brotherhood's support for the rule of the Revolutionary Command Council (RCC).[84] An open letter written by the *Murshid* was published on 28 July 1952 in *al-Ahram* newspaper, and was followed by the official announcement on 1 August 1952.[85]

The 'Revolution of 1952', which was, as Gamal al-Banna' pointed out, by definition rather a military coup than a people's rebellion, rearranged political relations, but did not, at least initially, demolish the existing system.[86] Until 10 December 1952, the constitution remained in force and it was only on 18 June 1953 that the Egyptian Republic was declared. However, King Faruq was forced to abdicate and the parliament was dissolved, thus effectively bringing the constitutional monarchy to an end. In the course of the year following the military coup, democratic institutions were gradually replaced. The Muslim Brotherhood initially hoped to participate actively in the new regime in one way or another, and the relationship between it and the new military rule progressed through phases.[87] In the first six months, relations were friendly, in spite of some degree of mistrust on both sides. During 1953, the façade of friendly cooperation began to corrode and was replaced by a strenuous power game. When an order of dissolution was issued against the Brotherhood in January 1954, it became clear that the relationship between the Revolution and the Brotherhood had turned sour. 'Abd al-Nasir, who by then dominated the RCC, clearly aimed to rid himself of any contenders. He finally succeeded; a staged attempt on his life provided the justification for ending any illusions of cooperation. The time of persecution (*mihna*) thus began with the so-called Manshiyya incident on 26 October 1954; it lasted for almost two decades, until 1971, when the 'people's president' died unexpectedly.

The rather short episode of cooperation between the Brotherhood and the RCC is in many respects crucial for the understanding of the Brotherhood's downfall and the rise of 'Abd al-Nasir. It shows that al-Hudaybi did not succeed in securing his leadership within the organisation. While many Brothers supported the RCC and were particularly fond of 'Abd al-Nasir, al-Hudaybi struggled to convince the organisation that his policies were in the best interests of the Brotherhood. At a time when the Brotherhood needed to demonstrate unity, the internal struggle made the organisation vulnerable. The final blow came when 'Abd al-Nasir used the Brotherhood's weakness against it.

In the following section we will look more closely at al-Hudaybi's role during the initial period of cooperation. The aim is to investigate his part in the gradual corrosion of the relationship with the state and ask questions about his responsibility for the time of persecution.

Cooperation with the Revolution

While the group of Free Officers under the leadership of Muhammad Naguib took power on 23 July 1952, personal links between these officers and a number of Brothers extended back to the war period.[88] Evidence of this tie can be found in several memoirs written by members of the Revolutionary Council; the most important sources to describe the relationship are those of Anwar al-Sadat and Muhi al-Din.[89] These memoirs show that Anwar al-Sadat, Gamal ʿAbd al-Nasir and Muhammad Naguib were personally acquainted with leaders of the Brotherhood's Secret Unit and with Hasan al-Banna'. Further, the growing crisis in Palestine gave Brothers and officers the occasion to fight side by side against British domination.[90]

Additionally, some authors interpret the pre-revolutionary links between army officers and the Brotherhood so as to argue that Sadat ʿAbd al-Nasir and Naguib were members of the organisation. They thus imply that the coup d'etat was in fact instigated by the Brotherhood. This view is put forward by Salah Shadi, who was the Head of the Brotherhood's Police Forces (*Raʾis Tanzim Dhabat al-Bulis*) and, as such, a member of the first rank. He points out that there were intensified talks between these leading Free Officers and al-Hudaybi.[91] According to him, the *Murshid* as well as those surrounding him were initiated into the plan. Muhammad Labib and ʿAbd al-Mun'im ʿAbd al-Ra'uf, who were both Free Officers and respected members of the Brotherhood, are mentioned as important go-betweens for the Brotherhood's leadership and the conspiring officers.[92] Shadi's insider opinion somehow challenges the view that al-Hudaybi was in favour of the monarchy. Why would al-Hudaybi, who was known to have personal links to the royal household, diminish his influence by siding with officers planning to destroy the social hierarchy? After all, revolution seems out of character for al-Hudaybi as a former career judge who emphasised the need to work within the state system. Moreover, while the coup d'etat unfolded, al-Hudaybi adopted a rather passive stance, waiting for the outcome rather than hastily welcoming the rule of the officers. In fact, it took al-Hudaybi almost a week to acknowledge the new government, while it was clear that the general membership of the Brotherhood was keen to support the RCC. It therefore seems unlikely that al-Hudaybi was really informed regarding the Free Officers' plot. It is much more plausible that leading members of the Brotherhood's Secret Unit such as Salih al-ʿAshmawi or ʿAbd al-Rahman al-Sanadi were in touch with the conspirators. Considering that army officers and members of the Secret Unit were brothers in arms, it is plausible that they were also working together on the idea of overthrowing the state. This view is also supported by the fact that al-ʿAshmawi and Sanadi showed revolutionary tendencies – or at least believed in an armed solution to the conflict with the state, if we take the involvement of the Secret Unit in the assassination of Prime Minister al-Nuqrashi into account. Since al-ʿAshmawi was competing with al-Hudaybi for influence over the Brotherhood, the change of governmental power played into al-ʿAshmawi's hands.

Whether Naguib and ʿAbd al-Nasir were indeed members of the Brotherhood cannot be answered with clarity, but it seems plausible that al-ʿAshmawi was

informed of an imminent strike against the constitutional monarchy and its institutions. Certainly, individual members of the organisation serving as soldiers and
officers were actively involved in the military putsch. Since al-Hudaybi did not
call on the Brotherhood to support the Free Officers while events were unfolding,
Mitchell's observation that the Society of Muslim Brothers' participation merely
amounted to passive support is thus correct, at least to a degree.[93] In any event,
it is not surprising that, while al-Hudaybi remained cautious, many Brothers
welcomed the coup d'etat.

Immediately after the Revolution, the *Murshid* met representatives of the new
leadership. Al-Hudaybi visited Naguib, who orchestrated the coup.[94] Also there
with him were 'Ali Mahir, who was still nominally the prime minister, and a
number of party leaders. During their talks, several stipulations were made, such
as the restitution of civil liberties, a constitutional reform declaring Islamic law to
be the basis of legislation and, finally, a land reform. After this first official visit, a
meeting between al-Hudaybi and 'Abd al-Nasir followed at the end of the month.
At this meeting both declared friendly cooperation between the Brotherhood and
the RCC.[95] On the basis of these terms of understanding, leading members of the
Muslim Brotherhood and the Free Officers kept in close contact.

However, the initial emphasis on goodwill and cooperation should not distract
from the fact that the revolutionaries and the Brotherhood under al-Hudaybi held
fundamentally different views on what constituted a just state system.[96] Nevertheless, the RCC was forced, at least initially, to work alongside the Brotherhood.
Being in need of wide public support, and considering that there was a level of
personal acquaintance, the Brotherhood seemed to be a good partner. The Brotherhood, on the other hand, was hoping to use the new distribution of power as an
opportunity to take an active role in Egypt's political arena. This way, al-Hudaybi
as well as al-'Ashmawi saw an opportunity to make a lasting impression on the
state, its system and laws, but also on the Brotherhood.

The opportunity to be actively involved in government and politics was generally welcomed by members of the Brotherhood. However, al-Hudaybi had not yet
managed to consolidate his position as *Murshid* and al-'Ashmawi had no intention
of retreating from the opportunity finally to regain his leadership. Considering
that the Brotherhood was suffering from internal disaffection at the highest level,
the new circumstances further widened the rifts within the organisation. While
the question of dissolving the Secret Unit was still unresolved, the future role and
involvement of the Muslim Brotherhood within the state system was an issue of
even more immediate importance in the period just after the Revolution.

The Brotherhood's relationship with the RCC was first put to the test at the
beginning of September 1952. It was at this point that the RCC decided to dismiss
the government under Prime Minister 'Ali Mahir, in spite of the fact that it had
gained a majority in the last elections. The officers called on the Brotherhood to
participate in the formation of a new government. The Muslim Brotherhood was
offered some ministries in the cabinet under Naguib. Apart from this piece of
information, accounts differ as to what took place. Shadi states that 'Abd al-Nasir
informed a close ally of al-Hudaybi, namely Muhammad Hasan al-'Ashmawi, that
the RCC had plans to involve the Muslim Brotherhood in government activities.[97]

In response, Hasan al-'Ashmawi recommended certain names; apparently, he also pointed out that the *Murshid*'s approval of the principle of participation was needed. Shadi remembers that al-Hudaybi was asked for permission on this matter but responded that it was up to the Guidance Council (*Maktab al-Irshad*) to make such a decision. The committee, which was to meet the same day, rejected the proposal. However, on the following day the RCC published a list of ministerial appointments; to the surprise of fellow Brothers, Hasan al-Baquri was declared Minister of Religious Endowments (*Wasir al-Awqaf*).[98] Al-Hudaybi then gave him the choice either to accept the ministry and leave the organisation or to decline and remain in the Brotherhood. He decided in favour of the post.[99]

According to Mitchell, al-Hudaybi was notified of the RCC's offer.[100] He agreed, with the RCC, on al-Baquri. He also negotiated over two additional posts for two of his closest associates, Hasan al-'Ashmawi and Munir al-Dilla, without actually consulting the Guidance Council (*Maktab al-Irshad*). Only after al-'Ashmawi and al-Dilla were rejected by the RCC did al-Hudaybi inform the Council that two further posts were part of the negotiations. The *Maktab al-Irshad* then refused the offer to participate in government, believing that the RCC did not fully meet the terms of a deal. When it became known that al-Baquri had already accepted the post of Minister of Religious Endowments, the latter was forced to leave the Brotherhood.

In yet another variant account of the same incident, Gordon relates that al-Hudaybi accepted the RCC's nomination of Hasan al-'Ashmawi and Munir al-Dilla.[101] However, the RCC then withdrew the offer and nominated al-Baquri and Ahmad Husni.[102] Following the dismissal of al-Hudaybi's favourite candidates, the Guidance Council under his leadership voted against approval of the new nominees. Al-Baquri was forced to leave the Brotherhood.

Commenting on the so-called al-Baquri crisis, al-Sisi, who was a prominent member of the Brotherhood, stresses that the RCC's offer of three ministries was merely a public ploy. The Brotherhood, he states, was aware of its tactics.[103] Although this viewpoint is an overstatement and only considers the events in retrospect, it contains a certain degree of truth. As-Sisi's statement correctly depicts the RCC and the Muslim Brotherhood as competing for public favour. Nevertheless, one needs to set against al-Sisi's theory the fact that the Brotherhood was not in the least aware of the situation. Proof of this are the various versions of the same account and the internal crisis which the discussion of the Brotherhood's involvement in government caused.

Not only does the al-Baquri crisis show that the Brotherhood had no real idea about the level of cooperation with the new regime, but the events also give a hint that RCC and al-Hudaybi had fundamentally different views of what constituted a just state system. Given their ideological and social backgrounds, this is not surprising. Most of the Free Officers were the product of the upcoming middle class, which benefited from secular education and the modernisation of the state and army. As mentioned above, the RCC was constrained to dealing with the Brotherhood, since it needed the organisation's influence over the masses, which saw religion as an important factor in their lives. However, the al-Baquri crisis shows that al-Hudaybi and the Brotherhood were not ready to take on governmental responsibilities. Al-Baquri's decision to choose the ministerial post over his membership in the Brotherhood suggests that he was not content with al-Hudaybi's handling of the situation. Indeed, the fact that al-Baquri was ready to switch sides implies that the Brotherhood could not be a political partner for the RCC. The al-Baquri crisis was, then, a first hint that ideological differences could not be overcome. The disagreement over ministerial appointments thus damaged the relationship.

While the issue of ministerial posts was under discussion, the debate whether al-Hudaybi's movement defined itself as a political party or as a religious association further widened the differences between the RCC and the Brotherhood. This issue had been a cause of internal debates in the past; as was shown above, dissidents had raised the issue of the Brotherhood's position in relation to politics during al-Banna's leadership.[104] As the political situation changed, with the RCC taking power, al-Hudaybi was confronted with this unresolved issue. On 9 September 1952, the RCC ordered all parties to register; this order became the trigger for new internal disputes on the status of the organisation.[105] The Consultative Assembly (*al-Hai'a al-Ta'asisiyya*), which is a body elected by direct vote of the Brotherhood's general members, recommended registration as a political party.[106] Al-Hudaybi, however, did not share the opinion of the Assembly's majority. He saw the Brotherhood as a religious association; since he could not overrule the vote of the membership, he resigned in protest and retired to Alexandria.

Again, accounts vary as to how this dispute was handled. Mitchell assumes that the Muslim Brotherhood indeed registered as a political party.[107] His statement is based on the fact that the Brotherhood was subsequently exempted from a decree issued in January 1953 which dissolved all political parties. Mitchell opines that the Brotherhood in fact had a say in this decision. Another account is presented by Gordon. Using references from the contemporary Egyptian press he states that al-Hudaybi returned to his office and submitted a new application which redefined the Society as a religious association. According to him, al-Hudaybi thus ignored the decision of the Consultative Assembly.[108] Shadi presents a third version; he states that al-Hudaybi put forward his objections at a second meeting of the Consultative Assembly, convincing it that it was better to withdraw the application for registration as a political party. Succeeding in putting forward his arguments, al-Hudaybi took up office once more.[109]

While it is impossible to discover whether al-Hudaybi managed to convince the Assembly, or whether he simply ignored their vote, some conclusions can nonetheless be drawn. The discussion on the party issue reveals a fundamental conflict within the Brotherhood. While the general membership, which was represented by the elected Consultative Assembly, was confident of playing an active part as a political party, al-Hudaybi rejected the idea of being part of the governing regime. This confirms that, even two years after his nomination as *Murshid*, he had failed to bring the differing wings of the Brotherhood under his control and to lead the organisation as a united body. In fact, the way in which he dealt with internal conflict shows that he did not aim to reach out to his constituency, but rather, adopted a top-down approach. As for the relationship with the RCC, it confirms that the

Brotherhood had no clear and consistent strategy. Al-Hudabyi's outwardly conciliatory attitude of friendly cooperation with the RCC contrasted sharply with
his actual mistrust and latent rejection of the new order. This, however, not only
widened the rift between the Brotherhood and the RCC (especially with 'Abd
al-Nasir), but also plunged the Brotherhood into further internal dissent. Al-Sisi,
for example, remembers that many Muslim Brothers believed at this stage that
it was best to remain loyal to the government. Thus, the affair had the result that
al-Hudaybi was criticised by both sides – internally and externally – and accused
of duplicity and incompetence.[110]

Al-Hudaybi's problem in providing clear leadership was the main factor in
the changed relationship between the Revolution and the Brotherhood. Facing a
situation whereby the Brotherhood could not be considered a tested partner of the RCC, but rather a possible contender for power, the ruling military
reconsidered its attitude. On the agenda was now to aim for constraining the
Brotherhood's influence in a similar way as had been done with other possible competitors, especially the Wafd party. The al-Baquri crisis and the party
issue were the starting-point for a deep mistrust between the Brotherhood and
the RCC, particularly between al-Hudaybi and 'Abd al-Nasir. In the course of
the next year, their political differences grew into dislike. Since 'Abd al-Nasir's
power increasingly dominated the decision-making process within the RCC, the
failing relationship between al-Hudaybi and 'Abd al-Nasir had severe political
implications.[111]

The *Murshid*'s perception that the Muslim Brotherhood was not a political
party did not imply rejection of direct involvement in contemporary state affairs.
On the contrary, al-Hudaybi wished the Society and himself, as its leader, to be
consulted.

As such, al-Hudaybi demanded the introduction of an Islamic constitution, with
the Qur'an as its foundation, and wanted to be involved in any negotiations on the
withdrawal of British troops.

Al-Hudaybi expressed the wish for constitutional reform in several public
letters, as well as in meetings with leading officials.[112] In preparation for a
proposal, Dr Muhammad Taha Badawi was given the task of working on the
text of the constitution, which was then presented to the Juridical Branch of
the Brotherhood and the Guidance Council, both of which accepted the draft.[113]
The RCC, on the other hand, had proposed constitutional reform from the very
beginning of the revolution. On 12 January 1953 a government commission of
fifty members was announced and, in recognition of the Brotherhood's demands,
three seats were offered to representatives of the organisation.[114] Regarding this
assignment, further research is required on the issue of the actual distribution of
the seats, i.e. to supporters or opponents of al-Hudaybi. According to Gordon,
Hasan al-'Ashmawi, Munir al-Dilla (both close associates of al-Hudaybi) and
Salih al-'Ashmawi (who was al-Hudaybi's opponent in the Brotherhood) were
nominated.[115] Somewhat different is the list of names mentioned by Mitchell,
who states that Salih al-'Ashmawi, 'Abd al-Qadir 'Auda (who opposed the
Murshid on certain issues) and Muhammad Kamal Mustafa were considered for

the posts.[116] While it is not impossible to verify the actual list of names, the incident shows that al-Hudaybi's position as the unquestioned leader of the Muslim Brotherhood was at stake.

As to the agreement with Britain on its right to station troops in Egypt, al-Hudaybi's anti-British rhetoric was as strong as that of his predecessor, al-Banna'. In almost every public letter issued during these days, al-Hudaybi mentions the British issue. In fact, next to the question of constitutional reform, the withdrawal of British troops and the talks on the relationship between Egypt and Britain proved to be matters in which he wanted to be directly involved. During April and May 1953, al-Hudaybi met the British Oriental Councillor, Trevor Evans, and representatives of the British embassy several times.[117] Al-Sisi claims that al-Hudaybi had the RCC's tacit approval to see Evans. Apparently, the ambassador had called upon the leader of the Brotherhood, since previous talks between the Egyptian and British governments had failed.[118] However, the official version claims that the *Murshid* interfered in state policies, making a pre-arrangement with the British and thus infiltrating the official talks.[119] Whoever initiated the talks between al-Hudaybi and British officials, al-Hudaybi seems to have acted beyond his call. His meetings with Evans and his aim of pushing for a deal were seen as interference in government matters. Al-Hudaybi's attitude certainly caused quarrels with the RCC, especially with 'Abd al-Nasir.

Being against direct participation, any coalition or union with the RCC on the one hand, al-Hudaybi's stance that the Brotherhood could not be ignored, because it represented the Egyptian people, was met with suspicion. At least superficially, the relationship between the RCC and the Brotherhood seemed to work; after all, both movements were dependent on each other. But soon a power struggle and competition for public favour showed through the façade, making cooperation impossible in the long term.

Disharmony

When the RCC ordered the dissolution of all political parties and associations on 16 January 1953, the Brotherhood was exempted.[120] The government was not able to give up the Brotherhood's support. In return, the Brotherhood welcomed the regime's assumption of direct power and the dissolution of all parties.[121] Instead of political parties, the 'Freedom Organisation' (*Hai'at al-Tahrir*) was established to represent the people directly. The Muslim Brotherhood was invited to join this national front.

The offer to be part of a national front effectively continued the unresolved question of whether the Brotherhood should actively participate in government. However, by now the stakes had changed. In fact, acceptance of the offer would have brought the Muslim Brotherhood under government control. Being part of the *Hai'at al-Tahrir* would mean that the Society would be subsumed into a government institution. It also implied that Hasan al-Hudaybi's power would be restricted, if not terminated. Yet to decline the offer would have denoted a clear end of the Brotherhood's cooperation with the RCC. As al-Hudaybi took the second option, a clash between the RCC and the Society was inevitable.[122]

While the relationship between the Brotherhood and the RCC turned sour, the controversy over al-Hudaybi's position as *Murshid* flared up. 'Abd al-Nasir, who by then was in charge of the RCC's dealings with the Brotherhood, began to openly show support for the *Murshid's* opponents within the Society.[123] 'Abd al-Nasir's strategy was clearly intended to undermine al-Hudaybi's position and to eventually have him removed as leader.[124] He shared this objective with al-Hudaybi's opponents within the Brotherhood. The voice that protested loudest was that of Salih al-'Ashmawi, former Deputy General of the Brotherhood and editor of the magazine *Majallat al-Da'wa*;[125] he was supported by 'Abd al-Rahman al-Sanadi, who was still leading the Secret Unit despite the fact that al-Hudaybi wanted the military subgroup dissolved. While al-Sanadi used his influence and network to persuade members of the Brotherhood to join ranks against al-Hudaybi, al-'Ashmawi's magazine was the mouthpiece for severe criticism of al-Hudaybi[126] Sharing the same goal, i.e. to force al-Hudaybi to resign, al-Sanadi met 'Abd al-Nasir during autumn 1953 to establish close a working relationship and to try to convince fellow Brothers that the *Murshid* was the main obstacle to possible cooperation.

While Salih al-'Ashmawi felt that he and not al-Hudaybi was the rightful leader, other Brothers were not convinced by the *Murshid*, for a different reason, which concerned the structure and administration of the Muslim Brotherhood. Opposing the hierarchical structure of the Brotherhood, they wanted a more egalitarian system which reflected their opinions in a democratic way. In the spirit of al-Sukkari, who had made similar demands in the late 1940s, these Brothers wanted reform of the Brotherhood's structure of command and administration. They demanded a greater right to speak and objected to al-Hudaybi's top-down approach, which the *Murshid* readily used against the decision of General Assembly in order to implement his own will.[127] In this regard, the democratic wing of the Brotherhood also asked for a time limit on the leader's term of office; they believed that the existing appointment for life was not in the interests of the Brotherhood. On 8 October 1953, disagreement broke out openly in a meeting of the General Assembly, which had been summoned to elect the representatives of the Guidance Council. At this meeting, al-Hudaybi managed to ward off attempts to limit his term of office to three years, which would have meant an imminent end to his leadership.[128] Although al-Hudaybi was successful in meeting the opposition on this occasion, there was no real solution to the cause of the discontent. In fact, the incident showed that al-Hudaybi's opponents were growing stronger and more vocal.

The assassination of Sayyid Fa'iz, who was the Deputy Commander of the Secret Unit, gave al-Hudaybi the opportunity to fight back and purge the Society.[129] Fa'iz was murdered on 20 November 1953, most likely by those members of the Secret Unit that he was leading. Supposedly, the motive for the assassination was that Fa'iz had allied himself with al-Hudaybi, thus turning his alliance away from al-Sanadi and al-'Ashmawi. The day after the murder, the Brotherhood's Guidance Council announced the expulsion of 'Abd al-Rahman al-Sanadi, Ahmad Zaki Hasan, Mahmud al-Sabbaj and Ahmad 'Adil Kamal, all influential figures in the Secret Unit.[130] In the official Brotherhood version, the charge was not related to the murder of Sayyid Fa'iz; since he was killed by a letter bomb, it would have been impossible, in any case, to prove that al-Sanadi was involved. The charge against al-Sanadi and his companions was of causing sedition (*fitna*).[131] Arguing that al-Sanadi had not followed orders to ensure that the Secret Unit was disbanded, the murder of al-Fa'iz was conveniently read as proof of the continuing negative influence and uncontrollability of the military group.

Considering that al-Hudaybi had to fend off opposition from many sides, and considering also that the expelled members were highly influential, al-Hudaybi's expulsion of al-Sanadi and his comrades was indeed a dramatic step to take. However, al-Hudaybi needed to take action against them, and he had, in fact, nothing to lose, as his support began to fade quickly. Admittedly, the expulsions were issued by the Guidance Council and not directly by al-Hudaybi; 'Abd al-Halim is right in pointing this out, but it needs to be considered that the majority of the Guidance Council was still behind al-Hudaybi. Fighting the inner opposition, led by al-Sanadi and al-'Ashmawi, al-Hudaybi risked alienating the lower ranks from the top leadership. In fact, the expulsions had won al-'Ashmawi and al-Sanadi wide support among younger, activist members, some of whom approved radical ideas; they also gained the approval of the marginalised democratic wing. Al-Hudaybi's authoritarian approach of fighting back thus risked alienating the membership from him even further.

On 27 and 28 November 1953, it was the turn of al-Hudaybi's opponents. A group invaded al-Hudaybi's house; a second group occupied the headquarters in Cairo.[132] The aim of the rebels was to force al-Hudaybi to resign. They also demanded the reversal of the expulsions. After some arguments, al-Hudaybi's supporters managed to gain control. Following this incident, twenty-one out of approximately seventy rebels were expelled. On 9 December an internal committee investigating the circumstances of the internal upheaval advised that the membership of Salih al-'Ashmawi, 'Abd al-'Aziz Jalal and Muhammad al-Ghazali, who were accused of being the leading figures, should be terminated.[133]

The events show that al-Hudaybi paid a high price, for his decision to break the opposition within the Muslim Brotherhood was actually achieved by authoritarian means. To begin with, the fact that he had succeeded a charismatic leader like Hasan al-Banna' put him in a difficult situation. Further, it is true that the circumstances of having influential contenders made it tricky to strengthen his position. Yet, al-Hudaybi did not respond adequately to the pressures of the post-revolutionary days. While he needed the unequivocal backing of his organisation in order to be an effective political player, he was unable to connect to the grass roots, and in fact increasingly lost his remaining support. Although al-Sanadi and al-'Ashmawi were clearly affiliated to the Secret Unit, not all of al-Hudabyi's opponents belonged to this subgroup. And while the Secret Unit was in command of the rebellion against al-Hudaybi, the expulsion of some of its leaders did not break the Secret Unit. In fact, the Secret Unit continued to exist and kept close ties to al-Sanadi and Salih al-'Ashmawi. Above all, al-Hudaybi missed the opportunity for a real resolution of the inner conflict by engaging in a fundamental reform of the organisation. Splinter groups (militant, activist as well as moderate, democratic and even quietist) continued to exist under the umbrella of the Muslim Brotherhood. Al-Hudabyi's top-down approach only temporarily silenced these factions, but opposition to his leadership remained a latent factor.[134] There was no open democratic decision making – a phenomenon which can be argued to be part of the general political climate rather than peculiar to the Brotherhood. The idea of obedience to the leadership of the *Murshid* was upheld. His regained authority, though, was only temporary.

The RCC attempted to take advantage of this internal crisis. On 14 January 1954, the RCC ordered the dissolution of the Muslim Brotherhood.[135] Al-Hudaybi was arrested and a press campaign was launched against him.[136] Mitchell points out "that Hudaybi was the prime target, and that the RCC intended to reconstitute the Society under more amenable leadership".[137] This was certainly the intention of a section of the Council influenced by ʿAbd al-Nasir, who by then was in charge of dealing with the Brotherhood.

Al-Hudaybi reacted by writing an open letter to Muhammad Naguib, who was officially still the head of the RCC and the president of the Republic. In his letter, al-Hudaybi defended the cause of the Muslim Brotherhood, pointing out that the accusations brought forward were untenable.[138] The letter opposed ʿAbd al-Nasir, accusing him of intending to build up an autocratic regime. Further, in this letter al-Hudaybi championed the reintroduction of the parliamentary system and public freedom. By issuing this public statement, the *Murshid* attempted align himself with the still-powerful Naguib, thus using the president as a shield against ʿAbd al-Nasir. After months of power struggle between Naguib and ʿAbd al-Nasir, a struggle which reached its peak at the beginning of March 1954, the president gained the upper hand. As Naguib regained his offices on 1 March 1954, the order of dissolution was withdrawn.[139] For a short period, it seemed that the Brotherhood could be reconciled with the RCC under Naguib.[140]

However, the dissolution of the Brotherhood in the period between January and March 1954 left its mark. Because of the imprisonment of leading figures, internal factions, which had already existed before the order of dissolution, drifted further apart. There were then a number within the General Assembly (*Majlis al-Shura*).[141] One group vouched for a closer cooperation and for reconciliation with the RCC and with ʿAbd al-Nasir. In their view, al-Hudaybi had led them into a dead end and the only way to overcome the differences of the past few months was to work with the regime. The spokesman of this faction was the Brotherhood's second in command, the Deputy *Murshid* ʿAbd al-Qadir ʿAuda. A second group firmly held on to al-Hudaybi. They wanted the Brotherhood to continue with al-Hudaybi's vision of a non-aligned pressure group acting particularly in opposition to ʿAbd al-Nasir and his influence in the RCC. A third group called themselves neutralists and did not join either of these opposing groups. Apart from these groupings within the General Assembly, one lasting effect of this period, during which the Muslim Brotherhood had been forced under cover, was that the idea of the Secret Unit was revived. In fact, there are even indications that al-Hudaybi changed his opinion insofar as he now wanted the Secret Unit to continue its recruitment and training, albeit under a leadership controlled by him. It was at this point that al-Hudaybi brought Yusuf Tal'at in to take on the command.[142] As one can imagine, this led to some internal confusion, since al-Sanadi and al-'Ashmawi still made use of their connections, despite the fact that they had both been expelled.

In many ways, the first period of dissolution was a precursor of what was to follow. It was a test of the Brotherhood's internal stability. 'Abd al-Nasir's strategy to further disrupt the unity of the organisation and play its factions against one another had worked. Al-Hudaybi became increasingly marginalised. And although the Brotherhood managed to get back into the political scene, it was now almost dependent on Naguib's backing. Despite Naguib's victory in March, 'Abd al-Nasir continued his power struggle against his major opponent in the RCC. His persistence and calculation paid off when Naguib signed his resignation; 'Abd al-Nasir was invested as prime minister on 18 April 1954 and thus came to dominate the regime.[143]

Although all the signs were against al-Hudaybi, he did not give up yet. At the beginning of May 1954, he approached 'Abd al-Nasir with a petition demanding a return to parliamentary democracy, and asking also for suspension of the state of emergency and the reinstatement of general rules of public freedom and insisting on the reinstatement of legal status for the Brotherhood.[144] However, it became obvious that a compromise between al-Hudaybi and 'Abd al-Nasir could not be brought about. The media, which was now under the control of the regime, launched a campaign against the Brotherhood.[145] Clashes between members of the Brotherhood's student organisation and the Liberation Rally on the premises of Cairo university, and incidents in the Canal Zone, were used to propagate the idea that the Muslim Brotherhood was endangering public security and undermining the interests of the state. Under these circumstances, the *Murshid* decided to step back from the scene. Probably advised that his presence constituted the main obstacle to an amicable solution between the regime and the Brotherhood, al-Hudaybi left the country on a business trip.[146] At the end of June 1954 he began a tour to several counties in the Middle East, where he visited branches of the Brotherhood and met fellow leaders of Islamist movements and state officials.[147]

While al-Hudaybi was on tour, 'Abd al-Nasir reinitiated negotiations between Egypt and Britain for withdrawal of the remaining British troops. To the surprise of most Egyptians, an agreement was reached and was published on 27 July 1954.[148] The news of the agreement reached the *Murshid* only a few days later. On 31 July, al-Hudaybi, who was then in Lebanon, published his first reaction in a newspaper article. Fiercely rejecting the conditions, he questioned the need for such a new agreement. His main concern was that the Anglo-Egyptian treaty of 1936 would expire within two years.[149] An official statement of the *Ikhwan* followed on 22 August 1954; in the absence of the *Murshid* it was signed by Dr Muhammad Khamis al-Humaydah.[150] Upon his return, the *Murshid* delivered a speech. It happened to be al-Hudaybi's last public appearance before the crackdown. Along similar lines to the statements, al-Hudaybi refuted any accusations that the Brotherhood intended to undermine state security and, further, publicly rejected the Anglo-Egyptian treaty.[151] In the month following his return to Egypt, al-Hudaybi retired to Alexandria.[152] His absence during the months of July to

September brought the confusion within the organisation to a peak.[153] Just when the Brotherhood was desperately in need of a leader, he chose to disappear from public life. With al-Hudaybi out of the way, it was then possible for 'Abd al-Nasir to take the final steps to get rid of the Brotherhood.

Several authors affiliated with the Muslim Brotherhood state that 'Abd al-Nasir had deliberately stirred up a controversy within the Society; conspiracy theorists even hold the view that the British were behind these plans and had asked 'Abd al-Nasir to fight back against the Muslim Brotherhood. While it is true that 'Abd al-Nasir benefited from the weakness of the Brotherhood, there is no proof of the involvement of the British government. After all, the only argument put forward by conspiracy theorists is that the British feared any interference which could jeopardise the negotiation of a new Anglo-British treaty. What speaks against this argument is that, only a year earlier, the British side had shown willingness to have the Brotherhood at the negotiating table. Only 'Abd al-Nasir was clearly against the idea of involving the Brotherhood, seeing al-Hudabyi's attempts as interference with government matters. The idea of conspiracy somehow also detracts from the real issue, namely that disunity within the Brotherhood contributed to the weakness of the organisation, which subsequently made it vulnerable to being outdone by 'Abd al-Nasir. Neither was Al-Hudaybi able to unify the Brotherhood under his leadership, nor did he give clear directives as to the organisation's political vision, strategy and level of cooperation with the RCC. As shown above, the Brotherhood was suffering from disintegration and crisis long before 'Abd al-Nasir's final strike against the organisation in October 1954.

On 19 October 1954 the Anglo-Egyptian treaty was signed.[154] A week later, on 26 October 1954, a former member of the Secret Unit, Mahmud 'Abd al-Latif, allegedly attempted to assassinate 'Abd al-Nasir during a celebration of the treaty in Alexandria. The incident ushered in the final stage of the relationship between the Revolution and the Muslim Brotherhood: the time of persecution.

1.4   The time of persecution: dissolved but not dispelled

The alleged attempt on 'Abd al-Nasir's life during his speech in celebration of the Anglo-Egyptian treaty in Alexandria on 26 October 1954 signalled the turning point in the relationship between the Revolution and the Brotherhood.[155] The Manshiyya incident, called after the place where the alleged assassination attempt took place, was used to push the Muslim Brotherhood off the political stage. Show trials painted the Muslim Brotherhood as a terrorist organisation, one which aimed to overthrow the political system.[156] While the trial was effective in branding the Islamist opposition, 'Abd al-Nasir purged the RCC of his opponents within the government. Muhammad al-Najib was pushed out of office as president of the Republic; he was accused of conspiring with the Muslim Brotherhood and was subsequently placed under house arrest.[157] With the opposition in prison or marginalised, 'Abd al-Nasir developed into the unquestioned leader of Egypt. His autocratic rule thus started with the defeat of the Brotherhood. The Muslim Brotherhood survived the next decades under the pressures of persecution. It is to this period, referred to as the period of *mihna* (humiliation, trial), that we now turn in our historical investigation.

After the Manshiyya incident

Following the assassination attempt, a wave of arrests was launched against the Society of the Muslim Brotherhood. Leaders of the Brotherhood, members of the Secret Unit (at least, those known to the government secret service), ordinary members and even those considered to be affiliated with the organisation were arrested within a very short time. The accuracy of the arrests implies that the operation was planned and well prepared.[158] Only a few managed to flee into exile, seeking refuge in other countries, in particular Syria, Iraq and Saudi Arabia, where they continued to work for the cause of the Muslim Brotherhood.[159] In Egypt, however, it seemed that the leadership of the Muslim Brotherhood had been effectively eliminated.

According to the official version, which was established through the show trials and is also supported by Mitchell, the Muslim Brotherhood was responsible for planning and executing an attempted coup d'etat.[160] However, this version of events must be handled critically. There is disagreement as to whether the Brotherhood was indeed behind the shots aimed at 'Abd al-Nasir or was framed. There are in fact indications that the attempt was instigated in order to create an opportunity to ward off the Muslim Brotherhood as well as Nasir's opponents within the RCC. The accused leaders of the Muslim Brotherhood, all of whom had been involved in the Secret Unit in varying degrees, adamantly denied any explicit involvement in the issuing of an assassination order.[161] This view is certainly promoted by authors affiliated to the Muslim Brotherhood.[162] Apart from these, there are also a number of experts who implicate 'Abd al-Nasir in the affair. Among scholars supporting the case in defence of the Muslim Brotherhood are Carré and Michaud.[163] They assert that 'Abd al-Nasir was the one who gained most from the event, while the leadership of the Brotherhood had no reason to jeopardise its position through a confrontation with the RCC. Keeping in mind that, only a few months earlier, in January 1954, 'Abd al-Nasir had failed in his attempt to rid himself of opposition and to claim absolute power, there is good reason to be suspicious about his sudden triumph. While relations with the RCC, and particularly with 'Abd al-Nasir, deteriorated in the months before the event, al-Hudaybi's conduct directly fed into the Brotherhood's vulnerability. He definitely lost all control over the organisation; this also meant that more radical elements within the organisation, closer to the ex-members al-Sanadi and al-'Ashmawi, had more room to conspire with 'Abd al-Nasir against al-Hudaybi. In other words, parts of the Secret Unit may have been involved in organising a plot, but this time they did not act under al-Hudaybi's command, but in fact were aligned with 'Abd al-Nasir. However, the picture becomes even more complicated, since there was also a split within the Secret Unit itself. In fact, the internal division created the perfect alibi for 'Abd al-Nasir. Those loyal to al-Hudaybi did not know about the plan, yet they were the ones who were addressed by the court as being responsible for the execution of the plot. Obviously, this is only a theory, and although there are indications that it could be an adequate description, it needs to be admitted that what really happened cannot be proved with absolute certainty. However, there can be no doubt that 'Abd al-Nasir clearly came out of the October events as the victor.

On 4 December 1954 the first verdicts were announced.[164] Seven defendants of the Brotherhood were condemned to death. These were Hasan al-Hudaybi, 'Abd al-Qadir 'Auda, Yusuf Tal'at, Hindawi Duwayr, Ibrahim al-Tayyib, Shaykh Muhammad Farghali and the alleged assassin, Mahmud 'Abd al-Latif. The next day, 5 December 1954, the Society of the Muslim Brothers was officially dissolved. On 7 December 1954 the death sentences were carried out, with the exception of that of the *Murshid*. Al-Hudaybi was pardoned; his verdict was commuted to life imprisonment. The Peoples' Tribunal announced a further nine death penalty verdicts in the following weeks, all of which were subsequently commuted to life imprisonment. Among these were seven members of the Guidance Council. The Peoples' Tribunal declared around 800 prison sentences, while the Military Court, which dealt with Brothers serving in the army, sentenced another 300 men.[165] It should be noted that a further large group, estimates suggest about 1,000 people, was incarcerated without any charges being made. These statistics provide a glimpse of the scale of the persecution. Prisons were filled with members of the Brotherhood. Most of the detainees arrested in 1954 were students, state employees and teachers, and thus belonged to the literate middle class.[166] As for the distribution of prisoners, the government had to consider how to accommodate such large numbers. Generally speaking, younger and lower ranking Brothers were sent to regional prisons such as that in Qanatir, which was known to house younger inmates. The leadership of the Brotherhood, such as most members of the Guidance Council and those considered as key actors, were detained in Liman al-Turra prison.[167] Most of the convicts there to faced long terms and were sentenced to hard labour. Conditions there were reportedly appalling and inmates had suffered abuse and torture.

Those who escaped the round-up lived in constant fear of being arrested or spied upon. Muhammad Hasan al-'Ashmawi, who was close to al-Hudaybi and a member of the Guidance Council, was one of the few leading members who managed to escape and live underground. He describes in his memoirs his fear of being discovered by the Egyptian Secret Service and how fellow Brothers were caught one by one. Living a secret life, he experienced isolation and mistrust.[168] Zaynab al-Ghazali also refers to this situation of fear and secrecy, mentioning that Brothers outside prison associated only on a very informal level.[169] Since it was not possible to meet in public, personal relationships were sometimes the only bond. Also, the Friday prayers, after which it is customary to sit and chat, were used as an opportunity to exchange news. As such, frequenting of certain mosques by the Brothers made it possible to maintain a loose network.[170] Different from the previous experience of persecution in 1949, there was no underground movement, nor the backup of a Secret Unit which could have kept the movement intact. Hearing about the hardship of imprisoned comrades, Brothers avoided any organised contact. The organisation seemed to have come to an end.

Silence is the most remarkable feature of the years until 1957. There are no signs of any organisational structure or of any activities.[171] There is no word of any groupings and their ideas. As mentioned, the memoirs of members of the Society talk about the injustice inflicted upon Brothers and the hardship of imprisonment and torture. A sense of desperation might describe the mood. Certainly, dispersing Brothers all over the country and separating them from the leadership led to a breakdown of communication. The experience of torture and the death of fellow Brothers under such circumstances contributed to the mood of despair, considering that twenty-nine Brothers were killed in the period October 1954 to April 1955. While the memoirs emphasise the Brotherhood's innocence, they do not elaborate on the organisation's failures. The reasons lie deep. In view of the fact that Brothers supported the RCC and ʿAbd al-Nasir in the lead-up to the October event, thus aligning themselves against their own *Murshid*, Brothers now turned inwards and reflected on their own responsibility for the debacle. The silence can therefore only be explained as a sign of disillusionment and internal collapse.

There is also no relevant information available on activities or discourse among the Brothers. The Brotherhood was not strong enough to maintain its opposition against ʿAbd al-Nasir in a systematic and organised way, nor was the feeling of hatred and rejection expressed in a consistent or well thought-out ideology. This could be described as an 'ideological gap'. At this point, a rigorous ideology which could provide answers to questions about the Brotherhood's future was missing. There is no evidence of any announcement on the part of Hasan al-Hudaybi, still *Murshid*. Qutb, who was to become the focal point of later discussions of radical opposition, had not evolved into an ideological leader, at least not at this stage. He just resumed work on his Qur'an commentary, *Fi Zilal al-Qur'an* (Under the Shade of the Qur'an); yet it seems that his thinking had not yet absorbed radical ideas.[172]

Phoenix from the ashes

By the year 1957/58, circumstances had changed for the Brotherhood. For one, the government loosened its policy of repression. A number of Brothers who were not sentenced to long-term imprisonment and those detained without any court case were released.[173] Those released were mostly younger and lower-ranking members of the Society. Another important concession made by ʿAbd al-Nasir was the pardoning of the *Murshid*, Hasan al-Hudaybi, for reasons of age and poor health. He was, instead, put under house arrest, where he lived with his family in Alexandria.[174] Most important, however, it was during this time that signs of reorganisation can be found.

The slight revision of government policy towards the Muslim Brotherhood is related to a change in Egypt's political circumstances. After the Suez crisis, the British presence in Egypt came to an end.[175] This was clearly a victory for ʿAbd al-Nasir and strengthened him to expand his regime. It made him a national, even an Arab, hero and enabled him to push forward his ideology of pan-Arabism. As many Egyptians supported the Brotherhood because of its resistance to the presence of British troops, 'Abd al-Nasir's victory was an implicit defeat for the movement. Hence, 'Abd al-Nasir may no longer have considered the Brotherhood as a threat. This change of government policy had an immediate impact; the release of Brothers accelerated the revival of the organisation.

The initial reaction among the Brothers to the dissolution was superseded by a new spirit of engagement only four years after the October event. First indications can be traced back to 1957, but they gained momentum from 1958 onwards. Ahmad 'Abd al-Majid, who was one of the leaders of the group which later was became known as 'Organisation 1965', provides a detailed account. He describes that from about 1957/58 onwards two small groups emerged independently of one another. One group gathered around 'Abd al-Fattah Isma'il and another around 'Ali al-'Ashmawi and Ahmad 'Abd al-Majid.[176] Eventually, the leaders of the two groups met; they decided to unite and to aim for a reorganisation of the Muslim Brotherhood. Therefore, contact with the *Murshid*, al-Hudaybi, was established.

According to al-Ghazali, 'Abd al-Fattah visited the *Murshid* to get his permission to reorganise the splinter groups of the Muslim Brotherhood outside of the prisons. Her account leaves no doubt that al-Hudaybi had no objections to the project.[177] 'Abd al-Majid confirms al-Ghazali's statement, arguing that the *Murshid* was fully aware of the plans of the group.[178] However, a somewhat different account is given by Ra'if, who notes that the *Murshid* advised 'Abd al-Fattah to act in accordance with the order of dissolution. Ra'if argues that 'Abd al-Fattah must have taken this vague advice as implicit support for his cause, since the *Murshid*, who was under constant surveillance, was hardly in a position to express his cooperation openly.[179] In his testimony during the later court case in 1966, al-Hudaybi also said that he responded to 'Abd al-Fattah that he needed to comply with the dissolution order. Hence, he implied that he was not responsible for the activities of Organisation 1965. Whether or not al-Hudaybi gave his permission is linked to the issue of whether and, moreover, to what extent, the *Murshid* was involved in the (re-)establishment of the organisation. While the sources are contradictory, it has nevertheless to be assumed that al-Hudaybi knew of the reorganisation. There is sufficient evidence, which indicates that he was in touch with the leadership of this group and that he did not object to the group. And why would he? At this point, when the idea of the Brotherhood was almost at an end, any revival must have been welcomed by al-Hudaybi. Thus, it can be argued that al-Hudaybi deliberately remained ambivalent and hid behind diplomacy and being out of reach.

According to 'Abd al-Majid, a committee of four was founded which had the aim of coordinating the work. The members of this committee were 'Abd al-Fattah Isma'il, Shaykh Muhammad Fathi Rifa'i, 'Ali al-'Ashmawi and Ahmad 'Abd al-Majid 'Abd al-Sami, the author of the memoir.[180] This account is verified to a great extent by Ahmad Ra'if, although he states that the committee consisted of five members.[181] He also recalls slightly different names, namely 'Abd al-Fattah Isma'il, Sabri 'Arafa al-Kaumi, Ahmad 'Abd al-Majid 'Abd al-Sami, Majdi 'Abd al-'Aziz and 'Ali al-'Ashmawi. Considering that Ra'if was not directly involved in the activities of Organisation 1965, but that 'Abd al-Majid was, there is no reason to question the latter's detailed report on the structure and division of duties. He puts forward the following list (directly translated from his book):

1 'Abd al-Fattah Isma'il (Trader): responsible for the area of Damietta, Kufr al-Shaykh and the Eastern Delta; contact to al-Hudaybi; contact to Sayyid Qutb; communication with Brothers in Alexandria, Bahriyya; contact to Shaykh Muhammad Fathi Rifa'i; fundraising.
2 Shaykh Muhammad Fathi Rifa'i (Lecturer at Azhar University): responsible for the Central Delta including al-Daqhaliyya, al-Gharbiyya, al-Manufiyya; compiling the educational and pedagogical programme.
3 Ahmad 'Abd al-Majid (Employee at the Department of Military Secrets) (Idara Katim Asrar Harbiyya): responsible for Upper Egypt (al-Sa'id); responsible for propaganda.
4 'Ali 'Ashmawi (Manager of the construction company Sambulkis): responsible for Cairo and Giza; sports education.

('Abd al-Majid (1991) 51–52, 55)

The list is interesting for too many reasons. It confirms that links were established to the leadership of the Brotherhood under al-Hudaybi and to the upcoming ideologue, Qutb. In the course of their activities they also built up relations with Brothers in exile, with like-minded supporters of the Islamist cause and with similar organisations.[182] The supporters abroad, especially those in Saudi Arabia, became the financial resource of the group. The list also indicates that the revival of the Brotherhood was not only confined to a small group in Cairo and Alexandria, but that circles were formed in other parts of Egypt which then came together under the network of Organisation 1965. This observation, then, somehow challenges the assumption that the revival of the Brotherhood occurred in prison. While Qutb may have had a role in providing a rigorous ideology for Organisation 1965, the prisons were not the loci of the Brotherhood's reorganisation. This observation obviously puts the basis of Kepel's and Sivan's analysis into doubt.[183] The focus on Qutb and his radicalisation of thought does not entirely explain the history of the Brotherhood's revival. In fact, their retrospective view on Qutb as father of the radical Islamist trend singles him out rather than putting his work and thought into context.

Communication, and this included interaction between those inside and those outside prison, was crucial for operations. A number of sources speak about how information was exchanged. Among these are Zaynab al-Ghazali's autobiographical account and also the aforementioned 'Abd al-Majid and Ra'if.[184] Some information can also be extracted from Fu'ad 'Alam, who was a brigadier general in the Egyptian army and a member of 'Abd al-Nasir's Secret Service. All of these sources agree that the wives and sisters of Brothers played an important role in maintaining the communication links. They were the backbone of a network which was built on personal bonds. Many of the women knew each other and were members of the Muslim Sisterhood (*al-Sayyidat al-Muslimat*), which was a branch of the Muslim Brotherhood led by Zaynab al-Ghazali. The structure of the Muslim

Sisters had remained intact after October 1954 and hardly any of the women were questioned. Obviously not considered a threat to the political system, the women attached to this group continued their activities. As such, Zaynab al-Ghazali was in touch with Qutb's sisters, Amina and Hamida Qutb, with al-Hudaybi's wife and his daughters, Khalidah, 'Aliyyah and Tahiyyah Sulayman, as well as with the wife of Munir al-Dilla, 'Amal al-'Ashmawi.[185] The Sisters were nominally engaged as a prisoners' support group.[186] The women did not play a passive role simply as mediators between prisoners and those Brothers living in hiding; beyond that they were involved in fundraising activities and the distribution of finances to members of the network, their families and individual members. Apart from the network provided by the Muslim Sisterhood, a few individual prison guards who were sympathetic to the cause of the Muslim Brotherhood occasionally helped or kept their eyes closed. Considering that exposure carried a high risk for these guards, this means of communication was only of limited use.

Communications within prisons were made difficult by the fact that Brothers were allocated to various prisons all over the country. However, the prison hospital at Liman al-Turra did provide a place where ideas could be passed on. Since sick inmates from other prisons were sent there for treatment and then returned to their own prisons, the hospital became a centre for the exchange of information and ideas. Qutb, who had to stay there for most of the time because of his poor health, wrote and revised his important works there, among them his Qur'anic commentary *Fi Zilal al-Qur'an* and his propagandistic work *Ma'lim fi al-Tariq*. While he was engaged in writing he talked to fellow Brothers, preaching his interpretation of Islam. His conversation with Muhammad Hawwash is an example of this discourse in the prison hospital. 'Abd al-Khaliq and Ramadan mention how Qutb's interpretation was thus passed on to the inmates and steadily distributed to other prisons.[187] While basic theological premises surrounding the idea of *takfir* (pronouncement of unbelief) were already current, Qutb incorporated this concept in drawing up some ideological guidelines for the revival the Brotherhood inside and outside prison.[188] It is reported by 'Abd al-Khaliq and Ramadan that Qutb's ideas were vividly discussed by younger Brothers and particularly inspired those incarcerated in Qanatir. It was also younger Brothers who were released and who directly fed into Organisation 1965.[189]

With a communication network in place, the committee of Organisation 1965 approached Qutb and asked him to support the reformation of the Brotherhood by drawing up an educational programme. Qutb's prison experience and the gradual radicalisation of his ideas directly fed into the ideological make-up of Organisation 1965. In fact, as will be shown below, there is reason to believe that his work *Ma'lim fi al-Tariq* was written for the purpose of providing spiritual guidelines to members of Organisation 1965. Within small circles, members studied the Qur'an and Sunna, as well as extracts from the works of classical scholars of jurisprudence. Al-Ghazali explicitly mentions works of Ibn Kathir, Ibn Hazm and al-Shafi' as being on the reading list.[190] 'Abd al-Majid gives a detailed list of the readings. The lengthy list includes works such as Ibn Taymiyya's *Risala al-'Ubudiyya* (Letters on Submission) and his *Risala al-Iman* (Letters on Belief); Hasan al-Banna's *Al-Aqa'id* (Creed); but also a number of works by Maududi, Sayyid Qutb, Muhammad Qutb and many others more or less well-known authors.[191] It is worth mentioning that the majority of books listed by ʿAbd al-Majid are by modern, non-classical authors of the Islamic revival. Obviously, parts of Sayyid Qutb's commentary on the Qur'an, and in particular extracts of Milestones (*Maʿlim fi al-Ṭariq*), were read and explained. The draft manuscripts of Milestones were smuggled out of the prison hospital with the help of his sisters Amina and Hamida Qutb.[192] According to al-Ghazali and ʿAbd al-Majid, al-Hudaybi was familiar with Qutb's writings, even with Milestones; whether he agreed with Qutb's point of view is, however, not altogether clear.[193] In any case, Qutb became the spiritual leader of Organisation 1965, although ʿAbd al-Majid states that Qutb was only asked to take the lead on spiritual matters once he was released from prison in 1964.[194] Describing the situation of the first meetings of the committee with Qutb after his release, he notes that the Qutb demanded that al-Hudaybi be informed about the plan to appoint him as their guide. Following this, al-Hudaybi was contacted. Apparently, the *Murshid*, who was surprised at the size of the organisation, gave his permission to go ahead.[195]

Organisation 1965 gathered not just for the purpose of studying. Certainly, the situation of the Muslim Brotherhood was the subject of discussion; considering the experience of the past, the question of how to bring the Brotherhood back to its glory was definitely a talking point.[196] There is no doubt that ʿAbd al-Nasir was seen as the prime cause of the *mihna* and was thus vehemently criticised. Incidents such as the killing of twenty-two Brothers in June 1957 left a profound impression, not only on Qutb but on other Brothers as well, and confirmed their postulation that ʿAbd al-Nasir was a tyrannical and anti-Islamic leader.[197] Ra'if states that plans to assassinate the president were talked of, but he indicates that these were merely speculative, the members of the groups neither being trained nor having the power to follow through a concrete plan.[198] Ramadan, however, argues that ʿAbd al-Majid and Qutb worked on plans to assassinate state officials which were to be carried out by an inner circle of followers (about seventy members).[199]

By the time Qutb was released in 1964, the mood of disillusionment and remorse had been replaced by a new spirit of Brotherhood activism.[200] The new communal strength led to a more solid rejection of ʿAbd al-Nasir's state system, which was by then underpinned by a more radical interpretation of what constitutes a just Islamic system. Qutb's radicalisation was part of this development of ideas.[201] The revival of the Brotherhood was not even stopped by the new wave of arrests which hit not only Organisation 1965 but the wider circle of Brothers.

The new wave of arrests and the beginnings of the moderate Brotherhood

In July 1965, a new wave of arrests began which targeted the Brotherhood in general and its activist sub-branch, Organisation 1965, in particular. ʿAbd al-Nasir ordered pervasive raids; anyone who was suspected of being a member of the Brotherhood was arrested. Possession of a copy of Milestones was enough reason

to be detained. Most of the leading members of Organisation 1965 had been cap-
tured by August. The main charge against them was high treason, which was based
on the accusation that members were attempting to assassinate ʿAbd al-Nasir and
thus planning to overthrow the state system.

Pointing out parallels to the situation of 1954, Muslim Brothers generally maintain that ʿAbd al-Nasir concocted the charge so as to put an end to the revival of
the Brotherhood.[202] They argue that the release of Qutb, whose rejection of the
state system was well known, was a pretence so as to expose the group and thus
take further steps on a larger scale against the Brotherhood. Several scholars pick
up this argument and point out that ʿAbd al-Nasir may indeed have chosen this
tactic to nip the regenerating opposition in the bud.[203] Certainly, ʿAbd al-Nasir
had an interest in wiping out his opponents. International relations may have been
one reason, since the Brotherhood's opposition to socialism and communism was
known. Moussalli thus argues that Egypt's relationship with Russia was the cause
of the persecution.[204] While ʿAbd al-Nasir established a closer alliance with the
East Block after 1962, the revival of an anti-communist opposition led by the
Brotherhood and Qutb would have brought about unwanted complications and
possible disruptions to Russian–Egyptian relations.[205] Also, when one considers
that Egypt was preparing itself for a war against Israel, another factor may have
come into play. As military preparations were in progress from at least 1965, the
persecution may also have been a consequence of the need to achieve internal
security. Of course, the Muslim Brotherhood and the followers of Qutb had an
anti-Israel attitude; however, there was certainly the risk that the Brotherhood
could take advantage to fight their chief enemy, ʿAbd al-Nasir. In short, there
are several factors which indicate that a move against the Islamist opposition,
and especially the group around Qutb and ʿAbd al-Fattah Ismaʿil, was in ʿAbd
al-Nasir's interest.

The military show trials established the expected, namely, that a number of
members of Organisation 1965 were guilty of planning to assassinate ʿAbd al-Nasir
and to attempt thus to overthrow the state system. In February 1966 the death penalties and prison sentences were announced. Among those condemned to death
were Sayyid Qutb, Hasan al-Hudaybi, ʿAbd al-Fattah Ismaʿil and Muhammad
Yusuf Awash.[206] Besides these high-profile cases, hundreds of prison sentences
were subsequently announced. The sentences against Qutb, Ismaʿil and Awash
were carried out on 26 August 1966. Al-Hudaybi's sentence was again suspended
and was then commuted to life imprisonment.

The persecutory measures are reminiscent of the beginning of the persecution
in 1954; the mood within the Brotherhood had changed. While the prisons were
filled once again, Brothers did not suffer disillusionment, remorse and speechless-
ness. Raʾif's account of the welcome given to those sentenced to death serves as
an example.[207] Upon their return to Liman al-Turra from the final court session at
which their sentences were announced, they were welcomed as heroes. The situation developed beyond the control of prison security; only the next day could
order be re-established. The uprising demonstrates that the short-lived revival
had left its mark: Brothers now had a clear sense of community and resistance,

which – at least for the moment – superseded even ideological differences. As such, the enforcement of the death penalty made Qutb a martyr for the cause and his legacy was subsequently venerated not only by proponents of radicalism but also by moderate Islamists.[208]

Despite, or rather because the Muslim Brothers did not suffer from remorse and self-criticism, ideological differences soon broke out. The centres of the debate were the prisons of Qanatir, Qina' and particularly Liman al-Turra. It was in Liman al-Turra that al-Hudaybi and the 'older generation' of members of the Guidance Council, but also key figures of Organisation 1965 were imprisoned. According to ʿAbd al-Majid, unresolved issues on the relationship of the Brotherhood towards the state, and also questions regarding ideological matters, were the cause of heated discussions. The dispute was set off when the *Murshid*, Hasan al-Hudaybi, demanded some clarifications from members of Organisation 1965.[209] Apparently, he asked for written statements on whether the group considered the idea of *takfir* as the core of its ideology. ʿAbd al-Majid further argues that the exercise had the objective of establishing whether Organisation 1965 was indeed planning to overthrow the state. However, ʿAbd al-Majid's assumption does not make sense if al-Hudaybi indeed knew of the Organisation, its leadership, its communications and its educational programme. In fact, ʿAbd al-Majid previously stated that al-Hudaybi had consented to Sayyid Qutb's spiritual leadership. Hence, the argument that al-Hudaybi intended to find out details may not be the reason. It is more likely that al-Hudaybi used the demand for statements as an occasion to re-establish his authority as leader. Soon after this incident, al-Hudaybi gave a speech in which he distanced himself from the activities of Organisation 1965. Al-Hudaybi's public declaration was not well received by members of Organisation 1965. ʿAbd al-Majid describes the frustration and disbelief at the *Murshid*'s withdrawal of his consent; some accused him of dishonesty and, with reference to 1954, questioned his leadership and judgement.[210]

Most importantly, this dispute surrounding al-Hudaybi's announcement was the beginning of a fundamental discourse about the Brotherhood's ideological and strategic premises. Al-Hudaybi, who was now sharing the cells with fellow Brothers, finally had the opportunity to speak directly to his fellow Brothers. Ra'if and ʿAlam tell us that Brothers addressed questions to him and sought his opinion and advice.[211] An example of al-Hudaybi's engagement in discussions is his Seven Public Letters (*Sabʿa Rasa'il min Sijn al-Turra*).[212] Al-Hudaybi's *Rasa'il* retain their original form of questions and answers. They thus provide a glimpse of the kind of theological, spiritual and implicit political concerns brought forward. They also show that al-Hudaybi and his circle tried to regain control over the Brotherhood by fighting back against an emerging radical trend.

At stake at this point was whether members of the Brotherhood defined the vision of the organisation as radical or moderate Islamist opposition. As for the radical option, it took the view that *jihad* as an offensive method and the establishment of an Islamic state was an immediate duty; this position sees it as a necessity to use revolutionary and militant means to bring about the establishment of an Islamic state. The moderate counterpart, however, argued that an Islamic state needs to be brought about through a gradual change of society. This is to be done through education (*ta'lim*) and missionary engagement (*da'wa*). While radical and moderate Islamists share the same objective, namely the establishment of an Islamic state system, the two are fundamentally different in their approaches. The Brotherhood thus stood at a deciding point in its future development. This was, however, not so much a decision for or against Qutb – even his work Milestones could have been interpreted either way. Yet it was a decision for or against Qutbists, i.e. radical members of the Brotherhood who claimed to follow Qutb's thought.

How deep the hatred of 'Abd al-Nasir actually was is illustrated by a story told by Ra'if.[213] Apparently, Muhammad Qutb was called on to make a public confession; instead of praising 'Abd al-Nasir, he chose to give a speech calling for resistance. The question was raised whether Qutb's concept of *jihad* against *jahiliyya* and against the regime was applicable in the event of an outside threat in the situation leading up to the war against Israel in 1967. Under circumstances of war, the division between Qutbists and those supporting al-Hudaybi became even more pronounced. Heated discussions arose when imprisoned Muslim Brothers were confronted with their willingness to support the struggle against the common enemy, Israel.[214] According to several sources, three major groups emerged in this situation.[215] First, the Qutbists, who denied that it was legitimate to support 'Abd al-Nasir; in their view he was an illegitimate, *jahili* leader, whose regime could not be redeemed.[216] Regarding a war against Israel, they argued that an illegitimate ruler – as they viewed 'Abd al-Nasir – could not be supported under any circumstances. Israel, therefore, was not the immediate enemy, but rather Egypt's leadership. In clear opposition to this point of view were the followers of Hasan al-Hudaybi, who argued that 'Abd al-Nasir's regime had done wrong, but that he was still a Muslim and must have support against a non-Muslim enemy. The alternative, so the argument went, leads to *fitna* (civil strife among Muslims). A third party, which did not wish to take sides for either al-Hudaybi or Qutbists, saw themselves in the tradition of Hasan al-Banna'. While the Qutbists clearly opted for a radical theology, the latter two factions, i.e. followers of al-Hudaybi and al-Banna', remained moderate in their approach and their differences were related to the issue of leadership rather than based on theological interpretation. Followers of al-Banna' were critical of al-Hudaybi and expressed their concern about his leadership through an emphasis on Hasan al-Banna's statements.

Egypt's defeat in 1967 had a devastating effect. 'Abd al-Nasir's popularity and confidence suddenly fell. As for the Brotherhood, the war left its mark here also. Qutbists clearly broke away from the mainstream under al-Hudaybi and the 'neutralists'. Claiming that the defeat was a sign of God's warning, they referred to the Qur'anic stories of punishment. They also saw Qutb's interpretation confirmed, insofar as they compared their struggle to that of the first Muslims and those true to God. As such, they took Qutb's interpretation literally, thus adopting the idea that they lived in a state of inner *hijra* (flight) during which they were preparing for the struggle of the realisation of God's absolute sovereignty (*hakimiyyat Allah*). In effect, they saw themselves exemplified as the vanguard (*tali'*) of which

Qutb spoke.[217] The split can be traced not only on an ideological level. Radical Brothers avoided the main community of prisoners and were eventually separated by the prison personnel, who allocated special cells to them at Liman al-Turra.[218] Both 'Abd al-Majid and Ra'if state that Mustafa Shukri was among those joining the Qutbists. When he was released from prison in the early 1970s, he moved on to establish the militant group named '*al-Takfir wa al-Hijra*' (the Predicament of Unbelief and the Refuge). Mustafa Shukri exemplifies that later militant Islamists had their roots in prison, where they broke away from the Brotherhood. The example of Mustafa Shukri and other radical Qutbists shows that it would be wrong to assume that this faction should be still considered as part of the Muslim Brotherhood.

As for the mainstream Brotherhood, al-Hudaybi now had to face the task of winning back mainstream members who were not convinced about his leadership and those who were still wavering between the arguments of the radical faction and the mainstream. Members of the Guidance Council such as 'Umar al-Tilmisani, Mustafa Mashhur and 'Abd al-'Aziz Attiyya supported him in this effort. Ma'mun al-Hudaybi, who was imprisoned with them, assisted his father as well. The work *Du'at la Qudat* (*Preachers not Judges*) was, then, a product of the efforts to rebuff the radical thinking of Qutbists. As we will see below, the work was not authored by al-Hudaybi. The circle of 'old guard Brothers' participated in the process of writing. However, most interesting is that several sources indicate that, besides them, some theologians of al-Azhar were also involved. Among these sources are 'Allam, 'Abd al-Majid, Ra'if, al-Tilmisani and 'Abd al-Khaliq.[219]

The participation of al-Azhar in the writing of *Du'at la Qudat* has fundamental implications. If it is indeed the case that trained theologians were taking part, as will be shown below in detail, this challenges the position that the rehabilitation of the Brotherhood only began under 'Abd al-Nasir's successor, Anwar al-Sadat. Since al-Azhar was effectively under state control from 1961, it would have been impossible for Shuyukh to enter the Liman al-Turra without the knowledge of the authorities.[220] It is even more unthinkable that they would have been able to discuss theological and juridical matters, and the writing of *Du'at la Qudat*, with members of the Brotherhood without 'Abd al-Nasir's approval. In other words, 'Abd al-Nasir must have approved and supported this arrangement. While scholarship holds it as a fact that state policy towards the Brotherhood only changed when Sadat came to power, there are a few indications that some negotiations between the arch-enemies al-Hudaybi and 'Abd al-Nasir were already aimed for after 1967. In fact, it fits in with the fact that 'Abd al-Nasir's rule loosened after the war.[221]

The question follows: what was possibly 'Abd al-Nasir's reason for changing his position? If we consider that his popularity took a downturn with the 1967 debacle, he was vulnerable to the possibility of growing opposition from Islamist circles. In fact, a new generation of intellectuals, students and middle-class bureaucrats started to turn their attention toward Islam as a political alternative.[222] It therefore makes sense that 'Abd al-Nasir should have tried for some level of appeasement with the Brotherhood. As for al-Hudaybi and the Guidance

Council, cooperation with al-Azhar on a book which refuted radical Islamist thinking was in their interests. At this stage, the circle around al-Hudaybi needed to reaffirm its leadership position and give clarity to the Brotherhood's ideological stance. Moreover, the public announcement that the Brotherhood did not pose a threat to the regime was the only conceivable means to end the time of persecution, since nobody would have thought that 'Abd al-Nasir would die.

Re-establishment under a new paradigm

On 29 September 1970 'Abd al-Nasir's died suddenly. Anwar al-Sadat, who was vice-president during 'Abd al-Nasir's presidency, was nominated to succeed him.

As president, al-Sadat aimed for a national policy which steered away from the political vision of his predecessor.[223] As such, he gradually distanced himself from Arab socialism as the overarching ideological framework of the Egyptian Republic, which eventually led him to break away from the alliance with the USSR. However, al-Sadat did not display the charisma of his predecessor and certainly did not command the same level of public sympathy, and he needed to build national alliances which allowed him to steer his course. Having been fairly close to the Muslim Brotherhood in the early 1950s, al-Sadat began to rebuild the relationship with the Muslim Brothers.[224] At the same time, he aimed to build a personal cult which depicted him as 'the Believing President'.

His reconciliation with the Muslim Brotherhood was part of his strategy for finding wide political backing for his political course. For one, he needed the support and influence of the organisation in society. Although the Muslim Brotherhood was persecuted and had lost some of its membership, it was still an organisation of considerable influence. In fact, the loss of the 1967 war had an impact on the revival of Islam as a factor in politics. While the public profile of the Brotherhood was re-emerging in the late 1960s and early 1970s, al-Sadat needed their support. Considering their growing strength, the Brotherhood's anti-Nasserite and anti-communist stance seemed to be in accordance with al-Sadat's larger plan to reintroduce a capitalist order which allowed the state to open up to Western investors.

From 1971 onwards, imprisoned members of the Brotherhood were gradually released. In 1975, a general amnesty was issued and all remaining Muslim Brothers were set free.[225] The introduction of al-Sadat's new policies allowed the Muslim Brotherhood to reorganise itself publicly. However, the official ban was never lifted. While the Brotherhood did adopt a public profile, legal limitations forced the organisation to adopt a 'half-official' status. The restraints did not allow the movement to be recognised as a social organisation or as political party.[226] However, the relative freedom of speech and the boost to its morale following the release of Brothers from prison provided the Brotherhood with the opportunity to rebuild its influence. Al-Hudaybi was engaged in this process of rebuilding organisational structures. His approach of engaging in missionary work and to thus influence politics through social structures and institutions was largely adopted as the new strategy of the organisation. One can argue that his legacy paved the way for the Brotherhood's success as Egypt's largest social movement. As such, the Brotherhood took on activities in student unions, professional organisations and institutions of civil society.[227] In that respect, there is a continuation of al-Hudaybi's manner of leadership, a legacy he has left to this day. He had a decisive influence on the moderate and conciliatory approach of the re-established organisation and his ideas are still discussed.[228] Indeed, his approach forms the basis of the modern-day Brotherhood's policy, albeit continuously challenged by those voices that demand a more activist or even a radical opposition towards the government.[229] The fact that there is an ongoing interest in him is demonstrated by the biographies written on him and in the memoirs of that period, in which his leadership is discussed – at times with some controversy. Nevertheless, he is mentioned on the official website of the *Ikhwan*, next to Hasan al-Banna', as one of the greatest leaders of the Society of the Muslim Brothers.[230]

When al-Hudaybi died on 11 November 1973 at the age of 82 the Muslim Brotherhood had regained considerable power in Egypt's political establishment.

2   The discourse of the prison years

Radical ideas and moderate responses

2.1 The discourse of the prison years: radical ideas and moderate responses

Sayyid Qutb is remembered as one of the leading figures of the Muslim Brotherhood. The books he is best known for were written or revised during his time in prison from October 1954 to August 1966. Since his works are more widespread than those of any other Muslim Brother, the assumption is often made that they represent the ideology of the organisation.

There is no doubt that Qutb's conceptions of Islam are significant sources of modern Islamic interpretation. However, there is a certain ambiguity with regard to the question of whether he contributed to the ideological framework of the Brotherhood. Defending his input, some Brothers point out that his legacy must not be reduced to his thoughts as presented in *Ma'lim fi al-Tariq* (Milestones). The diversity of his work is indeed impressive and encompasses several genres of literature, such as autobiography, poetry, literary criticism, religiously inspired analytical work and, last but not least, Islamist propaganda.[1] In particular, his commentary on the Qur'an is known as a modern contribution to the Islamic faith and not only referred to by members of the Brotherhood.[2] Nevertheless, many scholars, as well as Brothers, have pointed out that Qutb's writings contain the ideological basis for radical Islamic activism or even militancy.[3] In this respect, his Qur'anic commentary and, even more so, his book *Ma'lim fi al-Tariq* indeed contain the ideological foundations of radical Islamist thinking. As such, Milestones served as a theological guidebook for radical Islamist groups which first evolved in the 1970s and which eventually progressed to today's a Jihadist networks in and beyond Egypt.[4] The ambiguity embedded in Qutb's concepts and the diversity of his written expression led to a wide range of reactions, which vary from blind admiration to rejection.

Sayyid Qutb: father of radical Islamist ideas?

Sayyid Qutb was born in 1906 in Musha, a village in the district of Asyut, into a middle-class farming family.[5] His education could be described as rather secular in nature: he studied at the teacher's training college, *Dar al-'Ulum*, and hence had no particular background in the study of Islamic theology and jurisprudence.[6]

According to Abu Rabiʿ, Hanafi, Moussalli and Haddad, Qutb's literary work can be classified in stages.[7] Although the suggested divisions may detract from the fact that certain ideas were developed, but not used as material for ideological positions, these are tools – a type of guideline – that help to introduce Qutb's literary and ideological development. This development shows a gradual transformation from a politically aware modernist influenced by secular ideas to a rather radical thinking Islamist.

After finishing his degree in Education Arts in 1933, Qutb was employed by the Ministry of Education. At the same time, he was engaged as writer, journalist and literary critic. His first writings were on non-religious subjects.[8] During this period in the 1930s and early 1940s he was, indeed, highly influenced by ʿAbbas Mahmud al-ʿAqqad and Taha Hussain. He produced novels and poems, as well as two autobiographies. Further, he wrote articles of literary criticism and editorials, especially on education, advocating its modernisation.

During a second stage, lasting from around 1949 to 1954, he was mainly interested in social issues. It was then that Qutb adopted an Islamic perspective. During this time he published his first famous book, entitled *al-ʿAdala al-Ijtimaʿiyya fi al-Islam* (Social Justice in Islam), which was initially written in 1949 and revised repeatedly during later years.[9] It deals with religion and society in Christianity and Islam. Qutb herein explains that the separation of religion and politics is a characteristic of Western societies. He claims that it is actually the result of a legacy of struggle between Christian clergy, who were preoccupied with keeping their political power rather than instructing in faith, and secular leaders and philosophers, who doubted the ecclesiastic legitimacy. He counters that a separation of religion and politics would be inadequate for Islamic societies, because there is no hierarchy among believers and the ultimate authority lies with God alone. The Qurʾan, Qutb explains, gives guidelines, general principles and rules for life. Islam is thus the basis for social equality and true justice.

His experiences during a visit to the United States between November 1948 and August 1950 had an immense impact on his gradually growing anti-Western thought.[10] He was sent abroad by the Ministry of Education to study modern systems of education and training. In his subsequent works, the condemnation of Western thought and lifestyle, of its social, economic and political systems is a vocal and recurring point.

Upon his return to Egypt, Qutb became a member of the Muslim Brotherhood. Although authors of the secondary literature differ on the date of his entry, it can be noted that this was some time between 1951 and 1953.[11] Within a short period of time he took a seat in the organisation's Guidance Council (*Maktab al-Irshad*) and, further, held the position of head of the Propaganda Section (*Qism Nashr al-Daʿwa*).[12] Additionally, he became the editor of the weekly newspaper, *al-Ikhwan al-Muslimun*, in May 1954.[13]

Following the Revolution of 1952, the organisation of the Muslim Brotherhood had close links to the new governing body of the RCC (Revolutionary Command Council). Like many fellow Brothers, Qutb had, at first, a positive attitude towards the political change and cooperated with the leading Free Officers. In fact, he held the position of consultant for the RCC in matters of culture and education and was, therefore, a crucial link between the Free Officers and the Brotherhood.[14] However, when in the course of 1953 the power relations changed within the governing body of the RCC in favour of 'Abd al-Nasir, who resented the political influence of the Brotherhood, Qutb broke his ties with the RCC.[15]

In October 1954, following the alleged assassination attempt on 'Abd al-Nasir, Qutb was among those Muslim Brothers arrested and was sentenced to 15 years of hard labour.[16] Because of his poor health, which further deteriorated after torture and his stay in the state prison, Qutb spent most of his time of imprisonment in the prison hospital. There he had the opportunity to write and to revise his previous writings. The experience of imprisonment initiated a third stage. In the writings of the years 1954 to 1966, Qutb continued focusing on the subject of Islam, expressing his ideas, however, in a far more uncompromising way. He produced a tremendous output of books, which present ideological and political paradigms of Islamist political activism. Although most perceptions, such as the view that Islam is the only comprehensive and all-embracing system (*nizam*) and the notion that Western ideas as well as all deductive philosophies must be rejected, were present in previous writings, Qutb now put these ideas into a framework which suggests that belief coincides with active engagement in establishing an Islamic state system. This radicalisation can be seen in works like *Khasa'is al-Tasawwur al-Islami wa Muqawwimatihi* (The Characteristics of the Islamic Concept and its Elements), and also in *al-'Adala al-Ijtima'iyya fi al-Islam* (Social Justice in Islam), which he revised during these years.[17] The most important books of the prison years are the revised commentary on the Qur'an entitled *Fi Zilal al-Qur'an* (Under the Shade of the Qur'an) and the book *Ma'alim fi al-Tariq* (Signposts).[18]

In 1964 Qutb was released for a short time, probably through the support of the Iraqi president 'Abd as-Salam 'Arif. However, he was re-arrested shortly afterwards and accused of being the leading figure of a terrorist organisation which allegedly was planning an attempt on 'Abd al-Nasir's life.[19] After a military show trial, Qutb was hanged in August 1966.

As pointed out above, most of the authors of the secondary literature like Haddad, Tripp, Kepel and Hanafi see the period of imprisonment as a decisive phase in Qutb's life.[20] They argue that the isolation of imprisonment left a strong imprint on the radicalisation of his ideas. Hence, they seem to suggest that he lost touch with reality outside the prison walls.[21] However, this rather psychological explanation for the radicalisation somehow hides the fact that key ideas of his argument, as given in his later work, were already present in earlier stages. Additionally, by singling out Qutb's experiences and giving them a psychological explanation, one can easily overlook that his radical interpretation was also embedded in a debate among Muslim Brothers, a network of relations to other detainees and to supporters outside the prison. This also fails to notice that Qutb was indeed aware of news regarding national politics, such as the introduction of 'Abd al-Nasir's ideology of Arab socialism in 1962. Hence, Qutb's ideological development cannot be described as a conceptualisation which grew out of an experience of isolation. Thus, his ideas need to be brought into the context of a wider political Islamic discourse.

Although there can be no doubt that Qutb's argumentation of the prison years epitomises a radicalisation of thought, which exemplifies the perception of a particular group of rather young members of the Brotherhood, it must be pointed out that his work is embedded in the discourse on religion and politics. This subject of reforming Islam as a political entity was particularly fiercely discussed in Egypt throughout the twentieth century, be it from the point of view of proponents of modern Islamist activists, of associates of the theological institution of al-Azhar or of advocates of secularism.[22] The climate of unrest, even upheaval, and the attempt at what can be best described as (re) definition of identity in the face of social, political and economic challenges had certainly a strong impact on the debate about religion. Finally, the atmosphere of continuous deliberation on the subject of religion having a very strong value for most Egyptians must not be underestimated, even thought this ambience can hardly be pinpointed by means of 'historical facts'.[23] Overall, it can be said, without making assumptions, that the different contributors to the discourse attempted to (re)define the role of religion within the changing environment in which Egypt found itself in the second half of the twentieth century. In this respect, Qutb's entire literary output cannot be set apart from the intellectual disputes as a whole, and more specifically from the so-called Islamist reform movement and its contributors such as Muhammad 'Abduh, Rashid Rida, and Hasan al-Banna'. Certainly, it can be argued that Qutb continued al-Banna's call to activism and political engagement.[24]

On several occasions, al-Banna' described the Brotherhood in broad terms as an Islamic movement (*haraka Islamiyya*) which has a missionary outlet and has the aim to actively engage in political issues.[25] The underlying aim of his speeches was to take opposition to the state system of his time, calling for the (re-)establishment of an Islamic government.

While Qutb's work clearly represents a furtherance of this call to activism and opposition to the state system, it should not be overlooked that it may be equally argued that al-Hudaybi, who came up with an interpretation differing substantially from that of Qutb, continued al-Banna's missionary and diplomatic approach. Hence, Gomaa observed correctly that even though Qutb and al-Hudaybi may have shared an Islamist approach in succession of al-Banna', their interpretations regarding how to pursue this cause diverged.[26]

Further obvious influences on Sayyid Qutb are two Pakistani scholars: Abu A'la al-Maududi and Abu al-Hasan 'Ali al-Nadwi. The impact of al-Maududi has been pointed out by several scholars with particular reference to the ideas of *hakimiyyat allah* (God's absolute sovereignty) and of *jahiliyya* (ignorance).[27] In particular, the idea of *hakimiyyat allah* and his interpretation of activism as a essential requirement for being a Muslim can be found in al-Maududi's early works. The question, then, is when and how the Egyptian learned about these ideas from the Pakistani writers.

Al-Maududi, who was one of the founders and the leader of the Pakistani Islamist organisation *al-Jama't-i Islami*, was a prolific writer.[28] Some of al-Maududi's work was already available in Arabic translation from the late 1940s onwards.[29] In particular, his book *al-Mustalahat al-Arba' fi'l-Qur'an* was widely distributed and went through several editions. These considerations, however, are problematic for the genealogy of Qutb's ideas. It would mean that he was initiated into al-Maududi's interpretation as early as the late 1940s or the beginning of the 1950s.Abu'l-Hasan al-Nadwi was another writer who had a specific impact on Sayyid Qutb's interpretation. Al-Nadwi, who was an eminent scholar located at Lucknow, was in the 1940s and 1950s loosely attached al-Maududi's *Jama'at-e Islami* but later distanced himself from the organisation.[30] In the course of his long life, al-Nadwi developed into a respected scholar and a representative of the Islamic World League. Of interest regarding his influence on Qutb is his book entitled *Madha Khasira al-'Alam bi-Inhitat al-Muslimin*. The work was first published in 1949 in Arabic. Since it was remarkably successful, a second edition followed in 1952.[31] Al-Nadwi's book introduces the thought of a modern *jahiliyya*. This new reading of the term extends its meaning beyond the common reference to the pre-Islamic period. Instead, al-Nadwi sees the state of ignorance as an ever-existing phenomenon. It is this perception which Qutb made use of. Sayyid Qutb wrote an introduction for the 1952 edition, describing it as the first solid analysis of the reasons for the crisis of Islam and the rise of a modern age of ignorance.[32] The fact that al-Nadwi is known as one of the eminent critics of Maududi's and Sayyid Qutb's thought should not distract from the overwhelming evidence that, initially, Qutb incorporated his concept of *jahiliyya* back in the early 1950s.

The thesis that Qutb imported some of al-Maududi's and al-Nadwi's conceptions before his 'final stage' is in contradiction to the idea that he developed his radical conceptions only during his time of imprisonment. Effectively, the argument leads to a critique of the simplifying graduation of Qutb's ideological development into separate stages, and further challenges the line of reasoning that he developed the key ideas of *hakimiyyat Allah* and *jahiliyya* only in the last years of his life.

In fact, a continuum can be traced in his own work. Admittedly, his late work condenses its focus on certain key ideas. Yet, this already indicates that he maintained a stance taken in earlier books. The revisions of his Social Justice in Islam (*al-'Adala al-Ijtima'iyya fi al-Islam*) are a prime example and are evidence of this. Fundamental terms like 'Islamic system' (*al-nizam al-Islami*), 'Islamic path' (*al-minhaj al-Islami*) and even the demand for 'Islamic activism' (*al-haraka al-Islamiyya*), the concept of a modern time of ignorance (*jahiliyya*) and of God's absolute sovereignty (*hakimiyyat Allah*) can be found in Qutb's writings from the early 1950s.[33] Taking into consideration that Qutb maintained consistency throughout his writings, the fact that parts of his *Ma'lim fi al-Tariq* (Signposts) were extracted from his Qur'anic commentary *Fi Zilal al-Qur'an* (Under the Shade of the Qur'an) and that it seems to be in other parts a condensed summary of other previous writings sheds a different light on this late work in general and specifically on the issue of the aims of its composition.[34] It should, then, be asked whether *Ma'lim fi al-Tariq* was edited for a particular readership rather than being propagandistic material for wide distribution.[35]

Although Qutb's *Ma'lim fi al-Tariq* was intended as a guide for Organisation 1965, the work was first published in 1964. It was initially not censored. This may be surprising, since Nasser's government soon ordered it to be taken off the market. Nevertheless, it could be argued that its first publication created a demand. In fact, during the short period that the booklet was actually available it fed the radical Islamist trend with an essential source of reference. While publication of *Ma'lim fi al-Tariq* could be stopped, the evolution of a radical leaning with a clearly defined ideological agenda could not. Despite the threat that possession of *Ma'lim fi al-Tariq* was punishableby imprisonment, copies were available 'under the counter'. Although printing of the book stopped in Egypt, at least officially, copies were subsequently produced in a number of countries, among them Pakistan, Lebanon and Britain. For an impression of how important and influential the booklet was, one only needs to look at the list of languages in which it was available, among them Persian, Urdu and English.

2.2 Qutbists and their world-view

> The Rulers of this age are in apostasy from Islam. They were raised at the tables of imperialism, be it Crusadersim, or Communism, or Zionism. They carry nothing from Islam but their names, even though they pray and fast and claim to be Muslim. It is a well-established rule of Islamic Law the punishment of an apostate will be heavier than the punishment of someone who is by origin an infidel and has never been a Muslim. Hence, it is the view of the majority of the jurists that an apostate has to be killed.
>
> (Muhammad 'Abd al-Salam Faraj quoted in Jansen (1986))

These words were written by Muhammad 'Abd al-Salam Faraj in his *al-Farida al-Gha'iba* (The Neglected Duty). Faraj's booklet, which outlines his view on ideological principles of an Islamist engagement, was the guide for President Anwar al-Sadat's assassins.[36] Influenced by Sayyid Qutb, Faraj's pamphlet exemplifies how central is the issue of *takfir* (accusation of unbelief) to extremist interpretations of religion.

Referring to unbelief (*kufr*), radical Islamists such as 'Abd al-Salam Faraj, 'Umar 'Abd al-Rahman, 'Abdallah 'Azzam or Ayman al-Zawahiri not only draw on Qutb, but in fact make use of established orthodox Sunni legal opinion, which commonly sees unbelief as a severe transgression. This does not mean that radical Islamist ideologists are interested in the complexities of this legal discourse.[37] They selectively tap into orthodox legal tradition only to make use of its seemingly unified verdict that death is the appropriate punishment for a Muslim who consciously renounces Islam.[38] Drawing on a decontextualised legal consensus, they construct their particular understanding of belief and unbelief. While radical Islamist thinking draws upon traditional theology and jurisprudence, it would be wrong to reverse this observation and argue that traditional Muslim scholarship is responsible for the development of a radical ideology.

Obviously spurred by political convictions, radical Islamists go beyond traditional approaches. In fact they consider anyone who does not share their revolutionary aim as an unbeliever, including fellow Muslims. Following this kind of logic, Muslim political leaders commit the ultimate kind of *kufr*, namely apostasy (*ridda*). With regard to this ideological position, radical Islamists, or Qutbists as they are sometimes called, borrow key concepts from Qutb to further substantiate the foregoing premise of *takfir*. In order to provide a clearer picture, it is therefore necessary to return to Qutb and to elaborate on some of his ideas. It needs to be emphasised, however, that the discussion below merely focuses on *Ma'lim fi al-Tariq* (Milestones). This pamphlet is one of Qutb's last works and was written with the objective of giving Organisation 1965 theological and spiritual guidelines. What needs to be kept in mind, therefore, is the context of writing Milestones and the fact that the book is not representative of Qutb's overall work and his legacy. Nevertheless, Milestones had a particular impact on Qutbists. Therefore it should be clarified from the outsetthat radical Islamists such as 'Abd al-Salam Faraj, 'Umar 'Abd al-Rahman, 'Abdallah 'Azzam or Ayman al-Zawahiri actually made a reductionist reading of Qutb.

Jahiliyya and Jihad: cornerstones of radical Islamist interpretation

Qutb's argument in Milestones revolves around the key concepts of *jahiliyya* (lit. ignorance) and *jihad* (struggle). Upon these he builds a concise and uncomplicated interpretation. It emphasises that the true Muslim is obliged to counteract all non-Islamic influences, thus striving to implement *hakimiyyat Allah* (God's 'absolute' authority). *Jahiliyya* and *hakimiyyat Allah* are thus binary opposites and it is the duty of Muslims to engage in *jihad* to fight the first and to implement the latter.

Qutb's starting point is the Muslim profession of faith, the *shahada*. He argues that the meaning of the Muslim creed, which is epitomised in the phrase '*la illaha illa Allah wa Muhammad Rasul Allah*' (there is no God but Allah and Muhammad is God's prophet), contains not only a theological and spiritual message, but also calls for a commitment to action. Seeing faith and activism as one, he states that the underlying meaning of the first part of the *shahada*, namely the announcement that there is only one God, connotes that God possesses absolute authority on earth. Qutb therefore interprets the concept of *tawhid* (God's oneness) not only in a theological sense which emphasises the idea of monotheism, but also with immediate practical consequences in the social and political area sphere. Only God has the 'absolute power of judgment and command' (*al-hukm wa al-amr al-mutlaq*). Accordingly, God is the only legitimate sovereign. Although the concept of God as *hakim* (sovereign) is not disputed in traditional Muslim theology and jurisprudence, Qutb interprets this idea in a literal sense, with immediate political implications. For him, the laws of *shari'a* are God's way of establishing his rule in an Islamic society. God is the ultimate and supreme legislator and the laws which are set out in the Qur'an are obligatory. Qutb expresses this link between God and society clearly when he states:

No sovereignty (*hakimiyya*) but God's, no law (*shari'a*) but God's law and no power (*e*) of a person over another person, because all power belongs to God.

(Translated from Qutb (1993a) 25)

In accordance with his insistence that God is the absolute sovereign, Qutb argues that servitude to divine will (*al-'ubudiyya*) is an absolute demanded of humans. God stipulates that mankind or, to be more accurate, Muslims must derive their legitimate political existence from no other power except the authority of God. Qutb uses the Qur'anic avowal '*wa man lam yahkumu bi-ma anzala Allahu fa-ula'ika hummu 'l-kafirun*' (and whosoever does not judge by what Allah has revealed, such are the *kafirun*) as evidence for his interpretation.[39] Reading this statement in the literal sense, Qutb comes to the conclusion that any philosophies, social and political theories are '*jahili*'. Consequently the implementation and influence of '*jahili*' concepts into modern systems of state organisation are illegitimate (*taghuti*) and tyrannical (*zulmi*). Being based on '*jahili*' premises, they are obstructing God's *hakimiyyat*, which is – as stated – the only righteous basis of a social and political order.

The adjective '*jahili*' and the related noun '*jahiliyya*' are frequently used by Qutb in Milestones in order to emphasise his rejection of modern philosophies, concepts, attitudes and state systems. Literally, '*jahili*' means ignorant; likewise '*jahiliyya*' describes a state of ignorance. With the selection of this vocabulary, Qutb intentionally calls upon Qur'anic connotations. In the Qur'an, the term '*jahiliyya*' is used four times "… as the opposite of the word Islam, and which refers to the state of affairs in Arabia before the mission of the Prophet, to paganism (…) the pre-Islamic period and the men of that time".[40] While classical interpretations imply that the period of ignorance is equivalent to pre-Islamic times, thus arguing that ignorance was replaced by the knowledge, as presented in the revelation of the Qur'an, modern interpreters, starting with Abu 'Ala al-Maududi, Abu al-Hassan an-Nadwi and then Qutb, add a level to its negative connotation. In their view, *jahiliyya* cannot be restricted to pre-Islamic times. Next to the truthful Muslim way of life, they see the state of ignorance as an ever-existing phenomenon which is in opposition to Islam. The meaning of the term *jahiliyya* is therefore extended to refer to thought or practice which are held to be un-Islamic or antagonistic to Islam. Like Maududi and Nadwi, Qutb transforms the concept of *jahiliyya* from referring to the historical past to a means of condemning ideas and systems, particularly of modern and present times. As such, he sees Islam and *jahiliyya* as an ongoing battle, as a fight between good and evil.

Islam knows only two kinds of societies, the Islamic and the jahili. The Islamic society is a community that follows Islam in belief and ways of worship, in law and organisation, and in morals and manners. The jahili society does not follow Islam; it spurns the Islamic belief and concepts, Islamic values and standards, Islamic laws and regulations, and Islamic morals and manners.

(Qutb (1993b) 79)

It is worth noting that Qutb defines *jahiliyya* as antithesis towards Islam, but fails to give a definition of the term itself. In order to gain a clearer understanding it is therefore necessary to see how he uses the term in context.

Since being a true Muslim means submission to God's sovereignty, Islam is, as Qutb argues, active involvement in a movement which has as its goal the implementation of divine will. Being Muslim is therefore a lived reality which is devoted to God's rule. Islam thus cannot be reduced to rites. While some religious practices, such as the pillars of Islam, are indeed obligations, they are part of a holistic system of belief. In Qutb's view, the rules of practice and law build up an organic whole that links the individual to a spiritual and ideal environment governed by the divine. He emphasises that Islam is non-philosophical and alien to deductive reasoning, thus positing without any sophisticated theological or intellectual explanation that the doctrines of religion are comprehensive.

The reason for Qutb's adamant rejection of modern Western philosophy is that it allows the human to be at the centre of reasoning, thus questioning the legitimacy of the divine. In this sense Qutb is critical not only of Western theories of existence, he is also suspicious of the Muslim deductive theology and philosophy of *kalam* (Muslim scholastic reasoning). He argues that in *jahiliyya* societies, with Western society as a prime example, humans take it upon themselves to determine values and laws, thereby restricting the sovereignty of God. Qutb condemns philosophy and all deductive reasoning, making its approach responsible for alienation, loss of faith, economic and social injustice and political chaos. According to Qutb, human reasoning produces different ideologies, such as individualism or collectivism, capitalism or communism, all of which promise the way forward to improve living. Yet, Qutb is convinced that all these ideologies are not capable of satisfying the needs of human kind, because they are not in harmony with a divinely ordained 'cosmic' system. This universalistic approach to humanity's place in the scheme of things and his wholesale condemnation of philosophies goes beyond a plain critique of existing ideologies. The antagonism between Islam and *jahiliyya*, in Qutb's view, is not merely an ideological conflict, as Haddad pointed out.[41] Rather, Qutb sees *jahiliyya* as a living reality, in the sense that its theories determine the practices of daily life and the individual's relationship to life and community. The shortcomings in human logic and reasoning lead to unequal social relations, whereby some people are in position of power while others have to submit.

Defining *jahiliyya* merely by its opposition to Islam, Qutb merges his apprehension against philosophy in general and political theory in particular with social and political opposition. He writes that

> … jahili society is any society other than the Islamic society; and if we want a more specific definition, we may say that any society is a jahili society if it does not dedicate itself to submission to Allah alone in its beliefs and ideas, in its observances of worship, and its legal norms. According to this definition, all the societies existing in the world today are jahili.

> (Qutb (1993b) 66)

Qutb specifically mentions a range of societies and cultures as examples of the failed projects of modernity. Among those his lists are societies established on communist ideology, cultures based on idolatrous religious premises such as those in India, Japan, the Philippines and Africa, and also social orders influenced by monotheism, such as Judaism and Christianity.[42] Above all, he argues that all existing Muslim societies are *jahili*. While it is understandable that he rejects communism, polytheism, Christianity and Judaism, his condemnation of Muslim peoples is crucial for the turn towards radical Islamist ideology.

The reason for Qutb's rejection of Muslim societies is that sovereignty is, like in other *jahili* societies, illegitimately seized by human agents. He accuses Muslims of disregarding God's legislative power by adopting Western laws and Western values. Since there cannot be a compromise between *jahiliyya* and Islam, Muslim societies are thus usurping God's rights. For Qutb there cannot be a 'half-*jahiliyya*' or 'half-Islamic' system; any conciliation with *jahiliyya* is, in his view, a deviation from God's sovereignty. Qutb thereby forces every Muslim to decide for his vision of Islam, or otherwise be considered its enemy.

Qutb seems to have a clear vision of how to establish God's sovereignty, thereby breaking with *jahiliyya*. He argues that the kernel of success is to set up a vanguard, a motivated group of zealots who believe in the cause of the Islamist movement.

> ... we need to initiate the movement of Islamic revival in some Muslim country. Only such a revivalist movement will eventually – sooner or later get the world leadership. How to initiate such a revival of Islam? A vanguard must set out with this determination and then keep going, marching through the vast ocean of jahiliyya which encompasses the entire world.
>
> (Qutb (1993b) 9)

He then describes the Islamic concept (*tasawwur al-Islami*) which sets up this vanguard for success in future. For him it is the only way to overcome modern *jahiliyya*; it is also the natural way of establishing a true Islamic community, because its method (*minhaj*) was, he argues, devised by God. It was practised by Muhammad to guide the first generation of Muslims to build up a solid community within a period of thirteen years. This period can be broken down in distinct phases.[43]

The first step of the *minhaj* is that individuals accept their profession of faith and their servitude to God's absolute sovereignty. *'Ubudiyya* towards God initially means seeking knowledge, taking on and following strictly divine law. In Qutb's view, there is no question that once a person wholeheartedly recognises the Qur'an as the only source of law and as the ultimate guide in questions of daily life, he will unwaveringly turn his back on *jahiliyya* and its cultural, philosophical and scientific baggage. Once aware of their faith, members of the vanguard will build an organic activist group, a sort of nucleus of believers within the surrounding *jahiliyya* society. Their example will attract more and more people to join the group, making it into a force which eventually can no longer be ignored. At this moment the community will enter the second phase of the divine scheme.

As the ruling *jahiliyya* system will not take kindly to the growing number of true Muslims in their midst, it will try to restrict it. However, at this stage the vanguard is still too small and weak to be able to fight the *jahiliyya* society. The only recourse is to withdraw, to engage in *hijra* (withdrawal). Just as Muhammad left his home town of Mecca and took refuge in Medina, this withdrawal is a means of preventing destruction by the opposing system. It also allows the true Muslim community to avoid succumbing to the influences and attractions of *jahiliyya*. Through its *hijra*, the vanguard will strengthen its internal structures.

The third stage begins when they group finds its internal strength and reinforces its numbers. The sound structure and firm conviction allow the vanguard to prepare for the necessary confrontation with the *jahiliyya* society. Qutb thinks it impossible that the ruling tyrants will give up their power without a fight. For Qutb, battle against *jahiliyya* is at this stage politically legitimate, inevitable and necessary. He states:

> Preaching alone is not enough to establish the dominion of Allah on earth, to abolish the dominion of man, to take away sovereignty from the usurper and return to Allah, and to bring about the enforcement of the Divine shari'ah and the abolition of man-made laws. Those who have usurped the authority of Allah and are oppressing Allah's creatures are not going to give up their power merely by preaching.
>
> (Qutb (1993b) 47–8)

Jihad (struggle) is, as we can see from the quotation, an integral part of Qutb's vision of the Islamic concept.[44] It is the struggle to reinstate God's sovereignty and thus to establish an Islamic state system which is based on *shari'a*. It is thus congruent with the idea of bringing the Muslim creed (*'aqida*) into practice. However, although Qutb uses the term *jihad* frequently in Milestones, there is a certain ambiguity in how he employs it. Depending on the context, and congruent with the stage of the Islamic concept, it can take on different meanings. Playing on the idea of struggle in the path of God, it can entail engagement through preaching and learning, it can mean to join the community in its *hijra* from *jahiliyya*, but it can also mean militancy and war, as Qutb particularly envisions in the final stages of the *minhaj*. At any point of the *minhaj*, the vanguard is practicing *jihad*. Thus, in accordance with the stages in the development of the true Muslim vanguard, the command for jihad progresses:

> ... the Muslims were first restrained from fighting; then they were permitted to fight; later they were commanded to fight against the aggressors; and finally they were commanded to fight against all the polytheists.
>
> (Qutb (1993b) 52[45])

Overall, the means used is dependent on the developmental stage of the Muslim community. The ambiguity in this presentation of *jihad* leaves Qutb's view open to interpretation and is in fact at the heart of the difference between moderate and radical readings of Qutb. Militant interpreters certainly stress that they are ready to fight *jahiliyya*, while moderates put an emphasis on engagement through *da'wa* and political activism.[46]

Nevertheless, there should be no doubt that Qutb's concept of *jihad* has, at least in its final struggle against *jahiliyya*, connotations of fighting with arms.

> Anyone who understands this particular character of the din will also under-
> stand the purpose of jihad bil saif (striving by the sword), which is to clear
> the way for freedom to strive through preaching in support of the Islamic
> movement.
>
> (Qutb (1993b) 50)

Elaborating on the theme that *jihad* is not a defensive doctrine, he criticises Muslims who argue that it represents an inner struggle and a system of rituals. In his view, the theory of defensive *jihad* is an idea which is constructed through the influence of Orientalists. It is, in conclusion, a e reinterpretation which holds no truth for him. In fact, Qutb calls for a reinterpretation of the idea of defence, saying that Islamic *jihad* defends itself against the limitation of freedom by *jahiliyya*.[47] Completely turning on its head the argument that people have the right to defend their religion, he states that everyone has the right to break away from submitting to *jahili* ideas or institutions.

Qutb does not talk about concrete contents of the Islamic concept as a future Islamic state system or a constitution of such a state. He is of the view that this theme is not only unimportant; also, preoccupation with this subject is dangerous as long as the Islamic concept is not to be followed.[48] Over and above this, the moment that the Islamic concept is implemented it will automatically lead to an Islamic ideal society. Henceforth, answers on details will be unnecessary, because individuals who are freed from the slavery of human tyranny will intuitively understand the divine system.

Nevertheless, there are indications which confirm that Qutb's idea of the state has authoritarian, if not totalitarian, characteristics. For one, Qutb speaks of a strong leadership (*qiyada*) at the centre of the new society. He also says that believers need this authority (*sultan*) until humans are ready to respect and implement God's laws of their own accord. Obviously, the rules of *shari'a* are not open for discussion, but are delineated by the strong leadership. Apart from the issue of implementation of the law, Qutb's idea of *shari'a* itself is restrictive and fixed. He rejects, for example, any differentiation between *'ibadat* (religious observances, obligations) and *mu'amalat* (regulations pertaining to social life). In legal discussion, the area of *mu'amalat* is usually seen as the section of the Muslim legal framework in which humans have a certain freedom in constructing social law. Since Qutb rejects the very idea of *mu'amalat*, he consequently denies the idea of legal decision making. Overall, Diyab's critique that Qutb's theoretical basis is that of a 'theocratic fascism' is accurate.[49] In practice, this approach to Islamic law could lead to the totalitarian control of a group which claims to have the rightful and true understanding of the Qur'an and of the law. This attitude is not far from pronouncing *takfir* on anyone with a different understanding of the meaning of the Qur'an and a different interpretation of the law.

This discussion of Qutb's thoughts as set forth in *Ma'lim fi al-Tariq* helps in understanding the nuances in the ideological discourse on *takfir*. The concepts of *jahiliyya*, *hakimiyyat Allah* and *jihad* feed directly into the political position of Qutbists, who make use of these concepts to then formulate a simple but coherent ideology. The remainder of this chapter will present a brief overview of Qutb's impact on Egyptian radical Islamists. Before engaging with this topic, it needs to be emphasised that the direction of radical thought, which spurred militancy and violence from the 1970s onwards, should not be confused with that of the main body of Muslim Brothers.

Among those who were influenced in this way by Qutb are the ideologues of militant Islamist movements in Egypt and, subsequently, of the *jihad* movement. With the onset of the second wave of persecution, Mustafa Shukri, for example, was jailed and clearly developed away from the mainstream Brotherhood during his time in Liman al-Turra.[50] Subsequently, he became the founder of *Jama'at al-Muslimun*, publicly known better under the name a*l-Takfir wa al-Hijra* (Flight and Repentance). Qutbian thought can be also traced in the work of the above-mentioned 'Abd al-Salam Faraj. His *al-Farida al-Gha'iba* influenced *Jama'at Jihad al-Islami*e also known as *Jama'at al-Jihad*, which was behind the assassination of President Anwar al-Sadat.[51] 'Umar 'Abd al-Rahman, the blind theologian who issued the *fatwa* legitimising the assassination of Sadat, subsequently wrote several pamphlets, among them his *Kalimat al-Haqq* (The Words of Truth).[52] In these he put forward arguments similar to those of Qutb and Faraj. The Egyptian radical Islamist scene becomes increasingly complicated and confusing. Internal disputes led to factionalisation from the mid 1980s onwards.[53] For example, internal disputes within the Jihad group meant that al-Rahman was marginalised, with the result that he split away to then lead a group under the generic name *al-Jama'a al-Islamiyya* (Islamic Group).[54] Subsequently, al-Rahman became internationally known for his involvement in the 1993 World Trade Center attack. Without being able to dive into the political and social context, which had an impact on the onset of the idea of global *jihad*, it should suffice to mention that other radicalised Islamists whose genealogy of ideas can be traced back to Sayyid Qutb are 'Abdallah 'Azzam and, further, Ayman al-Zawahiri.[55]

If *jihad, kufr and ridda* lie at the heart of radical Islamist ideology, then what makes moderate Islamist distinctly different? Numerous scholarly observers have criticised that the distinction between radicals and moderates is merely one of degree and not one of actual substance.[56] They point out that both trends share the same sources of reference, whether of a juridical or an ideological nature, and that all Islamists, by definition of their cause, pursue the same objective, namely the establishment of an Islamic state system. The question of whether there is in fact a difference between radical Islamists, on the one hand, and moderate Islamists, on the other, goes right to the core of a dispute about whether to advise policy makers and politicians to negotiate and engage with Islamists – that is, with moderate Islamists. However, a narrow focus on the perceived political goal of Islamists tends to disregard the nuances of theological and juridical discussions. This is an immense shortcoming since, it takes no account of the rationale upon which Islamist movements are built, namely, religious ideas. Engaging with religious ideas, beliefs and creeds entails a careful analysis of the history and development of ideas. Only upon this basis can a careful and balanced assessment be made of whether particular Islamist interpretations contain radical or moderate positions and how this position relates to existing state systems.

The accusation of *kufr* is a widespread and popular means of silencing political opponents.[57] Although the use of *kufr* in populist rhetoric complicates the analysis of this concept and makes it difficult to set clear analytical markers, the ideas of unbelief and belief define, in many respects, the distinction between moderate and radical positions. On this point al-Qaradawi states that

> [E]xtremism reaches its utmost limit when a single group deprives all people of the right to safety and protection, and instead sanctions their killing and the confiscation of their lives and property. This, of course, occurs when an extremist holds all people – except those in this group – to be kuffar. This kind of extremism severs any bond between such a person and the rest of the Ummah. This is the trap into which the Khawarij fell during the dawn of Islam …
>
> (Qaradawi (1987) 43)

What is most striking is that al-Qaradawi also reverts to the framework of Sunni legal tradition and its theological distinctions between belief and unbelief. He uses the legal and theological framework, this time not to condemn 'all people', 'all Muslims' or 'all politicians', but to turn against radical Islamist thought. Effectively, he proclaims that radical Islamists are outside the limits of Islamic law. In other words, a kind of counter-*takfir* takes place, whereby proponents of radicalism are accused of unbelief and excess. While using law to combat radicalism, al-Qaradawi revisits theology and its intrinsic logic, a logic which indeed lies at the heart of Sunni Islam. In many ways, it could be argued that al-Qaradawi exemplifies a moderate Islamist position, one which clearly distances itself from revolutionary ideas and from the practice of a communal *takfir*. Nevertheless, al-Qaradawi also exemplifies why a clear description of the moderate Islamist position is difficult. After all, he also uses the same means and turns the idea of *takfir* against his opponents. Nevertheless, there is a moderate Islamist theology. *Du'at la Qudat*, which we turn to in the following chapter, is an outstanding example of a text which presents non-violent and non-revolutionary ideas while trying to remain devoted to Islamism.

3 Preachers not Judges

3.1 Text, composition and authorship

Hasan Isma'il al-Hudaybi's work *Du'at la Qudat* (*Preachers not Judges*) is one of the most significant sources for the Brotherhood's ideological premises. Yet, it is surprising that the book is ignored in scholarly evaluations of the Brotherhood. Almost obliterated from scholarly research on the Muslim Brotherhood, there is so far no in-depth analysis available. While there is much writing on Sayyid Qutb and his radicalisation of thought, only a small number of scholars have presented an investigation into the discourse among imprisoned Brothers. Nevertheless, this prison discourse on issues of belief and operational strategy, which directly fed into the writing of *Du'at la Qudat*, is the formative episode of the new Brotherhood.

Before analysing the book *Du'at la Qudat* in regard to its content, some remarks about its contextuality and, further, its composition have to be made. In investigating the questions how and why the text was composed and disseminated, a connection should be made between the historical situation, as set out particularly in the previous chapters, and the textual interpretation of *Du'at la Qudat* in the present chapter. The remarks are a first effort to illustrate the discourse among the imprisoned Muslim Brothers and give a genealogy of the communicative network. With this approach, one needs to go beyond hermeneutics, which seeks to link a specific text to its historical context. Hence, it is not the purpose of the following interpretation to isolate the book, to look into its composition solely from the perspective of its obvious content and its place in history, but rather to adopt as a leading query its interdependence with surrounding disputes and circumstances.

Aims and objectives of Du'at la Qudat

The introduction of the book *Du'at la Qudat* (*Preachers not Judges*), which will be the focus of our analysis in the following sections, describes its objective as follows:

> [The book contains] some discussions on the various opinions which have been expressed at different times. However, there is no evidence for their

correctness. We feel that we have to give a clarifying response referring to the mighty book of God and to the Sunna of the prophet (...) to give evidence of the truth in a very clear manner.

(al-Hudaybi (1977) 6–7)

The passage states clearly that the book is a response. Surprisingly, however, there is no clarification as to who or which concepts it deems to respond to. A summary of the ideas which *Du'at la Qudat* sets out to rebuff is also missing, and authors or proponents of concepts to which the book is opposed are not specifically mentioned.[1] One exception, however, is the reference to the Pakistani writer al-Maududi, who is quoted three times. Nevertheless, it is misleading to assume that *Du'at la Qudat* is simply a refutation of the latter's work. This leaves the reader, who may not be familiar with the historical circumstances of the text's composition, with some difficulty in reading and understanding the arguments put forward in the book. The task of grasping the content of *Du'at la Qudat* is made even more difficult by the absence of a rigorous structure. Al-Hudaybi constantly singles out topics without any particular indication of the relevance of the issue or explicitly demarcating a subject as part of a radical conceptual construct. When he presents an argument different from the issue he raises, it is difficult to understand how his point of view fits into a coherent theological and ideological framework. This pick-and-choose method jumps, at times, from one subject to another. Therefore, the reader can face a real difficulty in grasping the objective and meaning of the text.

Apart from its obvious deficiencies in terms of presentation and readability, *Du'at la Qudat* is a sophisticated work which combines spiritual instruction with Islamic jurisprudence (*fiqh*). Like in other texts of this category, the author makes heavy use of the sources of Muslim teachings: the Qur'an and Sunna. Using these sources to substantiate his argument, he applies traditional Islamic legal methodology: analogical reasoning (*qiyas*) and consensus (*ijma'*). The book uses orthodox interpretative methods whenever it is suitable to the argument. The aim of this approach is to establish authenticity and credibility beyond a sense of sophistication and literacy; to construct an aura of 'true' interpretation and the universality of its application.

Composition and editing

Du'at la Qudat was first published in 1977.[2] Hasan al-Hudaybi is named as its author.[3] According to the date given at the end of the text, the writing of the manuscript was completed on 23 February 1969.[4] Kepel, Sivan and Krämer have suggested that the text is a refutation of Sayyid Qutb's thought.[5] This thesis gives the book a unique quality: presuming that al-Hudaybi wrote it, it is the first negative response from a fellow proponent of Islamism to Qutb's conception of Islam. Although this aspect is remarkable in itself, the writing represents, consequently, a contribution to an inter-Muslim discourse with considerable reflection on the differing internal stances, as Krämer rightly argues.[6] Returning to the initial thesis that al-Hudaybi's writing is the first inter-Muslim refutation of Sayyid Qutb's radical thought, some corrections have to be made. Without diminishing the significance of the book *Du'at la Qudat*, the issue of authorship needs to be revised. Further, the thesis that the writing aimed to be an immediate response to Sayyid Qutb's conceptions must be reviewed.

There are, indeed, strong implications that al-Hudaybi did not write the book by himself, at least not entirely. This is pointed out by and 'Alam in his descriptions of leading members of the Muslim Brotherhood.[7] Some may view his account with suspicion, considering that he was part of the secret security forces. However, he is not the only person to have suggested that *Du'at la Qudat* was not written by al-Hudaybi. In fact, there are a number of Brothers, some close to al-Hudaybi, who also make this point. For example, 'Abd al-Majid, who was member of Organisation 1965, makes similar allegations.[8] 'Umar al-Tilmisani, who was a member of the Guidance Council while al-Hudabyi was alive and who was nominated *Murshid* after his death, mentions this detail in his memoirs. So does 'Abd al-Khaliq, a member of the Brotherhood who considers himself as a supporter of al-Hudaybi and who was imprisoned during the period under examination.[9] There is also Ahmad Ra'if, a Muslim Brother and playwright, who presents his recollections of his time in Liman al-Turra in his memoirs *al-Bawaba al-Sawda'* (The Black Gate). These voices cannot be ignored; there are too many and too detailed accounts by Muslim Brothers which lead to a belief that *Du'at la Qudat* was not written by al-Hudabyi. If it was not the *Murshid*, then who was engaged in the writing of the text and how was it compiled?

In the investigation of this question, some seven *Rasa'il* (Public Letters) by al-Hudaybi are of particular interest. These statements were also written during the second half of the 1960s, i.e. during the period of the second phase of persecution. The link between the text *Du'at la Qudat* and the *Rasa'il* is illustrated by the fact that the letters were attached to subsequent publications of the text.[10] Moreover, topics which were taken up in the letters were also the focus of extended analysis in *Du'at la Qudat* (*Preachers not Judges*). Also, the literary style of the *Rasa'il*, a rhetorical dialogue in the form of questions and answers, was retained in some parts of the book *Preachers not Judges*.[11] In summary, these facts point towards a relationship between the two sources, which is no coincidence. Accounts regarding the circumstances of writing the seven Public Letters give us a hint as to how *Du'at la Qudat* was compiled.

Generally speaking, *Rasa'il* issued by the *Murshid* are public announcements of the organisation's leader. They constitute the official line of the Brotherhood. In most cases, public letters are written versions of speeches the *Murshid* gave, or statements on a particular topic or in response to a specific incident.[12] In some cases during 1953 and 1954, al-Hudaybi used the method of writing letters to the president and to members of the RCC to make his opinion known.[13] The Seven Letters from Prison, however, are not written speeches or letters to the public; they originate in the time of the *Murshid's* imprisonment during the second *mihna* and are clearly addressed to his followers there. It is worth noting that the *Rasa'il* have a distinct format: a short leading question precedes a lengthy explanation.

They somehow remind one of *fatwas*, where a specific question is brought forward by a believer, who in return expects a theological explanation of the matter. The style and content of the letters are quite telling, considering the circumstances of imprisonment. They provide an indication of the Brothers' confusion over the Brotherhoods' strategy and hence mirror the dispute surrounding al-Hudaybi. As was shown in the historical outline, the *Murshid* was at the centre of discussions, particularly after he officially distanced himself from Organisation 1965. This contributed to uncertainty over the guiding principles of the Brotherhood, especially considering also that al-Hudaybi's announcement was seen as a rejection of Qutb's ideas. Yet, neither the Public Letters nor the script *Du'at la Qudat* mention Sayyid Qutb. Although it can be argued that particular mention of him was not necessary, since his arguments must have been know to most of the Brothers, it may well be that the *Rasa'il* and, more specifically, *Du'at la Qudat* had a more general aim: to refute circulating radical thought, rather than exclusively Qutb's interpretation. As we have seen, *Du'at la Qudat* clearly states this objective in its introduction.[14] The *Rasa'il* substantiate this argument; the answers are directed to fellow Brothers in order to clarify the leadership's guidelines and principles. This understanding of the purpose of the *Rasa'il* and of *Du'at la Qudat* also points to an underlying agenda: to reinstate al-Hudaybi's power and that of the old guard of leaders. Once we have tackled the issue of authorship, this thesis may become clearer.

As mentioned before, al-Hudaybi met during his incarceration in Liman al-Turra with fellow imprisoned Brothers in small circles and repeatedly gave his interpretation of Islamic issues and answered questions.[15] Primary sources, which are mostly in form of memoirs, seem to agree on this.[16] Interestingly, a number of these accounts also agree that *Du'at la Qudat* was not written by the *Murshid*, Hasan al-Hudaybi. The account of Brigadier General Fu'ad 'Allam may be the best known, but certainly not the only report on this issue. In fact, a number of Muslim Brothers, among them Ahmad Ra'if, Mahmud 'Abd al-Majid and Hasan al-Hudaybi's successor as Murshid, 'Umar al-Tilmisani, talk about it. Since their stories are slightly different, it is necessary to give a summative report before further commenting on the actual authorship of *Du'at la Qudat*.

Fu'ad 'Allam submitted his view on the subject in his book *al-Ikhwan ... wa Ana* (The Brotherhood ... and me).[17] He suggests that *Du'at la Qudat* was produced by the Secret Service once the government became aware that some members of the Brotherhood were turning towards the idea of *takfir* while in prison. He further argues that the writing of a theological refutation was commissioned with the aim of countering the spread of radical thought and revolutionary ideas. In particular, it was meant to rebuff the ideology of a group calling themselves Qutbists, among them reportedly Muhammad Qutb, Sayyid 'Ayyid Yusuf, Shukri Ahmad Mustafa and 'Ali 'Abduh Isma'il. *Du'at la Qudat* was thus written by al-Azhar. Moreover, 'Allam puts forward the accusation that Ma'mun al-Hudaybi, who was imprisoned with his father, was in fact a mole of the Secret Service. He received the finished copy, planted the book and convinced his father that it was in the best interest of the Brotherhood to sanction *Du'at la Qudat* as its public statement against radical Islamist thinking. Khatab takes up 'Allam's comments as sufficient proof of the thesis that *Du'at la Qudat* was not written by al-Hudaybi. Although Khatab comes to a conclusion which is supported by this study, it is problematic to only rely on 'Allam's story. His account of events is not only problematic because he used to be a member of the Egyptian Secret Service, but also because his revelations clearly have the aim of uncovering sensationalist 'truths'.

Brother Ahmad 'Abd al-Majid, who was one of the leaders of Organisation 1965, also puts forward that *Du'at la Qudat* was not al-Hudaybi's work.[18] In his version, Ma'mun al-Hudaybi was also at the centre of events. Apparently, the writing of *Du'at la Qudat* followed months of internal dispute. The initial spark of discontent was a consequence of the *Murshid's* demand to submit a statement describeing the ideological basis of Organisation 1965. He asked for clarification of the group's responsibility for the second *mihna*. This was followed by a speech during which Hasan al-Hudaybi distanced himself from 'those following al-Zilal'. 'Abd al-Majid explains that *Du'at la Qudat* was thus composed with the intention of containing the internal unrest ensuing from al-Hudaybi's declaration. He mentions that the notes were brought together by a circle of trustees around al-Hudaybi and that *Du'at la Qudat* was the result of this editorial work. Being imprisoned not at Liman al-Turra, but rather in Qina', 'Abd al-Majid was, however, not an eyewitness. Nevertheless, he claims that it was common knowledge among prisoners that Ma'mun al-Hudaybi composed the book with the help of some Brothers, but admits that Hasan al-Hudaybi may have given his ultimate consent. When comparing 'Abd al-Majid with 'Allam, it is interesting to note that there are some essential similarities. Both see the text as a response to radical thinking and discontent within the Brotherhood; both mention that the text was not written by the *Murshid*, but by aides; most importantly, both implicate Ma'mun al-Hudaybi.

Although 'Abd al-Majid's and 'Allam's are the two major accounts on this issue, at least in terms of length, there are others which may be of equal importance. One of these is by Ahmad Ra'if, a Muslim Brother and playwright who was incarcerated in Liman al-Turra.[19] Unlike that of 'Abd al-Majid, Ra'if's story is first hand. His account of the experiences and conflicts gives us some insight into the ideological shift within the Brotherhood during the period of the second *mihna*, which confirms some of the points made by 'Abd al-Majid. Like him, he mentions that members of the Brotherhood had to submit statements on their involvement with Organisation 1965 and its ideological underpinnings. This was then the source of an internal dispute which particularly came to the fore during and after the 1967 war. While he clarifies that it was the prison management and the Secret Service requesting these testimonies, he argues that the debates were directly connected to the writing of *Du'at la Qudat*. In his view, the book was compiled by Ma'mun al-Hudaybi and some Brothers, among them 'Umar al-Tilmisani, who cooperated with scholars of al-Azhar on the editing of the text.

'Umar al-Tilmisani, who was implicated by Ra'if, was a member of the Guidance Council and close to Hasan al-Hudaybi. Indeeed, Al-Tilmisani, who succeeded al-Hudaybi as *Murshid*, also submitted his account.[20] In his *Dhakkariyyat la*

Mudhakkirat (Memories not Memoirs), he mentions briefly the issue of authorship of *Du'at la Qudat* and tells that the leadership of the Brotherhood was increasingly alarmed by the influence of the idea of *takfir* on the thinking of younger Brothers. In this situation, the *Murshid* tried to combat radical ideas through open discussions. Out of this engagement, *Du'at la Qudat* was then drawn up with the help of Ma'mun al-Hudaybi and Mustafa Mashhur.

From the above accounts, it can be deduced with a great level of certainty that *Du'at la Qudat* was not written by Hasan al-Hudaybi, at least not single handedly. It was rather a joint project. As for its compilation, several sources affirm that Ma'mun al-Hudaybi took a leading role in the writing process. Key primary sources mention a few other names, such as Mustafa Mashhur and 'Umar al-Tilmisani, both of whom belonged to the Guidance Council and both of whom subsequently became *Murshid*s. Although it cannot be verified with certainty that they were indeed part of the editorial board, a case can be made that it is likely that members of the Guidance Council close to al-Hudaybi were involved.[21] Since key figures of the Guidance Council under al-Hudaybi later rose to the position of *Murshid*, this serves as an indication that those participating in the writing process were also those who continued and implemented this kind of theology.

As for the involvement of al-Azhar in the discourse and writing process, it appears that the scholars did have some input. The text of *Du'at la Qudat*, which is heavily based on traditional scholarship and methodology of interpretation, is evidence of this link. Nevertheless it is impossible to pinpoint names with any certainty. The primary sources do mention that al-Azhar scholars were part of the writing process, but do not once disclose any names. This leaves us guessing; the circle is considerably limited, considering that these scholars must have had the trust of the government and of the Brotherhood. Among those who come to mind are scholars on the highest levels of the Azhar hierarchy, such as Shaykh Hasan Ma'mun, who was the Shaykh al-Azhar at the time, Shaykh Ahmad Muhammad 'Abd al-'Al Haridi, who was the Mufti of Egypt, or Shaykh Mahmud 'Abd al-Majid, who was to become the Shaykh al-Azhar in the 1970s.[22]

It could also have included Azhar-trained scholars who were affiliated to the Brotherhood before the onset of the *mihna* in 1954 but who then turned to support 'Abd al-Nasir; fitting this description is Muhammad al-Ghazali or his pupil Yusuf al-Qaradawi.[23]

Despite these considerations, it must be emphasised that Hasan al-Hudaybi still bears responsibility for the authorship of *Du'at la Qudat*. Certainly, the *Murshid*, in his position as leader of the organisation, must have given his approval, given that *Du'at la Qudat* was issued in his name and distributed as an official statement. The finding that the book *Du'at la Qudat* is in fact a joint effort does not necessarily contradict these facts. Any organisation, particularly with large numbers of members, cannot be run entirely by only one person. The nominal head needs support and is to a large extent dependent on his close circle of companions. Given that the idea of authorship is interpreted loosely in this particular context, it is, in other words, not surprising that documents were drawn up by a number of trusted contributors and that these were then collated to form *Du'at la Qudat*. It is there-fore reasonable to assume that the writing process was headed by al-Hudaybi, as an editor-in-chief, so to speak. However, who exactly was involved in the process and who wrote which section or chapter can not be established.

Although the book *Du'at la Qudat* was not written by the *Murshid*, this does not diminish its importance. After all, the text is still significant for understand-ing of the discourse of the prison times. It represents a moderate stance against radical thought and can thus be regarded as a refutation of the latter. Above all, it provided the long-awaited guidelines for Muslim Brothers who remained, in their majority, moderate in their perception of an Islamist cause.

In regard to both the *Rasa'il* and *Du'at la Qudat*, another issue needs to be clari-fied: the question of distribution. The texts were initially not disseminated through the most common avenue of distribution, i.e. through being printed by a publish-ing house, as the organisation was, since 1954, officially dissolved and its pub-lishing houses closed. As mentioned above, the first publication of the book and the Public Letters was only years later, in 1977. Nevertheless, the texts reached their readership in prison as well as outside. The network of communication between the different prisons, which existed before 1965 and which was used to distribute Sayyid Qutb's interpretation among fellow Brothers, still functioned, as Mahmoud Ezzat's recent interview illustrates.[24] Ezzat was imprisoned in Qina' in late 1960. He managed to put questions to al-Hudaybi and was, like other Broth-ers, familiar with *Du'at la Qudat*'s content. Ezzat's remarks also evidence that the dispute about radical concepts did not just take place in al-Hudaybi's direct sur-roundings, i.e. in the prison of Liman al-Turra. Quarrels about Qutb's ideas were especially immediate for younger and disillusioned Brothers, who did not belong to the circle of leaders and who were desperately awaiting guidelines. Hence, the thesis that a communication network for the distribution of scripts and ideas was still in existence feeds into the argument of a broad discourse among imprisoned Muslim Brothers.

The publication of *Du'at la Qudat* in 1977 served a different objective from the writing of the text. This first official printing is set in a different political context and in fact is directly linked to the new circumstances.

It has been already mentioned that 'Abd al-Nasir's successor, Anwar al-Sadat, aimed to disassociate himself from the rule of his predecessor.[25] In the course of appeasement with the Brotherhood, al-Sadat lifted the censorship of publi-cations.[26] With the change in government policy, the Brotherhood was able to rebuild its publishing houses. A number of works on the events leading up to the persecution as well as memoirs, particularly on the years of hardship in 'Abd al-Nasir's prison, began to fill the market.[27] However, the reason for the publica-tion of *Du'at la Qudat* in 1977 is not only linked to the rebuilding of the Brother-hood's press. More than that, the first edition of the text appeared in response to the upcoming radical Islamist trend.

At the beginning of the 1970s, radical Islamist groups established independent organisational structures, distinct from the Muslim Brotherhood.[28] Groups like *al-Takfir wa al-Hijra* and *Jama'at al-Jihad* gathered around leaders who preached a religious ideology which called for an armed struggle against the existing state order. By the mid 1970s, these groups set off to engage in terrorist activities. In 1977, Shaykh al-Dhahabi, who was the Minister of Religious Endowments, was kidnapped and murdered by members of *al-Takfir wa al-Hijra*.[29] Shukri Mustafa, who broke with the Brotherhood during the prison years, gave the directives for this terrorist act.[30] In the attempt to distance themselves from the terrorist activities, the Muslim Brotherhood issued statements condemning these fanatical acts. Further, al-Hudaybi's writing was published as a clear theological guideline to counter Islamist terrorism.[31]

The historical context shows that there is a difference between the context of the writing process and the first publication of *Du'at la Qudat*. The altered context also signifies that not only had the target readership changed, but moreover the purpose of composing the text and the objectives followed in its distribution differ.[32] The aim of *Du'at la Qudat* changed with the publication of the text. Whereas it was originally conceived to refute the ideas of radicalised Brothers in prison, it now countered the ideology of radical Islamist movements. This more general application of the text remains meaningful for the Society of the Muslim Brotherhood today.

3.2 The ultimate question: Muslim or *kafir*?

After establishing the context of *Du'at la Qudat* we will now move on to the content. One of the central questions in *Du'at la Qudat* is the definition of Muslim and *kafir* (unbeliever). In order to fully appreciate al-Hudaybi's reasoning on this question a general understanding of these concepts is necessary.

If we agree for the moment that belief (*iman*) can only be defined through its opposite, it is essential to clarify the terminology related to unbelief. Without intending to go into any spiritual discussions, but rather remaining within the realm of Sunni theology, a simple definition of unbelief (*kufr*) includes non-belief in the concept of monotheism, which constitutes the ultimate principle in Islam, and/or rejection of Muhammad's prophecy. A *kafir* is therefore "a person [who] takes the position that there is no God, that He is not One, or that Muhammad was not a prophet."[33] This and similar variants of this broad definition set a useful working parameter for a further investigation, since it finds wide acceptance across Muslim religious tradition.

It needs to be said, however, that this definition sets a rather broad framework which leaves many possibilities as to how unbelief, in fact, manifests itself on an individual basis. One can immediately see that it leaves indeterminate, for example, whether a person does not recognise God, as for example atheists do, or whether the person believes in many Gods, as polytheists do. The concept of *kufr* also not does distinguish whether a person actually believes in a single God but rejects the revelation of the Qur'an or the position that Muhammad was a divinely inspired messenger. The working definition of *kufr* therefore does contain a combination of some basic characteristics, i.e. monotheism and prophethood. Yet it also shows that the idea of *kufr* is an umbrella concept which provides a relative definition rather than a concrete one. The reasons for this relativity of meaning can be explained through two separate developments; one lies within the history of the Qur'an as a text and the second relates to the advance of Muslim theology.[34]

As for the Qur'an, where the term is frequently used and in fact is part of the essential message, Waldman and Izutsu explained that the meaning of the term clearly changed during the process of revelation. Both point out that the term initially had the connotation of 'ingratitude to God'. In later Qur'anic, verses however, it came to represent a negation of the concept of *iman*.[35] While the meaning of the word varies within the chronology of the Qur'an, this transformation does not imply that the previous connotation was completely obliterated. Waldman therefore talks about an 'accumulation of meaning' and Izutsu calls the various semantic differences 'relational meaning'. What is important to note from this is that the Qur'an uses the term *kufr* frequently, but that it does not define what is meant by it. Moreover, the actual connotation of the word changes to such an extent that there is fluidity in its Qur'anic meaning. This fluidity transpires subsequently in theological and juridical discussions and is, as Saeed points out, the cause of much confusion today.[36]

As the discussion above shows, the concepts of *kufr* and Muslim are not exactly defined by the Qur'an. Hence, it is necessary to return to Islamic history, where the concepts where further shaped. Given that questions such as 'what is Islam?' and 'who is a Muslim?' were the most pressing issues of concern for the early community, the dispute surrounding *kufr* was the initiating moment of Muslim theological thinking.[37] The conflict of the early community was mainly fought out on battlefields rather than through scholarly disputation. The earliest movement that defined *kufr* by the sword was the Khawarij. The movement stood out through its fanaticism and egalitarianism. The Khawarij was the first movement to turn the concept of unbelief against fellow Muslims. As Izutsu rightly suggested, they thus widened its application.[38] It was part of Khawarij conviction that belief must manifest itself through action (*'amal*). It took the position that, in order to be considered Muslim, a person must actively engage in the community of the faithful. Rather than positively affirming who is Muslim it thus reversed the question, declaring anyone an unbeliever who did not belong to its particular community and share its zealous conviction.[39] With a fanatical desire to establish an uncorrupted Muslim community, it applied *takfir*, asking: 'Who are those that must be driven out of the existing community, which is corrupted and impure?'[40] A shift in the meaning of *kufr* thus took place which was extended to the idea of excommunication.

The reaction against Khawarij positions on belief and unbelief sets the tone for Sunni theology. The first theological movement to reject the application of *takfir* was the Murji'iyya.[41] While their theology was directed against the fanaticism of the Khawarij, it also legitimised the political system of the 'Ummayad caliphate, which in return championed this development.[42] The name Murji'iyya derives from the verb *arja'* meaning 'to suspend or postpone judgement'.[43] On the question of *takfir*, the Murji'iyya diametrically opposed the Khawarij. While the Murji'iyya deliberated on the idea of unbelief and sin, they developed the position that anyone who declares his/her belief as a Muslim must be recognised as such and will be ultimately judged by God. According to this principle, sin does not affect belief. A person who obviously contravenes rules as set out in the Qur'an and Sunna and who has therefore sinned must be still considered a Muslim. Emphasis is thus put on inner faith, and the Murji'iyya dismissed the idea of *'amal* as a defining characteristic of a Muslim.[44] During the period of dominance of Murji'ite thought, these theological principles were further elaborated and led to the first theory of belief in Sunni Islam. Although the 'Ummayad dynasty was eventually replaced, its protégé theological movement lais the fundamental building blocks for later theological discussions.[45]

Not entirely endorsing the misdemeanours of a sinner, the Mu'tazila took an intermediate position (*manzila bayna manzilatayn*) arguing that this person is neither Muslim nor *kafir*.[46] An important characteristic of the Mu'tazilite theology is that the individual is responsible for his/her actions. It thus amended the view of the Murji'iyya insofar as it disposed of any deterministic connotations which could be read into in the stance of the earlier school.[47] Since the idea of *manzila bayna manzilatayn* does not leave decisions on the status of sinners to the afterlife, it created an environment which furthered the development of jurisprudence and jurisdiction.[48] Also, its emphasis on human free will allows the individual to reason consciously about good or bad; the objective is to comprehend divine law through reason. It is on these grounds that Mu'tazila is called the movement of 'free-thinkers of Islam'. Ultimately, though, the stress on reasoning over literalist reading of revelation led them to conclude that the Qur'an as a text is created and that Hadith is not useful as a source of interpretation. As the leading school of theology during much of the rule of the 'Abbasid dynasty, the Mu'tazila was eventually superseded by an orthodox countertrend.[49] Yet, their interpretation on free will nevertheless left its mark on subsequent theological discussions on the nature of belief, sin and unbelief.

The orthodox traditionalism of the Ash'ariyya and Maturidiyya constitutes the final and lasting theological development in Sunni discussions on the distinction between *kufr* and *iman*.[50] Fairly similar in their overall approach, these two approaches represent the basis for the majority of works on Sunni *'aqida* (creed).[51] Just how influential these theological schools are can be seen by the fact that their elaborations on essential practice and beliefs are considered to be dogma. This includes their descriptions of the so-called five pillars of Islam or of the six articles of faith, which were firmly set as a framework by the Ash'ariyya and Maturidiyya. Their theology remains the underlying element of subsequent discussions and clearly had its impact on arguments of the major schools of law.

The impact of the traditionalist trend and its emphasis on Hadith and Sunna led the Ash'ariyya and the Maturidiyya to oppose the Mu'tazila, particularly with regard to its views on the createdness of the Qur'an and the use of Hadith as a primary source for interpretation. It is noteworthy, however, that the Ash'ariyya and the Maturidiyya took opposing positions on the issue of belief. Abu al-Hasan al-Ash'ari (d.330/ 942) essentially argued that belief is uncreated, since there was 'never a state in which there was no *iman* and *tawhid*, neither before not after the creation of the world'.[52] For him, the position that *iman* is created would contradict the principle of divine universality. Proponents of the Maturidiyya among the Abu Hanifa, held, however, that belief has its locus in the individual.[53] In this respect, the Maturidiyya were closer to the reasoning of the Mu'tazila than to the Ash'ariyya. This said it would be unfitting to claim that all aspects of Mu'tazilite thought were dismissed. It is thus interesting to see that the idea of free will was adapted by al-Ash'ari. He suggested a doctrine of 'acquisition', which put forward a compromise whereby the orthodox concept of God's Omnipotence could be reconciled with the idea of human responsibility.[54] He thus argued that all acts, good or bad, originate in God and humans acquire the choice of free will from God. It is then the believer's choice to decide. The theological rationale that the sinner is not an unbeliever also found continuation. In fact, Abu Mansur al-Maturidi (d. 333/945) further elaborated on the Murji'ite interest in whether and to what extent *'amal* is part of defining *iman*. Like the Murji'iyya, the Maturidiyya saw belief expressed through inner faith. But while the Murji'iyya was divided as to whether belief increases through good work and, conversely, whether it decreases through sin, the Maturidiyya clearly opted for the concept of 'degrees of faith' (*tafadul*).[55] This idea then became another constituting element of Sunni theology and was in its detail discussed by a diverse scholarly body, among them Ibn Hazm, al-Ghazali and Ibn Taymiyya.[56]

Looking back on the various theological trends of early Sunni Islam, it is then fair to say that the definitions of *kufr* and *iman* took centre stage and in fact form the defining moment of Sunni theological thinking. The survey above also shows that the terms *iman* and *kufr* cannot be simply set down as clearly definable concepts. Although they are clearly antonyms, they are umbrella concepts, which were variously discussed in terms of the content of their meaning.

Juridical considerations as to what constitutes *kufr* were directly informed by theology. Ash'ariyya and Maturidiyya delineations of *'aqida* had a direct impact on juridical thinking.[57] Thus not only was *kufr* discussed in theoretical terms of sin, but the various schools of law defined it as a punishable contravention of law. In the *fiqh* elaborations, *kufr* was an umbrella concept which contained a number of more specific offences.[58] Under its shade, then, are conceptions such as apostasy (*ridda*), polytheism (*shirk*), blasphemy (*sabb Allah or sabb al-rasul*), heresy (*zandaqa*) and hypocrisy (*nifaq*). Each of these concepts represents specific forms of *kufr*, all of them of a punishable nature. Defining these transgressions as major sins, most jurists followed with a harsh verdict. There seems to be thus a general accord that they justify the death penalty.[59] The underlying justification for the reasoning of the classical jurists is that hypocrites, blasphemers, heretics and apostates made the decision to turn against God and that they therefore made the decision to turn their backs not only on faith, but also on the community of Muslims. Being outside law, these sinners' lives are not considered to be protected by law. This logic not only is the common justification for the death penalty, but also permits any member of the community the right to act within the parameters of law to kill the assumed offender.[60]

A thorough analysis of the relationship between sin and crime shows that not all jurists agree that major sins equate to *hudud* offences, i.e. offences which demand punishment because they are mentioned as such in the Qur'an. In fact, of all the sub-categories of *kufr*, only apostasy (*ridda*) is listed as a *hadd*. This then begs the question as to why and how Muslim jurists came to decide that other forms of *kufr*, such as heresy, blasphemy and hypocrisy, are liable to penalty. The issue is even more complicated by the fact that unbelief, per se, is not necessarily reprimanded, as the example of Christians and Jews illustrates. The rejection of Muhammad's prophethood makes them *kuffar*, even though their non-belief in itself is not a punishable crime.[61] This sets the unbelief of Jews and Christians apart from Muslims who commit *ridda*, *zandaqa* or *nifaq*.

As we have seen, the debate about differing conceptions of belief and the dispute about them go back to the constitutive period of Islamic theological and juridical reasoning. While the Khawarij defined their position through excommunication of Muslims, the counter-movement of the Murji'iyya, and then later of the Mu'tazila and finally of the Ash'ariyya and Maturidiyya, laid the foundation for Sunni theology. Leaving aside for the moment the fundamental objection that the faith cannot actually be proven or, for that matter, challenged, the framework for *'aqida* as suggested by the Ash'ariyya and Maturidiyya sets the tone for Sunni orthodoxy. It is then interesting to see that moderate Islamists are informed by this theological orthodoxy and its prevailing system of dogmas and practices. Considering that radical and extremist Islamists have indeed much in common with the theological position of the Khawarij, the reference to conventional and accepted tenets of belief in *Du'at la Qudat* makes its alliance to moderation pronounced. The basis of belief is the crucial topic of dispute between moderate interpretation and that of radical and/or extremist Islamism. In fact, it marks the difference between these two modes of thought within the Islamist discourse.

Al-Hudaybi and the debate about belief

A great deal of the script *Du'at la Qudat* is dedicated to justifications of belief and unbelief. As pointed out above, the issue of a distinction between belief and unbelief goes right to the heart of Muslim theological thinking. By taking up the subject, *Du'at la Qudat* invokes Sunni *'aqida* as the ground rules and clearly associates itself with its theological principles. Rather than addressing the concept head on, at no point in the text is the word *takfir* even mentioned: *Du'at la Qudat* refers to traditional positions on the distinction between unbelief and belief. Via this route, the text aims to present conclusive arguments against radical thought. Referring to the traditional framework of Sunni theology, it aims to disprove *takfir*. Although the idea of *takfir*, which constitutes the logical conclusion of radical Islamist theology, is undermined merely by interference, it is most effective. As will be shown below in detail, its strength lies in the ability to call to mind familiar traditional stances on belief, unbelief and sin.

Profession of faith

The central issue of *Du'at la Qudat*, and indeed of the dispute between moderate and radical Islamists, surrounds the significance of the testimony of faith. The so-called *shahada* (sometimes also used is the dual form *shahadatayn*), is the commonly accepted profession of faith. It states "*ashhadu an la illaha illa Allah wa Muhammadan rasul Allah*" (I witness that there no god but God and Muhammad is God's messenger).

The testimony of faith is considered an essential part of Muslim creed. It is the first item in the list of the so-called pillars of Islam. The term *shahada* itself is used in several instances in the Qur'an. Although the actual formula of the *shahada* is not explicitly recorded in the Qur'an, the statement is seen as a verbalisation of the idea of *tawhid* (God's unity) and of the concept of *nabawiyya* (prophethood).[62] Both *tawhid* and *nabawiyya* are cornerstones of the Muslim faith and are, as such, at the top of the list of the so-called essential declarations of belief (*ma'lum min al-din bi-dhurura*). While the full sentence of the *shahada* is not written in the Qur'an, it is in its entirety transmitted through various Hadith, where it is described as the simplest form of testimony.[63] Following the evidence of Hadith, there is a general consensus among Muslim theologians and jurists that speaking the *shahada* publicly and with conviction initiates a person as a Muslim. In this respect, even orthodox scholars such as Ibn Taymiyya, who is often seen as the forefather of radical ideas, reflects this consensus. He writes that

> Whoever pronounces this 'Pure word' [the shahada] with his tongue, believes in it in his heart and does not combine it with any contradictory saying, act or belief, will join the Deen of Allah and depart from Kufr.
>
> (Ibn Taymiyya translated by Ya-Sin (2000) 182–3)

Once a person speaks the *shahada* he/she witnesses by this act of speech to be a Muslim. The centrality of the *shahada* and the act of declaring witness to *tawhid* and prophethood can be seen in the fact that "*la illaha illa Allah wa Muhammadan rasul Allah*" is shouted from the minarets whenever believers are called to prayer. It is also a formula often called out in gatherings, whether these be Sufi *dhikr* or demonstrations with an Islamist undercurrent.

While there is a consensus on the *shahada* as an act of speech which initiates to Islam, there is a continuous dispute on whether any requirements should be attached to the profession. As mentioned, different opinions were already being voiced by the early theological schools, notably by the Khawarij and the Murji'iyya. In the same vein, Clarke rightly points out that the debate as to whether there are requirements attached to the *shahada* has its root in early Islam.[64] The core of the dispute surrounds different claims as to whether it is sufficient to merely speak the *shahada* in order to qualify as a Muslim, or whether the act of speaking that one witnesses to belief in God and the prophet entails action (*'amal*). The issue of the relationship between belief and practice, which is at the core of the dispute over the meaning of the *shahada*, is not merely a question of whether a Muslim needs to perform ritual acts and practices which outwardly confirm his/her belief. Although this matter is part of the discussion, the issue lies deeper and is more essential. The question of whether active engagement is a requirement can be turned around to then ask whether Muslims who do not actively follow what is set as a requirement are by default not Muslims any longer. Can their lack of outward expression be constructed as apostasy? It is in answering this probing question that Islamists' opinions are divided. In fact, differing definitions of belief and unbelief, which are hidden behind fundamentally diverse interpretations of the profession, still mark different approaches, whether in relation to matters of daily life, to politics or to economy. These remarks bring me back to *Du'at la Qudat* and the interpretation of the *shahada*, and, more generally, of belief and unbelief presented therein.

Requirements of belief

In the discussion about the principles and requirements of belief, al-Hudaybi takes a clear stance in favour of a minimal definition. He emphasises that the only valid proof of being Muslim is by verbal profession, i.e. stating the *shahada*.[65] It contains, al-Hudaybi stresses, the most essential concepts of Islam, namely God's oneness (*tawhid*) and God's self-revelation through the prophet Muhammad. Therefore, once the individual has verbalised that he/she bears witness and devotion to God, there can be no doubt of his/her conviction.[66] One has to assume that Muslims know the content of the words of profession, even if they are not native speakers of Arabic. He maintains that it has to be spoken with commitment, and, in so saying, al-Hudaybi disdains hypocritical avowals. If someone does speak the *shahada* without conviction it is a sign of sin (*ma'asiya*), if not even an indication of unbelief (*kufr*). Emphasising that the act of speaking the *shahada* has not only an outward component, i.e. speech, but needs to correspond to an inward moment, *Du'at la Qudat* returns to the classical interpretation that two factors are involved in the act of bearing witness. One is the expression through speech (*bi'l-lisan*), inner conviction (*bi'l-qalb*) is the second.[67] That said, he admits that the outward expression is the only element which is verifiable, since the speaker's intentions cannot be put to test.[68] In his view, none but God has the ability to make a judgement on the underlying intentions of the narrator and it is for this reason that the verbalisation of the *shahada* must be accepted as the only and unquestionable doctrinal evidence of faith.

It is evident that this interpretation stresses the individual aspect of confession. In other words, the *shahada* is a verbalised expression of a bond between the believer and God. No mediation is necessary.[69] Clearly, al-Hudaybi resents positions that suggest that there are any obligations attached to the *shahada* which would give proof of 'rightful' belief and lawful conduct. Consequently, he repudiates any condemnation of unbelief (*takfir*) on those grounds. Al-Hudaybi's interpretation of the profession is fundamentally different from other currents of thought.

Al-Maududi and Qutb, for example, take the stance that it is not sufficient to verbalise the profession; in their view, faith must at the same time be put into practice. Hence, engagement in the establishment of an Islamic society is the measure of a Muslim's conviction. This activism, or vigorous participation in a movement, is therefore made a requirement for belief. The following words by Qutb exemplify the concept:

> A person who bears witness that there is no god except Allah and that
> Muhammad is Allah's Messenger should cut off his relationship of loyalty to

the jahili society, and to jahili leadership, whether it be in the guise of priests, magicians or astrologers, or in the form of political, social, or economic leaders, (…). He will have his complete loyalty to the new Islamic movement and to the Muslim leadership. This decisive step must be taken at the very moment a person says, *La ilaha illa Allah, Muhammadan Rasulu-l-lah* [sic] with his tongue. The Muslim society cannot come into existence without this. It cannot come into existence simply as a creed in the hearts of individual Muslims, however numerous they may be, unless they become an active, harmonious, and cooperative group, (…).

(Qutb (1993b) 39 (emphasis as in the text)[70])

Following this, the *shahada* is used to signify an ideology based on religious activism. In other words, political activism is spiritualised. Although al-Maududi and Qutb make no immediate connection to Islamic jurisdiction, the postulation is close to the radical assumption that activism is part of the category of *'ibadat* (religious observances).[71]

The dangers of this kind of connection between faith and action are obvious. Individual spirituality and faith only count in relation to a particular religious ideology as set out by a particular group or, more accurately, by its leader. The individual is made secondary to the interpretation of a specific community, which effectively takes the intermediate position between the believer and God. Hence, the Muslim loses the freedom of faith: the group or its head can accuse him/her of unbelief, whenever he/she does not follow the imperatives of the group.

Universal meaning vs lost understanding

In submitting necessary evidence that the profession of faith is the only acceptable evidence of belief, al-Hudaybi digresses and investigates Maududi's thesis on the reappearance of *jahiliyya*. The thrust of al-Hudaybi's refutation of *jahiliyya* is that the Qur'an is Islam's universal message. He stresses that because the Qur'an was sent as a book of guidance, the truth was never lost. Since the Qur'an gave meaning which was then accessible to all Muslims at any time, speaking the *shahada* is sufficient evidence that a person understood the core of Muslim belief. It becomes clear that two world-views clash: the idea of a lost understanding of the divine message against the conviction that religious meaning is embedded in the universality of the Qur'an.

At the basis of Maududi's view lies the conviction that the Muslim community has lost the 'rightful' understanding of central religious terms.[72] While the companions of the prophet, the *al-Salaf al-Salih*,[73] still comprehended the message of Islam, the generations to follow did not; they fell back into *jahiliyya*. Maududi's line of argument is used by subsequent Islamists, among them Sayyid Qutb, to show that it is necessary to turn against what they define as non-Islamic theories and practices. The ultimate aim is to reinstate a 'righful' understanding of Islam, one which returns to the ideal of the past. Clearly, Maududi and Qutb follow *salafi* footprints with their idea of present *jahiliyya*.

The reasons he gives for the decline of 'true' understanding are the lack of manners and the lack of deep understanding among those Muslims who entered Islam during the period of expansion. Islam developed immensely geographically and as a power-supported ideology, but even though people converted, the practice of idol worship continued. Consequently, members of the community who thought to follow Islamic rules knowingly or unknowingly committed polytheism (*shirk*).[74] Idolatry continued to exist beyond this pre-Islamic state of ignorance (*jahiliyya*).[75] According to al-Maududi, *jahiliyya* did not come to an end with the advent of Islam. This underlying state of unbelief remained unbroken and found an extension even into current times.[76] Even though the converts spoke the *shahada*, they were not enlightened with the 'true' meaning of the creed and faith. Al-Maududi concludes that it is not enough to bear witness to God and his prophet by verbalising the profession. A Muslim shows his/her conviction through action, in particular against an unjust, *jahili* (ignorant) system. He deduces from the creed that only those who stand up and actively participate in establishing an Islamic state system are the ones who rightly comprehend the meaning of the profession.[77]

Al-Hudaybi responds to Maududi's theory in an elaborate way, first quoting him at length to then counter his arguments on a linguistic and a theological basis. To illustrate his point, he focuses on the meaning of God's names, i.e. *Allah* and *al-rabb* (Lord), and also the meanings of the terms *'ibada* (worship) and *al-din* (religion).[78] The choice is deliberate: they correspond to al-Maududi's book *al-Mustalahat al-Arba'a fi al-Qur'an* (The Four Terms of the Qur'an).[79] In order to refute Maududi's idea that Islamic key terms were lost while *jahiliyya* was on the rise, al-Hudaybi applies the dogma of the universality of the Qur'an to the issue of understanding key words.[80] In general terms, this principle holds that the content of belief manifests in the Qur'an; it is comprehensive and timeless. The revelation of the Qur'an is the unquestionable source of reference for the individual Muslim; the Muslim can learn about the meaning of the key words through reading the Qur'an. Al-Hudaybi applies this doctrine and employs it to his advantage. He argues that the meaning of terms is fixed by the Qur'an. The believer, he concludes, has had (and continues to have) at any time and in an all-embracing way the opportunity to refer to the main and unquestionable source of Islamic faith. Hence, as the words of the Qur'an are set down and as the words contain divinely revealed truth, the individual is able to dissect its meaning.

The discussion of universal meaning versus lost understanding becomes even more interesting when taking into account al-Hudaybi's and al-Maududi's perception of Islamic history. Al-Maududi sees the period of Muhammad's leadership and the reign of the orthodox caliphs as a utopian ideal and therefore takes a revisionist stance on early Islamic history.[81] Indeed, this idealised vision of the time of the companions can be described as a *salafi* world-view. Quite different, then, is the perception of history as described in *Du'at la Qudat*. Al-Hudaybi draws a less idealistic picture of early Islamic history, one which avoids any connotations of perfection. Nevertheless, this does not mean that al-Hudaybi does not see Muhammad and his companions as a model; for him they are not perfect, not infallible, but exemplary humans.

It is interesting to note that depicting Muhammad's humanness is an approach which can be also traced in the works of 'Abduh and al-Afghani.[82] 'Abduh, for example, referred to the differentiation of the deeds of the person Muhammad, who was human and thus fallible, from his capacity as a prophet and mediator of divine revelation, which was characterised by infallibility (*'isma'*). Thereby he reformulated a division which was quiescently present in the traditional books of *usul al-fiqh*.[83] Gershoni and Jankowski relate the phenomenon of emphasising the human side of the prophet to a new Islamic mood in Egypt during the 1930s. They detect this shift in the portrayal of Muhammad in an analysis of a literary category they term 'Islamiyyat' literature. These include popular writings on the life of the prophet, such as by Muhammad 'Abduh, but also those of Muhammad Hussain Haykal, Tawfiq al-Hakim and 'Abbas Mahmud al-'Aqqad. These works, so Gershoni and Jankowski write, had an immense impact on common perceptions and were widely read.[84]

The modern presentation of the humanness, such as by 'Abduh, al-Afghani and al-Hudaybi, is distinct from its classical juridical use and its distinctions between Muhammad as prophet, military and political leader, judge and ordinary person. While these classical categories were used to resolve legal contradictions, this modern portrayal of Muhammad has the simple purpose of bringing the prophet's character closer to the average person living in the here and now. This objective coincides usually with a political aim.

Portraying Muhammad as a person who dealt with conflicts and made mistakes, al-Hudaybi suggests that misinterpretations were part of early Islamic history.[85] Contrary to the *salafi* idealisation, al-Hudaybi demystifies the past. This becomes even more obvious when he talks about Muhammad's companions, in particular the orthodox caliphs. He does not romanticise the rule of the prophet and of his close companions. He does not idealise it as a time when revelation and practice were the same, or as an ideal state and society.

Humanising the prophet presents a provocative concept. After all, it runs contrary to the commonly accepted idea of the prophet's infallibility. It could bring Muhammad's absolute status into question and could be constructed as blasphemy. It is apparent that al-Hudaybi avoids the offensive issue of the prophet's fallibility in a subtle way, but instead emphasises the imperfection of his companions and particularly of the later orthodox caliphs.

He argues that even those closest to the prophet were not familiar with every detail of Islam and the law.[86] Like every human, they made errors; they also misinterpreted the divine message and Muhammad's guidelines. In conclusion, their practice was not without mistakes. While he was still alive, the prophet still accepted them despite their shortcomings and did not exclude them from the community of believers. Certainly, al-Hudaybi argues, it would unreasonable to demand more from a Muslim today than the prophet did in his time.

It must be said that al-Hudaybi's line of reasoning contains an internal tension. As depicted above, he presents two opposing arguments in his polemic against al-Maududi. On the one hand, he brings forward that 'meaning' and, in the widest sense, 'truth' is delineated through the Qur'an. On the other hand, he gives in to the idea that misinterpretation is an actuality. The first position entails that the individual can derive and implement meaning immediately and only through reference to the source of revelation. At one point al-Hudaybi goes so far as stating that any distinction between original, true meaning as opposed to current, modified meaning of Qur'anic terms is unacceptable.[87] Holding on to the idea of the universality of the Qur'an, he gives the impression that meaning is fixed and that there is no interpretative flexibility. Through his second argument, however, al-Hudaybi implies that meaning cannot be drawn from the text of the Qur'an alone. He concedes that it is impossible to understand the Qur'an without elucidating and positioning its content in reference to other sources. Obviously, this means that there is the need to refer to the corpus of Hadith and Sunna. To understand the divine message and make corrections to their own practice, the companions approached the prophet to seek clarification. And while the companions were human and therefore made mistakes, the community continues to refer to their Sunna (practice), since it is assumed that they were closest to the prophet.

With his insistence on Hadith as an objective primary source, al-Hudaybi waters down his previous argument that all meaning necessary for understanding the divine can be deduced by reference to the Qur'an only. Conceding that Hadith and Sunna are central for understanding, it leaves one to wonder whether al-Hudaybi really sees the Qur'an as a universal whole; further, the admission that Hadith and Sunna are the important means of finding religious guidance begs the question whether al-Hudaybi's perception of the *al-Salaf al-Salih* really set him apart from *Salafi*s such as al-Maududi and Qutb.

Apart from this tension, al-Hudaybi's description of the prophet's humanness and the companions' imperfection raises a further, even more fundamental issue. Even if one takes for granted that Hadith and Sunna are the additional sources to be used to illuminate meaning, which is indeed the method of *fiqh* and also that employed in *Du'at la Qudat*, one could argue that al-Hudaybi's perception raises questions about the quality of these sources. In the face of fallibility, these references cannot uphold the assertion of being incontestable. The issue in question goes beyond objections regarding the problematic of the collection, verification and compilation of Hadith and, more generally, of Sunna during the first centuries. Admittedly the issue of verification is fundamental to the reliability of these additional sources and therefore to theological and juridical reasoning.

The problem al-Hudaybi ignores is rather essential. It is related to depicting the humanness, and hence the subjectivity and possible inaccuracy of the prophet and his companions, who after all stand at the beginning of the chain of authority (*isnad*) on which a tradition is based. Although al-Hudaybi does not stand alone in his portrayal of Muhammad and his first followers as human beings and, in fact, follows a trend in modern Islamic interpretation along with al-Afghani as the best-known proponent, the aspect implied in their fallibility contains immense theoretical implications. It would cast aside a long-held concept, some would argue even dogma, of the absoluteness and infallibility of the prophet's status (*'isma*) and, hence, the reliability of the content of Hadith and Sunna.[88] Consequentially, this has inferences for the method of Islamic juridical reasoning, and more generally for Islamic hermeneutics, and further for the reading(s) of the Qur'an as a historical text. Brown summarises the problem in the following words:

> But challenges to the infallibility also raise their own problems. For Muslims the question is quite direct and urgent: is it possible to question the infallibility without thereby completely undermining the authority of the Sunna? What will be left of Islam without the Sunna? Moreover, challenges to the infallibility lend special urgency to questions of human religious authority. If our sources of knowledge are not infallible, then who is to decide what to accept and what to reject?
>
> (Brown (1999) 63–4)

Al-Hudaybi's depiction of humanness inadvertently undermines the very basis of tradition theological and legal interpretations. Indeed, any critique of the verification process of Muslim scholars of Hadith is equivalent to questioning the objectivity of Muslim schools of thought. Muslim interpretative practice therefore would have to face the issue of the subjectivity of its claims, which would mean that their authority could be questioned. In conclusion, the schools of law and theology would have to face up to the humanness of interpretation.

Admittedly, the above critique of al-Hudaybi's positions on the universality of the Qur'an and his view of the *Salaf al-Salih* is rather harsh. One should not lose sight of the fact that his interpretation on these issues serves a purpose. As mentioned, the aim is to present a refutation of the idea of *jahiliyya*. Hence, his affirmation that the Qur'an is Islam's universal message directly opposes the idea of lost meaning. Since Muslims are able to discern meaning, it underpins al-Hudaybi's basic affirmation. He sees it as an objectionable step to pronounce *takfir* hastily. This aspect contains a political statement in defence of Muslims, particularly political leaders.[89]

Stages of belief

The *shahada* is the initiating moment for a Muslim and a constant reminder of the basic dogmas of Islam, namely monotheism and prophethood. As mentioned, al-Hudaybi considers it is unacceptable to ask for any further verification of a Muslim's faith, such as political activism or engagement for the Islamist cause. A person must be accepted as Muslim without any initial objections and requirements other than the verbalisation of the *shahada*. Nevertheless, al-Hudaybi adds to this ground rule a further aspect, namely the concept of 'stages of belief'. Although it is mentioned much later in the book, namely in connection with his interpretation of God's rule, it is closely interlinked with his definitions of belief, sin and unbelief.[90]

While he returns to the issue of whether intention and action are part of the belief in Islam, he puts forward the idea that belief verifies itself in stages. Referring to a well-known Hadith, he gives his opinion that the believer needs to work through layers of faith in order to reach a complete understanding of the faith.[91]

The believer enters the first stage through becoming aware of his/her conviction. Al-Hudaybi calls this step 'belief with the heart' (*iman bi'l-qalb*). At this stage, the believer does not yet have the knowledge of essentials of belief. The believer 'knows' with his heart that there is a divine purpose. It is only in the next stage that conviction is coupled with verbal expression of this faith; hence, he terms this stage 'belief with the tongue' (*iman bi'l-lisan*). It is at this stage that the believer speaks the *shahada*, thus verbalising that he/she is familiar with the core of Muslim belief, i.e. the belief in one God and the belief that Muhammad is God's messenger. As he pointed out above, in the explanation on the purpose of the *shahada*, faith is the prerequisite of entering Islam. Congruently, intent is within the heart of the professing Muslim, even though this intent cannot be subject to scrutiny, at least at this stage. Nevertheless, conviction and verbal expression allow the Muslim to then explore the last stage, where conviction and verbal expression will thus meet action. The manifestation of faith through action is therefore called 'belief with deeds' (*iman bi'l-'amal*).[92] Al-Hudaybi calls it the highest form of belief, since it is the lived expression of faith through deeds.[93]

The idea of stages of belief and action is somewhat reminiscent of Sufi ideas, which, as Lia points out, influenced Hasan al-Banna's conception regarding the establishment of an elite cadre of Islamist preachers and activists.[94] Similar, it could be argued, is also Sayyid Qutb's proposal of a *minhaj* (path) which gradually prepares the true believer for his duty of active engagement through withdrawal from society, during which the vanguard should engage in study and thus strengthen his conviction.[95] The manner in which al-Hudaybi presents his stages of belief, is however more closely connected to classical considerations. The idea that faith manifests itself was indeed discussed within *'ilm al-kalam* (speculative or philosophical theology) and continues to be controversially disputed among the Islamic scholars even today.[96] Although he argues, in regard to the centrality of the *shahada*, that action is not considered to be an actual requirement for belief, he adds that visible and physical manifestation of Islamic principles becomes a desirable goal.

The concept of stages of belief, which ultimately elevates action to be the best form of expressing faith, creates a contradiction in al-Hudaybi's interpretation. While he previously rejected the idea that *'amal* is a valid proof of being Muslim, he now reintroduces the idea of action. It is therefore fair to say that he is not entirely rigorous in his argument and, in effect, proposes conflicting definitions of belief.[97] In fact, the question of whether action is part of belief re-enters the arena of the discourse and leaves us to question whether al-Hudaybi's interpretation of belief is much different from those of radical Islamists and their emphasis on *'amal*.

The difference between al-Hudaybi's and activist approaches depends, then, only on the definition of the word *'amal* (deed, work, action). The question is, then, whether action signifies active participation for the establishment of an Islamic state or whether the concept stands for general practice such as praying, fasting, giving donations and going on pilgrimage. At one point al-Hudaybi indeed refers explicitly to these five pillars of Islam. Nevertheless, he walks a thin line. Because his interpretation reintroduces categories for the manifestation of belief, readers are left with the argument that activism is the sign of 'true' belief, i.e. the highest form of understanding. The hidden problematic is then whether political activism is a manifestation of true belief. Taking into account that al-Hudaybi sees active engagement in the establishment of an Islamic state system as a religious necessity, one is only left to wonder.[98] In this respect, his interpretation also shows an underlying glorification and hidden approval of political activism. Placing stress on action as the highest form of belief, al-Hudaybi supports a concept not dissimilar to al-Maududi's and Qutb's idea.

However, in defence of al-Hudaybi, one has to recognise that he is aware of the distinction between religious practice and belief. He qualifies that practice, even though it may signify faith, is not equal to belief.[99] This in itself is quite important and needs to be recognised. Following religious rituals and obeying the laws of the *shari'a* may be expressions of faith, but they are not faith in themselves. The Muslim grows in his/her faith by complying with the rules, thus reducing the possibility of committing sin.

Unbelief: the opposite of belief?

It must be said that al-Hudaybi's interpretations on belief and unbelief continue to follow conventional traits. Hence, he states that the opposite of belief (*iman*) is unbelief (*kufr*).[100]

Al-Hudaybi's description of unbelief would appear to be strict. The chief characteristic of *kufr* is, as he would have it, to deny God.[101] This denial is effectively the non-acceptance of God's divinity, expressed in the refusal to obey his law as set down in the Qur'an and Sunna. He even goes so far, in his definition of unbelief, as to argue that questioning the necessity of God's rule (by substitution of another deity, another being or one's self) is consequently the defiance of God's sovereignty. This implies, therefore, disregard for divine infallibility and absoluteness, being equal in al-Hudaybi's mind to *shirk*. Hence, he clearly uses the term polytheism synonymously to unbelief. This position makes him supportive of expulsion from the Islamic community upon commission of either *shirk* or *kufr*. Along this line, apostasy (*ridda*) has to be understood as a person's conscious perpetration of *kufr* or *shirk*.[102] In other words, following his point of view, it is not the community who banishes a person, but it is the individual committing the crime who ousts him/herself. The Muslim community merely reacts. Yet, in effect, 'a Muslim who left the community', using al-Hudaybi words here, signifies exclusion. Hence, the phrase he employs is only a euphemism for expulsion. Additionally, it is interesting to note that, while al-Hudaybi never explicitly uses the word *takfir* or openly calls for punishment beyond exclusion from the Islamic community, expulsion would also be indicated with the declaration of apostasy, i.e. *takfir*. At this point, it has to be asked whether his position is much different from the stance taken by radical Islamists and whether there are any contradictions of what he purports to stand for in regard to his liberal interpretation of belief.

The above shows that al-Hudaybi's interpretation is, like those of fellow Islamists, framed by these binary oppositions. However, his extensive but sometimes rather lengthy and (still) confusing explanations on terminology differ considerably from those given by proponents of radical Islam. Qutb, for example, clearly takes the position that belief must entail activism and thus implies that anyone who does not engage in political Islam is in fact an unbeliever. In Milestones, Qutb does not engage in philosophical or juridical deliberations on the basis of faith, but presents his version of a 'liberation theology'. He thus adopts a propagandistic line of argument, which leaves no place for defining a state between belief and unbelief. Similarly, the individual's conduct is measured against excommunication, and exclusion from the Muslim community.

Al-Hudaybi's approach, which is largely informed by classical theology and jurisdiction, is, however, essentially different. As we have seen above, al-Hudaybi's definition of belief (*iman*) aims to be inclusive. He takes a non-interventionist stance regarding the profession of faith and consequently puts stress on its individual quality. This allows the believer considerable freedom. Further, he delineates the terms *kufr* (unbelief), *shirk* (polytheism) and *ridda* (apostasy), all of these words denoting exclusion from the Islamic community. In doing so, he aligns himself with Sunni juridical and theological reasoning. Clearly well versed in *fiqh* (jurisdiction) and *kalam* (theology), his aim is to undermine a 'with us or against us' portrayal of Islam.

While al-Hudaybi tries to give the impression that Islam is an inclusive religion, he nevertheless clings to the idea that a Muslim is bound to religious principles and to the laws of *shari'a*. It is at this point that al-Hudaybi makes reference to an important theological distinction between transgressions which amount to unbelief and those which constitute sinful behaviour (*ma'siyya*).[103] Congruent with the theology of the Ash'ariyya, which was discussed above, al-Hudabyi sees the concept of sin as a 'buffer' between unbelief on the one hand and belief on the other. Not charging every transgressor with unbelief, the concept allows for the defence of the person's status as a Muslim. In cases of unbelief, al-Hudaybi agrees that the person needs to be excluded from the community. Yet, he argues that a decision on expulsion can only be passed if clear evidence is brought forward. He further stresses that banning someone, which equates to *takfir*, must be considered on an individual basis.[104] Al-Hudaybi therefore rules out the validity of announcing *takfir* against an entire society, which was indeed an approach suggested by Qutb.

This said, it needs to be emphasised that an act of transgression, at least if it is committed intentionally, can still be punishable under law. While misconduct is not necessarily enough reason for exclusion from the Islamic community, it does not protect from punishment. A sinner is still subject to the legal penalties in cases where Islamic jurisprudence has set rules. For example, Islamic jurisprudence (*fiqh*) tends to consider *hadd* crimes such as theft, illicit sexual intercourse or highway robbery as crimes which demand corporal penalties; the argument is that they are prescribed by the Qur'an.[105] Regardless of the act of transgression or the level of punishment, it is crucial to recognise that the transgressor remains part of the Muslim community.[106] This distinction between the transgressing believer and a person who can no longer be considered Muslim is informed by traditional Islamic jurisprudence and it is one al-Hudaybi adopts.[107]

As explained above, the distinction between *kufr* and *ma'siyya* is immensely important. It does not only have theoretical implications and al-Hudaybi is clearly aware of this. Exclusion from the community of Muslims is therefore clearly defined; there is, then, only one incident to ponder, namely *ridda* (apostasy). In other words, *takfir* can only be declared against an apostate, i.e. in cases where a person consciously leaves the community of Muslims. Considering the severity of the charge of apostasy, Islamic law demands clear evidence and cannot be proved by implication. While there is some clarity that apostasy needs clear evidence, it is, however, another area of debate whether apostasy is a *hadd* crime. Even though theology considers *ridda* a major sin, not all Islamic schools of law list *ridda* among the *hudud*.[108] Without wanting to foreclose the discussion, it should be noted that if *ridda* is not defined as a *hadd* crime, neither is punishment Qur'anically prescribed.

Apart from the juridical implications, al-Hudaybi's argument on belief and unbelief shows some shortcomings. Although the aim of the argument is to reject the concept of *jahiliyya* and of political *takfir*, al-Hudabyi falls back onto the common usage of *takfir* rhetoric. He also plays with threatening his opponents with *takfir*. The following extract, which represents an immediate response against al-Maududi, exemplifies this.

> We respond to those who go beyond (God's law) in claiming that people's misinterpretations regarding the creed lead to their expulsion from Islam: you depart from God's law because you make your own rules about what is actually set as law to all people. Your explanation (…) is a supposition, which bears no certainty at all.
>
> (al-Hudaybi (1977) 35)

Al-Hudaybi is clearly not content with limiting his response to a refutation of activist approaches based on theological and juridical reasoning. In various instances, he clearly tries to undermine the credibility of his opponents. Instead of facing up to the actuality of differing practices of interpretation, he puts the force of *takfir* behind his words. One could argue that he applies a similar doctrinaire position and accuses activists of dissenting from the 'truth'. Disregarding his own deliberations that *takfir* must not be pronounced without valid evidence, the passage above shows that he sends out the same threat.[109] This contradiction weakens his argument and sincerity. It leaves the reader to wonder whether al-Hudaybi applies the same dichotomies, those of belief and unbelief. Effectively, one could argue that his refutation is only superficially moderate and in fact contains the same dogmatism as radical interpretation.

3.3 Sin and crime

In order to appreciate al-Hudaybi's distinction between sin (*ma'asiyya*) and unbelief (*kufr*) and to understand the legal and political implications, one needs to revisit early Islamic history. Of importance is the conviction of the Khawarij movement, which professed the concept of *takfir* and thereby disregarded any differentiation between sin and unbelief. In opposition to this early Islamic zealot-ism, a gradually developing Sunni Islamic theology and jurisprudence developed a moderate stance, which ultimately gave stability to the political system of the 'Ummayad and 'Abassid caliphs. The distinctiveness of sin from unbelief not only confirmed the authority of the Sunni caliphate, but also had religious and legal inferences for the common believer.

In the search for some definition of sin and its distinctiveness from unbelief, Sunni descriptions are clearly interlinked with two areas: first, the issue of sub-sequent differentiation between minor and grave sins and second, Islamic penal law. Arguing his case with reference to these subjects, al-Hudaybi expresses his interpretation that there are a number of reasons which indicate that a Muslim who acted in contempt or disrespect for God's law must not be lightly charged with unbelief.[110] While referring to classical Sunni juridical ideas regarding sin, he takes a position against the idea of *takfir*. Although he does not mention the ideol-ogy of the Khawarij movement, he implicitly draws a line between their zealotry in the history of early Islam and modern radical Islamist conceptions.

Sin – minor and grave

Sin (*ma'asiyya*) constitutes the intentional breach of divine law.[111] However, this definition poses the question how to decide between what has to be seen as a sign of unbelief (*kufr*) or idolatrous acceptance of an authority other than God (*shirk*), and what violations are merely sinful behaviour. The issue is complicated by the fact that a few verses of the Qur'an indicate a distinction between two types of sin. In reference to verse 4: 31 of the Qur'an and in clarification of verse 42: 37, Sunni theology and jurisprudence inferred a supplementary differentiation of sin, namely grave offences (*kaba'ir*; sing. *kabira*) and venial infringements (*sagha'ir*; sing. *saghira*).[112] Further, since Hadith texts list idolatry (*shirk*) as the utmost case of grave sin, it posed the question of whether the trespasser (*fasiq*), in con-sequence of his sinful deed of acknowledging an authority other than God, must therefore be considered an idolater (*mushrik*).[113] In other words, the issue is that of whether grave sins are coequal to apostasy. In cases where a Muslim commits apostasy or idolatry, Islamic law foresees the death penalty. With the predicament of defining the difference between grave and minor sin, Sunni interpreters were thus continually drawn back to the initial problematic of differentiating sin from unbelief.[114]

Although the problematic seems to be highly theoretical, it is in no way born out of abstract theological reasoning. The origin of the quandary goes back to the formative period of Islam and indeed has a political cause. In opposition to the political objectives of the first sectarian movement of Islam, namely the Khawarij, Sunni theology established itself. In fact, as Izutsu points out, the issue thus constitutes the very beginning of theological reasoning.[115]

The Khawarij has its origin in the challenge to the validity of 'Ali's caliphal authority.[116] It accused him as well as his opponent Mu'awiyya, who in the course of history came to be the founder of the 'Ummayad dynasty, of *shirk* for the reason that both agreed to arbitration on the battleground of Siffin. Taking the stance that 'Ali and Mu'awiyya thus interfered in God's will, the Khawarij subsequently developed the concept that committing grave sin (*irtikab al-kaba'ir*) is reason enough to disqualify a person from the community of Muslims. In effect, this view proposes that sin and unbelief (*kufr*) are identical. Upon this interpretation, the movement established its concept of *takfir* (charge of unbelief). Consequently, any Muslim whom it considered as having broken *shari'a* law, i.e. anyone who did not follow the ideology of the Khawarij, was resolutely pronounced an apostate and thus deserved to be killed.

In response to this radical assertion, proponents of a developing Sunni theology took the stance that sin is distinct from unbelief, even though it comprises an intentional transgression of divine law.[117] The Murji'iyya put forward that the final verdict regarding one's belief lies with God alone.[118] Hence, they called for the postponement of eternal judgement. The Mu'tazila, which elaborated on Hasan al-Basri's concept of an intermediate position (i.e. *al-manzila bayna al-mansilatayn*), argued that a grave sinner (*fasiq*) is neither a believer (*mu'min*) nor an unbeliever (*kafir*) in a stricter sense, but occupies a position 'in between'.[119] The Mu'tazila's and Murji'iyya's stance of avoiding actual conclusions regarding the question of belief or unbelief had an immediate political application. Thus, early Sunni circles developed concepts, in defence of the orthodox caliphs' legitimacy, that minor sins did not affect their competence as leaders. Nevertheless, since the text of the Qur'an announces God's punishment for grave sins, it was generally assumed that a leader who had committed a severe transgression was no longer suitable for the post. The theological division made it possible to retain an affirmative image of the caliphal authority, even in consideration of the dispute over the question whether the fourth 'Ali had the right to agree to arbitration. Further, it was then possible to preserve the legitimacy of the orthodox caliphs while admitting that they might have sinned. Bearing in mind that the theological differentiation indeed indicated a political application, it had implicit consequences for later interpretations regarding the issue of whether a leader who sinned could remain in office or must be dismissed. The distinction between sin and unbelief became, then, a fundamental part of the moderate stance of the developing Sunni Islamic schools of thought. Classical Sunni theology and jurisprudence thus developed a theology of state which largely affirms actual authority.

Islamic penal code and the delineation of sin

Although the distinction between sin and unbelief lies at the core of Sunni theology and even though the differentiation between grave and minor sin had an immediate political application in defending Sunni authority against the religious zealotry of the Khawarij and the exclusiveness of the infallible imamate to the Shi'a, a definition of which offences fall into the one or the other category remained largely vague. In the attempt to find some clarity, Sunni *fuqaha'* thus turned to Qur'anic passages dealing with Islamic penal law.[120]

Islamic penal law distinguishes between three sets of crime, namely *hudud* (restrictions; sing. *hadd*), *qisas* (retribution), and *ta'zir* (castigation).[121] *Ta'zir* crimes comprise offences which are not mentioned in the primary sources of Qur'an and Sunna.[122] These are thus the product of human considerations of regulating society and are not divine law in a strict sense. Thus, breaking laws which fall into the category of *ta'zir* does not constitute sinful behaviour. Similarly, verdicts on their punishment and the severity of the penalty are traditionally left to the discretion of the judge. The second category, i.e. *qisas* crimes, demands requital, since the source of Qur'an and Sunna legally prescribe their retribution. Crimes of this type encompass offences such as murder, physical harm and battery.[123] Although the primary sources particularly mention *qisas* crimes as transgressions of divine law, they are distinct from the *hudud*, because of the right to insist on compensation to the victim or the next of kin (in case of the victim's death). Hence, the committer of a *qisas* crime is charged either with an equalising sentence (i.e. for the death penalty in case of murder), or alternatively is asked to give financial reparations (i.e. blood money). If so agreed, the penalty can be waived altogether. In other words, punishment for crimes of this category is not necessarily mandatory. The third section of criminal law is the so-called *hudud*.[124] The schools of Islamic jurisprudence commonly agree that *hudud* punishments are to be imposed for misdemeanours such as drinking wine (*shurb al-khamr*), for illicit sexual relations (*zina'*) and false allegations of illicit relations (*qadhf*), and also for crimes such as theft (*sariqa*) and highway robbery (*qata' al-tariq*).[125] Juridical interpreters of the various schools consider penalties for *hudud* transgressions to be mandatory, and thus agree that reprimands are divinely prescribed. The reason for this consensus is the shared opinion that the Qur'an sets these incidences out as punishable crimes. Although not explicitly elaborated in the Qur'an, classical jurisdiction proposed that the above-listed offences carry different penalties, which vary from public slashing, to amputation of a hand and to the death sentence.

Sunni juridical thinkers agree that *hudud* and *ta'zir* offences have to be considered as sinful behaviour.[126] With this emphasis on distinction of sin from unbelief, these transgressions against Islamic law do not immediately banish the offender from the community of believers, regardless of the severity of the crime and the vehemence of the punishment. With the development of Islamic law, classical Sunni legal interpreters aimed to translate the differentiation between minor and grave sins, and their distinctiveness from unbelief, into a legal framework. Because *hudud* punishments are described in the Qur'an as mandatory, classical jurists drew attention to this category in their explanations of grave sins. Yet, the proposition that *hudud* correspond to *kuba'ir* posed problems. For one, this link implies that crimes such as drinking wine and illicit sexual relations etc. are consequently on an equal footing with the most severe contravention of Islamic law, namely *shirk*. Moreover, not all the offences listed in the above-mentioned Hadith by Ibn Mas'ud fall into the category of *hudud*. Hence, attempts to define major violations of divine law in terms of *hudud* did not resolve the fundamental tension between sin and unbelief. Evidence that the problem remained unresolved in the

Sunni juridical rendering is the fact that categorisations into grave and minor sins continued to be disputed and that various attempts to set up catalogues of sins were not commonly agreed upon.[127] Nevertheless, the classical focus on *hudud* in explaining the content of grave sin continues to have an impact on modern Islamist interpretation.

Modern emphasis on crime, sin and apostasy

The challenges vis-àpvis renewal, reinterpretation and (re-)establishment of Islamic law as well as in competition with dissimilar approaches in Western law, made the Islamic criminal law the subject of fierce debates and disagreements.[128] The majority of today's Islamists generally follow the consensus of the schools of law insofar as they agree that actions explicitly denounced in the Qur'an must be penalised. While the authority of the (imagined) Islamic state as the executor of law is idealised to such an extent that Islamists generally fail to recognise that the issue of the Islamic law and Islamic penal code is not as clear cut as many wish it to be, a number of essential questions in regard to the applicability of the law remain unresolved.

Although it may in theory seem obvious which crime falls into one or the other classification of the Islamic penal law, it needs to be mentioned that there has existed at all times, during the course of Islamic juridical history, a dispute on the details of criminal law, particularly in regard to the *hudud*.[129] This for two major reasons: first, the schools of jurisprudence differed slightly on the list of activities which are punishable *hadd* crimes. Secondly, and more substantially, although there are a number of Qur'anic verses which indicate punishment, in most cases the passages do not specify the method of chastisement. Yet, the idea is particularly common among Islamists that *shari'a*, and penal law as part of it, consists of a corpus of objective regulations and clearly defined sentences. This is, however, a misconception.[130] In fact, penal law (just as *shari'a*) is the product of a history of meticulous Islamic juridical exegesis. During its course, juridical scholarship has developed and applied methods to extract and interpret information from the primary sources, claiming that these facilitate an objective determination of law in accordance with divine will. Still, the theoretical critique that the method of Islamic jurisprudence and, therefore its results, are exposed to human subjectivity is not given much consideration in Islamic juridical circles. Further, as much as there was a exegetical debate about the particulars of penal law, its implementation was dependent on various factors, namely, the strength or weakness of a (central) Islamic government during the reign of the various dynasties and houses; the directives of the juridical school prevalent in one region, which after all required acceptance by the ruling power in order to become executed law; and customs of different regions of the Islamic community (*umma*), which influenced the legal considerations of theologians and juridical experts. Hence, even though a central government represented by the caliphate (*khilafa*) existed nominally in Sunni Islam until the fall of the Ottoman Empire, the Islamic penal code was at no time a fixed code of law. In view of the fact that details of Islamic criminal law are embedded in human legal reasoning rather than specified in the Qur'an, the current discussion is related to the general debate about Islamic law (shari'a). Therefore, the issue of the feasibility of execution is embedded in the fundamental question of whether the actual penalties, as described in the various compendia of the classical schools of law, are indeed in accordance with the statements and the terminology of the Qur'an.

Ignoring these theoretical and methodological considerations, but also largely disregarding the delineation of transgressions as sinful behaviour and, further, the distinction of *hudud*, *qisas* and *ta'zir* which is integral to Sunni juridical reasoning, radical Islamism seems to put forward a simplified and politicised version of Islamic law. In the vocal call for an Islamic order, prominence is given to arguments for the enforcement of *hudud* punishments.[131] Thus, Islamists generally consider the application of Islamic penal law as the most effective means to prevent offences which are perceived as moral and social ills caused by sinful disrespect of divine law in modern society. The emphasis on penalties, which are seen as divinely ordained, exemplifies that orthodox concepts of sin and transgression remain a central issue in the modern Islamic discourse about law. Yet the lack of clarity in regard to the distinction between sin, grave sin and unbelief has left a theological and legal flaw in Sunni juridical tradition which persists to pervade the current politicised debate. Further, most proponents of radical interpretations do not have a specific juridical training and seem to be rather suspicious of extensive deliberations of *fuqaha'*, which often diverge from activism.[132] Hence, there is the tendency for the argumentation of radical Islam to focus on a limited selection of Qur'anic verses and segments.[133] Upon these key verses, proponents of radical Islamism commonly argue that any contravention of *shari'a* is in fact equivalent to *kufr*. This position, which indeed places any transgression on the same level as unbelief, effectively entails the far-reaching supposition that any kind of behaviour contrary to the convictions of the group must be demarked as a sign of unbelief or apostasy. Hence, as indicated above, a state between *kufr* and *iman* is not referred to and, overall, the question of sin is not discussed in radical Islamist thought. It is this position which allows for the possibility of *takfir* through reasons defined by politics, activism and the convictions of a particular group. It is this simplistic attitude which brings radical Islam close to the zealotry of the Khawarij and their concept of *takfir*.

Sin and crime in al-Hudaybi's interpretation

It is remarkable, then, that al-Hudaybi, as a leader of the largest religious–political oppositional movement, argues against this stance. Unlike his radical counterparts, his attitude towards penal law is heavily informed by traditional Sunni juridical thought and methods of exegesis. Although his juristic interpretation focuses on *hudud* crimes, he counters, in accordance with classical Sunni stances, that the issue of sin and the subject of legal penalties have to be discussed independently of the question of unbelief.[134] He points out as evidence that there is no reference in the sources of the Qur'an and *Sunna* which gives parity to punishable behaviour and unbelief. Still, al-Hudaybi holds on to the position that sentences for *hudud* transgressions are mandatory, since the Qur'an and Sunna demand them.[135] Thus, he supports conservative juridical ideas and takes a revisionist stance on the subject of punishment. From his point of view, *hudud* penalties are the appropriate measure for disciplining sinful behaviour. These are, according to him, not penalties at all, but rather penances which provide the offender an opportunity to atone to God and his law. Under no circumstance is the person who commits a *hudud* transgression an unbeliever; the offender is merely a sinner. The offender, he emphasises, remains within the realm of Islam. Even where the punishment for a given crime may be death, this does not, according to al-Hudaybi, conclusively mean that the perpetrator can be regarded as an unbeliever. From this standpoint, he adheres to classical Islamic law as elaborated in the four schools of jurisprudence.

From the above it follows that the question of punishment, and al-Hudaybi is clear on this point, goes beyond life. The actual penalty or reward is dealt out on the final day of judgement and is solely at the discretion of God.[136] Following al-Hudaybi, who with regard to this point seems to stick closely to orthodox juridical thinking, humans are merely the executors of the *shari'a* (*hudud* 'penances' being part of it); penalties for actions are not anticipated punishments, but rather part of repentance.[137] God is the final judge, law maker, and sovereign. The decision whether the perpetrator is an unbeliever or a believer is left to him. According to al-Hudaybi, it would be *shirk* to argue otherwise; the latter argument indicating a condemnation of radical thought.

Regarding the theological issue of sin (*ma'siyya*), al-Hudaybi thus emphasises that it is disobedience to Islamic law, and yet distinct from unbelief. Although sinners have broken *shari'a* law, they may still possess a fervent belief in God and his sovereignty even while sinning.[138] It is this fundamental recognition of God's authority that makes them part of the community of Muslims. Hence, wrongdoers cannot be regarded on the same level as unbelievers.[139] Al-Hudaybi states this position affirmatively and speaks thereupon regarding the Brotherhood's objective:

> We declared ever since we started our cause that we do not announce a Muslim as unbeliever because of sin (*la nukaffir Musliman bi-ma'siyya*).
>
> (al-Hudaybi (1977), 37)

Al-Hudaybi affirms the status of inclusion, even if a Muslim deliberately acts against God's law, but does not question the authority or the absoluteness of God; the believer is still merely sinning.[140] However, if the correctness or the reason for the law is called into question during the offence, the person is no longer a Muslim. This distinction is of major importance, since it makes the offence of unbelief, idolatry and apostasy an almost exceptional matter. It appears that there is only one possibility for passing an impeachment: the person must intentionally, publicly, willingly and consciously announce his/her break with the faith.[141] Al-Hudaybi admits that a person may hypocritically claim that he/she believes. Although the person is then, in fact, an unbeliever, it is yet impossible to check the hidden (lack of) conviction.[142] While recognising the impossibility of absolute certainty regarding a person's belief (or unbelief), the *Murshid* admits that it is not up to humans to make a final decision on the matter.[143]

Undoubtedly, al-Hudaybi's description of crime, sin and their distinction from unbelief shows considerable knowledge of Sunni jurisprudence. He mentions the modern Egyptian proponent of the Hanafi school of jurisprudence Abu Ja'afar Ahmad al-Tahawi as well as the ninth-century theologian Hasan al-Basri (forerunner of Mu'tazila) as references for his subsequent analysis of sin.[144] Nevertheless, al-Hudaybi takes a critical stance on the distinction between grave and minor sin.[145] He posits that this differentiation is obsolete because *kufr* and *hudud* transgressions (and therefore even severe cases of sinful behaviour) describe two different states of affairs.[146] Referring at length to classical juridical positions, he dismisses their suggested analysis with the argument that the classification of sins is not supported in the sources of the Qur'an and Sunna.[147] In this argument, al-Hudaybi differs from commonly held Sunni interpretations. This is surprising, since he usually tends to agree with and repeat classical and generally accepted theological stances. While he does not mention verses such as 4: 31, which indicate a distinction between grave and minor sin, he counters that the concept is merely a juridical construct.[148] It was, he argues, introduced to even out obvious interpretative discrepancies which became manifest once the idea arose that certain *hudud* crimes signify unbelief. Yet he does not specify with this statement whether he is referring to ideas brought forward by the Khawarij and their rigid stance, which ignores not only any distinction between *hudud* transgressions and unbelief, but more generally between sin (regardless whether minor or grave) and unbelief. More probably, then, referring to a movement of early Islam, he implicitly targets stances put forward by Sunni interpreters of modern times and in his immediate milieu which also show a radical tendency to perceive *hudud* crimes and (grave) sins as equivalent to *kufr*.

While dismissing the distinction of grave and minor sins, al-Hudaybi introduces a number of possible excuses.[149] He maintains that these need to be taken into consideration in the description of sinful behaviour, since they may provide explanations for the believer's wrongdoing. Indeed, the mitigating factors are significant in marking out the difference between belief and unbelief, since the idea of excuses emphasises the aspect of intent. The advantage of this depiction of sin and its differentiation from *kufr* is that it is not static; whereas radical attitudes tend to put forward rigid concepts in defining who can be seen as a Muslim and who should be considered outside the realm of Islam, al-Hudaybi's interpretation leaves considerable room for defending actions and misdeeds. Without categorising transgressions as grave and minor sins, he reaches a similar conclusion: he is able to call for the incorporation of offenders into the Islamic community and yet, he does not dispute that their deeds need to be punished in those cases where the Qur'an marks out the sin as one of the *hudud* crimes.

Ignorance, error and force as excuses

Entwined with al-Hudaybi's description of sin and its distinction from unbelief is his proposition that there are potential mitigating factors. These include ignorance (*jahl*), the related issue of misinterpretation (i.e. mistake, *khata'*) and force (*ikrah*).[150] Congruent with classical interpreters, he suggests that there are some instances which provide justification for actions which appear to be against the law.[151] Although the Muslim is principally bound to abide by God's law, these justifications excuse the transgressor. The wrongdoer cannot be considered to be an unbeliever and is, to an extent, pardoned. Thus, according to al-Hudaybi, the person is merely a sinner. His subsequent interpretation of potential excuses rests on a basic consensus among orthodox Islamic juridical interpretations, which perceives intention as a significant aspect of criminal law.[152] Hence, his elaboration on *jahl*, *khata'* and *ikrah* is line with the general opinion that the intention to do good and to avoid wrong is a sufficient defence for someone who committed an apparent act of unbelief. Yet, while al-Hudaybi gives an account of the details of possible excuses, he concedes that there are differences among the various legal interpreters in defining the aspect of intentionality. In effect, there is no agreement on the extent to which excuses are to be applied.[153]

The first motive al-Hudaybi gives is that the person may not have been aware of disregarding God's law and thus is not able to uphold the required obligations. This may be due to a lack of knowledge and education. He calls this exception ignorance (*jahl*).[154] Even though lack of awareness is a defence, it does not imply that any disrespect of God's law can be excused by this means. Al-Hudaybi makes the issue of any pardon dependent on the principal admission on the part of the wrongdoer that God is absolute. Since the prerequisite of respect for God's will requires knowledge of his commands, it is also a duty (*fard*) to learn about these. There are two levels upon which to meet this responsibility, namely the individual and the collective obligation.[155] Primarily, the believer has an individual duty (*fard al-'ayn*) to fill the gaps in his/her knowledge and to inform him/herself about God's law.[156] Additionally, the community of believers has a collective duty (*fard al-kifayya*) to engage in the examination of the Qur'an and Sunna, to interpret the sources and to make them understandable to fellow Muslims.[157] This obligation calls upon the Islamic community to generate and support a number of experts in the fields of theology and jurisprudence who in turn, through their knowledge and advice, serve the public. This way, the preservation of religious knowledge is provided for.

Although al-Hudaybi introduces the idea of ignorance (*jahl*) as a mitigating factor, he reintroduces the intention to learn as a personal duty and responsibility (*fard al-'ayn*). Implicitly, he thus opposes the idea that a Muslim only needs to follow the authoritative opinion (*taqlid*).[158] Al-Hudaybi's emphasis on divine obligation effectively means that the individual Muslim is forced to study the tenets of Islam. Disregard of this duty makes the person an unbeliever. However, this stress compromises the purpose of *jahl* as a possible defence. Further, his emphasis on personal duty creates some tension with his initial statement regarding the *shahada* as the only tangible requirement for being considered a Muslim. In other words, al-Hudaybi reintroduced the idea that a Muslim is bound to fulfil a particular obligation, namely engagement in learning, and is therefore defined by it.

Yet it should be admitted that al-Hudaybi's viewpoint regarding ignorance as a possible excuse introduces reality and practice into the theoretical framework of theology and jurisprudence. Although, ideally, all individuals of the Muslim community should be learned and informed about God's law and its requirements, the reality of life is rather different. Certainly, there is a lack of education, particularly in Egypt of the twentieth century; and unquestionably, not everyone is able engage in training, be it for personal, economic or any other reasons. Hence, al-Hudaybi's presentation of a possible defence can be applied to the majority of common people, who would be charged with *takfir* according to radical interpretation.

The obligation to overcome ignorance and, therefore, to engage in learning is interlinked with the second excuse that al-Hudaybi mentions: error (*khata'*).[159] Errors in understanding, which particularly includes mistakes in the exercise of Islamic juridical interpretation, are, according to al-Hudaybi, the main reason for false practice.[160] Al-Hudaybi introduces here the idea that 'faults' in interpretation and understanding are a natural part of reading. He acknowledges that since humans are not infallible, their reasoning is subject to mistakes. In fact, misinterpretations have always existed. Al-Hudaybi gives as examples the legal interpretations of the orthodox caliphs, particularly the first two, Abu Bakr and 'Umar.[161] Yet they were not seen as unbelievers or even as sinners. Further, al-Hudaybi counters that a rigid interpretation of *kufr* would mean that there were no Muslims except for the infallible prophet; this, he concludes, cannot be a correct interpretation.[162]

The legal interpreter (*faqih* or *mujtahid*) has the duty and responsibility to attempt to convey the divine law truthfully.[163] In order to avoid errors, and thus to ensure exactness and objective an explanation of God's law, some prerequisites are indispensable. The requirements for correct interpretation as al-Hudaybi lists them are, overall, congruent with the classical proposals on methodology.[164] The most outstanding preconditions are proficiency in Arabic and knowledge of Muhammad's biography. Additionally, the interpreter of law must be acquainted with formal aspects of presentation, argumentation and evidencing. In other words, the legal interpreter must be familiar with the traditional methodology of Islamic jurisprudence using the four principal sources of reference.[165] Related to the formal aspects of presentation and argumentation, al-Hudaybi states that the *faqih* needs to limit his interpretation to his particular subject of expertise and so avoid the possibility of giving a verdict in a field with which he is less familiar.[166] Finally, but no less importantly, al-Hudaybi mentions personal qualities, such as a sense of justice.

In the passage dealing with errors of interpretation, al-Hudaybi emphasises that the task of a legal interpreter is merely to transmit and explicate God's law (*shari'a*). He stresses that it is a misconception that the *ulu al-amr* (men in charge) have the right to pass laws, to lay down the law or to establish an order which Muslims are obliged to obey.[167] On the contrary, interpretation is, he states ardently, restricted by the constraints of the Qur'an; the principles are defined by God.

It is quite obvious that al-Hudaybi defends trained legal and theological interpreters, i.e. to *fuqaha* and *'ulama'*. These have particular responsibilities, as we will see in our analysis of the *Murshid*'s stances on the issue of an Islamic state and the delineation of the content of *shari'a*, Moreover, his elucidation on the sinful character of unintentional mistakes of interpretation could be also applied to proponents of radical Islam. Yet, his explanations contain a twofold signification. They are critique and excuse. The emphasis on formal methodology and on requirements for correct juridical investigation can be understood as implicit disapproval of radical thought. Nevertheless, because al-Hudaybi sees their propositions as erroneous rather than intentionally misleading, his explanation on *khata'* marks them as sinners. It is through this perception that he is able to make a hefty critique against fellow Brothers who sympathise with the idea of collective *takfir*, but without expelling them from the organisation or even claiming that they positioned themselves outside the community of believers.

Still, al-Hudaybi's handling of error as a possible excuse raises questions about what constitutes a truthful, objective and universal reading, or whether understanding is linked to subjective interpretations which are influenced by the factors of time, space and personal views. At least in this paragraph on interpretative errors, he seems to propose that objective understanding is possible through the correct and rigorous application of the methodology of Islamic hermeneutics and legal interpretation. This stance supposes, then, that the meaning of revelation is static. The *faqih* and *'alim* only transmit and explain God's revelation and divine will as embedded in the text of the Qur'an. However, in another passage, which deals particularly with the content of the *shari'a*, al-Hudaybi indicates that there is room for human reasoning. This stance challenges the description of objectivity as he presents it here.

Lastly, al-Hudaybi mentions physical or mental force (*ikrah*) as a third possible excuse. He argues that a person who has been compelled to defy laws of the *shari'a* or even to deny the faith is not to be considered an unbeliever.[168] This justification for an incidence of seemingly obvious disobedience of God follows on from the subject of denying religion under duress in order to avoid the threaten of damages (*taqiyya*).[169] Al-Hudaybi admits that the Qur'an does not define clearly the difference between and the boundaries of *ikrah* and *taqiyya*. He points out that classical Sunni interpretation therefore also differs on these topics.[170] With this remark on Sunni jurisdiction, he avoids mentioning that the issue of *taqiyya* is cheifly used in Shi'a jurisdiction and, indeed, was considered as a point of critique of the latter. Ignoring the difference between Shi'a and Sunni tradition, the point al-Hudaybi deduces from the lack of consent is that God sets the limits individually. Arguing that the final judgement lies in his hand, the Muslim has to aim to prove the strength of his/her faith to the extent of his/her capability, since this signifies the strength of conviction.[171]

It is interesting that al-Hudaybi brings arguments forward which are similar to Shi'i positions on the right to self-preservation at the expense of religious commitment. Nevertheless, he also maintains that a person who adheres to a political system, even if it is oppressive, is not an unbeliever as such.[172] Yet it is a sign of weakness if the Muslim is obedient to a leadership which violates divine law. Other temptations, such as money, glory, power and social status, but also illness or death, are other ways in which God tests the conviction of a Muslim. Indeed, the believer must aim to withstand these psychological pressures, although the measure of whether a Muslim went beyond the limits of the excuse lies only by God.

Although final judgement is a divine matter, al-Hudaybi points out that believers should follow as a guideline the general consensus of classical interpretation that the boundaries of this excuse are reached when the Qur'an undoubtedly rules out the option of apology.[173] In particular, another person must not be negatively affected through one's denial of belief – for example, must not fear loss of life or physical harm, or the impairment of their honour. Although al-Hudaybi puts forward that humans are not allowed to judge whether a person is an unbeliever in respect of *ikrah* as a legitimate excuse, it is remarkable that he holds on to the idea that *hudud* may still be applicable penalties for repentance. In effect, the person does not loose his/her status as a Muslim, but may have to be subject to penance, which could in certain circumstances be as severe as losing his/her life.

Al-Hudaybi encountered the effects of persecution and torture on fellow Muslim Brothers during his period of imprisonment, and his interpretation on *ikrah* has a most immediate application. It can be seen as words of support to those imprisoned or in hiding, that they should not despair and should hold on to their belief. Al-Hudaybi even suggests, somewhat, that *taqiyya*, i.e. the act of disclosing faith in order to avoid persecution, is a justifiable act. His interpretation on force as an alleviating aspect also provides some comfort to those members who, in the course of their torment, found themselves forced to disclaim their faith and their convictions. Nevertheless, it entails a message of warning. The Muslim who is forced to break divine law or who is compelled to deny his faith must not take it upon his conscience to be responsible for the harm of others.

Al-Hudaybi's interpretation on *ikrah* not only gives the assurance to his fellow Muslim Brothers that they still belong to the community of believers, even though they may have transgressed the law or even denied it, but also defends the passivity and conformity of the majority of people who follow the established social and political power without questioning. It is this argument which stands in opposition to the radical stance that anyone who does not participate in Islamic activism and therefore does not engage in resistance to the current regime of ʿAbd al-Nasir as well as to dominant ideologies and economic systems such as capitalism or socialism, has to be charged with unbelief.

3.4 *Shariʿa* – divine law or human construct?

There is no dispute among Muslim legal interpreters of the past and present, and no discontent among Islamists, about the necessity of applying *shariʿa*. However, the content of the term is debated in modern Islamic discourse, as Burgat rightly points out.[174] As a result, the call for its application attracts differing aspirations. In order to introduce the subject of the discourse on Islamic law, we need to examine the problematic of defining *shariʿa*.[175] On this basis, we shall outline the debate on the relationship between obedience to divine law and freedom of decision making. This subject is interconnected with the fixed and the flexible aspects of the Qur'an, which is at the core of the modern discourse on the content of the *shariʿa*. Here, Muhammad ʿAbduh's, Rashid Rida's and Mahmud Shaltut's proposals are of particular interest to us, since their contributions are likely to have made an impact on al-Hudaybi's position, and hence on his description of *shari'a*.

The problematic of defining shari'a

As Hooker rightly observes, the term *shari'a* has a range of meanings.[176] Being used once in the Qur'an, it refers here to a divinely prescribed way (of conduct).[177] The metaphor of a divinely guided path has been applied in Islamic theological and juridical tradition, where it refers to a set of rules and regulations which are extracted from revelation.[178] The erudition whereby Muslim juridical scholars attempt to acquire knowledge about the content of *shari'a* is called *fiqh*. Using the Qur'an as the primary text of analysis and reference, a methodology developed in Islamic legal scholarship (*'ulum al-fiqh*) with the purpose of establishing these guiding principles for the conduct of a Muslim. Hence, *fiqh* is intrinsically inter-connected with the delineation of *shari'a* as a whole and of its particular laws and rulings (pl. *ahkam*, sing. *hukm*). However, the Qur'an is in itself not a legal text-book.[179] It is therefore work of the *faqih* to extract legal meaning from the verses of the Qur'an. The context of a verse plays an important role in the interpretation of law. The causes of revelation (*asbab al-nuzul*) need to be clarified as well as the linguistic meaning of words and phrases, or any links to other verses, including incidences of abrogation as expressed in the method of *al-nasikh wa al-mansukh*. In order to carry out this hermeneutical investigation, traditional scholarship sees it as necessary to consult the Sunna as an additional primary source. With the Qur'an and Sunna as primary sources, consensus (*ijma'*) and analogical reasoning (*qiyas*) are part of the traditional interpretative methodology which tries to explain an objective meaning of the text.[180] Traditional scholarship thus describes these four sources of knowledge as the roots of juridical analysis (*usul al-fiqh*). The approach to the text of the revelation, with the underpinning objective of extracting positive law, was first formulated as a methodology by the ninth-century scholar al-Shafi'i in his treatise entitled *al-Risala fi Usul al-Fiqh*, and found common approval in Sunni juridical scholarship.[181] Following his con-cept of legal knowledge, definitive answers to the quest for Islamic rules and regulations can be found through the application of this 'objective' methodology. Consequently, laws of the *shari'a* can be formulated for every aspect of a Muslim's life. Further, laws can be categorised into what is required (*wajib*), prohibited (*mahzur* or *haram*), recommended (*mandub*), disapproved of (*makruh*), or merely permissible (*mubah*).[182]

Even though *fiqh* "designates a human activity, and cannot be described to God or (usually) the Prophet",[183] the notion of an exact methodology – put into writing by al-Shaf'i and practised throughout Islamic legal scholarship – underpinned the common conjecture that rules and regulations emerging from Islamic juridical rendering are explanations of God's prescribed path as revealed in the Qur'an. The problematic rests in the presupposition that truthful extraction and the deduction of rules can be brought about by the use of an objective methodology. Once for-mulated and evidenced with reference to Qur'an and Sunna, many legal findings appeared as truthful and almost infallible, as dogmas or principles, needing to be observed. This shift of paradigms was established particularly when legal findings gained wide acceptance through application, reiteration and finally common acceptance.[184] Hence, the term *shari'a* is widely recognised as a synonym for divinely given laws. Yet the term denotes a body of widely accepted rules which are derived through the legal interpretations of classical *fiqh*.[185] The fact that the term *shari'a* is used both for a divinely ordained way, on the one hand, and for rules and regulations emerging from juridical rendering, on the other hand, is an indication of the deep-rooted problematic surrounding the usage of the term. It further signifies a lack of distinction between the source and the bulk of (classical) Islamic juridical interpretation that gained widely accepted authority through reiteration and application. Hence, the term *shari'a* is used as 'meta-signification' which disregards – or at least puts aside – disputes regarding the actual theoretical and practical questions on the content of the term, even without giving an explanation as to which particular set of rules it refers to.

The discourse about *shari'a* shows that the content of the term is indefinite. The paradox of meaning gives the term an immense potential for its utilisation. It is, for example, common practice in Islamist literature to substantiate interpretation with an emphasis on the acknowledgement and respect of *shari'a*. Often, the mere declaration that the *shari'a* is a set of divine laws is used to reassure the reader that their particular interpretation is truthful. The problematic becomes even more complicated, though, when an opposing interpretation is either downgraded as *fiqh* (i.e. hereby stressing that the opponent's position is merely the result of human reasoning) or, more so, when it is dismissed as illegitimate innovation (*bid'a*). In summary, the ambiguity of definition and, therefore, meaning, as well as the term's use for various political objectives, is at the core of the modern discourse about the content of *shari'a*.

Obedience and reasoning

Leaving aside for a moment the issue of the content of *shari'a*, it can be said that obedience (*ta'a*) to God's will marks the difference between an unbeliever and a Muslim. There is hence an unequivocal agreement that submission to God is set as a fundamental duty (*fard* or sometimes *usul*) of Islamic belief.[186] Hence, the view is common that this relationship between God and humans defines all aspects of a Muslim's life, with the result that obedience to God's supremacy is seen as the core of Islamic concepts of state and government.[187] Even though the distrust of separating the 'religious' from the 'secular' is deeply rooted and common among the majority of Muslim interpreters, Islamist attitudes seem to go even further and, to all intents and purposes, politically 'substantialise' the relationship between God and human.

The fact that the word *islam* translates as 'submission to God's will' is often reinforced in Islamic writings. Further, the idea of *tawhid* (belief in the unity of God) serves as a theological basis for explaining the notion of obedience. Since God is one – as, for example, the profession of faith clearly states – and since

God is universal, beyond the human and worldly, *tawhid* is frequently, and with much greater emphasis in modern Islamic interpretation, declared as confirmation of the inevitability of God's supremacy.[188] Being one of the major subjects of the revelation, Qur'anic statements such as "there is no judgement except for God" and "whoever does not pass judgement according to what God has revealed, those are indeed the unbelievers" are given as evidence in support of the concept of the absoluteness of God's rule.[189]

Bringing this into relation with the debate about *shari'a*, the question is not whether obedience to God's will and law is a duty. Further, for most Muslim contributors of the past and of the present, it is beyond doubt that *shari'a* in its totality is tantamount to divine law (or at least, the summary of objectively extracted law). The disagreement among interpreters is, rather, on the issues of what this submission entails and whether and to what extent humans have freedom to identify their own regulations. In other words, the source of discontent among modern Muslim interpreters regards the unchangeable substance of divine law and whether (and, if yes, to what extent) there is a flexible element embedded therein.

In fact, classical juridical interpretation already rose this problematic. The distinction between the fixed (*thabit*) and the flexible (*mutaghayyir*) was expressed through the theoretical categories of fundamentals (*'usul*) and derivations (*furu'*).[190] This means that, while maintaining that there is an unchangeable essence, jurisprudence acknowledged (at least on a theoretical level) that changing circumstances have their impact on *shari'a* and that the application of law demanded a continuous (re-)reading and interpretation of the sources. In theory, this relative feature of *shari'a*, embedded in the flexible aspect, needs to be met with human reasoning in order to be meaningful and applicable. In this respect, human decision making and freedom of will are a complementary part of the fundamental obligation of submission to God's will. One could even conclude that a frequent practice of reinterpretation in the realm of the flexible makes a constant reinvention of law in its entirety probable. The idea that Islamic juridical scholars (*fuqaha*) and theologians (*'ulama*) were those learned in the sources, trained in the skill of methodological exegesis and therefore those with the ability to fulfil the flexible aspect by innovative reasoning, also gave them a major responsibility and opportunity. This even more so, since a central agency for interpreting the textual sources does not exist in Sunni Islam. Although the flexible realm may have suggested openness to reasoning, 'free' *ijtihad* (legal reasoning) was, in the historical practice of application, not explored. This is for several reasons. First, during the time when Islamic jurisdiction was evolving, the customary laws and legal ideals of the occupied territories found an entrance into Islamic jurisdiction. Although these rulings were often based on the opinion (*ra'y*) of the early *'ulama'*, they eventually constituted the framework of Islamic legal rendering.[191] Once the four schools of Sunni Islam had taken shape and been instituted as the guiding juridical establishment, the exegetical results of highly recognised scholars of one or the other school, and therefore regulations and laws, were continuously reapplied and gained in themselves a somewhat unquestioned authority.[192] Following one of the four schools of jurisprudence, *fuqaha* were not only constrained by the textual sources, but were also somewhat attached to previously made choices of particular verses and Hadith for evidencing, and bonded to argumentation as well as to embedded theoretical attitudes and, finally, judgements of outstanding representatives of their school. Further interlinked with this issue is the fact that the methodology of interpretation, particularly regarding consensus (*ijma'*) and analogical reasoning (*qiyas*), which conceptually could have been used in explaining rules of change within the flexible realm, instead imposed a certain prevailing attitude in legal theory and, one could say, even stagnation.[193] The pressure against 'free' use of *ijma'* and *qiyas* in the classical juridical dispute was due to a growing textualism, which set out that reasoning and interpretative human involvement needed to be rigidly restricted, otherwise they would endanger the primacy of the text. Textualists assumed that in this way God's will could be preserved without distortion. Their approach found support in the idea that the early Islamic community represented an example which should be re-enacted; hence, a tendency was cultivated that a return to the ideal makeup of this society was essentially possible. Above all, the distinction between the fixed and the flexible notions of the *shari'a* was irrelevant insofar as the interpretation of the content was relatively dependent on the various Sunni caliphs of Islamic history (with the decline of the caliphate, even reliant on rulers).[194] Corresponding to the power of the ruler and the demand to obey his leadership, all law and regulations executed under his responsibility as the guardian of Islamic law were marked out in their totality as *shari'a*.

In regard to modern times, the issue of interpretation gained new relevance. With the abolition of the caliphate, the introduction of independent nation-states, and particularly with modernity, proponents of so-called Islamic revival saw themselves challenged to respond.[195] The fact that a recognised central authority in (Sunni) Islam, whether in the interpretative or juridical, executive or political field, is absent, is one of the main reasons for the problematic of defining *shari'a*. Subsequently, the issue of obedience and self-determination, and thus the question of the fixed and flexible component, gained renewed significance. Although that the notion of an objective textual analysis is dominant through the continuing prevalence of al-Shafi'i's methodology of exegesis, modern Islamic interpretation seems to be wrestling yet again with the content of obedience and freedom of reasoning. Hence, even though rigid voices argue that the revelation, and therefore *shari'a*, does cover every aspect of life, since they also perceive it as a timeless, unchangeable and universal set of divine laws, in actuality they overlook the fact that human reasoning comes into play in the reading, understanding, extraction and application of the text. If one accepts (and Muslims do, since this is the essential distinction) that there is a divine foundation which has to be obeyed, this leaves open the issue of its interpretation. In other words, there is a continuous problem of defining the content of *shari'a*, or which laws are considered to comprise the unquestionable core, and to what extent free will is a factor. Within the Islamic discourse, there is not yet an absolute answer to this search. Yet there is a strong tendency among modern Islamic legal interpreters such as 'Abduh, Rida and Shaltut, and also more current ones such as Muhammad Sa'id al-'Ashmawi and Fahmi Huwaydi, to give priority to human interpretation rather than to doctrine.[196] Hence, these modern thinkers revitalise rationalist approaches to the text and counter a certain stagnation of thought which for many centuries presided, with its focus on dogmatic law, over discussions on Islamic law. Their emphasis on *ijtihad* signifies their call to give religion fresh value in accordance with the demands of modern times.

A moderate interpretation of Islamic law

In this section we will focus on al-Hudaybi's perception of law as presented in his work *Du'at la Qudat*.[197] We will see that his opinion is shaped by various sources of reference, each embedded in a network of contexts. The most obvious link is al-Hudaybi's opposition to uncompromising concepts regarding the divinity of law, as put forward by members of his organisation – Sayyid Qutb could be seen as a proponent of these. In this respect, al-Hudaybi responds to the context of the radical Islamist discourse of his time and milieu and targets the concept of *hakimiyyat Allah* (God's absolute sovereignty). Yet, it must be noted that al-Hudaybi's argumentation incorporates previous contributions on the subject submitted by proponents of the Islamic resurgence.[198] This instance represents a second level of contextuality. Moreover, his approach must be set in relation to traditional scholarly and juridical interpretation. The link can be seen in the methodology al-Hudaybi applies to support his reasoning; it can be described, by and large, as approaches of *fiqh*. Further, he not only employs the established methodology of Islamic juridical interpretation, but also uses readings of classical interpreters of Islamic jurisprudence whenever it is appropriate to his purposes. Overall, his interpretation can be described as an ambivalent stance: it is a modern interpretation which struggles with the issue of human reasoning and is still embedded in a tradition of classical Islamic juridical thought which suggests the universality of *shari'a*.

The fixed and the flexible aspect of law

By no means does al-Hudaybi question the premise that God is the ultimate source of law. In accordance with the general perception of Muslim jurisprudence, he sees obedience to the *shari'a*, and thus to God, as a conceptual prerequisite for belief.[199] Indeed, he repeatedly stresses this, to the extent that the reader may consider him to be particularly unwavering in this respect. Further, he is in line with the radical Islamist perception that disregarding God's sovereignty is a characteristic of *shirk* and therefore the ultimate sign of unbelief. Hence, he also sees implementation of *shari'a*-law and, congruently, the establishment of an actual form of governance which represents God's will as a duty (*fard*). Following this, it has to be asked whether al-Hudaybi is any different in his approach from other modern interpreters of political Islam, since Islamist concepts are built on this line of thought. The essential question needs to be asked whether and – if yes – why al-Hudaybi can be considered a supporter of a moderate stance within the realm of Islamism. The difference will then mark the dividing line between his and radical stances and, hence, implicitly contain a critique of the latter.

An interesting aspect of al-Hudaybi's description of the content of *shariʿa* is the attempt to reconcile two seemingly opposing notions: freedom of reasoning and the obligation of obedience. He begins by putting an emphasis on worship of God and hence the absolute submission (*ʿibada*) to divine will and laws.[200] Duties (sing. *fard*, pl. *furud*) and prohibitions (sing. *haram*, pl. *hurum*) which are explicitly specified in the revelation define this realm of unquestionable obedience. Hence, this area comprises the sphere of *ʿibadat* (religious observances, obligations) and therefore constitutes the fixed body of the *shariʿa*.[201] Distinct from the sphere of *ʿibadat*, al-Hudaybi identifies a further category. A quotation should exemplify his stance:

> The truth is that God (praise him and let him come) left many worldly matters to us in order to regulate these in line with our reasoning. These are framed by general aims and limits, which he [i.e. God] (praise him and let him come) set out for us, and according to what we were ordered [to do] for its realisation, and under the condition that we do not allow what is forbidden and that we do not forbid what is allowed. Hence, there are actions in the shariʿa, namely duty, prohibition and permissible actions.
>
> (al-Hudaybi (1977) 73)

The legalists have, according to his view, some freedom in shaping their affairs and therefore their positive code of law. Al-Hudaybi identifies the sphere of *mubahat* (indifferent, permissible actions) as a category of the *shariʿa* which supports human decision making.[202] He writes:

> It is up to the Muslims to shape these [mubahat] with the use of reasoning, which takes the form of regulations, rules and laws.
>
> (al-Hudaybi (1977) 73)

Yet, al-Hudaybi stresses that the results of this engagement in self-governance must not contravene divinely ordained law, since God's will supersedes all human reasoning and any legal conclusion deduced solely from it. The realm of *mubahat* comprises regulations, which are not explicitly mentioned in the Qur'an as prohibitions and duties, i.e. which therefore do not fall into the sphere of *ʿibadat*. The limits of interpretative liberty lie, al-Hudaybi believes, in the qualification that secondary regulations of the *mubahat* must be in harmony with the essential field of the *ʿibadat*.[203] Therefore, divine laws are set above human decisions and interpretations. Even though obedience to divine law and free choice were, in orthodox Islamic interpretation, handled as somewhat mutually exclusive notions, it is al-Hudaybi's perception that they are not in opposition to each other. In his view, obedience and reasoning correspond, as long as the Muslim accepts that at the foundation of human rationale stands the recognition of God's will, law and supremacy.[204] The key to understanding this position is that divine will itself is the source of freedom. In summary, it can be said that he attempts to accommodate both – obedience and freedom of reason. In other words, al-Hudaybi puts forward that the *shariʿa* encompasses submission to divine command and yet divine law is concurrent with justice, freedom and human will as long as the Muslim observes obedience to God.

The area of *'ibadat* represents the fixed element of *shari'a*, whereas the *mubahat*, according to al-Hudaybi, is the field where human decision making is permissible, or is even a necessity in order to adapt law to change. Being part of human self-governance, consultation (*shura*) is permissible in the field of *mubahat*, *shura* being a concept of the internal process of finding an agreement among equal participants in a council.[205] Further, since regulations within the sphere of *mubahat* are a result of human reasoning rather than explicitly originating from revelation, they can be challenged without blaspheming. This, however, does not mean that the individual is in actuality not bound to execute these laws and regulations; however, the need for their observance is solely based on respect for a social contract, rather than on religious obligation.

With a classification of *haram* and *fard* as comprising the fundamental category of necessary religious obligations, al-Hudaybi does not present any new ideas and concepts. Indeed, he is in accord with orthodox legal interpretation and its classification.[206] Further, the distinction between *'ibadat* and *mubahat*, the first sphere signifying a fixed (*thabit*) and the second representing a flexible (*mutaghayyir*) notion of law, seems to correspond – in principle – to the classical juridical differentiation between fundamentals (sing. *asl*, pl. *'usul*) and derivation (sing. *far'*, pl. *furu'*).[207] As such, the classifications demonstrate the theoretical attempt of classical Muslim theological and juridical scholars to come to terms with two seemingly divergent concepts: to reaffirm the concept that the *shari'a* is universal (*shamila*) and yet also has the ability to adapt to changing times and circumstances, i.e. it is also flexible (*marina*). For example, the classical scholars of law Ibn Hazm (d. AD1063) and Ibn Qayyim al-Jawziyya (d. AD1350) already distinguished between *ibaha*, on the on hand, and *haram and fard*, on the other.[208]

As Kerr and Krämer point out, the classification of law into the fixed and the flexible found revival in modern times through the contributions of Muhammad 'Abduh, Rashid Rida and Mahmud Shaltut.[209] The latter was a contemporary of al-Hudaybi and Rector of al-Azhar from 1958 to 1963. These modern reformers of Islamic law argued that, next to the obligatory *'ibadat*, a certain flexibility of law is guaranteed in the area of regulation of social life (*mu'amalat*). Following, to an extent, the Hanafi school of law, 'Abduh and Rida saw ritual duties, religious struggle (*jihad*), laws of taxation and penal law as part of the *'ibadat*, whereas law of personal status, inheritance and private financial law fall into the realm of *mu'amalat*.[210] Shaltut went even further and limited the *'ibadat*, in his interpretation of law, to ritual duties.[211] Consequently, his interpretation left vast areas to be determined through human reasoning. Similarly to these reformers, al-Hudaybi argues that humans can make decisions upon many matters. As mentioned above, the term he puts forward to describe the area of (limited) free will is *mubahat* (indifferent, permissible actions). Although *mubahat* is used as another technical idiom, it is interesting to note that al-Hudaybi includes herein regulations pertaining to social conduct (*mu'amalat*). One even gets the impression that he sometimes employs the terms *mu'amalat* and *mubahat* synonymously.[212] But are these indeed interchangeable terms? Since his predecessors 'Abduh and Rida and his contemporary Shaltut had already described the area of *'ibadat* and *mu'amalat*, an answer to the above question could be that al-Hudaybi demarcates these spheres in a manner not dissimilar to his contemporaries. Hence, a comparison between their interpretations of *'ibadat* and *mu'amalat* may then give a clue as to how far-reaching al-Hudaybi proposes the realm of free decision making to be, as against normative obedience.

Before embarking on a comparison between the various definitions of *'ibadat* and *mu'amalat*, it must be recognised that some laws which traditionally fall into the realm of *mu'amalat* are in fact fixed by statements in the Qur'an.[213] In particular, there are some regulations concerning family law and inheritance law. Hence, a clear distinction between *'ibadat* and *mu'amalat*, in terms of one standing for the fixed and the other representing the flexible, is only a theoretical ideal which is, in actuality, not adhered to. Whereas 'Abduh does not explicitly recognise this problem regarding the moment of overlap of both categories, Rida and Shaltut try to resolve this obvious discrepancy by making the issue of moral significance the decisive criterion for possible changes of laws within the realm *mu'amalat*.[214] Al-Hudaybi, like 'Abduh, does not consider the issue of possible intersections. In fact, al-Hudaybi's insistence that the text is the source of final authority suggests that his idea of *mubahat* does not in fact correspond with 'Abduh's, Rida's or Shaltut's characterisation of *mu'amalat*. Further proof of this point is al-Hudaybi's description of the practical application of the category of the *mubahat*. He explicitly mentions within this realm matters of traffic control, public health, agriculture and irrigation.[215] This seems to suggest a very restricted sphere for human decision making. Hence, it shows that 'Abduh's, Rida's and Shaltut's descriptions of *mu'amalat* are, regarding their content, much more controversial and disputed, yet their accounts are bolder in supporting the idea of human reasoning and self-governance than is al-Hudaybi's category of *mubahat*.

Indeed, al-Hudaybi struggles in his work *Du'at la Qudat* to describe a distinction between obedience, on the one hand, and freedom of will and human reasoning, on the other. This raises considerable issues of critique. First, al-Hudaybi uses the term *shari'a* in a confusing and sometimes conflicting manner. On the one hand, he refers to law in general, almost giving the impression that there is a body of Islamic positive *shari'a*-law. This attitude to *shari'a* as a unified system is seemingly influenced by a long tradition of classical interpretations of *fiqh*, the works and compendia of the schools of law, which saw their legal analysis as the epitome of Islamic law. The common usage of the word in terms which originate in this stagnant outlook on law certainly had an impact on al-Hudaybi. Yet, on the other hand, he restricts *shari'a* to a number of rules which find particular mention in the Qur'an, i.e. those describing *aharam* (prohibitions) and *furud* (obligations). Thus, he confines the term to the category of *'ibadat*. Even more confusing is al-Hudaybi's usage of the term when taking into account his comment that *shari'a* is not only composed of *'ibadat*, but also includes regulations which are derived through human reasoning (i.e. the laws he proposes within the realm of *mubahat*). However, he explicitly points out that regulations within the *mubahat* are not to be regarded as divinely ordained. To conclude, his handling of the term *shari'a* shows major inconsistencies, even to the point of contradiction.

Apart from the confusion regarding the use of the term *shari'a*, some critique regarding his description of *'ibadat* and *mubahat* must be made. His work shows both a progressive and a conservative attitude regarding these. Speaking merely on a theoretical level, which avoids issues of practical application, al-Hudaybi's definitions of *'ibadat* and *mubahat* are kept rather vague. In other words, the reader may still be puzzled as to the question of the extent to which both – obedience and free will – are to be imputed. Subsequently, this leaves open the issue of positive law, which is derived from the categories of *'ibadat* and *mubahat*. Al-Hudaybi's hesitancy does not help to answer central issues of Islamic theory of law: first, how can the fixed and the flexible within Islamic law be ultimately defined? Who has the legitimacy to do so? Al-Hudaybi does not touch this subject at all, but rather gives the impression that *'ibadat* comprises an already well-defined entity.[216] Second, even though one may consider the realm of *'ibadat* to be defined through the text of revelation, the conversion from sacred text into positive law (i.e. its translation into paragraphs and sections and application of sanctions for transgression etc.) requires the involvement of human reason. Hence, the realm of *'ibadat* in the sense of immutable divine law is in fact merely an ideal. Al-Hudaybi, though, gives this issue no consideration. Third, even if one subscribes to the concept of limited decision making within the framework of Islamic law, i.e. within the sphere of *mubahat*, it remains unresolved as to how far this concept is to be practically applied. The impulse to engage in decision making, however, continues to be only hypothetical, because the realm of the *'ibadat* remains ill defined. Al-Hudaybi is considerably hesitant to give any definite clues and leaves it almost up to the reader to establish his/her definition. Hence, one could still read into his text that he sees the sphere of *'ibadat* as encompassing the body of all laws regulating human life, particularly if one follows his recurring remarks regarding the all-encompassing nature of *shari'a* and examples of regulations which fall under the realm of human decision making.

Obviously, the hesitant nature of al-Hudaybi's account of *'ibadat* and *mubahat* raises serious questions regarding the actual significance of his initially quoted position, that many matters are open to human decision making. In his defence, it has to be pointed out that it is not the aim of *Du'at la Qudat* to present a meticulous and original work of Islamic *fiqh*. Its objective lies, and this needs to be mentioned again, in the refutation of radical trends within the Muslim Brotherhood. Considering his interpretation in this context, his position on the right to make decisions is, indeed, a rejection of rigid applications of the concept of *hakimiyyat Allah*.

3.5 The theology of an Islamic government

The most crucial issue for Islamist movements is the call for the establishment of an Islamic state; this issue is the defining point of their activity. According to proponents of political Islam, it is the presence of Islamic governance that guarantees the application of *shari'a*.[217] While calling for the implementation of what most

Islamists consider to be a divine body of law, they envisage the construction of an order which reflects God's will, and hence establishes justice, peace, freedom, equality and security. It is, moreover, inferred that the execution of divine law is regarded as a duty. Consequently, Islamists consider the demand for an Islamic state system and the application of *shari'a* a necessity.[218] '*La hukm illa bi-llah*' (no law except that from God), a line from the Qur'an, seems to confirm this perception. In the view of Islamists, divine law supersedes the state. This means that *shari'a*, which for most Islamists constitutes God's law, not only forms the foundation of a (yet to be established) state system but is, moreover, unconditionally and universally valid. For this reason it is applicable to Muslims, independent of its implementation via a form of governance. For most Islamists, this superiority of Islamic law, and at the same time its interconnectedness with the issue of state, is evidence for the soundness of the proposed 'divine order'.[219] It is this logic of the ideal that is the driving force for their demands.

Yet, as was shown above, the issue of the content of *shari'a* is ardently discussed. Generalising the underlying contentions of the dispute, there are oppositng answers to the question of whether to view Islamic law – in its essence as well as in its particulars – as a defined, fixed body or whether it constitutes a flexible and (in time) changing organism. This also leaves its imprint on the quest for an Islamic state and on evaluations as to whether existing state systems are in congruence with Islamic law. Further, since divine will, and subsequently Islamic law, precede the issue of state, the theoretical and practical problematic of constructing a structure of inter-human organisation, to be unanimously regarded as reflecting God's order, becomes apparent. Even more so, since there are diverging positions regarding the issue of whether a state needs to be built first, in order to deliberate on factual and practical matters of *shari'a*, or whether details of Islamic law ought to be explored and defined before a state can be formed on its basis. The latter issue also indicates conflicting positions regarding the strategies of Islamist movements in their attempts to describe *shari'a* and in their struggle to implement their interpretations; it further reveals disagreement among Islamists regarding the acceptance or rejection of existing state order. Also, dependent on the approaches to *shari'a*, and particularly the issue of permanence and/or flexibility of law, are the various propositions on the formal aspects of an Islamic state; an example thereof is the question of whether Islamic governance is compatible with, or even identical to, democracy, or whether it should be led by a single authority and therefore epitomises an autocratic state system. In other words, even though there is agreement on the essential point that the establishment of an Islamic system of governance is a requirement, opinions regarding the administrative form and the means of reaching the objective vary irreconcilably.

In the writings of modern contributors within the Islamic world, the issue of Islam and state has received special attention.[220] This is especially evident among proponents of the so-called 'Islamic revivalism' or 'neo-Salafiyya', who engage anew with the text of the revelation in order to find a fresh and yet original understanding which is congruent with the challenges of modern times. Nevertheless, the many contributors present essentially differing approaches. Further, although particular organisations such as the Muslim Brotherhood may appear as cohesive Islamist movements, differences of opinion on these very matters are perceptible within the groups. Indeed, a number of Muslim Brothers did write on Islamic law and state, presenting at times rather differing attitudes.[221] Generally speaking, the unifying bond that holds the Brotherhood together as a religious–political movement is the agreement on the need for an Islamic state and for the introduction of divine law, since these are seen to institute the representation of divine will in society. Yet the actual nature of a state (caliphate, parliamentary system or state led by legal experts) and, subsequently, the make-up of a corpus of law are central points of dispute among the various factions of the *ikhwan*. The viewpoints also delineate dissimilar positions regarding related issues, such as strategies of action to implement a suggested Islamic government, or means of opposition to current state systems.[222] These express simultaneously divergent attitudes to an existing order. Sayyid Qutb and al-Hudaybi are two representatives of the Brotherhood, and they exemplify dissimilar positions.

This section addresses the dispute within the Muslim Brotherhood regarding the issue of state. Since the premise of most Muslim and Islamist contributors of the past and present is that the existence of Islamic governance is a necessity, the theology of the state and its problematic is the starting-point of this investigation. The issue leads us to investigate the institution of the caliph, as he historically personified the succession of the prophet and was seen as the guarantor and protector of the *shari'a*. With this background information, we enter into discussion on al-Hudaybi's view of an Islamic state. It must be noted that his approach is largely shaped by a classical interpretation of the issue of state and governance. Yet, modern influences can also be found. Although this leads to certain discrepancies and contradictions in his explanations, we will see that he focuses not so much on suggesting an original interpretation on the issue of state, but rather uses well-established juridical opinions to refute the radical attitude of other Muslim Brothers. It is this negative response which provides proof of the discontent even within a seemingly unified Islamist organisation.

Theology of the state

Seeing God as the defining focus of belief, there is a general agreement among Muslims that the Qur'an, as his revealed word, contains his ultimate will regarding a just order. According to the classical theory of the state, it is the objective and therefore the characteristic of an Islamic state to accomplish the implementation of essential principles, which are to be deduced from the primary sources.[223] These principles coincide with the so-called *maqasid al-shari'a* (lit. intentions, spirit of law).[224] Interpretations on state and government are inspired by this premise. Yet the basic question follows, on how to formalise the relationship of God, on the one hand, and politics, society and the individual, on the other, in such a way that the premise of divine supremacy is respected, and the actual and temporal authority of humans, who run the state, is made possible. Indeed, it is this motivation that has led Islamic legists to engage in theological and functional aspects of the state.

Basic features and key verses

In terms of theology, classical as well as modern writers agree that it is the paramount religious tenet at the foundation of Islamic governance which makes this system of rule distinct from other, secular, state systems.[225] Since monotheism is one of the major themes of the primary sources of the Qur'an and Sunna, it congruently points to the first premise of the Islamic theology of state, which argues that God is the holder of utmost power.[226] This characteristic is expressed in the imperative of *tawhid* (unity), which explicates God's oneness, universality, omnipotence and omniscience.[227] Thus, Qur'an 5: 44 is often referred to as evidence of God's active command through the presence of the revelation: *"wa man lam yahkumu bi-ma anzala Allahu fa-'ula'ika hummu 'l-kafiruna"* (whoever does not pass judgement according to what God has revealed, those are indeed the unbelievers).[228] Yet, only a limited number of Qur'anic verses deals with juridical issues; these are therefore specifically known as *ayat al-ahkam* (juridical verses). Of these, even fewer refer to the discussion surrounding issues of state. Further, these specific verses do not elaborate on the questions regarding the organisational form of an Islamic state order. Hence, it is fair to say that verses of the Qur'an which could be employed to construe a positive state order are scarce and undefined. This leads to the dilemma that, apart from the essential notion that God is the bearer of utmost authority, basic constituents and issues need to be shaped by humans.

The question of who is eligible to supervise the implementation of the order is largely unresolved through the text of the Qur'an and has, therefore, been differently answered in the history of Islamic interpretation.[229] A key passage in the discussion should serve as an example. Qur'an 4: 59 states *"Ya ayyuha 'lladhina amanu atiyy'u 'llaha wa atiyy'u 'l-rasula wa uli 'l-amri minkum"* (O you who believe! Obey Allah and obey the Messenger, and those of you who are in authority). This passage was indeed at the centre of discussion regarding the issue of delegation of authority (*wilaya*), which was in legal terms closely related to personal law of guardianship. Yet, it still leaves the issue open as to who is meant by the term *uli 'l-amr* (those in authority).[230] Historically, the passage was used to evidence the command of the caliph.[231] While maintaining this interpretation, later classical works extended the understanding of the term to rulers within the Islamic realm who held actual power.[232] In this respect, contributors such as al-Mawardi, but also al-Ghazali, adjusted their reading to the reality of the gradually declining institution of the caliphate, and thus remained true to its conceptual construct despite the fact of its disappearing political power. Hence, they broadened the meaning of an essentially religious terminology and conclusively included 'secular' leadership, such as the authority of the sultan (*sultan*; regional ruler). This extended understanding survived, to an extent, the abolition of the caliphate in 1924. Thus, this created a variance of opinions regarding the legitimacy of regimes and the power of autocrats, such as the rule of 'Abd al-Nasir. Yet it is interesting to note that the same verse, Qur'an 4: 59, is brought into play by some modern liberal Islamists who argue in favour of democratic power sharing and against the rule of a single authority.[233] Khalafallah, for example, particularly calls attention to the grammatical plural of *uli 'l-amr* (those in authority) and to the reflexivity of *minkum* (among them), deriving from this reading of the text his demand for a democratic system of power sharing. Next to the classical, hierarchical and the modern, rather egalitarian interpretation stands a third way of understanding verse 4: 59, which was employed throughout Islamic history. Theologians (*'ulama '*) and legists (*fuqaha '*) have used the term *uli 'l-amr* to confirm their own position as those empowered through knowledge.[234]

Summarising these examples, it becomes clear, therefore, that the meaning of particular Qur'anic terms and passages which are central to the discussion about the form of an Islamic political order is still disputed. Hence, it gives indication of the fluidity of understanding of relevant passages of the Qur'an which may result in conflicting interpretations of subjects, such as the formal aspects of an Islamic state and governance.

Since there are only sparse and rather vague statements on the actual structure of an Islamic state, but many references on *tawhid*, formal and practical matters of an administrative and organisational structure merely form a subsidiary aspect of theological investigation.[235] Moreover, the organisation of a state system is indeed somewhat akin to a social contract between humans which has to achieve one end, i.e. respect of God's supremacy. Or, in other words, at the core of reasoning on state affairs is the quest to bring the religious principle of subordination to God's law into accord with the necessity of governance on a human level. For this reason, attempts to formulate and formalise an Islamic state system have to face the constant possibility of theological critique; since the relationship between God and humans is the focus, any suggestion on a positive, formal state order runs the danger of being dismissed on the grounds that legislative and executive power is given to human institutions, which subsequently would entail restriction of God's supremacy. This, then, explains the unbroken dispute over the form of governance, not only between proponents of secularism, but even more so between advocates of Islamist ideas.

A modern theological approach

As we have already seen, the vast majority of Muslim contributors writing on the subject of Islam, governance and state touch organisational aspects merely in relation to theological issues. Al-Hudaybi is, indeed, no exception. His arguments are, to a large extent, limited to outlining the purpose of institutions of governance and, further, to giving justification to the necessity of building an Islamic state.[236] Hence, even though he refers to state institutions, such as the caliphate (*khalifa*) or Imamate (*imama*),[237] council (*shura*) and judges (*quda '*) as constituting components of a just Islamic system, al-Hudaybi does not go into particulars about formal issues. For example, he elaborates on the requirement of the caliphate and gives details regarding prerequisites of the post, but neglects to explain issues concerning procedures for their installation in office. And although he points out that *shura* (council) needs to be practised as an essential part of the elective process, he does not specify the nature of the body.[238] Hence, he leaves important (and controversial) questions, such as whether members of the council are chosen according to their political or their religious status, or whether they should be appointed through general, free and confidential elections, unanswered. Additionally, matters regarding the interplay of institutions are not explicitly addressed; for instance, he avoids giving a definitive answer on whether *shura* is merely to be seen as an equivalent to a consultative council to one side of the caliph's central authority, or whether it is akin to a parliamentary forum with powers to pass positive law. Consequently, al-Hudaybi's interpretation only abstractly describes issues of the internal executive structure and administrative organisation of a state system.

Leaving aside the fact that it is not his intention to write a treatise on formal matters of an Islamic state, the lack of defining interpretations on these formal questions is a cause of puzzlement and inconsistencies. This becomes particularly evident when the general reader of *Du'at la Qudat* hopes for an evaluation of the extent of institutional powers, such as the authority of the ruler. Thus, even though the issue of the purpose and function of the caliphate is extensively dealt with from a theological point of view, the text does not attempt to define specific constitutional rights and their limitations.

Bearing these problematic remarks in mind, al-Hudaybi's dealing with the issue of Islamic governance echoes traditional positions and simultaneously reflects modern disputes over the Qur'anic text, its interpretation, the theology of state and its laws. It is this combination of a modern moderate, yet modern conservative, interpretation that makes his deliberations unique. Indeed, he tries to stress the continuing relevance of the classics to the renewed discussion on key issues. It is thus not surprising that he takes the arguments of classical juridical interpreters such as Abu al-Hasan al-Mawardi (AD 974–1058a), Abu Hamid al-Ghazali (AD 1058/9–1111) and 'Abd al-Rahman Muhammad Ibn Khaldun (AD 1332–1406) into account.[239] Along with these, modern positions on nationhood and state are endorsed. In his explanations on the issue of state, al-Hudaybi frequently quotes his contemporary, the Egyptian legal scholar Muhammad Diya' al-Din al-Rayyis.[240] Other modern interpreters find their way into his elucidations on Islamic governance, even though he singles out the latter through explicit reference. Since the caliphate is a major component in al-Hudaybi's exposition on Islamic governance, the issue of its decline and final dissolution has left impressions in the *Murshid*'s writing. Thus, the concept of the revival of the caliphate is fundamental in al-Hudaybi's writing as much as in his engagement with the Muslim Brotherhood. His reformist approach connects him to proponents of Islamic resurgence, a movement that was (and is) particularly strong in Egypt. For example, contemporaries such as 'Abduh, Rida and Shaltut left their mark on his discussion of *shari'a*.[241] Without doubt, their opinions on this subject are directly linked to the question of state organisation. Further, we can assume that Islamist positions in discussions on the re-establishment of this institution, which were particularly ardent in monarchist Egypt, provided a benchmark for al-Hudaybi's position. Important reformist thinkers such as Rida, 'Abd al-Raziq and Khallafallah wrote on the subject. Although these works on the caliphate are not directly linked with al-Hudaybi's, it needs to be noted that *Du'at la Qudat* refers to a wider context of roaming ideas. However, more particular is the influence of the Brotherhood's post-Revolutionary experience. This is the context of al-Hudaybi's leadership, during which the Muslim Brotherhood's immense influence gradually clashed with 'Abd al-Nasir's growing position in the RCC. His collected public statements of the pre-1954 episode provide evidence of al-Hudaybi's continuous propagation of an Islamic state and of his resentment regarding the idea of secular law and rule.[242] Moreover, the immediate context of the years of persecution, which coincide with 'Abd al-Nasir's autocratic rule, gave al-Hudaybi the incentive to dedicate parts of his *Du'at la Qudat* to the issue of governance. Most important in this context is the dispute within the Brotherhood on how to react to the state system. The internal quarrel was stirred by the experience of persecution, which undoubtedly was the main cause for reservations put forward by many Brothers regarding the legitimacy of the state system.[243] Under the circumstances of persecution and internal dissent, al-Hudaybi responded to radical arguments. Particularly in the prison environment, rather uncompromising proposals became part of a debate on theologies and means of Islamist resistance. During the dispute the *Murshid* maintained a rather moderate stance. Nevertheless al-Hudaybi's theology of state and his support for the caliphate can equally be read as opposing 'Abd al-Nasir's secular rule.

Although the network of influences is not explicitly referred to in *Du'at la Qudat*, it is indeed at the core of his contribution on the issue of state and society. Overall, the quality of al-Hudaybi's interpretation on the issue does not lie in suggesting original ideas regarding the establishment of an Islamic state system, and even less in proposals for formal aspects of state organisation, but rather it retains its importance in countering radical ideas while combining traditional and modern stances, which equally challenge the legitimacy of 'Abd al-Nasir's rule.

The rule of the 'imam al-haqq'

It is wrong to assume that the dispute surrounding a divinely guided state system is a phenomenon of modern Islamic interpretation. The issue of governance is undeniably a focal aspect in Muslim juridical and political reasoning throughout history. Even though the major intent of most writings is to investigate issues of congruency with divine law, and hence engages in outlining the purpose rather than the formalities of an Islamic state system, it needs to be admitted that interpretations by various contributors contain indications about formal features of a supposed state organisation. For example, classical interpretations on the subject of an Islamic order validate the central religious–political governance of the caliph without questioning the institution itself.[244] Modern liberal interpretations, however, strive to prove that a democratic order is the appropriate form of governance of state affairs, so long as the religious paradigm of God as the absolute power is acknowledged.[245] Al-Hudaybi's interpretation lies, as we shall see, in between these lines of thought.

Classical theory of the caliphate

As indicated above, the Qur'an does not particularly elaborate on the organisation of an Islamic state. However, the caliphate was, historically, the leading institution and even the epitome of Islamic governance. Statements of the Qur'an such as verses 2: 30 and 38: 26 were read accordingly.[246] Even though the term *khalifa* is mentioned in these particular passages, Watt rightly remarks that "it is curious that this office, though one of the distinctive marks of Islam, has no basis in Islamic ideation".[247] Hence, the caliphate presented in fact a socially agreed entity, resultant of customs and of the political organisation of early Islam, and one which was given religious justification by Islamic juridical interpreters in retrospect and in acknowledgement of the given reality.[248]

This retrospective interpretation looked on the events of the early Islamic community, particularly the rule of Muhammad and the leadership of his orthodox successors – Abu Bakr, 'Umar, 'Uthman and 'Ali – as a past ideal and a future example for the purpose of the state and the function of leadership.[249] However, this period of time, which is central to explanations of the caliph's legitimacy, was not at all a peaceful time of consent. Indeed, similar and, in fact, related to the discourse on the content of belief, ideas of Islamic governance go back to the constituting period of Islamic history.[250] After Muhammad's death, and with the quest of his succession, Abu Bakr was chosen as the first caliph.[251] Yet the continuance of authority was not undisputed, as the so-called *ridda* wars which raged during his reign as caliph show.[252] Still, Abu Bakr managed to implement his authority and thus continued a religious–political leadership. The title *khalifat rasul Allah*, which was subsequently carried by the orthodox caliphs – Abu Bakr (r. AD 632–34), 'Umar (r. AD 634–44), 'Uthman (r. AD 644–56) and 'Ali (r. AD 656–61) – signifies the idea of guardianship as much as the theological limitation of the institution, which after all specifies that the post of the caliph is built on the succession of the prophet rather than as an immediate representation of God.[253] Further, it can be argued that *shura* (council), which has a special place in the elective process of Abu Bakr and 'Umar and (although arguably) in Islamic ideation, points to the 'profane' source of caliphal legitimacy. Nonetheless, the orthodox caliphate established itself as a hierarchical order which accumulated the power of leadership in one person. However, the root of power for their rule was to become the focal issue of difference in the discussion about legitimacy. The issue erupted with the events of the battle of Siffin, when 'Ali faced his challenger Mu'awiyya.[254] Rather than letting the fate of the sword decide, 'Ali sought arbitration. However, some of his followers withdrew their support, arguing that leadership and legitimacy are divinely given and cannot be an element of negotiation. This group, which then came to be known as Khawarij (secessionists), caused the first split. Indeed this group was the first movement to raise theological questions as to the origin of power and authority. They saw their position of divinely appointed legitimacy and authority evidenced through their understanding of "*la hukm illa li-llah*" (no judgement except for God).[255] In the following history, 'mainstream' denominations, i.e. Sunni Islam and Shi'a, developed in response to 'sectarian' movements such as the Khawarij, but also in opposition to each other.[256] In fact, the issue of legitimacy represents the self-defining moment of the movements and their particular theologies. Hence, the gradually evolving theologies of these denominations, movements and sects had not only a religious, but moreover a political purpose. This demonstrates that the issue of the source of legitimacy was already disputed during the period of the orthodox caliph's governance, which in Sunni Islam serves as a prime example of an ideal. Yet this does not entail that autocratic leadership was in doubt. The Khawarij, as well as Shi'a and Sunni Islam, continued to argue that authority must be accumulated in the hands of a caliph, although they developed different concepts on the source of his legitimacy, and hence on prerequisites for the post.[257] Within the realm of evolving Sunni Islam, the concept that the caliph has to be of Quraysh descent became integrated into the theology of the state and was adopted as one of the pre-requisites of the office. As a further development of this aspect of legitimacy, the 'Umayyads, who prided themselves on their 'aristocratic' line of Quraysh descent, implemented a dynastic rule. Effectively, the vaguely defined assembly of a council (*shura*) was reduced to an oath-giving body having no actual influence on the election of the caliph.[258] Adapting and continuing the hierarchical form of governance, the 'Umayyads broadened the source of their legitimacy by deriving their authority directly from God. Hence, they took on the title *khalifat Allah* (God's Caliph).[259] Even though the rule of the 'Ummayads was eventually replaced by the 'Abbassids in the year 133/750, the foundations were laid for a gradually developing concept of state in Sunni Islam which delineated the caliphate not only as a hierarchical but also as a de facto dynastic form of government.[260]

The focus of the many classical Sunni works on Islamic governance, such as those of al-Baqillani, al-Baghdadi, al-Mawardi, al-Ghazali and Ibn Taymiyya – to name just a few important names – was to provide theological explications regarding religiously sanctioned state organisation.[261] Not doubting the institution of the caliphate, interpreters of classical *fiqh* aimed to provide a reading which was true to the premises of God's divinity and, simultaneously, facilitated the legitimacy of single leadership. Since, as we have seen, the Qur'an and Sunna provide only few concrete disclosures, and since the history of the orthodox caliphs was not at all peaceful, classical contributions constructed an imagined model which rested not only on their reading of the primary sources but even more on a blend of what they considered to be the outstanding example set by the orthodox caliphs, as well as by Arab customs and, additionally, Greek and Persian notions of perfect leadership.[262] In other words, classical writers gradually created an ideal conception of the state, which was epitomised in the leadership of the caliph or rightful imam (*imam al-haqq*). But it would be too presumptuous to argue that a consistent conception of state organisation developed with the passage of time. Rather, it was changing circumstances which necessitated continuously new engagements with the issue of state at different marking-points in the history of the caliphate.

It is with this background that, for example, the thesis of the requirement of a strong, central leadership must be read. Facing the decline of the institution of the caliphate, an eminent supporter of this argument was the eleventh-century theologian ʿAli Ibn Muhammad al-Mawardi.[263] His work *al-Ahkam al-Sultaniyya wa al-Walayat al-Diniyya* is a deduction of laws that pertain to Islamic government, giving a systematic description of the requirements and responsibilities of its major institutions.[264] Since the actual power of mediaeval caliphs gradually deteriorated, its de facto authority being steadily substituted by the control of 'secular' (regional and military) leaders, the legitimacy of the institution and of those in concrete command had to be consistently redefined. An example of this adjustment of theory to the actual distribution of power is al-Ghazali's contribution to the subject, particularly as put forward in his *Iqtisad al-Iʿtiqad*, where he argues that the leadership of the *sultan* (regional military leader) must be accepted purely out of necessity.[265] Recognising the actual state of power distribution, he not only gives theological ground to tyrants but also wards off questions regarding the ultimate purpose of an institution in decline.[266] Another important example of the relationship between the historical situation of the caliphate's incapacity and the engagement with the subject of state is Ibn Khaldun, who proposed that the nature (*fitra*) of human beings requires the leadership and guidance of an *imam*.[267] In his most influential writing, entitled *al-Muqaddima* (Introduction), which actually constitutes a preliminary part to his major work on Islamic history, he outlines his perception of society.[268] He states that religion cannot be pursued without safety and security – safety and security cannot be implemented without power (*sultan*).[269]

The accommodation with political realities is the major feature when comparing classical works on the issue of state. However, modern Islamist contributors on this issue largely ignore this contextuality, and hence the interpretative side of their works. In fact, parts of Ibn Khaldun's, as well as of al-Mawardi's, writing are widely quoted and referred to as if they were objective evidence rather than interpretative opinions. Thus, two points need to be clearly stated regarding concept and reality. First, even though the Caliph was generally seen as the head of the community (*umma*) within Sunni Islam, the de facto executive power did not at all times, and not in all regions, lie within the hands of those holding the office. Reality was, as Islamic history exemplifies, quite different from classical theories of state. Second, even though the model suggests at first sight the centrality of a politico-religious leadership, the caliphs could not, according to the theology of state, claim absolute authority, since this would have been in contradiction of the religious premise of the absolute supremacy of God. Obviously, classical theology of state largely describes a constructed model. The discrepancy between the conceptual ideal and historical reality leaves some puzzlement as to how to approach modern Islamist interpretations. This problematic is even more pertinent, because many modern works refer to classical opinions regarding Islamic governance in order to make statements about its continuous applicability.

A number of aspects need to be commented on, which – as we progress to al-Hudaybi's modern interpretation – allows us to further explore differences and commonalties between classical and modern interpretations. It also may give us hints regarding the distinction between radical and moderate positions. First, as already pointed out, the caliphate was an existing institutional reality, although its power changed in the course of time. Classical theology of the state was therefore less concerned with the issue of how to construct an Islamic state system but, rather, affected by the question of how to accommodate its theological ideal into existing realities. Classical works of al-Mawardi, al-Ghazali, Ibn Taymiyya and Ibn Khaldun show, when compared to each other, adaptations to the gradually declining central caliphal authority, while contra-caliphates were established and the power of regional political and military rulers rose, which governed more or less independently, although they nominally gave the oath of allegiance and obedience to the caliph.[270]

Modern writers, such as al-Hudaybi, had to face a different reality. Hence, modern interpretations on the state were concerned with the critique of existing secular state systems and ultimately proposed the (re)construction of what they considered Islamic governance. This call for the establishment of just, divine governance poses questions, which classical interpretation had to meet only to a minor extent. Since, in classical writings, the caliphate and conclusively Islamic governance was an established preliminary, the premise that *shari'a* supersedes the state was merely a theological abstract. Even though classical writings emphasise that divine law is superior to the state, the argument served merely to stress the religious limits of the caliphal institution in relation to God's absoluteness. Because, in classical Islamic history, the state (at least nominally) guaranteed the execution of *shari'a*, the concept of its application outside Islamic governance was not discussed as an actual possibility. In modern interpretations, though, the emphasis that *shari'a* comes before the state did indeed gain different significance.

With the abolition of the caliphate, Islamic interpretation on law had to come to terms with the fact that the execution of *shari'a* does not necessarily coincide with the implementation of law through the state. New prominence is given to the concept that *shari'a* is to be carried out on a personal level, as part of Muslims' belief. Effectively, much greater emphasis is given to the idea that *shari'a* essentially outlines a relationship between God and humans. Whereas some modern Muslim interpreters adopted this move away from institutionalised execution of Islamic law and presented this trend as 'secular Islam', Islamists refused to adopt concepts, which suggested a separation of religious law from its execution through the state. They not only showed a disapproving stance toward secular trend, but also used classical notions, such as the divine obligation of the presence of Islamic governance, to refute this concept.

In doing so, modern Islamist contributors presume to find orientation in the example of a past ideal, i.e. the time of the orthodox caliphs. Yet Lambton rightly points out that the development of the doctrine of the caliphate or imamate was "a gradual process which extended over the first four and a half centuries and took into account developments not present in the early days of the caliphate".[271] Taking their observations further, it can be argued that the premise of the obligatory presence of Islamic governance and caliphate was part of this gradual development of the classical theories. In the light of the construction of classical theories, it would indeed seem to make questionable the Islamist claims of the *divine obligation* to establish Islamic state organisation. This is even more evident when considering that classical interpretations do not make a clear distinction between the requirement of the state and the issue of the necessity of its establishment. In fact, because Islamic governance was reality, there was no need to deliberate on the contingency of constructing an Islamic state. Even though the statements of classical works are often uncritically referred to as authoritative proclamations, their conceptualisations regarding the requirement to establish an Islamic state are part of a modern phenomenon.

In summary, classical and modern writings on the state differ in essential points because the contextual circumstances of their deliberations are dissimilar. In other words, the statements of the classics may have a new and slightly different reading and meaning in modern context. This needs to be borne in mind when analysing modern contributions such as that of al-Hudaybi, who indeed uses extensively classical arguments to prove his point.

Supporting the caliphate

Al-Hudaybi's exposition on Islamic governance (*al-hukuma al-Islamiyya*) leads him to raise his voice in support of the re-establishment of the caliphate. In fact, he sees the institution of the caliphate (*al-khilafa*) as corresponding to the Islamic state system.[272] Synonymously to the word *khilafa*, and actually more frequently, he uses the term *al-imama* (imamate). Further, he draws an immediate line between the institution and the person holding the office. Thus, Islamic governance is, in his view, personified in the office of the rightful imam (*imam al-haqq*), whom he occasionally also identifies as the caliph (*al-khalifa*) or the bearer of command (*wali al-amr*).[273]

This line of argument is reminiscent of classical writers.[274] Like these, al-Hudaybi tends to ignore a distinction between institution and office, as well as between the terms 'caliph' and '*imam*'. Bearing in mind that a considerable number of recent Muslim and Islamist contributors detach themselves from the theory that an Islamic state needs to be constructed on the basis of autocratic or hierarchical structured leadership, al-Hudaybi's position is indeed comparatively orthodox.[275] This observation is further supported by the fact that he does not even consider the possibility of an Islamic state without the leadership of the *imam al-haqq*. In fact, al-Hudaybi's interpretation shows that, for him, an Islamic state system without the imam as its ruler is unthinkable. Although he acknowledges that the *shari'a* precedes the state and indeed is universally valid, i.e. independently of whether Islamic governance exists or not, he does not subscribe to the idea that a state system which adopts and adjusts Islamic laws as part of its legal code can be considered Islamic. For him, an Islamic state system coincides with the application of the *shari'a* as its fundamental law and with the governance of the *imam al-haqq*. The orthodoxy of this approach becomes particularly pointed when one considers the contribution of other modern Islamic interpreters who stress that the Egyptian legal and governmental system is essentially congruent with Islamic principles.[276] Further, there are other modern interpretations, which regard the compliance to the *shari'a* as merely as a private matter. Proponents of this view stress that the Islamic law gains recognition through the practice of Muslims in their daily lives rather than through state-imposed ordinances.[277] Although the various Islamic interpreters of modern times admittedly show grades of resemblance to aspects of orthodox interpretation, al-Hudaybi's position, which assumes an immediate equivalence between Islamic state, Islamic governance and the rule of an Islamic leader, in comparison stands out because of its conservativeness.

Purpose, function and nature of the 'imam al-haqq'

The impact of classical contributions, particularly those of al-Mawardi and Ibn Khaldun, becomes evident in al-Hudaybi's description of the purpose, function and nature of the state. Indeed, al-Hudaybi quotes both classics.[278] Additionally, he cites the modern Egyptian jurist Diya' al-Din al-Rayyis. References from the latter's work *al-Nazariyya lil-Siyasa al-Islamiyya* are particularly used to comment and further expound on classical interpretation.[279] However, because of extensive quoting, the reader loses the distinction between classical interpretation, Rayyis's commentary, and which parts in fact form al-Hudaybi's interpretation. While using classical authority and contemporary expertise, al-Hudaybi manages to give the impression that there is a consensual description on the objective of Islamic governance and uniformity on the purpose and function of the *imam*.

Accordingly, it is supposed that Islamic government, which is personified in the caliph as its head, has the function of succeeding the prophet and of providing protection of religion and the law as well as of its lands and people.[280] These functions define, then, the distinctiveness of Islamic rule.

Drawing on Ibn Khaldun's differentiation between three forms of rule (*hukm*) – natural, political and Islamic – al-Hudaybi expresses the superiority of Islamic governance.[281] He emphasises that, in comparison to natural and political rule, which are based on greed, personal interest or reason, Islamic rule rests on God's will as embodied in the *shari'a*. It is this description of the excellence of Islamic rule which leads him to speak out against secular influences and profane definitions of divine law and order. Al-Hudaybi initiates his critique with an assessment of the classical writer al-Mawardi, arguing that the latter's *Ahkam al-Sultaniyya* puts too much emphasis on the worldly postulate of the caliph's office. Therefore al-Mawardi fails to put the accent on the religious nature of the caliphate. This contention seems to be rather far fetched. However, al-Hudaybi in fact uses this point of argument against the classical writer to then target conventional modern interpretations, which see the *shari'a* as an Islamic equivalent to secular constitutional law (*dustur*).[282] While pointing out the divinity of the *shari'a* and thereby stressing that it supersedes all human-made law and institutions, the *Murshid* rejects any kind of definition which equates or compares Islamic governance to secular order. Hence, he argues that statements are essentially void which delineate the Islamic political order as "governance, in which the Islamic *shari'a* is its law (*qanun*)."[283] Thereby, al-Hudaybi implies criticism of widespread images within Islamic circles which either demand modernisation of Islamic concepts of law and state or compare secular ideologies with Islamic ideals.[284] It can hence be assumed that Islamic reform of Islamic governance has a different meaning for al-Hudaybi, which indeed demonstrates traditional, *re*-formist features.

His rigid and conservative stance brings back the substantial question of what Islamic governance is and how it can be 're-'established. While al-Hudaybi retreats to an unrefined theological model of the *shari'a*, almost every attempt (including his own) to submit a theory which can be practically employed to construct a positive state order could be dismissed on the grounds that its actual laws are not congruent with divine rules. In effect, al-Hudaybi's critique is indeed not constructive. Instead, he hides behind classical ideal notions of the state and merely describes Islamic governance in broad terms as the following quotation exemplifies:

> Islamic government or 'the Rightful Imam' is a governance which encompasses Islam as its religion and which is in charge of the execution of shari'a laws ... It is these shari'a laws, which order us to protect and defend the religion and which (demand) the empowerment of Muslims on earth and the rejection of enemies, who took control over them. (It also demands of us) to work for the spread of God's mission and the struggle (al-qital) so that God's word is the greatest (according to Qur'an 8: 39 which states) 'and fight them until there is no discord (fitna) and the religion will be all for Allah'. It is the laws of shari'a, which order us to (recognise) what is restricted for us in terms of related laws regarding the organisation of the relationship between the ruler (al-hakim) and the ruled (al-mahkum), the specification of form and system of the state and the freedom granted to the individuals and to the communities; it is (the shari'a), which orders us to acknowledge and execute what is restricted in terms of laws governing the social, economical life and the relationship of the Islamic *umma* with other communities. Further, it encompasses the life of the *umma* and its individuals in different ways and therefore makes a connection between this all, between the life of the *umma* and its individuals and the afterlife. It is (the shari'a) which confirms everything demanded in it.
>
> (al-Hudabyi (1978) 132)

This passage shows that al-Hudaybi merely sketches Islamic governance in terms of its purpose. Further, he appropriates its function to a purely idealised notion of *shari'a*. It also exemplifies that he maintains the conventional image that a just ruler symbolises a righteous system of truthful Islamic governance, which is indeed sustained by orthodox presentations. Drawing heavily from these, he repeats the commonly acknowledged idea that it is the duty of the imam to enforce *shari'a* laws and thereby to safeguard the subjects through security and justice. It is not unusual, then, that he argues also that the lack of a strong central leadership leads to injustice and discord.[285] This state of sedition is then described with the term '*fitna*'.[286]

It has to be said, al-Hudaybi's description of the purpose, function and nature of the Islamic state confirms the previous thesis, that his definition only moves within the nonspecific framework of theology of state. What becomes most apparent is that his traditional approach, which is heavily drawn from classical interpretation, does not give precise indications regarding its practicability in a modern environment. One could even go so far as to argue that his deliberations on this subject indulge in images, rather than giving constructive prescriptions.

Prerequisites for the office

Having thus established the necessity of an Islamic leadership, al-Hudaybi sets out to describe the prerequisites for the post of the *imam al-haqq*. He puts forward that the candidate must be male, must not be a minor in age, must be Muslim and must be of full physical and mental health.[287] The endeavour to report on qualifying preliminaries for the office reminds strongly of classical works such as those of al-Mawardi or Ibn Khaldun.[288]

A closer look shows that al-Hudaybi's description differs from these in a number of points. Without intending to overstress this point, it seems that al-Hudaybi's account of essential prerequisites for the office of the *imam* is similar to commonly accepted provisions for the vocation of the judge (*qadi*).[289] However, in an important instance he does re-evaluate the classics' opinions. On the question of whether descent is a prerequisite, he distances himself from the position that the imam has to be from the tribe of Quraysh.[290] Since this issue was ardently discussed in modern times, particularly in Egypt, al-Hudaybi was most probably influenced by contributors of his time.[291] For example, one of the most outstanding critics of descent as a precondition to a candidacy for the caliphate was Rashid Rida.[292] Nevertheless, al-Hudaybi disguises the impact of modern stances on this point. Instead, he refers to the historical dispute of the early Islamic community, particularly on the conflict surrounding 'Ali's appointment. Al-Hudaybi stresses herein that the orthodox caliphs were chosen from among those who had joined Muhammad in his exile (*hijra*) and who simultaneously had tribal ties to the Quraysh.[293] Thus, the *rashidun* combined the eminence of belonging to the so-called group of *ansar* (helpers) with the prominence of noble lineage. Their excellence lies in the quality of representing the most outstanding groups of their time. Al-Hudaybi then turns to explain that the central constituent of legitimacy is the oath (*bay'a*). This qualifying element was the issue of dispute in the case of the fourth caliph. Hence, al-Hudaybi continues, it was not the institution as such which was in doubt, nor was 'Ali's genealogy or his companionship to Muhammad a point of argument, but what was questioned was the obligation to comply with the oath to a ruler who was implicated in the assassination of his predecessor. This was the inflammatory issue regarding 'Ali's legitimacy, and thus the initiating point for the various denominations. Al-Hudaybi thus emphasises the significance of the oath as the legally binding aspect of legitimacy and draws the attention away from lineage. Accordingly, he sees his reservations regarding genealogical affiliation confirmed in the lack of consent on this point.[294] He concludes that descent cannot be considered as a qualification.

It is interesting that al-Hudaybi leaves the reader with the impression that the authority of the orthodox caliphs was based on a harmonious vote, which is signified through the oath. In other words, he implies that election, which is finalised through the oath, is a constituent requisite of the office. Yet al-Hudaybi's account of early Islamic history turns away from reality and practice: even though he avoids the common idealisation of the orthodox caliphs' rule, the focus on this period underpins the idealisation that events of this time are the source and measure of all questions regarding succession and leadership. This attitude ignores the fact that the 'election' of the orthodox caliphs was not at all a smooth and univocal process.[295] In other words, al-Hudaybi reiterates the constructed classical ideal of the orthodox caliphs and aims to support a rather modern concept of elected leadership. Moreover, al-Hudaybi's focus leads to a disregard of the actuality of caliphal dynasties throughout the centuries; during this time, the oath was reduced to being merely a ceremonial formality. Analysing further al-Hudaybi's point that there is no consensus (*ijma'*) on descent, it is noteworthy that in his argument he places 'outlawed' non-Sunni movements, i.e. the Khawarij and the Shi'a, on equal footing with the four Sunni schools of law.[296] This last aspect is certainly a remarkably unorthodox approach for a supporter of traditional Sunni opinions. By drawing attention to these, al-Hudaybi omits to mention the fact that the issue of lineage to the Quraysh used to be more or less unquestioned by orthodox Sunni schools. Indeed, the re-evaluation of this point in Sunni Islam is rather a modern theme, which developed its particular importance only after the abolition of the Ottoman caliphate in 1924. In the attempts to re-establish the institution (and, indeed the Egyptian king of the time was discussed as a possible candidate), the issue of descent was particularly fiercely discussed in Egypt.[297] An outstanding contributor to this discourse was Rashid Rida, who opposed the interpretation that the caliphate needed to be from the tribe of Quraysh, because it would legitimise the possibility of a dynastic rule.[298] Although he does not make explicit that he adopted Rida's line of argument, it is probable that al-Hudaybi was familiar with his work. It can be said, then, that the *Murshid* joins the modern opposition to descent and, instead, opts to argue for an elective procedure, which is finalised in the oath as a prerequisite for the caliphal office.

Taking this stance, there is the question of who participates in the election of the caliph and who gives this circle of representatives their legitimacy. Although al-Hudaybi does not suggest any concrete answers, it seems that his stance regarding the issue is rather exclusive. Indications for this notion are somewhat hidden behind interpretations of Qur'anic verses and the extensive use of quotes. For example, in the summary of his interpretation of Qur'an 22: 41, he states without further explanation that "the one we choose to represent the Islamic governance or the rightful imam is based on a contract between the *fuqaha'* (Islamic legists)".[299] While al-Hudaybi drops this remark in the context of his analysis on the contractual nature of the imam's office (rather than descent), it does nevertheless point to the privileged rank of Islamic jurists. Hence, it seems that al-Hudaybi implies yet another prerequisite for the office of the imam, namely affiliation to the circle of the 'learned'. Indeed, the suspicion of an elitist attitude in his writing is deepened when taking into account his explanation of the collective rather than the individual nature of the obligation to establish an Islamic state. We will come back to this subject and its critique at a later stage.

Contractual nature of leadership

As already noted, an important point in al-Hudaybi's assessment of the early Islamic discourse on leadership is his interpretation that the continuous presence of the institution of the caliphate is based on a consensual vote for and the oath to a person who subsequently takes the office of the imam. To put this stance differently, it can be said that he sees institution and office as purely contractual. However, the interpretation of the contractual nature of leadership bears some problems regarding the primary source of authority, i.e. God, and hence stands in contradiction to his previous strict opposition to describing Islamic governance and leadership in terms of worldly affairs.[300] Yet, al-Hudaybi ignores this theoretical conflict and does not mark his statements on the contractual basis of worldly authority in contradiction to the Qur'an and Sunna or to what he outlined before regarding the divine nature of state and rule. On the contrary, he sees the contractual nature of leadership, and thus the necessity of Islamic governance, substantiated through the primary sources.

In order to explain worldly authority, al-Hudaybi refers, like the orthodox interpretations, to the passage of Qur'an 4: 59 which states "O you who believe! Obey Allah and obey the Messenger, and those of you who are in authority".[301] As mentioned above, there are differences of opinion regarding the meaning of this passage. Central to the dispute is the understanding and interpretation of the phrase "*uli al-amri minkum*" (those among you who have authority). Without going into detail about the various interpretations, al-Hudaybi opts to understand it as an idiom for the caliph, since he should be the holder of actual power.[302] This is hardly surprising, since it matches with the opinions of the classics, which are formative for his stances on the purpose, function, necessity and duties of the imam.[303] The *Murshid* then turns to interpret Muhammad's rule, arguing that the prophet was in charge of the larger community, while regional chiefs kept their domestic power. He depicts Muhammad as the *wali al-amra'* (holder of authorities) among a number of *awla al-amr* (holders of authority). It seems that he hereby attempts to describe the prophet's rule as a relationship of *pars inter pares*. The association al-Hudaybi implies is quite remarkable. Following this account, the caliph cannot claim absoluteness for his position, first because he is bound by the *shari'a*, but also because he is one among a group over which he takes precedence. With this line of thought, al-Hudaybi seems to maintain a classical tenet regarding the involvement of the so-called *ahl al-'aqd wa al-hall* (lit. the group of binding and dissolving). Although he does not explicitly use this *terminus technicus*, he certainly expresses the notion embedded in this classical idiom, that a selected group representatively enters into the binding contract between the leader and the community of Muslims.[304]

Using this theory of 'power delegation', which was only a theological construct, since the *ahl al-'aqd wa al-hall* had in fact hardly any choice other than to give their oath, al-Hudaybi attempts to bridge between classical and modern theology of state. Indeed, his understanding of leadership shows some novelty and can be described as contemporary. Another aspect, which is closely related, is al-Hudaybi's portrayal of a 'humanised' Muhammad. This depiction of the prophet is a theme of modern Egyptian literature, particularly of the 1930s, but can already be seen in 'Abduh's work.[305] Although it is disturbing that al-Hudaybi moves between picturing ideals (e.g. the construct of the caliphal ideal) and dismissing or at least reinterpreting them (e.g. the humanisation of the prophet) whenever it is most suitable for his argument, he employs these conflicting perceptions to adjoin classical and modern concepts. Hence, he applies the idea of *pars inter pares*, which is immediately connected to the humanisation of the capacity of the prophet's leadership, to construct the notion that caliphal power emerges from 'the bottom' rather than 'the top'. In other words, he tries to stress that the leadership has its substance in the common people rather than being divinely ordained. Largely disregarding what he stressed before regarding the divine nature of Islamic governance, he now implies that the leader is equal to all, except that he is non-contentiously singled out from among a group of representatives and given the oath of allegiance. This perception is somewhat reminiscent of a system of elected representation or even of a form of power delegation, although – as we will see – it is rather doubtful that al-Hudaybi has the concept of 'democratic' power representation in mind. Leading to this suspicion are the crucial issues of who constitutes the group of communal representatives, of who is therefore eligible to participate in *shura*, and therefore of who decides on and/or gives the oath to the leader.

Islamic governance as a collective duty

As we have already seen, al-Hudaybi delineates Islamic governance and the office of the imam as a divine institution, and yet purposes that the appointment of the leader is essentially a contractual issue. This indeed creates a conflict in al-Hudaybi's interpretation. The matter is seemingly further complicated when al-Hudaybi elaborates on the necessity of an Islamic state. Herein, his interpretation refers to the distinction between collective and individual duty, i.e. *fard al-kifaya* and *fard al-'ayn*.[306] Indeed, like classical legists, he argues that the Islamic state falls into the category of collective duties.[307] He therefore explicates the conventional stance that the existence of the Islamic state is a religious duty. In other words, he responds to the paradigmatic thesis that the application of *shari'a* requires Islamic governance and subsequently the presence of an Islamic political and administrative order. Reasoning that it is a collective divine order assumes, then, that the single Muslim is excused from individually discharging the obligation as long as the demand is vicariously met.[308] Al-Hudaybi's recognition of the concept itself is quite remarkable, not because this – once more – confirms his steadfastness in classical thought, but more essentially because it links the notion of the divine origin of the Islamic state with the idea of investiture through the community, indicating a contract between society and the chosen leader. Hence, the concept of *fard al-kifaya* (collective duty) constitutes for al-Hudaybi the missing link between the two diverging premises. The reference to the theological concept of *fard al-kifaya* is further notable because numerous other modern Islamist contributions, in particular those of radical proponents (most of them having no training in Islamic jurisdiction or theology), tend to disregard this juridical concept entirely. Most of all, al-Hudaybi's argumentation indeed supposes, in comparison to other Islamist writings, a moderate and rather pragmatic approach. Considering that radical Islamists tend to demand a zealous dedication to the Islamic cause, which stresses that every Muslim bears the responsibility to work actively for the establishment of the state, the *Murshid* tries to relieve the individual and instead places emphasis on communal motivation. He therefore refutes the notion that all Muslims must be considered unbelievers as long as the obligation does not meet fulfilment. Still, as the concept of *fard al-kifaya* implies, individual representatives of the communities have to engage in the objective; on condition that at least one believer strives for the establishment of Islamic governance, others are excused to a certain extent, leaving them to be sinners rather than unbelievers. Nevertheless, al-Hudaybi's interpretation also stands in opposition to secular state systems and is, in particular, antagonistic to ʿAbd al-Nasir's rule; the demand for the construction of Islamic governance is strongly upheld. Additionally, taking into account that radical perceptions largely speak in terms of Islam as a contra-ideology, al-Hudaybi attempts to give a theological explanation. Although his approach, as has been repeatedly pointed out, fails to give precise guidelines, it is comparatively more sophisticated in tackling conflicting notions resulting from the endeavour to meet the divine, the individual and the state, but also bringing together classical and modern interpretation.

This should, however, not deflect from the fact that al-Hudaybi's distinction between *fard al-kifaya* and *fard al-ʿayn* also bears some problems, especially when comparing his interpretation with its classical application. Like traditional treatments, he describes a number of the imam's executive responsibilities as collective duties, since he performs these vicariously as the leader of an Islamic state organisation.[309] Similar to these he counts war (*jihad*), the supervision of the market (the juridical idiom: *hisba*), the requirement to do good and to avoid malevolence (*al-amr bi'l-maʿaruf wa al-nahy ʿan al-munkar*), council (*shura*) and the care of the poor (*sadd hajat al-fuqara'*) as examples in which the state, i.e. the leader, intervenes on behalf of the community, i.e. all Muslims.[310] The common rationale given by jurists is that these duties cannot possibly be executed individually and hence must be fulfilled by a common authority (*sulta ʿamma*) which is sufficiently backed by an administration and which stands above individual desires. Classical proponents of this justification subsequently infer from this line of thought a reciprocal duty, namely the obligation to be obedient to the authority of the imam so that he, in return, can discharge collective duties on their behalf.[311] Al-Hudaybi, who alludes in his description to al-Ghazali but also to the modern interpreter al-Rayyis, is unsurprisingly conventional in this respect.[312] As already mentioned, al-Hudaybi opines that the community of believers at large is excused from the obligation to construct the Islamic state, as long as a few Muslims engage actively in this enterprise. Yet this argument goes beyond classical characterisations of the collective duty. Overall, it must be said that al-Hudaybi's deliberations on the collective duty to choose the *imam*, as well as his explanation on the representative nature of Islamic governance, merge immediately with the topic of the construction of an Islamic state. Indeed, these subjects coincide in his thinking. Because he sees no distinction between classical descriptions of the installation of the imam and the present situation, he is led to extend the idea of *fard al-kifayya* to the current case of Islamist endeavour, in which the Islamic state would have to be constructed from scratch. Yet it is startling that, in this instance of building the state system, al-Hudaybi reverses the idea of collective duty. The following quotation should illustrate this.

> The presence of Islamic governance or the righteous imam is one of the collective duties (furud al-kifayya); this means that it is a duty the entire community [which is composed] of the total of its individuals is required [to obey] until it is fulfilled. Every person is individually [to be considered] a sinner as long as this duty is not fulfilled. There is no doubt that every single person of the Islamic community is individually accountable towards his Lord on whether he was negligent in regard to the effort he could have made on the path in order to fulfil the duty, which God (…) made a requirement.
>
> (al-Hudaybi (1977) 136)

This statement is quite astonishing and leads to considerable confusion and puzzlement. Admittedly, the particular passage can be read in various ways. Each of these readings is contingent upon the reader's emphasis and none of them is entirely conclusive or in accordance with the general meaning of the collective duty. Al-Hudaybi's words could indicate that the community at large is asked to fulfil the obligation, whereby it is left to the reader himself to reflect on whether his engagement is sufficient. However, what speaks against this interpretation is al-Hudaybi's persistent stress on the responsibility of individual Muslims in the process of constructing an Islamic state. It is this focus on personal accountability which reminds rather of a description of an individual duty (*fard al-'ayn*).[313] The observation that his interpretation is adjacent to *fard al-'ayn* is also fed by a reference to al-Rayyis. The latter remarks that the idea of *wahda mutasamina*, which might be best translated as 'unifying solidarity', does not fall into the category of *fard al-kifayya*.[314] By stressing that all individuals of the *umma* rather than a selected group such as the *fuqaha'* or individual members are all asked to meet the obligation, by also pointing out that every individual is personally responsible, and by further suggesting that every person is a sinner, al-Hudaybi implies to the reader that that he/she is required to engage in the construction of an Islamic governance. This reading, however, is in contradiction of the classical concept of *fard al-kifayya* and feeds the suspicion that he makes some concession to radical interpretation. Further, it has to be asked what exactly al-Hudaybi means with his emphasis that this duty demands discharge. The puzzlement on this matter originates in the lack of clarity regarding phrases like "*illa 'an yatahaqaq*" (until it is fulfilled) or in "*ma dam dhalik al-fard lam yatahaqaq*" (as long as it is not fulfilled). In conclusion, it has to be asked what the *fard* itself entails. The question is, then: does he denote that the obligation is discharged when an Islamic state is finally reinstated, or is the duty fulfilled by the active engagement for its construction? The text does not give any clarification on this point.

This poses a main problematic for the interpretation of his statement, particularly when brought into conjunction with the issue of excuse. According to the conventional idea of *fard al-kifayya*, a person is exempted from personally fulfilling a duty when the obligation is met vicariously. Generally, this implies several things: first, and this supposedly accounts for any kind of divinely imposed duty, is that Muslims have fulfilled the duty when the objective is accomplished. A simple example is that the collective obligation to perform a funeral prayer is fulfilled when the ceremony is finished; in classical Islamic thought, the collective duty of the presence of Islamic governance was met when a new caliph was installed in office. Yet, considering the situation al-Hudaybi finds himself in, the application of this classical notion would mean that every Muslim remains unexcused until an Islamic state has been established. This stance goes contra to the proposal of an exemption, which is embedded in the conception of *fard al-kifayya*. This objection leads on to the second point: there seems to be a shift of paradigm regarding the issue of excuse. Whereas classical interpretation proposes that the Muslim is exempted from responsibility when the duty is fulfilled on his behalf by someone else (i.e. there is a stress on the *attempt* of meeting the obligation), al-Hudaybi seems to indicate that every Muslim remains a sinner *until* the objective is accomplished. This stance imposes some difficulty. Since an Islamic state is, in al-Hudaybi's view, not a present reality, it conclusively means that he charges all Muslims collectively with sin. Considering that radical proponents announced a collective charge of unbelief, the reader could come to the conclusion that al-Hudaybi is more moderate in this respect. Yet a similar objection needs to be made regarding the *Murshid*'s version. Indeed, he puts forward a collective judgement of sin. However, this contradicts his initially stated principle that a charge needs to be made on the individual case rather than the whole community. Further, on the theological level of the *fard al-kifayya* it must to be said that al-Hudaybi is not congruent with the rationale of the collective duty, which suggests to the Muslim a reasonable exemption from a divine obligation.

That al-Hudaybi is indeed putting forward a modern interpretation of *fard al-kifayya* can be further seen in a few remarks regarding the process of the imam's institution into office. He argues that the installation of a leader, and therefore the obligation to set up Islamic governance, must be a representative vote of all Muslims.[315] Yet, because al-Hudaybi shows compassion for the ideal constructed in classical writings on the state, he takes no notice of the fact that hardly any imam – not even all orthodox caliphs – was chosen through communal representation. Further, his empathy with classical treatments leads him to pay no attention to a differentiation between the presence of an ostensible Islamic state in the past and modern issues regarding the construction of a state order. As described above, classical contributors do not tackle this aspect. They lived with the reality of the caliphate as an existing order; their accounts on the collective duty therefore describe merely principal aspects regarding the installation of the imam, as well as his function as a vice-guard of the law and as representative of community, who takes on certain communal obligations. Al-Hudaybi, conversely, applies the concept to put forward his version of the necessity of engaging in the construction of Islamic governance, i.e. from its very preliminaries, including institutional, administrative and executive details. This is indeed a shift of thought and, hence, a modern re-interpretation, which takes the contention into account that the caliphate, as the only legitimate form of Islamic state order, ended with the last ruler of the Ottoman dynasty.

Because al-Hudaybi does not take the distinction between the necessity of its presence and the perceived demand of the construction of Islamic governance into account, he throws together subjects, which admittedly are related to each other but still shed light on different issues of state and leadership: first, he sees the imam, who heads the administration of the Islamic state, as responsible for the vicarious discharge of certain obligations. He also implies that there is a selected group of *fuqaha'*, who choose the imam from among them and in so doing fulfil the collective obligation. Al-Hudaybi hereby silently introduces a further characteristic of the imam and a prerequisite for his office, namely that he has to be educated in juridical reasoning. This can be seen particularly in his inference that a selected group plays an outstanding part in the choice and election of the imam. It seems at first sight that he again follows classical contributions, insofar as these also promote the idea of an exclusive assembly of the so-called *ahl al-aqd wa al-hall*.[316] But there is a crucial difference. Classical legists endorsed this notion to model an ideal which they saw retrospectively exemplified in the appointment of the orthodox caliphs; while recalling this epitome they simultaneously tried to find a theological vindication, which facilitated verification of the legitimacy of the caliphs of their period, whose appointments in fact largely rested on dynastical preference and the oath of allegiance of a few selected people in the successor's milieu. Obviously, modern Islamist interpretations do not have to deal with the issue of theologically validating an election procedure, but rather have needed to work out a new system, which is executable under the current situation and which is simultaneously true to the assumed ideal.

Al-Hudaybi's modern re-interpretation needs to be seen in this light. Of course, he refers to the ideal of the orthodox caliphs and to the classics, since these are the signposts of an Islamic state system in the past. However, his as well as other modern reinterpretations on the matter of the elective procedure show some novelties. The crucial problem here is that the *ahl al-aqd wa al-hall*, the group of voters, needs to be (re)defined.[317]

In attempting to do so, al-Hudaybi proposes an exclusive attitude. His quite 'elitist' opinion can already be surmised in statements on related topics such as the contractual nature of Islamic leadership and his opposition to descent as a defining prerequisite for the office. In both examples he interprets Qur'anic passages, i.e. Qur'an 4: 59 and Qur'an 22: 41, to denote that the circle of *fuqaha'* are those who should ultimately have the right to decide on the leader, and that the latter is chosen from among this group.[318] Linking this to his description of *fard al-kifayya*, the suspicion of a hidden elitism in al-Hudaybi's interpretation, which would give decisive powers to Islamic legists, is furthered. Drawing on Qur'an 2: 286, which states "Allah does not burden a person beyond his scope", the *Murshid* aims to prove that the mass of people do not have the capacity to make decisions.[319] Hence, he implicitly supposes that common believers are not able to vote on leadership. Additionally, he endorses his opposition toward a broad and equal involvement in the elective process with a quotation from al-Rayyis, who herein argues that humans are prone to differences in opinion; this leads, so the latter argues, to conflict and consequently paralyses religion.[320] He refers to al-Ghazalis's well-known explanation that religion cannot be brought to fruition without security and that the latter is only provided through an executive power (*sultan*) – without it, the community is doomed to discord (*fitna*).[321] While al-Hudaybi takes al-Ghazali's statement out of context, his aim is to defend a position which obviously favours a 'priestly class', namely the class of the learned would have the 'sanctity' and influence over political control. Thus, al-Hudaybi promotes a conception that somehow reminds of al-Khomeini's *welayat-e faqih* (authority of the jurists).[322]

It would be interesting to know how al-Hudaybi identifies individuals who supposedly have the required insight into Islamic jurisdiction. On this crucial point, the text of *Du'at la Qudat* is silent. The straightforward proposition would be that al-Hudaybi points to those who have formal education in Islamic theology and jurisdiction. However, if recognised scholarly training (for example in the form of the study of Islamic jurisprudence at a well-known institute such as al-Azhar) were the determining factor, al-Hudaybi himself would fail to fall into the group of *fuqaha'*. Apart from this remark, and on a more serious theological level, it can be said that al-Hudaybi's proposal goes contrary to Islamic conceptions that there is no rank of priests. Learnedness, so it is commonly proudly announced, is an individual engagement with the primary textual sources and matters of belief. These points only indicate that the definition of knowledge and learnedness is undeniably a difficult matter in Islamic thought, even more so since – at least theoretically – pious insight and religious understanding cannot be measured, let alone evidenced, through an academic degree.

That al-Hudaybi indeed intends to respond with his interpretation of *fard al-kifayya* to currents of Islamist thought becomes evident in a few remarks, which should – because of their importance as evidence – be quoted at length:

> The obvious is evidence of the rightfulness of what we outlined, namely that the absence of a Islamic governance and of the imam of Muslims (imam al-Muslim) as well as the diffusion of all Muslims, their weakness and their discord led to discord (fitna), shame (hawan), conditions of suppression (al-mazalim), rottenness (fasad) and the situation of Muslim countries of these days.
>
> (al-Hudaybi (1978b) 136)

Indicative in this statement is that al-Hudaybi supposes Islam to be in decline.[323] Indeed, the notion of decline was a much-discussed subject in the Islamic world of the twentieth century. In fact, the writers of the so-called Islamic revivalism had their origin in the objective to counter this perception and to face up to what they took on as the challenge of modernity. Although the subject of decline is at the core of Islamic resurgence, one must not imagine that responses to this matter are alike. Indeed, political Islam or Islamism represents only one of many explanations by making an immediate link between political leadership and religion. Al-Hudaybi's brief account summarises, therefore, a view which was prevalent among Islamists, who argue that the problem and its cure lie in the presence of an Islamic state. In these terms, he does indeed not differ from radical voices of his time. Of particular significance are remarks such as the following, where he distances himself from those he responds to:

> The past generation said: 'Religion is the basis, and power is the guardian. If there is no basis then it (i.e. power) is destroyed; and if there is no guardian then it (i.e. religion) is lost.' We respond to this statement that we believe that the Islamic imamate and caliphate or the Islamic governance is a symbol for Islamic unity and the manifestation of the interconnectedness between the communities of Islam. (Further we believe) that Islamic consciousness (sha'ira Islamiyya) makes it necessary for Muslims to think about it and to give it relevance. (…) Therefore, the concept of the caliphate and the work for its reconstruction is a fundament, which is a requirement for us. We hence believe that this takes a lot of preparations, which are a must, and that immediate steps for the reconstruction of the caliphate indeed have to be preceded by other steps.
>
> (al-Hudaybi (1977) 137)

Even though al-Hudaybi's interpretation of *fard al-kifayya* is not quite substantial and conclusive in its argument, it has to be admitted that the above statements show some moderation, especially when seen in contrast to positions in his immediate milieu. His attempt to apply the collective duty to the issue of the construction of an Islamic state is directed against the position taken by radical interpretations, which saw the Egyptian government under 'Abd al-Nasir as the prime enemy. While they adopted Qutb's, al-Nadwi's and al-Maududi's assessment on the causes of political inadequacy, radical proponents argued that Islamic society at large lives in the state of modern *jahiliyya*. Thus, radical thought disqualified all existing societies collectively; their antagonism against secular influence was, however, particularly directed against their own societies. In order to return to faith and justice, they pronounced that the establishment of an Islamic state is the utmost duty of every Muslim. This line of thought, indeed, suggested immediate activism and a revolutionary overthrow of the existing state system. In reaction to this, al-Hudaybi's argument on the construction of an Islamic state does indeed show some temperance and an emphasis on a strategy of gradual, moderate and well-discussed transformation towards an Islamic order.

3.6 Obedience or opposition?

The questions as to whether Muslims have a right or even a legally prescribed duty to stand firm against leadership, which transgresses *shari'a*, or whether the

Muslim community is bound to obey it for better or for worse, was given particular impetus through the establishment of secular state systems. Religious–political movements such as the Muslim Brotherhood in Egypt attracted their membership because they provide a forum for dissidence and a voice of opposition to the government. Yet, in situations of immediate confrontation, such with the parliamentary system and the revolutionary regime, quarrels over the strategies and means of opposition arose within the movement.

The difference of opinion among members of the Brotherhood became obvious after the first disagreements with the regime in 1953. The years of persecution were not only a time of administrative crisis, but also of ideological challenges. The hounding, imprisonment and torture of a large number of Brothers, often without charges and trial, started off heated discussions on how to respond to ʿAbd al-Nasir's autocratic governance, which was perceived by many as the epitome of evil and injustice. Central to the dispute was the question regarding the limits of lawful Islamic resistance and whether Islamic law commands obedience after all. Inspired by works suggesting a right of resistance – present, for example, in writings of ʿAuda and Qutb – a group claimed a religiously sanctioned duty of activism and even the right of combating 'illegitimate' leadership with violent and armed means.[324] In his capacity of *Murshid*, al-Hudaybi's response to this radical interpretation was of particular importance. However, his account on this matter is rather short and is disguised as a purely juridical treatment. It deals with notions of obedience to the imam – a subject which would appear to have nothing to do with the current situation. Nonetheless, it contains practical implications on the quest among Muslim Brothers for strategies of opposition.

In order to fully understand al-Hudaybi's argumentation on the subject, any analysis needs first to address the classical handling of concepts of *al-amr bi'l-maʿruf wa al-nahy ʿan al-munkar*. The so-called *ahkam al-bughat* (laws of rebellion), which form the basis of classical juridical theory of rebellion, come into play only to a minor extent.[325] Because the act of revolt obtained in the course of development a rather negative nuance, i.e. some schools of law count *baghy* as a *hadd* crime, these laws are scarcely referred to and subject of reinterpretation in modern literature. Our focus will thus be on the principle of *al-amr bi'l-maʿruf wa al-nahy ʿan al-munkar* (commanding good and forbidding wrong), since it is this concept which is used in modern interpretation to explain the right of opposition. The postulate suggests, at least in theory, the duty of opposition to injustice and 'un-Islamic' leadership.[326] Following a briefing on the understanding of this command in classical interpretation, the analysis focuses on the *Murshid*'s interpretation thereof: the study engages in measuring al-Hudaybi's position on opposition to the theoretical framework of the *amr*. We will see that al-Hudaybi tries to find a balance between the notion of obedience, which finds particular emphasis in orthodox interpretations, and the idea of resistance, which is strongly supported by proponents of radical Islam. Further, juridical explanations of the meaning of the term *hukm*[327] build the foundation of his final critique against radically politicised understandings of Islam and the importance of Islamic governance. Thus, he discards interpretations which raise ideas such as *takfir* to the status of a divinely commanded duty.

Commanding good and forbidding wrong

Islamic theories of opposition are inferred from and closely connected to the so-called *al-amr bi'l-ma'ruf wa al-nahy 'an al-munkar* (commanding good and forbidding wrong).[328] Indeed, the command has its root in the Qur'an, where the idiom is mentioned several times.[329] Although – or perhaps because – the religious–moral command appears in the primary source without its content being particularly explicated, jurists and theologians were faced with the need for further exegetical delineation. In the attempt to define the meaning of the *amr*, Islamic theorists of the past and present apply it to two major areas.

First, because of the ethical connotation of the command, the *amr* serves to establish and codify values and moral modes, as religiously sanctioned.[330] In this regard, the command to do good and to forbid wrong is a powerful tool in determining what is in accordance with Islam and what is not. An indication for its use in defining moral regulations, which are subsequently seen as divinely ordained, is the still-prevalent understanding of its meaning as *commanding good and forbidding evil*. However, it must be noted that the classification of what is to be considered good or wrong, divine or evil, acceptable or unacceptable, and therefore a religious norm rests to a large extent on interpretation, and hence on the convictions of those defining the content of law.[331] Yet, the power of interpretation should not disclaim that the command contains strong emphasis on the individual's accountability to God.[332] Indeed, the believer carries, in the face of the Day of Judgement, a personal responsibility for his/her conduct in order to fulfil rightfully his/her duty. In these terms, the *amr* describes a dutiful and obedient relationship between the individual and God, which does not require mediation through the priestly class. This indicates, at least in theory, a certain sense of autonomy on the part of the Muslim to consider what is good and what is wrong. Nevertheless, it generally did not lead to individualistic rationalisations on the meaning of the *arm*. On behalf of the believer, submission was and to a certain extent still is identified through the exegetical deductions of theologians and jurists. One thus could argue that a priestly class exists as a matter of fact.

The second area in which *al-amr bi'l-ma'ruf wa al-nahy 'an al-munkar* finds expression is the issue of economic, social and political control.[333] The general moral–religious conception is hereby extended and applied to the framework of organising inter-human relationships. For example, al-Mawardi explains in his *Ahkam al-Sultaniyya* (Ordinances of Governance) the role of the *muhtasib* (lit. someone who can expect reward in the hereafter). He hereby applies the *amr* to a governmentally instituted official who acts as an overseer of 'rightful' conduct in public spheres such as markets, mosques and streets.[334] Al-Mawardi exemplifies a tendency in classical interpretations, which see the command as applying merely to a governmentally instituted 'watchdog'. The function of the *muhtasib* is to keep order, and thus underpins the structure of authority through the execution of what are considered moral laws. However, this approach to the *amr* and, more generally, to supporting an institutionalised power structure, had restrictive consequences for the political rights of individuals. Emphasising dutiful compliance to the leader, classical interpretations hence did hold back from exploring the *amr* in terms of a theory of resistance, which acknowledges civil liberties to question the power of a transgressing leadership. Nevertheless, *al-amr bi'l-ma'ruf wa al-nahy 'an al-munkar* could be interpreted as a concept for disobeying leadership which transgressed *shari'a*-law. Hence, it could be also be employed as a basis for defining the boundaries of Islamic leadership.[335] Although this theory of opposition to an unjust leader (i.e. one who disobeys *shari'a*-law) was ubiquitous in the Islamic theology of state, it only received detailed discussion in modern Islamist discourses.[336] 'Abd al-Qadir al-'Auda, for example, made a connection between the *amr* and Islamic criminal law, and concluded that opposition to a transgressing leadership is legitimate.[337] Others, such as Muhammad 'Abd al-Salam Faraj and 'Umar 'Abd al-Rahman, developed a more drastic understanding of illegitimacy of non-Muslim rule and subsequently see the command of doing good as the basis for a religious duty of resistance.[338]

A theory of opposition stands, however, in conflict with the concept of obedience. For both instances, relevant passages of the Qur'an and Sunna can be brought forward. Apart from the textual references of *al-amr bi'l-ma'ruf wa al-nahy 'an al-munkar* in the Qur'an, the idea of opposition commonly finds support in verses 26: 151–52, which indicate that it is necessary to contest those who act against divine will.[339] Also relevant are the passages which seem to refer to the struggle against disbelief and transgression, such as verse 5: 44.[340] Further, the so-called *aya al-baghy* (verse of rebellion, i.e. verses 49: 9–10), and the so-called *aya al-hiraba* (verse of fighting, i.e. verses 5: 33–4) are taken into account by some interpreters.[341] On the other hand, the notion of obedience can be derived from and evidenced through Quranic verses such as verse 4: 59.[342] This conflict between compliance and resistance finds its continuation in Hadith.[343] In the discussion about the *amr*, a prophetic statement which affirms three means of opposition is commonly brought forward. This highly relevant Hadith, which talks about defiance through hand, tongue and heart, is at the centre of the dispute regarding appropriate measures of opposition.[344] Yet, in support of obedience, Hadith traditions warning about the dangers of discord and dissolution (*fitna*) gained explicit importance in classical juridical thought.[345]

Led by the notion of order, classical Sunni theories on the state tended to stress obedience to the *imam*. Although the *amr* was mentioned in treatises on the caliphate, the logical conjecture that the command demands open resistance to a leader who violates law show juridical deficiencies. For example, al-Mawardi's classical work lists a number of points which indicate that compliance with the contractual nature of the caliph's power has its limits; yet the passage counts mostly for physical disabilities and, moreover, does not elaborate on any means of power control and even less on legal procedures of abdication.[346] Hence, even though the idea that the caliph, like all other human beings, is subject to God's authority and that the leader therefore equally had to be obedient to the *shari'a* constituted the fundamental premise of Islamic theories of the state, the classics were reluctant to elaborate on the *amr* as a theory of power control or of resignation, let alone rebellion. In effect, a theory that formulated particular guidelines on these issues did not evolve.

Reasons for the contradictory relationship between the 'ideal', classical juridical theory and the historical caliphate must be sought in the social and political developments of medieval Islam as well as in its complicated relationship to Islamic jurisprudence.[347] Whereas the historical caliphate progressively deviated from the imagined ideal of the orthodox caliphs, it was also a political reality that the caliph's de facto power gradually declined. In fact, provincial rulers replaced his authority.[348] In attempting to counter this moment and aiming to uphold the constructed ideal of a just caliphate, the writings of classical contributors show an increasing stress on the issue of submission to the institution of the *imam*, even to such an extent that, in later accounts, obedience was considered a religious duty and *baghy* (rebellion) was considered a crime.[349] The latter interpretation clearly challenged and limited any possibility of opposition or resistance. The growing discrepancy between historical model and theory, as well as between theory and reality, can be explained insofar as the classics attempted to uphold a constructed ideal of the just rule, using the orthodox caliphs as their example. Yet they needed to make amendments where either reality demanded adjustment (e.g. in the gradual acknowledgement of provincial leaders), or they saw the possibility to boost the image of the declining caliphal institution, which after all represented the unifying bond of the *umma*.[350] Hence, theoretical writings on the subject of the state had the objective of underpinning the authority of the caliphate by stressing the duty of obedience rather than of undermining it by emphasising the right of resistance. Subsequently, the *amr* had only marginal significance and was presented merely in general terms, without further elaboration; instead, strong emphasis was put on obedience to leadership, arguing that the lack of a common authority leads to the disintegration of the Islamic community at large. For example, al-Ghazali wrote the following almost in denial of a concept of opposition:

> An evil-doing and barbarous sultan, so long as he is supported by military force, so that he can only with difficulty be deposed and that the attempt to depose him would create unendurable civil strife, must of necessity be left in possession and obedience must be rendered to him, exactly as obedience is required to be rendered to those who are placed in command.
>
> (al-Ghazali quoted in Gibb (1955) 19)

In modern Islamist discourse, the concept of opposition to 'unjust' leadership gained new relevance. However, there has been a shift of paradigm. The question was no longer whether and how a transgressing Islamic leader could be contested, but rather of the legitimacy of resistance to secular rule. The debate among Muslim Brothers regarding the legitimacy of 'Abd al-Nasir's regime is hence loaded with a theological controversy regarding the classical emphasis on obedience and ideal notions of Islamic justice.

Most proponents of the modern Islamist opposition (in Egypt, but also in the Muslim world) referred to the fundamental issue of unbelief in order to find a religious justification for their defiance of the state. Qutb is an example thereof. His concept of resistance builds on the simple premise that unbelief (*kufr*) and the state of ignorance (*jahiliyya*) need to be contested, since these constitute an illegitimate occupation of God's supremacy. Implying the charge of *takfir*, he suggests the defying of present (secular) systems and their leaders. It is striking that Qutb makes no effort to reinterpret the *amr*. However, there are a few writers, such as the Egyptian lawyer and leading member of the Muslim Brotherhood 'Abd al-Qadir 'Auda, who provided a fresh interpretation to the *amr*. In three volumes entitled *al-Tashri' al-Jina'i al-Islami*, he argues that the principle of commanding good and forbidding wrong is an essential part of Islamic criminal law.[351] While he attempts to revive the moral component of Islamic justice, he explicates that the *amr* is also fully applicable and executable in regard to the leader. Unlike classical interpretation, he therefore concludes that opposition to those in authority is religiously endorsed.

A modern theology of opposition

Considering that the book *Du'at la Qudat* was written by al-Hudaybi in his position as *Murshid* of Egypt's largest religious–political opposition movement, one would expect his statement to represent a clear vision of the Brotherhood's mission, particularly regarding the central issue of opposition. Under the circumstance of political persecution, members of the Brotherhood fiercely discussed religious justifications for the opposition to secular (rather than Islamic) rule. In this environment, the question of deploying means of religiously sanctioned resistance was important. Considering this, al-Hudaybi's brevity on the subject of opposition, with a consequent retreat to classical approaches, is most striking. Indeed, the lack of definite verdicts and conclusive remarks on this integral subject may disappoint those looking for transparent directives. Instead, al-Hudaybi's statements on resistance are concealed within lengthy juridical deliberations which appear to deal merely with the limits of compliance to the rule of the *imam*. In respect of the classical issue of divesting the leader of Islamic governance, one might be left with considerable uncertainty as to whether and, if so, how al-Hudaybi's interpretation is relevant to the situation of modern times.

It is the objective of the following analysis to show that the few remarks do still contain a modern stance. While al-Hudaybi purports to focus on the boundaries of obedience to the *imam*, it is interconnected with the wider issue of resentment to any kind of 'non-Islamic' leadership, particularly secular, non-religious authority. Al-Hudaybi again uses the classical notions of obedience to respond to the modern situation. In this we find an implicit refutation of concepts which support radical activism, upheaval, anarchy and militant opposition in the name of Islam. But, as we shall see, inconsistencies, which are the result of his attempt to reapply the classics to modern issues of state, find their peak in his interpretation of opposition. For example, al-Hudaybi struggles with the precedent of the (historical and ideal) Islamic order and the actuality of secular governance. Moreover, he tries hard to bring together the conflicting notions of obedience and opposition. The problematic becomes apparent in his emphasis on the paradigm of the need to respect authority; otherwise the community faces disintegration (i.e. *fitna*). This position, however, leads to the question of whether indeed *Du'at la Qudat* contains an adequate response to the situation in which the Brotherhood found itself during the time of persecution, when the issue of religiously sanctioned opposition to a regime which was perceived by many members of the organisation to be an illegitimate occupation of God's supreme rule was most pressing. Indeed, al-Hudaybi attempts 'a dangerous walk on the ridge': since he is the *Murshid* of the Muslim Brotherhood, he has to defend the political–religious activism and the attitude of legitimate opposition which are a constituent continuum of the organisation's subsistence. Yet, he makes it his objective to put forward a moderate stance which calls for a restrained confrontation. It is the latter aspect which makes his interpretation distinct from radical understandings of the Islamist cause of the modern time and which, conclusively, stands out in his critique of the latter.

The conflict between obedience and opposition

It is quite telling that al-Hudaybi's statements are presented under the heading '*al-sama' wa al-ta'a*' (listening and obedience). This shows that he sees the issue of opposition as supplementary to the matter of obedience. Indeed, the *Murshid*'s juridical remarks on opposition are preceded by an extensive repetition of the classical positions, so stressing the duty of submission before setting out to explain his position on opposition.[352] Conventional theological and juridical paradigms, such as the duty of submission to the *imam*, are reiterated; recapitulated also is the notion that respect for leadership is crucial for the continuous existence of Islamic governance and for the prevention of discord (*fitna*). Yet he also reminds the reader of the premise that the *imam*, like all human beings, is not infallible. Hence, the leader too must submit to God and his law and should merely oversee the execution of the *shari'a*.

Having rehearsed these preliminary points, al-Hudaybi then puts forward his interpretation of opposition. Since obedience is essentially directed towards God, conformity, he states clearly, is only authoritative as long as the *imam* acts in accordance with the preset divine law. In effect, the duty of respect towards the *imam* is annulled if he sins.[353] Herein, his interpretation departs from classical works, which commonly refrain from this position. In evidence of his interpretation, al-Hudaybi refers to verse 4: 59 of the Qur'an.[354] The citation of this particular verse in connection with the issue of religiously sanctioned opposition is indeed remarkable. As mentioned before, it is this verse which is commonly used to substantiate the notion of obedience. Most works refer particularly to the first half of the verse, which speaks of obedience to God, to the prophet and to those holding authority. Al-Hudaybi points to the entire verse and stresses its less-cited part, which states in translation: "So if you differ in anything among yourselves, refer it to Allah and his messenger, if you believe in Allah and in the Last Day. That is better and more suitable for final determination."[355] With reference to this passage, al-Hudaybi thus evinces that disagreements may include issues regarding obedience to worldly authorities. This theological argument is then used to underpin the concept that submission to the divine is the guiding paradigm; while retaining that obedience to worldly authority is immensely significant, he also points out that the position of (political) leadership is not unquestionable and therefore has its limitations. Still, one can argue in response to this religious argument that al-Hudaybi has not delineated the parameter of the *imam*'s rule or of non-divine leadership. If we disregard this aspect for now, the interpretation of this particular verse in terms of boundaries applicable to those in authority is significant, particularly because Qur'an 4: 59 frequently appears in the discourse of Islam and leadership. Whereas classical readings used the passage mainly to substantiate the notion of unqualified obedience to the caliph, modern radical interpretation aimed to show that resistance to secular rules is legitimate. The latter focused on God's absolute supremacy and the authority of leaders of their Islamic movement, who claim to actively engage in the establishment of their envisioned ideal state. Al-Hudaybi's interpretation is therefore out of the ordinary. It is a strong indicator of his intention to find a balance between obedience and resistance.

Al-Hudaybi's tendency to synchronise conflicting notions is also the reason behind his reference to a number of Hadith. These convey that submission – important as it may be – must not be upheld in the case of the leader's transgression of divine law.[356] The references to Hadith seem to indicate that al-Hudaybi fully supports opposing the wrongdoings of the *imam*; in fact, they imply that it is a religious responsibility to defy any leadership which transgresses Islamic law. One can even gain the impression that al-Hudaybi backs the activist interpretation of the 'command to do good and to forbid wrong' (*al-amr bi'l-ma'ruf wa al-nahy 'an al-munkar*). The following quotation demonstrates this:

> However, the command (al-amr) goes beyond a merely passive attitude, whereby one must resent to listen to [someone committing] sinful behaviour and to obey. [It is] an active command, which contains the necessity to reject injustice (al-baghy), to forbid sin, to change wrong (al-munkar) and [to bring about] its elimination. (God), honour and pride be on him, said: 'And if two parties among the believers fall to fighting, then make peace between them both. But if one of them outrages against the other, then fight against the one that outrages until it complies with the command of Allah.' The Supreme commanded to fight (bi-qital) the tyrannical group until it retreats and gives obedience to God's authority and his rule.
>
> (al-Hudaybi (1978) 139[357])

In this quotation, al-Hudaybi makes a link between the *ahkam al-bugha* (the laws of rebellion) and the *amr bi'l-ma'ruf wa al-nahy 'an al-munkar*.[358] This interpretation is, compared to classical stances on the law of rebellion, quite pioneering. He not only withdraws from the negative tendencies in the understanding of revolt that predominate in most classical works of law; but further, he re-evaluates the concept as a legal precedent that allows opposition to unjust rule. Moreover, he turns around the idea of *baghy* (rebellion). For him, rebels are not those who oppose the leader, but it is the transgressor who revolts against law. Thus, it is the law-breaking ruler who commits the crime. While al-Hudaybi puts forward that resistance to the ruler is in dutiful compliance with the *amr*, he stresses that active engagement to correct this wrong, even if it may entail the use of force, is a legitimate means. Yet, he then partially withdraws his far-reaching statement.

> (But,) the unjust group (al-fa'a al-baghiyya), which tries hard, remains protected (ma'jura) in its ijtihad, even though it is therein mistaken.
>
> (al-Hudaybi (1978) 139)

Indeed, al-Hudaybi tones down his initial position. He points out that intention is a significant aspect of evaluating whether the transgressing leader should remain in office.[359] His assertion is connected to what he previously stated on the topic of the distinction between unbelief and sin, and particularly regarding his account of possible excuses. Herein he argued that someone who obviously committed a severe offence against clearly defined divine law might find justifying exemptions from being charged with unbelief.[360] Hence, his account of excuses elaborates on the basic attitude of Islamic criminal law, which sees intention as a quintessential aspect of legal allegations against the accused offender.

Nevertheless, the aspect of intention poses a problem, particularly when a ruler applies it to defend his actions, although they are obvious offences against what is generally considered to constitute divine law. One objection is that intentionality is impossible to determine, and therefore constitutes an ill-defined parameter. Hence, it is a questionable guideline to monitor the illegality or the legitimacy of leadership. Indeed, this raises questions regarding the issue of whether to choose obedience to a transgressing leader or whether to decide for opposition. In simple terms: how could one be sure of the good intentions of a leader? Ultimately, continuous compliance to a ruler would be based on the testimony of the transgressing *imam* that he has the intention to comply with divine law. Moreover, in order to give justification to his actions, the apparently sinning leader could make reference to the theory of *al-maslaha al-'amma* (public interest). In connection with the juridical principle of *la darar wa la dirar* (no harming and [hence] no reciprocating harm), there is the possibility of bringing forward that it was necessary in the public interest to disregard *shari'a*-law.[361]

In effect, the reference to intention makes any attempt to dispose of the leader extremely difficult, because the accused can repudiate any charge resting on his actions. Since there is hardly any real possibility of discharging the *imam*, al-Hudaybi effectively reaffirms the stress on submission to the leader's authority, even though this may be at the expense of lawful conduct. Therefore it can be said that although al-Hudaybi attempts to accommodate conflicting notions (i.e. active resistance and the use of force, on the one hand, and the determination to resolve a conflict and the desire to meet the terms of obedience as far as possible, on the other hand) he falls back onto ideas of the late classical period (e.g. those of al-Ghazali), which have the tendency to support absolute submission to the authority of leaders, regardless of whether they comply with law or not.

Patience as a strategy of opposition

Al-Hudaybi attempts to use the command to do good and to forbid wrong (*al-amr bi'l-ma'ruf wa al-nahy 'an al-munkar*) to bring forward an interpretation which legitimises opposition to unjust authority. Yet it can be argued that he reverses his statement, introducing the aspect of the *imam*'s intention to comply with divine rule as a measure of whether his leadership is legitimate or not.

Leaving aside the already mentioned problematic of challenging the legitimacy of the *imam*'s rule, al-Hudaybi picks up the *amr* to give an explanation of the issue of means and strategies of opposition. Herein, he engages in a discussion on active versus passive resistance. Stressing that *al-amr bi'l-ma'ruf wa al-nahy 'an al-munkar* is unequivocally accepted, al-Hudaybi admits that there is disagreement on the means of executing the command.[362] In his following a purely juridical approach he constructs his argumentation around the above-mentioned Hadith, speaking of three ways of responding to wrongdoings, namely through hand, tongue and heart. These three means are metaphors signifying, first, action, which could in its extreme form be interpreted as physical or even armed intervention (i.e. *bi'l-yad*; lit. with the hand); this means may involve the intention to actively fight and possibly kill the transgressing leader. *Bi'l-lisan* (lit. with the tongue) then corresponds to resistance in the form of speech or writing; thereby, the aim is to convince the wrongdoer to renounce or maybe to pressure him to resign. Third, the weakest measure is then passive opposition (i.e. *bi'l-qalb*; lit. with the heart), whereupon insubordination is expressed through quiet and individualistic withdrawal of support and through non-participation.[363] Al-Hudaybi identifies these three ways as being central to the various understandings of strategies of opposition.

With reference to early Islamic history, al-Hudaybi points out that the dispute surrounding the manner of executing *al-amr bi'l-ma'ruf wa al-nahy 'an al-munkar*, and in particular the application of force, was the cause of the split into the major denominations and sects, and the reason for divisions among the schools of thought within Sunni Islam.[364] He admits that, depending on the emphasis applied to hand, tongue or heart, past interpretations came to different conclusions regarding the validity of one or the other means. His analysis leads him to look into early Islamic history; al-Hudaybi identifies two opposing approaches. Some jurists inferred from the Hadith that passive opposition (i.e. *bi'l-qalb*) is an inescapable obligation, whereas verbal opposition (i.e. *bi'l-lisan*) should be used if one is able to do so.[365] Among proponents of this position are famous names such as Ahmad ibn Hanbal, Sa'd ibn Abi Wa'qas, Usama ibn Zayd, Ibn 'Umar and Muhammad ibn Muslima. He explains that proponents of this reading emphasised that force (i.e. *bi'l-yad*) should only be considered as a last resort. The sword should be drawn (*salla al-suyuf*) when absolute certainty is established: evidence must be given that the leader undoubtedly admitted having left the community of Muslims; further, the case against the leader can then only be processed when all prosecutors – who must belong to Sunni Islam – personally witnessed that the leader announced his disaffiliation from Islam.[366] Although force remains a final option, it is not necessarily a method to be striven for. This means, however, that a forceful eviction of the leader is almost impossible. Hence, opposition to a transgressing leader is (almost) restricted to passivity.

As mentioned, al-Hudaybi identifies a second group, which views force as a necessary instrument to respond to wrongdoing, particularly if there is no prospect that the transgressing *imam* will be stopped by other means.[367] To this group belonged, so al-Hudaybi states, not only jurists accounted for as proponents of the Zaydiyya and Khawarij movement and moreover the majority of Mu'tazila, but, most importantly, a number of luminaries of early Islamic history, such as ʿAli, ʿĀʾisha, and also Muʿawiyya and ʿUmar, Hasan, Husain and many companions (*sahaba*) and helpers (*ansar*) of the prophet.[368] Characterising then their position, al-Hudaybi points out that they see vigorous intervention as the most appropriate means of conducting the *amr*, making activism the utmost option of resistance that a believer should strive for. Hence, unlawful conduct, regardless of whether the issue of leadership is at stake or whether it applies to the protection of ownership rights, can be legitimately contested by forceful means. In other words, stress is hereby placed on the issue of correcting transgressions against divine law through energetic engagement, which could include physical and armed aggression.[369] This interpretation thus opens possibilities to legitimating violent means and, thereby, less attention is given to peaceful and less aggressive solutions.

Interestingly, al-Hudaybi does not comment further on the prominence of those listed as proposing force, and moves on to criticise the attitude. He argues that the evidence of this group lacks any consideration of other means suggested by the Hadith that mentions hand, tongue and heart as means of resistance.[370] Al-Hudaybi thus rejects concepts which suggest that vigorous oppositional activism is the utmost means of showing one's conviction. Instead, he subscribes to the premise that force is only the last of all options. Nevertheless, he also distances himself from ultimate passivity. He explicitly criticises the inference that the Hadith indicates a purely peaceful response, arguing that there is no evidence to uphold a reading which suggests unchallenged compliance.[371]

Before further commenting on al-Hudaybi's objectives in regard to his presentation on opposition, it may be beneficial to engage in an analysis of the Hadith, or rather the orthodox Sunni interpretation thereof. It is striking that juridical thinkers did not make the execution of one or the other form of opposition dependent on the severity of the *imam*'s offence against *shari'a* law. Further, the idea of a gradual increase of measures for executing the *amr* somehow reverses the sequence of the Hadith. In the original Hadith, a decrease of measures is indicated, whereby active resistance (i.e. *bi'l-yad*) is mentioned first; passive resistance (i.e. *bi'l-qalb*) is described as the weakest; inferentially, active challenge to the transgressing leader requires the 'true' conviction. Setting aside whether al-Hudaybi's portrayal of these two opposing views regarding the Hadith is correct or merely a simplification of the variations within Islam on the topic of opposition, it is the purpose of his characterisation of two opposing views to prepare for his presentation of an intermediate position. Accordingly, al-Hudaybi argues for a gradual increase of measures; foremost, the Muslim should resent the *imam* with his/her heart, before speaking out or even moving on to forceful means as a final resort. Hence, he shows reservations on both approaches and yet sets out to argue for an understanding which combines elements of both interpretations. In partial agreement with passive resistance, he calls for patience (*sabr*) before engaging in more forceful and possibly violent actions.[372] Explaining that *sabr* is an essential aspect of belief and, indeed, is demanded through divine revelation, he infers that endurance in waiting is also an essential element of opposition. Conclusively, he warns, a Muslim who violates this obligation is a sinner (*fasiq*).[373] But al-Hudaybi draws on the second approach when he tries to affirm that fighting (*al-qital*)[374] is legitimate, although its application is regulated and it can only be a final solution. It can thus be assumed that al-Hudaybi supports the concept of gradual increase of force. This conjecture is furthered by the fact that he uses the very same Hadith to evidence his interpretation of the stages of faith and steady growth of the Muslim's belief.[375]

Accommodating obedience with opposition

As outlined, it is al-Hudaybi's objective to find a balance between the conflicting notions of obedience and opposition. Although he focuses his analysis on the authority of the *imam*, his explanation contains implications for how Muslims are supposed to react to any political leadership, including secular. The differing conceptions of obedience and resistance inevitably incorporate seemingly incompatible strategies with regard to how a believer should react to transgressing leadership. As we have seen, the question at stake is whether the Muslim needs to comply with the ruler, even though he acted in contradiction to the basis of his authority, or whether it there are legitimate means of active resistance, which might include combating his power. Al-Hudaybi suggests that obedience to the leader, even if he transgresses, is a primary duty. However, supplementary to deference, active opposition is a last resort to challenge leadership if the accused cannot be convinced by non-violent means to abide by divine law. In addition to his interpretation of *al-amr bi'l-ma'ruf wa al-nahy 'an al-munkar*, al-Hudaybi turns to the juridical theory of abrogation for further evidence.

Abrogation (*al-nasikh wa al-mansukh*) can briefly be described as a theory and method of Islamic jurisprudence which puts forward that Qur'anic verses or passages which were revealed later in time override or abrogate earlier texts.[376] Additionally, the technique of abrogation was applied to *sunna* as the second fundamental source.[377] Although the juridical concept entails a deep-rooted conceptual problem, as we will explain below, it is evident that the formulation of such a theory was of major importance for the development of Islamic jurisprudence and the harmonisation of contradicting precepts.[378] It was a necessary component to establish the basis for applied, practical law, since it proposed a solution to the problematic of some occasional contradictions in the textual sources.

Yet, without going into full detail about fundamental theological and theoretical critique of the concept itself, it needs to be pointed out that the theory bears the problematic that the essential belief in the absoluteness of every single sentence and verse of the Qur'an is made somewhat relative. This is for a number reasons:

first, since the concept of *al-nasikh wa al-mansukh* is a part of the wider field
of what can be described as Islamic hermeneutics, it is obvious that its employment requires some investigation into the historical event (i.e. the occasions of
revelation; *al-asbab al-nuzul*) and therefore into the chronology of revelations.[379]
Although the historical order of the revelation is a subject of considerable dispute
in itself, it is a fact that Islamic jurisprudence applied, practised and used hermeneutical tools to deduce *shari'a* laws. This shows that, for practical purposes of
deducing positive law, the Qur'an was scrutinised under the paradigm of the text's
contextual, historical and therefore relative event of its disclosure. Yet, at the same
time and in contradiction to the relativity embedded in this manner of handling
the revelation, Islamic interpreters also stressed the universal, timeless and divine
nature of the text. Even more complicated and controversial is the historical event
of Hadith and their relation to incidents in Muhammad's life. Yet, without the
clarification of the contextuality, a dispute about the abrogating authority of particular Hadith remains. Second, the application of *al-nasikh wa al-mansukh* effectively supposes the classification of revealed text. On the one hand, there are
continuously valid verses, which are timeless and universally applicable; on the
other hand, there are a number verses which were only applicable for a restricted
period of time, since these were overruled by the revelation of another verse.
However, the classification of verses into universally applicable and time limited,
into valid and overruled, constitutes a grading of divine text. In effect, through
the application of juridical hermeneutics, which is a fundamental element of the
theory of abrogation, one text is made more relevant for juridical purposes than
another. The implications of qualifying text, which is in its entirety regarded as
divinely given, is a theological and theoretical concern largely ignored, or at least
downplayed, in Islamic jurisprudence in favour of a practical exegesis of law.
Further, the abrogation of Qur'anic verses through *sunna*, or more specifically
through Hadith texts, is inevitably problematic, since the Qur'an is considered to
comprise God's revealed word, whereas Hadith consist of statements from and
about the prophet and his companions. Hence, the latter textual category had no
divine origin. Nevertheless, the theory and method of *al-nasikh wa al-mansukh* is
an important tool of Islamic jurisprudence for eliminating contradictions within
the textual sources. Only on these premises is it possible to discuss and deduce
positive law.

   In a complicated theological evaluation of Hadith texts, some indicating a verification of the use of violent action and others pointing to a refusal of it, al-Hudaybi
attempts to find proof for his intermediate position regarding the means of opposition. The following quote should give an impression of how al-Hudaybi handles
the concept of abrogation and comes to his conclusions.

> We found those Hadith that propose the refusal (al-nahy) of fighting
> (al-qital) coincide with the well-known principle that a [peaceful] resolution
> [to conflict] was in place at the beginning of Islam. Hence, the rejection of
> hostile action (radd al-'adwan) was [expressed through] divine law, which
> was made an obligation and was authorised through no less than the text

of the revelation (al-nass). However, later Hadith were mentioned to affirm an additional divine law (shari'a za'ida) to the well-known principle and it [allows] fighting. There is no doubt about this. Therefore, it is right (to say) that the meaning of these Hadith abrogate the refusal regarding fighting (nasakha ma'na al-aHadith al-munhi fi-ha 'an al-qital) and it is made a rule on this point by (the prophet) may blessing and peace be upon him through other authoritative statements on fighting.

(al-Hudaybi (1977) 142)

His considerations lead him to argue that amiable efforts are at the foundation of Islamic belief and practice. However, this essential was complemented by supplementary Hadith, which affirmed the restricted use of violent action and fighting. Therefore, active resistance is legitimate. Although it is, as we have established already, al-Hudaybi's stance that force is only a means of last resort in cases where a peaceable solution cannot be brought about, the question arises as to whether al-Hudaybi's application of the juridical principle *al-nasikh wa al-mansukh* indeed helps to support this view.

In this respect, the application of the juridical principle of abrogation is indeed problematic. Concerns can be raised on various levels, which include purely theological and theoretical apprehensions against the conception in general, as well as more specifically regarding al-Hudaybi's attempt to apply and use the juridical tool. Apart from the aforementioned fundamental theoretical and theological problems, which al-Hudaybi unavoidably inherits when using *al-nasikh wa al-mansukh*, there are more concrete points of critique regarding his specific treatment. It must be said that his elaborations are complicated to the extent of being almost incomprehensible. The reader is taken back and forth between abrogative and abrogated text, with the result that it is almost impossible to follow the argument. Admittedly, this is only a superficial observation.

On a more serious level of critique however, it needs to be pointed out that his evaluation of abrogating and abrogated Hadith texts could be questioned as to its accuracy. Although the textual category of Hadith is not of divine origin, prophetic statements are nevertheless a fundamental complementary source of Islamic exegesis. Hence, when using them for hermeneutical purposes, a degree of certainty about the contextual event of the Hadith is needed. Yet, even if one does not question the authority of prophetic statements, there is still significant room for speculation about when, where and why a particular Hadith originated. Hence, although al-Hudaybi sets out to find solid grounds for his position, his application of *al-nasikh wa al-mansukh* on particular Hadith-texts is susceptible to challenge on its correctness. Hence, even though he attempts to provide theological evidence for his theses, his verification through Hadith is constructed on somewhat vague grounds.

More significantly, the above quote, which exemplifies al-Hudaybi's employment of the concept, shows that is not entirely consistent with the juridical theory of *al-nasikh wa al-mansukh*. In the passage, he outlines that peaceful means are the premise, verified through revealed texts and put into practice during the years of early Islamic teaching. In later times, additions were made to this principle; Hadith statements show that the restricted use of forceful means was permitted. It is clear that it is al-Hudaybi's aim to find a balance between the notions of obedience and of opposition through the application of abrogation. However, on a purely theological level, al-Hudaybi's understanding of the concept of *al-nasikh wa al-mansukh* needs to be called into question. In fact, there are two ways of analysing his use of abrogation. In the first instance, one could conclude that forceful actions are sanctified through later text. This understanding of al-Hudaybi's proclamation sees peaceful resolutions overruled through fierce and activist means of opposition. Yet, this reading contains a major problematic. It implies that Hadith overrule the more weighty textual source of Qur'anic verses. This way of understanding it would then disregard the juridical rule that divine text is superior to any other source. The second possibility of understanding his explanation is more likely. It suggests that the objective of finding a peaceful solution is more significant. The use of force is merely a last resort. This reading proposes that the earlier state of affairs, which was affirmed through revealed texts, continues to be valid and comprises the essential premises regarding the issue of opposition. Consequently, later Hadith statements constitute merely supplementary information. Yet, if one understands the quotation along these lines, it could be critically remarked that he does not use the concept *al-nasikh wa al-mansukh*.

In one or the other case, al-Hudaybi's employment of *al-nasikh wa al-mansukh* fails to give clear, juridical support to his thesis. Nevertheless, the fact that he attempts to find equilibrium between obedience and opposition, which acknowledges the primary importance of compliance to leadership but also approves of gradually increasing force regarding the means of resistance, is in itself remarkable. Yet, it is perturbing that radical Islamists may see additional legitimisation of the use of violence, particularly if al-Hudaybi's interpretation of abrogation of peaceful actions is taken further.

Resistance or subordination to secular state systems?

In his summation on issues of Islamic governance and the concept of resistance, al-Hudaybi launches his most explicit critique against the radical interpretations of his time.[380] The point of departure is the often-quoted verse 4: 65, which reads in translation as follows: "But no, by your Lord, they do not believe until they make you judge (*tahkim*) in all disputes between them, and find in themselves no resistance against your decisions, and accept them with full submission."[381] The Qur'anic statement, as al-Hudaybi would have it, cannot verify a theory of opposition to (secular or unjust) rule. In explaining his position, he first turns to the essential paradigm that divine law precedes the state. According to the theology of Islamic governance, just governance is built on legal rules as set out by God. This argument comprises an obvious fundamental principle of Islamic interpretation, as we have previously shown. Al-Hudaybi's fresh engagement with the subject stresses that *shari'a* laws are applicable beyond their execution through an Islamic state system.[382] This emphasis bears most interesting conclusions. Indeed, al-Hudaybi hereby aims to undermine a single-minded focus on the indispensability of an Islamic state as the institution executing *shari'a*. He explicitly directs his words against the focus of (radical) Islamist interpretation, which argues that it is essential for the believer to actively engage in the establishment of an Islamic political system in order to remain part of the community of Muslims.[383] With reference to the verse, al-Hudaybi then puts forward that proponents of radical interpretation construe a number of incorrect assumptions regarding its meaning. The most crucial erroneous supposition is their inference that a person who does not actively engage in the construction of a just and divinely guided state system and conclusively defies secular rule cannot be called Muslim. First, this interpretation suggested by radical Islamists commences with an erroneous understanding of *tahkim*; they hence deduce incorrectly that the execution of law through the institution of Islamic governance is an inevitable necessity for validating the belief of a Muslim and religion itself.[384] This does not mean, as we have previously seen, that al-Hudaybi does not value the existence of the Islamic state as a religious duty. However, he differs from radical interpretation in stressing that Islamic governance is the sole means of carrying out divine law. The obdurate focus on the state, he argues, bears the false assumption that the authority of divine law is dependent on its enforcement through a state institution or the power of a *wali al-amr*.[385] This position thus connotes wrongly that there are no Muslims outside an existing Islamic state. Al-Hudaybi points out that this reading contains threatening conjectures which cannot be tenable, since it in fact implies that there were no Muslims at any time of Islamic history. First, even if one assumes that divine justice was instituted in the past in the form of an Islamic governance which administered parts of the world, a rigid understanding would entail that everyone – including those living under the rule of justice – would have continued to be unbelievers, since divine rule was in fact not established all over the world and among all people. Second, even if one accepts that Islamic governances existed in the past, history has shown that the existence of an Islamic state is in fact no guarantee of a just enforcement of divine law. Likewise, the radical position implies that even if a ruler aimed to act justly and in accordance with God's demands, all humans would have remained unbelievers. Al-Hudaybi opines that the reason for this paradox lies in the fact that the leader, having come to power through military force, actively occupies the position which should legally be reserved for the rightful *imam*.

The meaning of Qur'an 4: 65 thus emphasises the power of revelation, which forms the basis of *shari'a*. According to this fundamental paradigm, divine law is the dominant and universal feature. Islamic governance is built on this prerequisite and merely fulfils the duty of executing the God's will, as is subsequently explicated in the *shari'a*. Following this, the state is a secondary result, but not the essence.[386] Since divine law is superior to the contractual nature of a social and political structure among humans, it is also independently valid. In order to further explicate his opposition to this understanding of verse 4: 65, al-Hudaybi indulges in a lengthy analysis of the meaning of *tahkim*.[387] It leads him to assert that one needs to differentiate between the execution of law (*tanfidh shari'a*) through Islamic governance and the act of making God judge (*tahkim*) in all matters of life. Whereas *tanfidh* explicitly refers to an institutionally decreed obedience to *shari'a* through its enforcement by the state, *tahkim* emphasises the individual quest for meaning and truth. It is the subjugation to divine will, al-Hudaybi reminds the reader, which is the fundament of belief. Hence, *tahkim* implies that it is the responsibility of every Muslim to follow the demands of religion and law, regardless of whether their execution is guaranteed through a state order. While al-Hudaybi evidently interprets the meaning of *tahkim*, he thus challenges concepts supposing that the term necessarily carries a political content. Thus, he opines, every Muslim holds the status of a *hakim* (judge) in regard to his/her own life and practice.[388]

In conclusion, al-Hudaybi's focus on the individual brings his interpretation of the bond between belief, practice, law and the issue of Islamic governance to its peak. His elucidation indeed contains a refutation of the radical stance that political action or even violent opposition are an inescapable necessity. It also goes against the attitude that a believer is obliged to engage in the struggle for the establishment of an Islamic state or otherwise loses his/her status as a Muslim. In this respect, the *Murshid*'s understanding also serves as a dismissal of the idea of communal *takfir* or, more generally, any sweeping verdicts which announce that modern Muslim society is overshadowed by unbelief and the return to a state of *jahiliyya*. This indeed highlights his refutation of radical Islamic interpretation. Indeed, al-Hudaybi uses the past and the theory of Islamic governance to exaggerate the implications of radical exegesis. Therefore, he almost ridicules their conclusions. Yet it is doubtful that his statements point to non-involvement and passivity. Certainly, he does not purport that Muslims have to submit to a system of rule which he regards as tyrannical and against Islamic principles. One can thus draw the conclusion that the *Murshid* of Egypt's largest opposition movement opts against (violent) resistance at all costs. Rather, the movement needs to first strive for peaceful, non-violent solutions. It can thus be said that al-Hudaybi sees the major aim of the organisation as lying in engagement in missionary activities. It seems evident that he favours a strategy of preaching in order to create a basis for the construction of an Islamic state. Further, his ideas of resistance show that the movement needs to first exhaust every possibility of non-violent opposition before stepping up force. On the question of when and how the resources for diplomacy are exhausted, al-Hudaybi remains ambiguous.

Conclusion

Hasan al-Hudaybi remains one of the most influential figures in the Society of Muslim Brothers. The ideology of today's largest politico-religious organisation, which has its main base in Egypt, draws its concepts of non-violent opposition from al-Hudaybi's writing *Du'at la Qudat* (*Preachers not Judges*). Although al-Hudaybi played a decisive role in the development of a conciliatory concep, which aims to gradually change the existing state system(s) toward an Islamic order, the second *Murshid* has not received much attention in the annals of the Society. Indeed, his name is tainted because he is linked to a period of near defeat for the organisation. Accordingly, the focus of Western scholarly interest is on Hasan al-Banna' and Sayyid Qutb. They were variously described as the leading ideologists of the Muslim Brotherhood who paved the way for radical interpretation and action. Their lives as activists, their propagandistic writings and their association to political violence are used to portray the organisation's political engagement and creed. Less recognised, however, is al-Hudaybi's theological and juridical approach, which takes a firm stance against radical Islamist activism. This creates a gap in scholarly descriptions of the Muslim Brotherhood. The focus on al-Banna' and Qutb cannot explain the ideological foundation of today's official statements against radical thought. Also, the focus cannot explain the objective of today's Brotherhood, to engage in national politics on an institutional level, or its aspirations to gain recognition as a political party.

Hasan al-Hudaybi was nominated as the Brotherhood's second *Murshid* in 1951. He took over an organisation which was in great disarray. The order of dissolution issued in December 1948, the following mass arrests and a number of court cases, one of them over the Brotherhood's involvement in the assassination of Prime Minister al-Nuqrashi, brought the organisation to the brink. Further, the death of Hasan al-Banna' weighed heavily on the organisation. During the period 1949–51, when the survival of the Muslim Brotherhood was at stake, a circle of close associates, to which Salih al-'Ashmawi, 'Abd al-Rahman al-Banna' and Hasan al-Baquri belonged, managed to run the organisation in secrecy. Putting aside their differences for the time being, they set their primary focus on the pending court cases. Only after the juries had delivered their verdicts, which were overall in favour of the Brotherhood, could attention be given to the unresolved issue of nominating a new General Guide. It was the inner circle of leaders, each of them possible contenders for the post, which negotiated on the candidacy. Realising that an election from within their circle could eventually threaten the unity of the Brotherhood, they accepted Munir al-Dilla's proposal to bring in an outsider. Indeed, the approval of this suggestion was the result of a number of calculated considerations regarding the advantages al-Hudaybi would bring. As a high-ranking member of the judiciary he was well connected to the network of influential public personalities and the government. Further, his brother-in-law was the chamberlain of the royal household. With an eye to al-Hudaybi's personal connections, it seemed them that he would be the perfect choice to reconcile the dented public image of the Brotherhood and (re)introduce the organisation to leading circles of national politics. Al-Hudaybi's links to Egyptian society must have been a convenient factor. However, the actual leaders were looking only for a symbolic figurehead, someone who would enable them to pursue their own agendas in future. When al-Hudaybi was nominated, his appointment was a surprise to many members.

The newly elected *Murshid* soon made it clear that he had no intention of downplaying his role. Thus, one of his first steps was to reorganise and reshuffle top administrative positions, which he filled with candidates of his own choice. Although this tactical move reaffirmed the position of the newcomer, it had the disadvantage that al-Hudaybi broke the administrative continuity during precarious period when the Brotherhood was in greatly need of unity. Not surprisingly, he made enemies for himself within the leading circle. Both factors were crucial in the period after the coup d'etat in July 1952.

Relations between the Revolutionary Command Council of the Free Officers, which took power in 1952, and the Muslim Brothers were initially amicable. In fact, a number of Brothers had personal connections to the new leaders which went back to the warfare in Palestine. Hence, at least in the beginning, an atmosphere of broad support prevailed. Al-Hudaybi gave in to this enthusiasm and offered his cooperation. The *Murshid* hoped that the political change would enable the Brotherhood to have a decisive say in the construction of a state system, which would bring the vision of an Islamic order into reality. However, within the following two years the alliance with the RCC gradually deteriorated, while 'Abd al-Nasir progressively strengthened his influence within the circle of leading officers. The major events, which indicated growing differences, were the issue of registration as a political party, the rejected offer of participation on a ministerial level in the new government, and the question of participation in a constitutional council. With the failure to come to an accord on these central points of involvement, the differences between al-Hudaybi and the RCC, and therein particularly 'Abd al-Nasir, became increasingly obvious. Further, these crucial events were also the cause of the dissent breaking out within the Brotherhood. Al-Hudaybi's major internal opponents, Salih al-'Ashmawi and 'Abd al-Rahman al-Sanadi, publicly criticised the *Murshid* for non-democratic decision making. They were not only influential voices with an extended network of relations, but also figureheads in the Secret Unit, which still existed, against the *Murshid*'s wishes. While Salih al-'Ashmawi used his magazine *Majallat al-Da'wa* to influence the opinion of many members against al-Hudaybi's style of leadership, he secretly allied himself with 'Abd al-Nasir. The latter skilfully applied a policy of 'divide and rule'. Internal revolts against al-Hudaybi's authority openly broke out in autumn 1953. Al-Hudaybi managed to regain control over the organisation, and this led to the expulsion of Salih al-'Ashmawi and some fellow members of the Secret Unit. However, the image of a unified Brotherhood was destroyed. Moreover, the evictions of these Brothers who were linked to the Secret Unit could not prevent their continuing ties to the military wing. Further, 'Abd al-Nasir managed to exploit the internal rift to his advantage and pressed the RCC for the dissolution of the Brotherhood. The order was announced in January 1954. Yet, this first attempt to rid himself from the influence of the Muslim Brotherhood and of his most influential opponent within the RCC, namely the president of the Republic, al-Najib, failed because of strong support for the leader of the Revolution Yet, it introduced finale of 'Abd al-Nasir's efforts to gain autocratic power. In April 1954 Naguib resigned. Only a few months later, during the celebration of a treaty with Britain, 'Abd al-Nasir had his closing scene with a staged assassination attempt against him.

The incident which took place on 26 October 1954 in Alexandria marked the beginning of the time of persecution. The Muslim Brotherhood was accused of attempting the assassination in order to overthrow the state system; a number of death sentences were carried out, thousands of Brothers were imprisoned, many of them without charge, and some were able to flee into exile. Indeed, it seemed that the Muslim Brotherhood was defeated. Al-Hudaybi, who was initially among those sentenced to death, was then put under house arrest. Being separated from the rest of the organisation, for a while he almost entered into oblivion. The Brotherhood was able to continue only on the informal level of personal relations. While those Brothers with no or only minor sentences began to be released in the late 1950s, individual members outside the prisons started to engage in a secret re-formation. With al-Hudaybi's knowledge, they met in small circles, apparently to read and learn. The reading materials contained extracts from classical works of Sunni theology and jurisdiction, but also passages of a number of modern works, among them Maududi and Qutb. Sayyid Qutb's Qur'anic commentary *Fi zilal al-Qur'an* and his propagandistic work *Ma'alim fi al-Tariq*, which was specially composed for the circle, were part of the curriculum. Funded by exiled Brothers and like-minded supporters, the clandestine circle had the intention to gradually build up a vanguard, which eventually aimed to target their prime enemy, 'Abd al-Nasir. Yet the group most probably did not have the strength and experience to be an actual threat. In 1965, the group, which was hereafter called 'Organisation 1965', was exposed. A new wave of arrests shocked the Muslim Brotherhood and its members again filled the prison camps. The show trial of Organisation 1965 concluded with a number of death sentences, among them against al-Hudaybi and also Sayyid Qutb, who had only been released the year before. Sayyid Qutb was hanged in August 1966. The *Murshid*'s sentence was commuted to life imprisonment.

With the challenge of the renewed situation of persecution, questions about the means and strategies of opposition were raised. A radical wing which focused on Qutb's conception of modern *jahiliyya* and *jihad* put forward that there is a clear distinction between believers and unbelievers (*kuffar*; sing. *kafir*). The true Muslim is defined through active engagement, which legitimises violent resistance against what is seen as unjust rule. It was in this environment that al-Hudaybi was able to participate in discussions on the theological and juridical foundation of opposition and the strategy of the Muslim Brotherhood. The book *Du'at la Qudat* is evidence of this discourse, as much as it is the foundation for today's movement. The work was not, as generally assumed, written by Hasan al-Hudaybi. It was a joint project, composed by a circle of Brothers close to al-Hudaybi who was worked on the text in conjunction with scholars of al-Azhar. Among those participating in the writing process was Ma'mun al-Hudaybi, but most likely also 'Umar al-Tilmisani and Mustafa Mashhur. Since *Du'at la Qudat* was issued as the official declaration of the Brotherhood led by Hasan al-Hudaybi it is, however, still correct to attribute it to the second *Murshid* of the Brotherhood.

After the death of 'Abd al-Nasir in 1971, al-Hudaybi himself led the Muslim Brotherhood into a new phase of reorganisation. When he died in November 1973, his concept of a conservative yet moderate Islamist movement was carried on by his successors some of whom were certainly engaged in the writing of *Du'at la Qudat*.

It has been variously argued that al-Hudaybi's writing *Du'at la Qudat* responds to concepts put forward by Sayyid Qutb in his final stage of ideological development. Yet the analysis shows that the book does not immediately target Sayyid Qutb. For one, Qutb is not once mentioned in the text. It could be argued that it was a tactical move to deliberately avoid naming him, since he was considered a martyr for the cause of the Brotherhood. But, as the historical context of composition evidences, it is most likely that al-Hudaybi saw it necessary to head a board of editors which wrote *Du'at la Qudat* as a reply to a radical conceptual construct which was developed by a marginal group within the Brotherhood in consequence of a second wave of mass arrests after 1965. It was in this situation that proponents of zealous activism raised their voices against the continuous state persecution. It was also in the environment of discourse among those imprisoned that al-Hudaybi saw it as necessary to provide guidelines which called for political moderation.

The main objective of the text is to refute the collective condemnation of unbelief (*takfir*) as the most striking consequence of the extreme position. However, the issue of *takfir* is not referred to in the text; in fact, the term itself is not once mentioned. Instead of responding explicitly to this particular subject, *Du'at la Qudat* rather looks back at the foundations of Islamic faith. It thus undermines the basis upon which radical concepts are built. Still, sharing the same premise that God is the supreme being who lays down laws through the revelation of the Qur'an, the two interpretations (i.e. the radical and the moderate) pose contrary definitions of basic religious ideas such as belief *(iman)* and disbelief *(kufr)* and subsequently terms such as duty *(fard)*, rule *(hukm)* and Islamic law *(shari'a)*. However, al-Hudaybi has to face the same essential problems of giving meaning to 'belief' as it is in itself a very subjective value presupposition, which seems to be easiest to define in terms of opposition to 'disbelief', and only then from the subjective understanding of one who believes. As a result, he is caught up in the same structural, binary oppositions of belief versus unbelief and in correlating these paradigms to Muslim versus unbeliever (*kafir*).

Although there are theoretical issues regarding the manifestation of belief which are not the subject of the argument of the analysis, it has to be said that, in the way both notions (i.e. belief and unbelief) are presented, al-Hudaybi suggests a greater diversity within the realm of belief. The matter of finding a sound juridical definition for 'belief' is explored throughout *Du'at la Qudat*. For example, al-Hudaybi engages in the issue of whether there are requirements attached to the profession of belief (*shahada*) or whether it is enough to bear witness to Islam verbally. Opting for the second assertion, he clearly responds to the radical attitude that only those who actively engage in the Islamic cause (i.e. in the establishment of an Islamic state) can be called Muslim. Another section engages with a differentiation between unbelief and sin (*'asin*). Therein it is argued that, even though someone may have committed a sin for which Islamic law may require punishment, the person cannot be considered an apostate. The sinner is still a Muslim unless it can be proven otherwise. Bearing these essential distinctions in mind, the argument then moves on to examine the issue of delineating 'unbelief'. Al-Hudaybi reasons that a condemnation can only be justified in an individual instance and, even then, only when there is no doubt about the submitted evidence. Hence, he insinuates that there can be no ultimate proof, since reasoning is exposed to error; the final judgement lies, in conclusion, only in God's hand. Although it may seem that al-Hudaybi speaks only in the framework of theological, abstract theory, his stance has indeed practical and political implications.

The initial definitions are consistently taken up in later stages of the book. Some outstanding sections should be mentioned, namely those where al-Hudaybi pushes the theological distinctions further. Outlining first the principle of Islamic jurisprudence that God only demands obedience to rules to which the person has been introduced *(hukm al-jahil bi-l-awamir wa-l-nawahir)*, he then emphasises this concept, elaborating on possible excuses. In other words, if it is the case that someone is not aware of a law (i.e. is *jahil*), he/she can be forgiven and therefore should be not considered outside the community of believers. Similarly, additional supplementary exemptions have to be addressed, such as cases of unintentional mistakes within juridical exegesis (*khata'*) and instances of confessing apostasy under unsustainable duress (*ikrah*). Through the differentiated mode of scrutinising the foundations of faith, al-Hudaybi thus advocates a defence of Muslims who would, in the eyes of radical proponents, be regarded as apostates. In this respect, chapter seven of his *Du'at la Qudat* is of particular interest. Herein, he juxtaposes his interpretation against arguments which are clearly brought forward by proponents of the radical position.

Arguing within this framework, the book examines the declaration that God is the ultimate law maker. By no means does *Du'at la Qudat* question the idea of God's 'oneness' (*tawhid*) and its inference that he is the originator of just and divine rule. Yet, al-Hudaybi abandons the radical position. He sees this interpretation as an undifferentiated, reductionist understanding of God's authority, which is epitomised in the concept surrounding the phrase '*hakimiyyat Allah*' (absolute sovereignty of God). As a starting point, al-Hudaybi rejects the term itself, arguing that the phrase '*hakimiyyat Allah*' has no reference in the sources of Qur'an and Sunna. But his argument does not stop here. In contention with the view that any kind of human decision making is an illegitimate penetration of divine law, *Du'at la Qudat* propounds greater freedom for individual self-determination under the realm of God's supremacy. Similar to al-Afghani and other modern Islamist interpreters, al-Hudaybi suggests that one has to differentiate between divinely decreed, incontestable acts of worship and variable rules of practice. He argues that rules of the first category, i.e. *'ibadat*, are rendered precise in the Qur'an and Sunna; they are unchangeable, timeless, and hence represent a constant in Islamic law. The indisputable commandments within the realm of the *'ibadat* can subsequently be classified into duties (sing. *fard,* pl. *furud*) and sanctions (sing. *haram,* pl. *hurum*). The second category of rules, which al-Hudaybi calls *mubahat* (permissible actions)*,* comprises changeable laws. These regulations have to be congruent with the Qur'an and Sunna, but rather derive from reasoning. Hence, they are in no way equivalent to divine law. *Mubahat* are subject to possible errors of interpretation; further, they are situated in time and can be reversed. As only a few laws are explicitly defined through divine revelation and can therefore be considered to be incontestable laws (*'ibadat*), there is a large sphere of permissible actions in which humans have authority to make their own decisions. This domain particularly includes civil laws. Human decision making should take place in a consultative council (*shura*).

Al-Hudaybi and other writers support the distinction between fixed and flexible and argue that the division is not in conflict with Islamic law (*shari'a*). Following their position, self-determination (although it is somewhat limited) is actually part of Islamic jurisprudence. Islamic law cannot, then, be understood as a set of canonical, universal rules, but must be understood, to a major extent, as an adaptable system of regulations derived through deductive reasoning. A position which argues against the possibility of human decision making in the name of God is, according to al-Hudaybi, a misinterpretation or even a denial of divine supremacy. Yet al-Hudaybi does not recognise the theoretical implications of accepting individual involvement and reasoning to facilitate the construal of Islamic law. Even though he demonstrates a quite differentiated stance towards the make-up of *shari'a,* he continues to have trust in the possibility of objectivity and truthful extraction of law, which therefore is of divine nature.

Al-Hudaybi's deliberation of God's legislative supremacy surrounds the issue of whether divine rule is recognised only in an Islamic state system. Notwithstanding that the objective is the establishment of governance in which Islamic law is the source of legislation, it is argued in *Du'at la Qudat* that obedience to divine law is independent of its application on a state level. Indeed, God's law must be followed individually. And, even if Islamic law was nominally at the foundation of a state, as it has been in the past, it is no absolute guarantee of a just system. Whereas radical proponents emphasise the correlation of law and politics to the extent of 'sacralising' politics, al-Hudaybi tries to disentangle the two. It is obvious that *Du'at la Qudat* presents an entirely different reading of belief and unbelief. It also expounds a very distinct perception of the aims and objectives of an Islamic movement, which are very well described in the title itself: *Preachers not Judges.*

Notes

Introduction

1 The mentioned authors wrote a number of scholarly works, for example Esposito (1991), Halliday (1995), Burgat (2003) and Krämer (1993).
2 See for example al-Ghazali (1987), Rizq (1977), Ra'if (1986).
3 See for example al-Sisi (1987a), al-Sisi (1987b), al-Sisi (1989); Shadi (1981); 'Abd al-Halim (1979), 'Abd al-Halim (1981), 'Abd al-Halim (1986); 'Abd al-Khaliq (1987).
4 See al-Hudaybi (1977). Although al-Hudaybi appears to be the author, it has to be questioned whether he in fact was.
5 It is part of the aim of this book to analyse the issue of whether *Du'at la Qudat* can, indeed, be considered as an immediate response to Qutb's ideas and, further, whether al-Hudaybi can be considered the author of the writing.
6 Mitchell (1993); Kepel (1985).
7 See 'Abd Rabbah (1987).
8 See Sayyid Ahmad (1977). A summarised biographical outline given in Sayyid Ahmad's book (1977) 49–51, which is also in Rizq (1991).
9 The correct title of the leader of the Society of the Muslim Brotherhood is *al-Murshid al-'amm*.
10 'Abd al-Halim (1979), 'Abd al-Halim (1981), 'Abd al-Halim (1986); 'Abd al-Khaliq (1987); 'Abd al-Majid (1991); Shadi (1981); al-Sisi (1987a), al-Sisi (1987b), al-Sisi (1989); Ra'if (1986); Ramadan (1982).
11 For example, Mitchell and Gordon both use documents and newspaper articles in their work without considering that these sources may reflect a certain point of view, which is in most cases the viewpoint of the then current regime (which I call the official version).

1 The Muslim Brotherhood during the years 1949–73

1 See e.g. the Ikhwan's official website and particularly its history section: (last accessed 7 March 2008) and, in Arabic, www.ikhwanonline.com/Section.asp?ID=111 (last accessed 7 March 2008).
2 Halpern (1965) 49.
3 See for example www.ikhwanonline.com/Article.asp?ArtID=147&SecID=453 (last accessed 8 March 2008).
4 See statements on the Ikhwan's official websites: www.ikhwanonline.com (last accessed 7 March 2008) and www.ikhwanweb.com (last accessed 7 March 2008).
5 See Forstner (1988).
6 For a selection of his speeches see www.ikhwanweb.com/SectionsPage.asp?SectionID=74 (last accessed 7 March 2008).

7 Interview with Mahmud Ezzat, in: www.ikhwanweb.com/Article.asp?ID= 14456&LevelID=1&SectionID=87 (last accessed 7 March 2008).

8 Hasan al-Banna reflects in his memoirs on the establishment of the organisation. See al-Banna' (n.d.) 83–5 and al-Banna (1982) 141–2. This account finds large acceptance, see for example Commins (1994) 125–33, Harris (1964) 143–8, 'Abd al-Halim (1979) 53–70, 183–90 and al-Sisi (1987a) 120. Yet, others raise serious doubt regarding al-Banna's report; see Mitchell (1993)1–8 and Carré (1995) 195. Carré assumes that the organisations developed out of the Hasafiyya order. Indeed al-Banna' had close links to Sufi movements; see al-Banna' (n.d.) 81–2 and al-Banna (1982) 67–109. Similarly, Zahmul maintains that al-Banna' kept up his links until his death; see Zahmul (1985) 5, 8 fn 2. Still, the issue of the Brotherhood's initial affiliation remains unclear when one takes Mitchell's statement into account that the relations to these Sufi orders had a rather informal character; see Mitchell (1993) 214–16.

9 There is much literature about Hasan al-Banna' and the growth of the organisation. For further reading in the English language see Mitchell (1993) 1–34, Lia (1998) and Harris (1964). See further: Heyworth-Dunne (1950) 55–70, Commins (1994) 125–33, Carré (1995) 195–8. For accounts written by Muslim Brothers consult 'Abd al-Halim (1979) 53–70, 1: 183–90 and al-Sisi (1987a) 120. The main source regarding al-Banna's ideas is his speeches collected and published in a single volume. See al-Banna', H. (1990). An additional main source is his memoirs, see al-Banna' (n.d.). There is a translation into English: al-Banna (1982). A further set of sources, which are not yet adequately recognised, are letters by Hasan al-Banna' to his father Ahmad al-Banna'. These were collected and edited by Jamal al-Banna', Hasan al-Banna's brother. See al-Banna', J. (1990).

10 Harris (1964) 159; see also Carré and Michaud (1983) 20–1, Zahmul (1985) 8 and Heyworth-Dunne (1950) 17; also of interest are the statistics presented by Lia (1998) 295.

11 Jansen points out that al-Banna's earliest pamphlets indicate that the initial focus was on educational reform (Jansen (1992) 254–8). In this respect, he followed the footsteps of Islamic reformists such as Muhammad 'Abduh (1849–1905) and Rashid Rida (1865–1935); on the connection, see Mitchell (1993) 5 and 246. Only with the 3rd General Assembly of 1935, during which organisational and administrative structures were implemented, and the 5th General Assembly of 1939, during which al-Banna gave his famous speech on the goals of the organisation, were some constitutional guidelines defined. See al-Banna', H. (1990), but also 'Abd al-Halim (1981) 117–22 and Carré and Michaud (1983) 221–2.

12 On the political struggle see al-Sayyid Marsot (1985) 82–106; Deeb (1979) 123–50,182–92, 357–70, who comments on the other parties; and Goldschmidt (1990) 55–77, Schulze (2000) 169–73. The declaration of the 22 February 1922 is published by Hurewitz (1979) 2: doc. 68.

13 On 22 February 1922, the British government, which was represented by Allenby, ended its mandate over Egypt. However, Britain asserted its interests through the Ango-Egyptian Treaty. The declaration is published in Hurewitz (1979) 2: doc. 68.

14 Goldschmidt (1990) 64–7; al-Sayyid Marsot (1977), al-Sayyid Marsot (1985) 96–9, Deeb (1979) 331–44 and Abdel Nasser (1994) 30–1. The treaty is published in Hurewitz (1979) 2: doc.113.

15 Palestine was part of the Ottoman Empire until 1917, when British troops occupied the territory. For the history of Palestine, the British–Palestinian struggle and the Israeli–Palestinian conflict until the establishment of State of Israel see Nafi (1998). On the strike of the year 1936 see Nafi (1998) 191–310, Gershoni and Jankowski (1995) 167–91, Goldschmidt (1990) 70–1 and Schulze (2000) 97–101.

16 See Gershoni and Jankowski (1995) 167–91, El-Awaisi (1998), Mitchell (1993) 16–17, 55–8 and Carré and Michaud (1983) 31–2. The Muslim Brotherhood called

its members to volunteer in armed struggle for the liberation of Palestine and started to build training camps. Furthermore, financial contributions to the Palestinian cause raised by supporters of the Brotherhood were partly used to develop the administrative structure of the organisation. See Harris (1964) 177–80, Heyworth-Dunne (1950) 22–3, Mitchell (1993) 16, 'Abd al-Halim (1979) 90.

17 Goldschmidt (1990) 72–4, al-Sayyid Marsot (1985) 99–101 and Abdel Nasser (1994) 38–90. Egypt became one of the major battlefields of the Second World War. Although it had no relevance to the outcome of the war and the struggle of dominance in Egypt, some Egyptian officers and politicians, who had anti-British sentiments, established contact with the German Army. Among them was Anwar al-Sadat. See Mitchell (1993) 24–6.

18 See Deep (1979).

19 Regarding the official line of rejection of the party system see, for example, al-Banna's speech entitled *Nizam al-Hukm* (System of Rule) in al-Banna', H. (1990); further, see 'Abd al-Halim (1979) 123–30, Shadi (1981) 20–1 and Commins (1994) 125–53.

20 See Mitchell (1993) 27–8, 33.

21 Lia (1998) 93–128 and Mitchell (1993) 328–31 On the representation of the Muslim Brotherhood among students see Abdalla (1985) 46–9. 'Abd al-Halim points out that al-Banna's course was more successful and hence more attractive to the masses than was the intellectual Salafiyya movement of 'Abduh and Rida; this, because it presented a religious message in a more comprehensive and all-encompassing way. See 'Abd al-Halim (1981) 2: 393–401. However, Ayubi and Kramer point out that the lack of clarity was frequently criticised; see Krämer (1999a) 2: 8 and Ayubi (1991), 134. It can therefore also be argued that the breadth was not only a factor and tactic in attracting the masses (see Ayubi (1991), 134, but eventually also played a part in the spread of internal conflict (see below)).

22 In October 1944 the Wafd government under al-Nahhas was replaced by the Sa'di government of Ahmad Mahir. From then onwards, minority governments ruled the country. Mahir was assassinated in February 1945. See Mitchell (1993) 33.

23 See Mitchell (1993) 30–2, 52–79, 205–8. There are a number of statements of Muslim Brothers regarding the establishment of the Secret Unit; consult, for example, the works of Ramadan (1982), Kamal (1989), Shadi (1981), al-Sisi (1987a), and 'Abd al-Halim (1979).

24 Mitchell (1993) 205–8.

25 About the authoritarian leadership of the Secret Unit see Shadi (1981) 32–4, 115. He particularly criticises Salih al-'Ashmawi's successor al-Sanadi.

26 Mitchell (1993) 55.

27 They also developed a network of personal relations with young officers, which eventually had some importance after the Revolution of 1952.

28 Mitchell (1993) 55–71.

29 For a list of names of those arrested in connection with the jeep case see al-Sisi (1987a) 272–4.

30 The decrees are edited in Shadi (1981) 337–46.

31 'Abd al-Halim (1981) 419–20.

32 Mitchell (1993) 67.

33 Mitchell (1993) 55–8 and Carré and Michaud (1983) 226.

34 Mitchell (1993) 55–8 and Carré and Michaud (1983) 226.

35 See Mitchell (1993) 55–8, Abdelnasser (1994) 39, Shadi (1981) 169–79, 'Abd al-Halim (1979) 258–60, 263–4, 409–34 (on the Secret Unit and their involvement in the Palestine war), al-Sisi (1987a) 195–8, 207–46, 255–7 (on Muslim Brothers fighting in the Palestine war).

36 On al-Sanadi's and al-'Ashmawi's growing influence see Mitchell (1993) 54–5, 58–71 and Carré and Michaud (1983) 226.

37 Shadi (1981) 32–4, 115. See Carré and Michaud (1983), 226.
38 Mitchell (1993) 17–19; further see Heyworth-Dunne (1950) 30; Carré and Michaud (1983) 26–7; Zahmul (1985) 41–3 and Shadi (1981) 2–21, 47.
39 See Mitchell (1993) 52–4.
40 Shadi (1981) 2–21, 47.
41 Carré and Michaud (1983) 26–7.
42 On the imprisonment of leading members see ʿAbd al-Halim (1981) 419–20.
43 Mitchell (1993) 71–84.
44 Indeed, parallels to the persecution between the years 1954–71 could be drawn.
45 See ʿAbd al-Halim (1981) 422–4, Shadi (1981) 79–80, see also the interview with ʿAbd al-Badiʿ Saqr, in: Rizq (1991) 61.
46 Mitchell (1993) 165.
47 Carré (2003)
48 Mitchell (1993) 71–84.
49 Quoted in Mitchell (1993) 76.
50 Quoted in Mitchell (1993) 78.
51 See Mitchell (1993) 85, Husaini (n.y.) 113.
52 There is no proof that the palace was involved in his nomination, yet rumours say that al-Hudaybi's candidacy was put forward by the palace; see e.g. Halpern (1965) 149 and al-ʿAsal (n.y.)13–14 (I wish to thank Jamal al-Bannaʾ for giving me a copy of this unpublished study).
53 See ʿAbd al-Halim (1981) 451–3, Shadi (1981) 82, Husaini (n.y.) 114–15, Mitchell (1993) 84–5; see also interviews with Ahmad Malat, in: Rizq (1991) 77; with ʿAbd al-Badiʿ Saqr, in: Rizq (1991) 62; with Jamal Fauzi, in: Rizq (1991) 54–5; with Salah Shadi, in: Rizq (1991) 47.
54 See Krämer (1999a) 251. According to Shadi, al-Hudaybi refused the proposal at first, stating that his weak health did not allow him to assume the responsibility of the position, see Shadi (1981) 82–3.
55 See Shadi (1981) 80–3.
56 The literary translation of the institution would be 'Foundation Council' (*al-Hayʾat al-Taʾsisiyya*). The term used in the text follows Mitchell (1993) 165 as it describes more precisely the function of the council. On the structure and administration of the Muslim Brotherhood see Mitchell (1993) 162–84, also Carré and Michaud (1983) 24, Zahmul (1985) 162–82 and Lia (1998) 98–112, 161–81.
57 See Mitchell (1993) 87, Rizq (1991) 29–33, Husaini (n.y.) 115.
58 ʿArab al-Suwaliha is a village near the town of Shibin al-Qanatir, north-east of Cairo.
59 Mitchell gives no quotation for this source; see Mitchell (1993) 86.
60 Interestingly, Hasan al-Bannaʾ and Sayyid Qutb also underwent secular education; this piece of information is not merely a fascinating coincidence, but hints at the fact that a large number of those being attracted by the Islamist trend do not have a background in theological training. On the relationship between secular education and Islamist conviction see Gorman (2003) 99; for further reading on the secular training of Dar al-ʿUlum, where al-Bannaʾ and Qutb studied, see Reid (1990) 146–9.
61 Goldschmidt (1990) 50–1.
62 Rizq (1991) 13–14.
63 Mitchell (1993) 86 and Rizq (1991) 13.
64 With regard to his working life see Mitchell (1993) 86, Rizq (1991) 12 and also the interview with Hasan al-Hudaybi's son Ismaʿil al-Hudaybi in: Rizq (1991) 125.
65 Rizq (1991) 13; also see the interview with Ismaʿil al-Hudaybi in: Rizq (1991) 126; and further ʿAbd Rabbih (1987) 12.
66 See Rizq (1991).
67 Al-Hudaybi (1978) 6, 19–20, Rizq (1991) 19–20.
68 Al-Hudaybi (1978) 52–5. This source is also edited in: Rizq (1991) 125–8.

69 Al-Hudaybi (1978) 53; further information is given by Isma'il al-Hudaybi in: Rizq (1991) 125–7. As well as by Jamal Fauzi in: Rizq (1991) 53.

70 Mitchell (1993) 87; Rizq (1991) 21–5; 'Abd Rabbih (1987) 35. Shadi (1981) 82–3 states that al-Baquri and 'Abidin, whom al-Banna delegated to run the affairs of the Brotherhood shortly before his death, knew about the contacts with al-Hudaybi. Yet, a number of interviews substantiate that he was not known at the time to the majority of the Brothers; see e.g. Muhammad Hamid Abu al-Naṣr, in: Rizq (1991) 38; Salah Shadi, in: Rizq (1991) 46, Hamza al-Jami'i, in: Rizq (1991) 84, Ahmad al-Malat, in: Rizq (1991) 85–6 and Ahmad al-'Asal, in: Rizq (1991) 105.

71 Sayyid Ahmad (1977) 12.

72 Ahmad and Husaini give 17 October 1951 as the date of his resignation; see Sayyid Ahmad (1977) 22 and Husaini (n.y.) 115. 'Abd Rabbih mentions that he had already quit in 1950; see 'Abd Rabbih (1987) 13.

73 Mitchell mentions that the position of the vice-leader was introduced after differences appeared between al-Hudaybi and 'Auda. See Mitchell (1993) 87–8. For some biographical notes on 'Abd al-Qadir 'Auda see Krämer (1999a) 255–6. 'Auda was a lawyer, like al-Hudaybi, who became well known in the 1940s for his writings. Humayda was a lawyer as well.

74 See Mitchell (1993) 87, Ramadan (1982) 119. Shadi states that al-Hudaybi intended to reform the unit. The disintegration was, according to him, just a rumour. See Shadi (1981) 99.

75 See 'Abd al-Halim (1986) 189.

76 On the authoritarian leadership of the Secret Unit see Shadi (1981) 85–94.

77 'Abd al-Rahman as-Sanadi was the second leader of the secret apparatus after Salih al-'Ashmawi, who was the deputy of the Brotherhood during Hasan al-Banna's leadership. Al-'Ashmawi lost his position after the appointment of Hasan al-Hudaybi, who invested 'Abd al-Qadir al-'Auda instead. On the internal conflict between al-Hudaybi and the secret apparatus and/or al-Sanadi and al-'Ashmawi see Ramadan (1982) 119; Mitchell (1993) 88, 119–20; see also the interview with 'Abd al-Badi' Saqr, in: Rizq (1991) 63.

78 The meetings took place on 14 November 1951 and 16 January 1952. See Mitchell (1993) 90–2; Ramadan (1982) 93–4. Mitchell states that al-Hudaybi was accompanied by thirteen members of the Brotherhood, among them Salih al-'Ashmawi and Muhammad al-Ghazali.

79 His insistence that he should be consulted in current political and religious affairs is to be seen in accordance with his attitude that the Muslim Brotherhood represents the 'true Islam', which cannot be abolished by any government, e.g. see Al-Hudaybi (1978) 162–71.

80 On the historical background see al-Sayyid Marsot (1985); al-Sayyid Marsot (1977); Goldschmidt (1990) and Hail (1996).

81 On the history of the Sudan question see Hail (1996) 59–77, Goldschmidt (1990) 86–8, Gordon (1992) 26–8. As an example of the *Murshid*'s anti-British statements see Al-Hudaybi (1978) 147–53 and an extract from a speech edited by 'Allam (1996) 87, 89.

82 See Mitchell (1993) 89–90, 92–3. Early commentators on the events as well as the official Egyptian press of these days see the Muslim Brothers as organisers of the great fire; see for example Kaplinsky (1954) 384. There is, however, no conclusive proof that there was an organised involvement.

83 See 'Allam (1996) 89.

84 Brief accounts of the events are to be found in Gordon (1992) 63–78, Goldschmidt (1990) 88–99. For further reading on the Revolution see Beattie (1994), Gordon (1992), Abdel-Malek (1968) and Dekmejian (1971).

85 The letter is edited in Zahmul (1985) 203–16. The announcement is to be found in: Shadi (1981) 347–56. See also Mitchell (1993) 104–5.

86 Only after ʿAbd al-Nasir gained absolute presidential power in November 1954 did the term *inqilab* (revolution) become synonymous for the events of July 1952. See al-Banna' (1988) 66–85. For the constitutional and legal system after the 'revolution' see Fahmi (2002) 44–65.
87 See Gordon (1992) 98. Further, see Mitchell (1993) 106–7.
88 See Mitchell (1993) 55–6, 96–101; Abdelnasser (1994) 38–43; Shadi (1981) 84, 116–20, who describes the relations between the Brotherhood and the officers, and al-Sisi (1987) 76–7.
89 Al-Sadat wrote several accounts, some of them translated into English. Only the first two, published in 1954 and 1956, are of greater importance regarding the events leading to the Revolution. See al-Sadat (1954) and al-Sadat (1956). On the relationship with the Brotherhood see El-Sadat (1978) 22–4 and El-Sadat (1957) 22–31. Apparently, his accounts differ slightly regarding the first encounter with the Brotherhood and especially on the importance of the Brotherhood in preparation for the Revolution. For another account of events, see Mohi El Din (1995) 20–33.
90 See Mitchell (1993) 55–8; Abdelnasser (1994) 39; Shadi (1981) 169–79, 258–60, 263–4, 409–34 on the Secret Unit and their involvement in the Palestine war. See al-Sisi (1987b) 195–8, 207–46, 255–7 on Muslim Brothers fighting in the Palestine war.
91 See Shadi (1981) 169–76.
92 See al-Sisi (1987b) 77 and Mitchell (1993) 96–101.
93 Mitchell (1993) 101–4.
94 See Gordon (1992) 98; Mitchell (1993) 107 and also Shadi (1981) 182, ʿAbd al-Halim (1986) 115–25. See also the articles in *al-Misri* 28 August 1952 and *al-Ahram* 15 January 1954.
95 Different dates are given for the first meeting. Shadi gives 30 July 1952 as a date; see Shadi (1981) 182. ʿAbd al-Halim mentions 28 July 1952 as a date; see ʿAbd al-Halim (1986) 141.
96 About the attitude of Brothers to the new people in charge see ʿAbd al-Halim (1986) 117–30; Shadi (1981) 32, 116–18,169–89, 203–16, 347–56. See Mitchell (1993) 209–94 (for a general introduction) and ʿAbd al-Halim (1986) 73–111, 115–25 (with regard to the historical situation after the Revolution).
97 See Shadi (1981) 190–3. Muhammad Hasan al-ʿAshmawi, who was a supporter of Hasan al-Hudaybi, should not be mistaken with Salih al-ʿAshmawi, his opponent.
98 For an account of his life see al-Bazz's interviews with al-Baquri in: al-Bazz (1977). Hasan al-Baquri was a member of the Guidance Council but seemingly did not attend the meeting nor contact the Brotherhood on the issue of the proposed position – only after he accepted the offer; see al-Bazz (1977) 97.
99 Shadi's account largely correlates with al-Baquri's statements; see al-Bazz (1977) 97–100.
100 Mitchell (1993) 107–8. Mitchell points out that the actual happening escaped precise detection, mentioning in his footnotes another variant of the incident, which is again completely different from those given here.
101 Gordon (1992) 99–100.
102 Ahmad Husni was not a member of the Muslim Brotherhood, merely a close associate.
103 See al-Sisi (1987b) 157–8.
104 Mitchell (1993) 17–18.
105 Mitchell (1993) 109–12 and Gordon (1992) 100. See also Shadi (1981) 198–9 and ʿAbu al-Nasr (1987) 73–5.
106 Mitchell (1993) 109–12. Gordon mentions that during the session of the Consultative Assembly a group calling themselves the Free Brothers appeared. They voted for registration as a party and, additionally, demanded al-Hudaybi's resignation, proposing new by-laws – which sets a time limit of three years to the position of the *Murshid*. See Gordon (1992) 100.

107 Mitchell (1993) 110.
108 Gordon (1992) 100.
109 Shadi (1981) 191–2 and ʿAbu al-Nasr (1987) 73–5.
110 See al-Sisi (1987b) 91.
111 Mitchell (1993) 108–9, on the mistrust and antipathy between al-Hudaybi and ʿAbd al-Nasir.
112 See the official statement dated 28 July 1952, in: Zahmul (1985) 203–16; and the statements dated 1 August 1952, in: Shadi (1981) 347–56; also edited in ʿAbd al-Halim (1986) 117–30. On the context of the proposed reform see ʿAbd al-Halim (1986) 85–7, 101–11, al-Sisi (1987b) 89–90; see also Mitchell (1993) 109, 260–3.
113 See Zahmul (1985) 42–159, 209–211; Mitchell (1993) 109. The text is published in Zahmul (1985) appendices 1–37.
114 Mitchell (1993) 109 and Gordon (1992) 101.
115 Gordon (1992) 101.
116 Mitchell (1993) 109. Salih al-ʿAshmawi was the editor of the Muslim Brotherhood's magazine *Majallat al-Daʿwa*, Hasan al-Banna's deputy and predecessor of al-Sanadi in his position as leader of the Secret Unit. ʿAbd al-Qadir ʿAuda, like al-Hudaybi a former judge, was invested by the latter with the position of vice-leader of the Society, but soon got into dispute with the *Murshid* on the issue of cooperation with the regime and issues of power sharing and decision making within the Brotherhood.
117 See for an excerpt of the meeting ʿAllam (1996) 90–3; further see the minutes and memoranda of conversation of the British Embassy, published by ʿAllam (1996) 554–5, 564–6; see also Mitchell (1993) 113–14,139 and al-Sisi (1987b) 89–91. The fact that al-Hudaybi met with representatives of the British Embassy was later used against the *Murshid*, during the court cases of November and December 1954.
118 al-Sisi (1987b) 89–91.
119 Mitchell (1993) 113. This reproach apparently came up in the order of dissolution of 13 January 1954. See appendix 3 in: Shadi (1981) 61–362. During the court case of 1954 against al-Hudaybi the same accusation was used to show his duplicity. See *al-Jumhuriyya* 15 January 1954, 28 August 1954 and 16 September 1954.
120 For historical accounts of the struggle see Gordon (1992) 63–78; Goldschmidt (1990) 88–99; Mitchell (1993) 109–10. For the Muslim Brotherhoods' perspective, see al-Sisi (1987b) 94–6.
121 Gordon (1992) 102 and Mitchell (1993) 109.
122 See al-Sisi (1987b) 135; Shadi (1981) 211–13, 173–6 and the interview with ʿUmar at-Tilmisani, quoted in: Gordon (1992) 102–3.
123 Mitchell (1993) 116–25 and Gordon (1992) 103.
124 ʿAbd al-Halim (1986) 201–2.
125 *Majallat al-Daʿwa* was published from 1951 to 1956. It was owned by Salih al-ʿAshmawi and was the semi-official magazine of the Brotherhood until his expulsion from the Society in December 1953.
126 Mitchell (1993) 116–25 and ʿAbd al-Halim (1986) 173–8.
127 Mitchell (1993) 120 and ʿAbd al-Halim (1986) 189–92, who defends al-Hudaybi's position.
128 Mitchell (1993) 120–5. Even before, al-ʿAshmawi pledged for a time limit on the office in several articles.
129 Mitchell (1993) 121 and Gordon (1992) 103.
130 Mitchell (1993) 121–2; Shadi (1981) 101–4; Zahmul (1985) 257–9; al-Sisi (1987b) 138–40. ʿAbd al-Halim states that there was no political disagreement between as-Sanadi and al-Hudaybi. According to him, personal dislike was the reason for al-Hudaybi's decision. Personal aversion may have played its part, but it was certainly not the motivating factor. ʿAbd al-Halim (1986) 203–8.
131 ʿAbd al-Halim (1986) 205–8 and Shadi (1981) 106–7.

132 Mitchell (1993) 122–3 and ʿAbd al-Halim (1986) 211–21.

133 Mitchell (1993) 124; Shadi (1981) 105–7; Zahmul (1985) 257–9. The application for the expulsion and the decision are edited by al-Sisi and ʿAbd al-Halim. See al-Sisi (1987b) 144–9; ʿAbd al-Halim (1986) 223–5, 229–37. On al-Ghazali's career during ʿAbd al-Nasir's rule, see Abu Rabiʿ (2004) 223–55.

134 It would be interesting to make further studies on whether these splinter groups reappear later in prison. The work would have to include a study of the membership of the Brotherhood and the personal network within. Considering that the Muslim Brotherhood did not keep an official list of members, also that many of the active Brothers are of an advanced age or even dead and, lastly, that it might be difficult to get information on members because of their fear of being exposed, it seems to be almost impossible to get a clear picture. Another possibility for approaching this question of internal splinter groups before the time of persecution would be to study files of the Egyptian secret service, which, as a source of information are certainly biased.

135 Mitchell (1993) 126; Shadi (1981) 367–8; Zahmul (1985) 221–9 and ʿAbd al-Halim (1986) 259–86. The order of dissolution is edited by Shadi (1981) 357–66.

136 Al-Hudaybi was charged of being the leader of an illegal, militant organisation.

137 Mitchell (1993) 127.

138 Al-Hudaybi (1978) 164–6.

139 Mitchell (1993) 144–7, 159–60; al-Sisi (1987b) 188–9; Zahmul (1985) 246–51 and ʿAbd al-Halim (1986) 277–315. The reasons for the power struggle between them focused on different opinions within the Revolutionary Command Council on the future political system. The clash was then triggered by the attempt to dismiss Naguib from his positions. Mass demonstrations in support of the president followed and Naguib was able to restore his power, which led to the re-enacting of political parties and political freedom.

140 See *The Times*, 1 March 1954, 7 March 1954 and 9 March 1954.

141 Mitchell (1993) 144–7.

142 For more detail see Mitchell (1993) 148–9.

143 See *The Times*, 28 March 1954 and 18 April 1954.

144 The statement is dated 4 May 1953. See al-Sisi (1987b) 178–82, Shadi (1981) 369–71 and ʿAbd al-Halim (1986) 308–10.

145 The press, which regained relative freedom from censorship at the beginning of March with the restoration of al-Najib's power (see *The Times*, 5 March 1954), was purged a month later (see *The Times*, 6 April 1954) and brought under government control.

146 Mitchell (1993) 135, ʿAbd al-Halim (1986) 317, see also *al-Jumhuriyya*, 17 November 1954. He visited Saudi Arabia, Palestine, Jordan, Syria and Lebanon.

147 Mitchell (1993) 135.

148 See *The Times*, 27 July 1954 and 28 July 1954. Parts of the agreement, which was then signed on 19 October 1954, were published in *The Times*, 19 October 1954 and *al-Jumhuriyya*, 19 October 1954. See also Gordon (1992) 168–74 on the Anglo-Egyptian negotiations.

149 Parts of the article are published in ʿAbd al-Halim (1986) 318.

150 The text of the statement is published in: ʿAbd al-Halim (1986) 322–9 and Zahmul (1985) 239–45. See also Mitchell (1993) 136.

151 The speech is published by Shadi (1981) 382–4. See also Mitchell (1993) 137–8.

152 al-Sisi (1987b) 259–61; Shadi (1981) 269–70, 382; al-Sisi (1989) 31.

153 See Ramadan (1982) 208–16.

154 See *The Times*, 19 October 1954 and *al-Jumhuriyya*, 19 October 1954.

155 On the attempt on ʿAbd al-Nasir's life, see Mitchell (1993) 148–51; Carré and Michaud (1983) 59–63, 399–405; Rizq (1977) 20–8; Zahmul (1985) 261–7; Ramadan (1982) 239–4.

156 See ʿAbd al-Khaliq (1987) 105–6; Zahmul (1985) 267–74; and Ramadan (1982) 239–309. See also Mitchell (1993) 154–60.

157 See *The Times*, 14 November 1954 and *al-Jumhuriyya*, 14 November 1954.
158 As an example of the view of a Muslim Brother, see ʿAbd al-Halim (1986) 399–400 and ʿAbd al-Khaliq (1987) 105–7. The reproach that the attempt on ʿAbd al-Nasir's life was staged was not only put forward by Muslim Brothers: see also the studies of Carré and Michaud (1983) 59–63. Al-Hudaybi, for example, was taken into custody only three days after the incident on 29 October 1954, although he was hiding in Alexandria. See al-Sisi (1989) 31.
159 See al-Bayyumi (1987) 64–5.
160 See Mitchell (1993) 148–51.
161 See also some interrogations of Mahmud ʿAbd Latif (the alleged perpetrator), Hasan al-Hudaybi, ʿAbd al-Qadir ʿAuda (the deputy of the Brotherhood), Yusuf Talʿat (the Head of the Secret Unit after al-Sanadi's expulsion), Hindawi Duwayr (Head of the Imbaba section of the Secret Unit) and Ibrahim al-Tayyib (head of the Cairo section of the Secret Unit). All of them were sentenced to death in the main court case against the Brotherhood accusing them of planning the assassination attempt. For statements of the court case in extracts, see Kamal (1989) 417–22; Ramadan (1982) 239–309; and al-Sisi (1989) 71–6, 79–80, 83–5.
162 See ʿAbd al-Halim (1986) 399–405; Zahmul (1985) 261–7; Rizq (1977) 20–8 as examples of the view of Muslim Brothers.
163 Carré and Michaud (1983) 59–63.
164 Kamal (1989) 417–22; Ramadan (1982) 239–309, 307. See also Mitchell (1993) 154–60 and Zahmul (1985) 267–4.
165 The numbers are just approximations, as the different sources give different numbers. See Davis (1984) 134–57; Mitchell (1993) 160–2 and Carré and Michaud (1983) 68.
166 Davis (1984) 142–3; Kogelmann (1991) 46 and Carré and Michaud (1983) 68.
167 ʿAbd al-Khaliq (1987) 109; Kamal (1989) 387–92 and Kepel (1985) 28.
168 Al-ʿAshmawi (n.y.) passim.
169 al-Ghazali (1987) 28–30.
170 It is almost impossible for an outsider to pinpoint mosques which were/are commonly frequented by Brothers. However, there were/are certain areas of residence which can be considered to be strongholds of the organisation. A sociological study by a Muslim Brother written in 1954 can give a clue to the question of which mosques were gathering centres. See Zaki (1954) 112–15. In contrast to voluntary institutions of the Brotherhood, which had to be closed after the order of dissolution, the mosques were privately owned and therefore not under governmental control. Of course, ʿAbd al-Nasir tried to get mosques (most of them were run privately) under his control or instrument them for the Revolution's own aim. See Crecelius (1989) 304–15. Connected with this issue is the status of al-Azhar, which ʿAbd al-Nasir also tried to bring under state supervision.
171 There are a number of personal accounts by members of the Brotherhood writing about their experiences during the time of persecution. The most famous accounts of the life in prison are al-Ghazali (1987) and Rizq (1977). Additionally, see also the above-mentioned memoirs of ʿAbd al-Halim (1979, 1981, 1986); al-Sisi (1987a, 1987b, 1989), Kamal (1989); Ramadan (1982) and ʿAbd al-Majid (1991). As examples of introductory secondary literature are to be noted Kepel (1985); Choueiri (1990); and Sivan (1990); on the development of ideas see Gomaa (1983) 143–58. See also the below-mentioned literature on Sayyid Qutb.
172 Sivan points out that only a few inmates were apprised of Qutb's ideas at this stage. See Sivan (1990) 26. The first volume of the commentary was published in 1952, then completed and revised in prison. The eight-volume work is the basis for his most influential writing, "Maʾalim fi al-Tariq" (Signposts), which Qutb revised and completed in prison. Parts of both scripts were distributed from the early 1960s onwards.
173 ʿAbd al-Khaliq (1987) 109; Ramadan (1982) 313–14; and al-Ghazali (1987) 28.

174 Kepel (1985) 46 and Sivan (1990) 108.
175 In the years 1956–58, Egypt underwent a major political and ideological change: the Suez crisis, the shift of alignment and closer relationships with the Eastern bloc, union with Syria, and pan-Arabism are aspects of this change which cannot be further discussed in this book. Therefore, see al-Sayyid Marsot (1985) 110–17; Goldschmidt (1990) 100–13; and Gordon (1992) 189, 196–8.
176 ʿAbd al-Majid (1991) 45–7; Raʾif (1986) 236; al-Ghazali (1987) 32–3, 36–8; and Kepel (1985) 29–30.
177 See al-Ghazali (1987) 35–6; also Raʾif (1986) 238–9. This statement tallies with al-Hudaybi's testimony during the court case of July 1966. See ʿAllam (1996) 131.
178 ʿAbd al-Majid (1991) 59–60.
179 Raʾif (1986) 238–9. Raʾif's statement tallies with al-Hudaybi's testimony during the court case of July 1966. See ʿAllam (1996) 131.
180 ʿAbd al-Majid (1991) 51–2, 55.
181 Raʾif (1986) 236.
182 ʿAbd al-Majid (1991) 49–50.
183 Kepel (1985) 26–67 and Sivan (1990) 40–3, 83–129.
184 See al-Ghazali (1987) 32–4; also ʿAbd al-Majid (1991) 59–60 and Raʾif (1986) 237. Although al-Ghazali played an important role, it seems that she sometimes exaggerates. Her story needs to be taken with caution. For a critical analysis of al-Ghazali's biography see Cooke (1994) 1–19. See also ʿAllam (1996) 193–203. It has to be noted, though, that Fuʾad ʿAlam was an officer working for the secret service.
185 al-Ghazali (1987) 28–9.
186 al-Ghazali (1987) 28–30 and Kepel (1985) 29–30.
187 Qutb (n.y.); ʿAbd al-Khaliq (1987); and Ramadan (1982).
188 ʿAbd al-Khaliq (1987) 109–12 and Ramadan (1982) 313–14. For the implications of *takfir* see Karawan (1995) 178–9.
189 A list 43 members of the Organisation in s1965 gives an idea of the age of members: 27 members were 20–30 years of age, 7 were 30–40 years old, 6 were older that 41 years, none was under 20 years of age and for 3 members no age is given. It is also interesting to note that most of those named in the list had a higher education, being engineers, teachers and students of professions. The list is edited in ʿAbd al-Majid (1991)175–80.
190 See al-Ghazali (1987) 32–3.
191 See ʿAbd al-Majid (1991) 76–7.
192 See al-Ghazali (1987) 36–8.
193 See al-Ghazali (1987) 36–8; ʿAbd al-Majid (1991) 69–73.
194 See Diyab (1987) 104–5; Kepel (1985) 30. See also ʿAbd al-Majid (1991) 69–71.
195 See ʿAbd al-Majid (1991) 69–73.
196 See Raʾif (1986) 241–2 and Ramadan (1982) 318–19.
197 See Kepel (1985) 28; Moussalli (1992) 38; and ʿAbd al-Khaliq (1987) 107.
198 See Raʾif (1986) 241–2, 253.
199 See Ramadan (1982) 319.
200 See Diyab (1987) 104–5; Moussalli (1992) 36 and Abdelnasser (1994) 57–8 state that Qutb was released on the intervention of the Iraqi president, ʿAbd al-Salim ʿArif.
201 There are a variety of critical studies of Sayyid Qutb. Most of the biographical literature of Arab scholars gives an insight on his work as novelist, literature critic, journalist etc.; e.g. see Diyab (1987); al-Khabbas (1983); Hamuda (1996); Hanafi (1989) 167–300. Most of the biographical accounts in English or French stress the ideological aspect of Qutb's later work, see e.g. Moussalli (1992); Abu Rabiʿ (1996); Carré (2003); Binder (1988) 170–205; Tripp (1994) 154–83 and Haddad (1983).
202 See ʿAbd al-Halim (1986) 399–405; Zahmul (1985) 261–7, 24–6; further see Kepel (1985) 34.

203 See Moussalli (1992) 36, 172–75, 193; and Abdelnasser (1994) 172–8.
204 See Moussalli (1992) 36.
205 For a historical survey on the relations between the UDSSR and Egypt see Goldschmidt
     (1990) 103–35. On the Brotherhood's anticommunist attitude see Abdelnasser (1994)
     221–5, 172–8; and Moussalli (1992) 172–4, 193 on Qutb's anticommunist perceptions.
206 For details on verdicts see ʿAbd al-Majid (1991) 193–8.
207 See Ra'if (1986) 400–6.
208 E.g. Sayyid Qutb is listed in the Muslim Brotherhood's website as one of the major
     thinkers of the organisation. As mentioned before, it would be inadequate to reduce
     Sayyid Qutb's work to his radical proposal of the later years, even though they had
     a major impact on the development of radical thought. Some authors go so far as to
     explain away Sayyid Qutb's radical approach as being a result of his time of imprison-
     ment; see e.g. Hanafi, (1989) 167–300 from the point of view of a left-wing, Islamic
     philosopher. Further, others defend Sayyid Qutb's arguments, saying that his concept
     has been misinterpreted. One of the best-known defences was put forward by his
     brother, Muhammad ʿAli Qutb; see Qutb, M. (1974).
209 See ʿAbd al-Majid (1991) 251–69.
210 See ʿAbd al-Majid (1991) 254–69.
211 See Ra'if (1986) 500–6 and ʿAllam (1996) 219–27.
212 See al-Hudaybi (1977) 183–7 and also *Sabʿa Rasaʾil min Sijn al-Turra* (Seven Letters
     from the Prison al-Turra), in: Al-Hudaybi (1978) 209–38.
213 See Ra'if (1986) 353–6.
214 See Ra'if (1986) 400–6; further, see Kepel (1985) 17–19, 47–8, 108–9, 131–5.
215 See e.g. Ra'if (1986) 409–37 and ʿAbd al-Majid (1991) 220–2. On Mustafa Shukri see
     Moussalli (1999a) 216–17 and Kogelmann (1991) 118–38.
216 On Mustafa Shukri see Moussalli (1999a) 216–17 and Kogelmann (1991) 118–38.
217 See Qutb (1993a) 2, 14–17, 86–7.
218 See ʿAbd al-Majid (1991) 220.
219 Refer to Chapter 3.1 for details on the composition of the text.
220 On the reform of al-Azhar and the implications of the Azhar law of 1961 see Skovgaard-
     Petersen (1997) 182–98.
221 See Wickham (2002) 21–35.
222 See Abu Rabiʿ (2004) 43–92; and the accounts of Tariq al-Bishri, Rashid al-Ghannoushi
     and Adel Hussain in Burgat (2003) 26–42. See also Wickham (2002) 21–35.
223 For al-Sadat's politics see Baker (1990); Beattie (2000).
224 Regarding his policy towards the Brotherhood see Kogelmann (1991) 99–107, Abdel-
     nasser (1994) 62, Forstner (1988) 386–422.
225 Kogelmann (1991) 100.
226 Krämer (1999a) 2: 20.
227 Wickham (2002); Clarke (2004); Hafez and Wiktorowicz (2004).
228 See for the impact a declaration issued on 30 April 1995 by the Muslim Brother-
     hood. The declaration was available (but no longer) on www.ummah.org.uk/ikhwan/
     questions.html (last accessed 26 March 2005). Especially on the subject of non-
     violent political opposition, see al-Tilmisani, in: *al-Wafd* 5 July1984 and *Ruz al-Yusuf*
     14 May 1984.
229 Leiken and Brooke (2007) 107–21.
230 See al-Ikhwan al-Muslimun "al-Mustashar Hasan al-Hudaybi", in www.ikhwanon
     line.com/Article.asp?ArtID=147&SecID=453 (last accessed 7 March 2008).

2   The discourse of the prison years: radical ideas and moderate responses

  1 Diyab (1987); al-Khabbas (1983); Hanafi (1989) 167–300; Carré (2003); and Abu
     Rabiʿ (1996).

2 This stance towards Qutb's concepts is particularly present among some supporters of political Islam, who see his ideas as an example of an Islamic liberation theology. Yet, this positive, non-scholarly interest in his ideology is not easy to evidence. However, the internet gives an impression of Sayyid Qutb's continuous influence on current Islamic interpretation. See e.g. www.muslimedia.com/archives/features99/qutb.htm (last accessed 17 February 2008).

3 Haddad (1983) 67–98; Kepel (1985) 26–69; Moussalli (1992); Tripp (1994) 154–83; and Khatab (2006).

4 On the impact of Qutb's writing on the development of radical groups see the above-listed works and further consult Hanafi (1989) 167–300; Sivan (1990) 83–94, 117–29; Roy (1994) 35–42; and Kogelmann (1991) 118–38.

5 Within the framework of this study a comprehensive biography cannot be given; for a detailed description consult Diyab (1987) 280–3, 80–107; al-Khabbas (1983) 77–109; Tripp (1994) 155–65; Moussalli (1992)19–38.

6 Dar al-'Ulum is a secular institute for higher education which offers a teachers' training programme. In Qutb's time, Rashid Rida ran the school. The latter had considerable impact on the Islamic reform movement through his writings. Further, it should be mentioned that Hasan al-Banna', the founder of the Muslim Brotherhood, used to be a student at the very same institute during these days. Although is a remarkable incident, there is no evidence that Qutb and al-Banna' knew each other then.

7 Abu Rabi' argues that Qutb's work is focused on the following subjects, which coincide with stages of his ideological development: 1. Poems and literature; 2. Qur'anic aesthetics; 3. Philosophy of social justice; 4. Sociology of religion; 5. Qur'anic exegesis; 6. Islam and the West; see Abu Rabi' (1996). Quite similar is Hasan Hanafi's periodisation: 1. A literary period from 1930 to 1950; 2. A social period from 1951 to 1954; 3. A philosophical period from 1954 to 1962; 4. A political period from 1962 to 1966. See Hanafi (1989) 167–300, esp. 169–71. Moussalli (1992) 44 counts two major phases and Haddad (1983) 67–98 describes three stages.

8 Abu Rabi' (1996); Diyab (1987) 92–3.

9 Qutb (1949). On the continuous revision of the text see Shepard (1989) 31–50.

10 Qutb wrote an account of his experiences titled *Amirika allati ra'aytu* (America, which I visited). The writing was first published in 1951 as a series in the magazine *Majalla al-Risala*. Later, the series came out as a book. It should be noted that Qutb conceptualised his anti-American attitude in later works with a rejection of capitalism. His *Milestones* serves as an example; Qutb (1993a) 81–4.

11 See al-Khabbas (1983) 105; Diyab (1987) 83, 226; Tripp (1994) 159.

12 See Moussalli (1992) 31. Apparently, his appointment to the Guidance Council was against the Brotherhood's constitution. According to Mitchell, members of the Guidance Council had to be previously members of the Consultative Assembly for more than three years. See Mitchell (1993) 166. Yet, Mitchell does not mention that Qutb was a member of the Guidance Council after all; see Mitchell (1993) 141.

13 Diyab (1987) 101; al-Khabbas (1983) 105, 210–13. The magazine was only published between May and October 1954, see Mitchell (1993) 141, 187.

14 Diyab (1987) 100–1; al-Khabbas (1983) 107–8; Moussalli (1992)32–3; Haddad (1983) 73; and Gordon (1992) 99.

15 Diyab (1987) 100–1; al-Khabbas (1983) 107–8; Moussalli (1992) 32–3; Haddad (1983) 73; Gordon (1992) 99.

16 Diyab (1987) 102; Moussalli (1992) 34; Tripp (1994) 160; al-Khabbas (1983) 108 (the latter mentions 13 years).

17 See Qutb (1978); the two volumes are also available in translation; see Qutb (1991); further, compare the texts of Qutb (1949) (1st edition) and Qutb, S. (1974) (an edition of the revised text). See also Shepard (1989) on the different versions of Qutb's *Social Justice*. Further, Qutb revised previously published books such as *Hadha al-Din*

(This Religion), *al-Mustaqbal li-Hadha al-Din* (The Future is for this Religion) and *Nahwa Mujtama' Islami;* see Moussalli (1992) 46–55 for a list of Qutb's later works and descriptions of their content.

18 See Qutb (1979). It has to be noted that Qutb had already finished parts of his commentary before his imprisonment and engaged then in a revision, which also has the mark of a radicalisation of his ideas. His *Milestones* is based on extracts of the commentary; see Qutb (1993a).

19 See Moussalli (1992) 36–8.

20 See Haddad (1983) 67–98; Tripp (1994) 154–83; Kepel (1985) 26–69 and Hanafi (1989) 167–300.

21 Hanafi describes the last stage of Qutb's life in terms of a psychological struggle; see Hanafi (1989) 167–300. On the experience of isolation see also Ra'if (1986) 329–30.

22 See the anthologies of Kurzman (1998), Kurzman (2002) and Donohue and Esposito (1982) to gain an impression of the discourse.

23 For an impression regarding the growing interest in religion see Gershoni and Jankowski (1995) 54–78 and the anthropological study on Islamic preaching in contemporary Egypt by Gaffney (1994).

24 See Gomaa (1983) 143–58.

25 Gomaa (1983) 143–58. Of particular interest is al-Banna's speech at the 5th General Assembly, where he described the aims and structure of the organisation; see al-Banna', H. (1990) 167–208 and Mitchell (1993) 18–19, 163–208.

26 See Gomaa (1983) 143–58.

27 See Hanafi (1989) 123–65; 'Ammara (1987) 181–221 and 'Ammara (1985) 147–54; Diyab (1987) 127–30; Binder (1988) 174–85; Kepel (1985) 47–51.

28 On al-Maududi's life and the organisation, which was the major platform for the distribution of his ideas until his death in 1972, see Seyyid Vali (1996), Seyyid Vali (1994b) and Seyyid Vali (1994a) 98–124, Adams (1969) and Adams (1983) 99–133, furthermore Ahmad and Ansari (1979) 359–81.

29 See Ahmad and Ansari (1979) 3–14 present a list of al-Maududi's works and their translations. The list contains a number of works which were available in Arabic during the 1950s. Further, see Seyyid Vali (1994b) 78–80.

30 Schulze (1990) 200–1; Seyyid Vali (1996) 40, 115; Hartung (2004) passim. In 1962, al-Nadwi was one of the founding members of the Islamic World League.

31 First published in 1949, the book is still popular and reached its eighth edition in 1989. It is translated into English under the title *Islam and the World* (Nadvi (1981)).

32 The introduction is reprinted in the later editions; see al-Nadwi (1980) 12–17.

33 See the collection of articles dating from this period titled *Dirasat Islamiyya*. Qutb (1992) esp. 62–75. Further see Shepard (1989) 31–50.

34 Qutb himself mentions the relationship between both works; see Qutb (1993a) 10. For example, the entire chapter "Tabi'a al-Minhaj al-Qur'an" is taken from the commentary on Sura al-In'am (6), see Qutb (1979) 7: 1004–15.

35 An indication for this thesis is Zainab al-Ghazali's description of the gathering of small circles of interested Brothers. See al-Ghazali (1987) 40–1.

36 For an analysis and translation of *al-Farida al-Gha'iba* see Jansen (1986); see also Cook (2004) 106–10.

37 See Abou El Fadl's analysis of the classical interpretation on the *ahkam al-baghy* (laws of rebellion) and on *ahkam al-hiraba* (laws of warfare); Abou El Fadl (2001). There are a number of useful works on the classical concept of *jihad*, for example, Firestone (1999) and Peters (2005).

38 Ibn Taymiyya's Kitab al-Iman is an often-quoted source; see Ibn Taymiyya (1997) 191–211. See also Peters (2005) 53–5, 64–5 and Saeed and Saeed (2004) 36–7, 56–68

39 The phrase is part of Qur'an 5: 44–7 and Qur'an 4: 65.

40 See *Djahiliyya* on CD-ROM of *Encyclopedia of Islam*.

41 See Haddad (1983) 67–98.
42 Qutb (1993b) 66–8.
43 See Qutb (1993b) 53–7.
44 For further reading on Qutb's interpretation of *jihad* see Cook (2005) 102–6.
45 See further Qutb (1993b) 53–7, where he elaborates on the idea of stages for *jihad* and links the concept to the development of the Muslim community in Mecca and Medina.
46 47 See Qutb (1993b) 50–1.
48 49 See Diyab (1987) 180–6.
50 See Ibrahim (1980) 423–53; and Jansen (1997) 75–9; See further Mahfuz (1988) 98–128 for an 'insider' description of Shukri Mustafa's ideology.
51 Jansen (1997) passim; Ibrahim (1980) 423–53; Cook (2005) 106–10; Rubin (1990) 63–78.
52 See 'Abd al-Rahman (n.y.), which is also available in translation Abdurrahman (1990).
53 OEMIW under Jihad Organisation, Strategy Report
54 One needs to be careful not to confuse the mentioned *al-Jama'a al-Islamiyya* (Islamic Group) with the generic term 'al-Jama'at al-Islamiyya' (Islamic Groups); the latter describes a loose framework of Islamist groups which first appeared in the early 1970s, particularly on university campuses.
55 For a summary on the evolution of political violence in Egypt in the 1980s and 1990s and its impact on global jihad, see Hafez and Wiktorowicz (2004) 61–88 and Kepel (2004). For an anthology of writings on jihad, including proponents of radical and global jihad see Bonney (2004). The writings and statements of Ayman al-Zawahiri have been translated by Mansfield (2006).
56 Oliver Roy exemplifies this position in his work *Globalized Islam* (Roy (2004)). The assumption that there is no factual distinction between moderate and radical Islamists seems to be particularly dominant among political and social scientists, but is also the underlying conjecture of conservative scholars of Islam. It includes well-known scholars such as Halliday (2005), Kepel (2004) and Lewis (2003).
57 See Saeed and Saeed (2004). Since the early 2000s, a legal loophole has allowed the accusation to be brought before the Egyptian family courts; for further information see Berger (2003).

3 *Preachers not Judges*

1 An exception is the reference to the Pakistani writer al-Maududi, who is quoted three times. However, it is misleading to assume that *Du'at la Qudat* is simply a refutation of the latter's work. The extracts quoted in *Du'at la Qudat* are taken from al-Maududi's book *al-Mustalahat al-Arba' fi al-Qur'an*; see al-Hudaybi (1977)16–18, 25 and al-Maududi (1993) 8–11, 72.
2 al-Hudaybi (1977).
3 As pointed out, *Du'at la Qudat* was most probably a joint effort of members close to Hasan al-Hudaybi. Still, it can be considered an official statement of the *Murshid* as it was compiled under his supervision and distributed in his name. Therefore, I will continue to refer to al-Hudaybi as the writer, or rather the editor, of the book.
4 al-Hudaybi (1977) 170.
5 See Kepel (1985) 61–3; Sivan (1990) 108–10; Krämer (1994) 183–91 and Gomaa (1983) 143–58.
6 Krämer (1994) 184.
7 'Allam (1996) 219–27.
8 'Abd al-Majid (1991) 252–4.
9 Interview with 'Abd al-Khaliq, 30 April 1998; interview with Gamal al-Banna, 3 May 1998 (recorded by the author with permission to use the information).

10 al-Hudaybi (1977) 183–7. See also *Sab'a Rasa'il min Sijn al-Turra* (Seven Letters from the Prison al-Turra), in: al-Hudaybi (1978) 209–38.
11 For example see al-Hudaybi (1977) 74, 75, 76.
12 Most famous are the Public Letters of the founder of the Muslim Brotherhood, Hasan al-Banna'. These were initially speeches the latter held, which were then compiled and edited as a book. See al-Banna', H. (1990).
13 See al-Hudaybi (1978).
14 al-Hudaybi (1977) 7–10.
15 Ra'if (1986) 500–6 and 'Allam (1996) 219–27.
16 On the literary genre, see Hafez, "Torture, Imprisonment, and Political Assassination in the Arab Novel", in www.aljadid.com/TortureImprisonmentandPoliticalAssassination.html (last accessed 15 February 2007). See also Kupferschmidt, "Literacy, Illiteracy and Censorship in the tradition of the Muslim Brotherhood, in: http://pages perso-orange.fr/colloque.imprimes.mo/pdf/UKT0.pdf (last accessed 7 March 2008).
17 al-'Allam (1996) 193–203.
18 'Abd al-Majid (1991) 259–69.
19 Ra'if (1986) 586–8.
20 'Umar al-Tilmisani, *Dhikriyat la Mudhakkirat* (Cairo: al-Islamiyya, 1985), 123.
21 Interview with Jamal al-Banna', 28 April 1998; interview with 'Abd al-Khaliq, 30 April 1998, (recorded by the author with permission to use the information).
22 For information on some of the scholars mentioned above see Skovgaard-Petersen (1997) 193–6 and 'The Grand Imams of al-Azhar', in: www.sunnah.org/history/Scholars/mashaykh_azhar.htm (last accessed 7 March 2008).
23 At this stage of the research, these names are only based on informed conjectures, but cannot be verified.
24 See interview with Mahmud Ezzat, in www.ikhwanweb.com/Article.asp?ID=14456&LevelID=1&SectionID=87 (last accessed 8 March 2008).
25 Regarding the change of early years of al-Sadat's rule and his policy towards the Muslim Brotherhood see Kogelmann (1991) 87–99 and Forstner (1988) 386–422.
26 See Kupferschmidt, in: http://pagesperso-orange.fr/colloque.imprimes.mo/pdf/UKT0.pdf (last accessed 3 March 2008).
27 Abdelnasser (1994) 62.
28 See Kogelmann (1991) 118–71; Kepel (1985); Sivan (1990) 117–52.
29 See Abdelnasser (1994) 62.
30 See Jansen (1997) 75–94
31 See al-Qaradawi (1985) 10.
32 The different contextual readings could serve as an outstanding example of Gadamer's hermeneutical theory, which he lays out in his work *Wahrheit und Methode*; see Gadamer (1981).
33 Saeed and Saeed (2004) 42.
34 Izutsu (1980) 22.
35 Ibid; Waldman (1968) 453.
36 Saeed and Saeed (2004) 44.
37 Izutsu (1980) 1–16.
38 Izutsu (1980) 6–10.
39 Izutsu (1980) 11.
40 Ibid.
41 On the theology of the Murja'iyya see Izutsu (1980) and Watt (2002). Shorter and more accessible descriptions can be found in Rippin (1999) 62–3.
42 Hodgson (1974) 264–5.
43 Izutsu (1980) 83.
44 See Izutsu (1980) 92–102.
45 Rahman (2002) 86–7. For further reading see Martin et al. (2003) passim.

46 For a detailed description of the Mu'tazila see Martin et al. (2003); for shorter descriptions see Rahman (2002); Saeed (2006) 65–7 and Rippin (1999) 64–9.
47 See Rahman (2002) 87–90.
48 Hallaq states that "[F]rom the field of theology (*kalam*) were appropriated certain fundamental elements that became an integral part of many, if not most, legal theories. Indeed, the prevailing epistemology in mainstream legal theory owes much to theology, although it is at times difficult to determine which of the two, legal theory or theology, influenced the other in this particular area" (Hallaq (1999) 134).
49 See Hallaq (1997) 135–6 and Martin et al. (2003) 31–3.
50 For a detailed description of the Ash'riyya and Maturidiyya see Izutsu (1980) 205–27.
51 The term *'aqida* (creed) is, in the widest sense, equivalent to belief, since it denotes what Muslims believe in. It must be added, though, that it developed into a *terminus technicus* which delineates the details of dogma and practices. Hence, *'aqida* is more than belief in the commonly used sense. It generally includes articles of faith such as the belief in *tawhid* (God's oneness; i.e. God's universality and all-prevailing powerfulness), *nubuwwa* (prophethood; i.e. sending of prophets to deliver God's message), *kutub* (books; i.e. the revelation of God's message), *mala'ika* (angels; i.e. the existence of angels) and *qiyama* (Judgement Day). Part of *'aqida* are also the so-called 'five pillars of Islam', which are the practices a Muslim needs to observe; these are *shahada* (profession of faith), *salat* (prayer), *zakat* (paying of alms), *zawm* (fasting) and *hajj* (pilgrimage).
52 Izutsu (1980) 207.
53 Izutsu (1980) 210–14. Abu Hanifa stated: 'We acknowledge that man, his works, his verbal confessions, and his knowledge, are all created' (cited from Izutsu (1980) 211); Wensick (1965) 128.
54 Rahman (2002) 92.
55 Izutsu (1980) 179–80.
56 Izutsu (1980) 179–93.
57 Hallaq (2005) 150–77.
58 Peters (2005) 35–43.
59 Saeed and Saeed (2004) 36–43.
60 Christian and Jews have a special status since they are protected monotheistic religious communities, the so-called *ahl al-kitab* (people of the book). Because they do not profess to be Muslim they are not obliged to observe shari'a law.
61 Orthodox scholars and their neo-orthodox counterparts consider Jews and Christians' unbelief as non-punishable only so long as they accept that Islam is the basis of the state system they are living under, or so long as they are in some form of alliance with a Muslim state if they are living outside of the so-called *dar al-Islam* (abode of Islam). This interpretation has been challenged by more progressive thinkers such as Tariq Ramadan (Ramadan (2004) 63-77).
62 The first part, i.e. '*la illaha illa Allah*', is found in verses 37: 35 and 47: 19. Similar to the second part of the creed is verse 63: 1.
63 See Clarke (1995) 4: 41–2.
64 See Clarke (1995) 4: 41–2.
65 See al-Hudaybi (1977) 11, 31 and *passim*.
66 al-Hudaybi (1977) 14–16, 30–4.
67 Clarke (1995). However, al-Hudaybi's definition of a believer seems to somewhat contradict his preliminary argument. Referencing a *Hadith* transmitted by Ibn Mas'ud, al-Hudaybi (1977) 29 defines a believer as 'someone who strives with his hand, tongue and heart'.
68 al-Hudaybi (1977) 14, 34.
69 The stance reminds one of the Sufi tradition, which is indeed very strong in Egypt. However, it is impossible to evaluate whether or to what extent al-Hudaybi was influenced by this tradition.

70 The passage corresponds to the original Arabic text in Qutb (1993a) 50–1.
71 Moussalli (1992) 160–1. For a closer investigation of al-Hudaybi's suggestion of a distinction between *'ibadat* (religious observances) and *mubahat* (indifferent, permissible actions), see chapter 6.
72 al-Maududi (1993) 10. Cited by al-Hudaybi (1977) 25. Similar to al-Maududi's perception of early Islamic history and the continuous existence of *jahiliyya* is al-Nadwi's interpretation regarding the reasons for the decline of Islamic civilisation; see al-Nadwi (1959).
73 Explanation of the term; see Wiktorowicz (2005) 189.
74 See al-Maududi (1993) 10–11; cited by al-Hudaybi (1977) 18.
75 Wehr (1976) 144 translates the term *jahiliyya* as 'state of ignorance; pre-Islamic paganism, pre-Islamic times'. The translation of the term as 'ignorance' is common and therefore used in this book; see Doumato (1995) 353 and Shepard (2002) II: 487–9 for further explanation of the term. Izutsu (1964) rightly points out that *jahiliyya* is not opposite to the term *'ilm* (knowledge), but rather to *hilm* (understanding, reason).
76 Al-Maududi cited in al-Hudaybi (1977) 16–18. The passage is taken from al-Maududi (1993) 8–12.
77 See al-Maududi (1993) 11–12, 126–30. Al-Maududi, al-Nadwi and Qutb have similar interpretations on modern *jahiliyya* and a comparable perception of history. Indeed, the latter was influenced by the Pakistani writers; for example, compare with Qutb (1993a) 83–4. For additional literature see Binder (1988) 170–205, esp. 177–81; Haddad (1983) 67–98, esp. 85–7; and Moussalli (1992) 19–20, 36, 213–30.
78 See al-Hudaybi (1977) 16–19.
79 The passages al-Hudaybi quoted are to be found in al-Maududi (1993) 8–11.
80 al-Hudaybi (1977) 19–28.
81 Brown (1999) 60–80.
82 al-Hudaybi (1977) 89–94 and regarding 'Abduh and al-Afghani see Brown (1999) 60–80.
83 Classical works of *usul al-fiqh* categorise Muhammad's actions as those of 1. prophet (nabi), 2. leader of the military and of politics (*qa'id 'askari wa siyasi*), 3. judge (*qadi*) and 4. ordinary person (*insan 'adi* or *bishr*). Furthermore, it needs to be added that the concept of the prophet's infallibility was first constructed in the context of the early Christian–Muslim dispute about miracles (particularly of the second century *hijra*) and was then further developed in Islamic theology. On the development of the concept of *'isma* see Brown (1999) 60–80.
84 Gershoni and Jankowski (1995) 54–78.
85 al-Hudaybi (1977) 89–94.
86 al-Hudaybi (1977) 30–1.
87 al-Hudaybi (1977) 32. In this context he uses the phrase *shari'a za'ida mustahditha* (excessive novel interpretation of law). The accusation is equivalent to *bid'*. On *bid'* see Zaman (1995) 1: 215–16.
88 Regarding the reinterpretation of the concept of infallibility of the prophet in modern Islam, see Brown (1999) 60–80.
89 al-Hudaybi (1977) 77–81.
90 al-Hudaybi (1977) 29, 157–8.
91 The Hadith is based on the authority of Abu Sa'id al-Khudri and states: "I heard the Messenger of Allah (…) say: Whoever of you sees an evil action, let him change it with his hand; and if he is not able to do so, then with his tongue; and if he is not able to do so, then with his heart – and that is the weakest of faith." Quoted in al-Nawawi (1977) 110.
92 al-Hudaybi (1977) 193.
93 Al-Hudaybi explicitly refers to Ibn Taymiyya, see al-Hudaybi (1977) 193.
94 Lia (1998) 117, 172–7.

95 Qutb (1993b) 14–17, 86–8.
96 Krämer (1999a) 290–1. Al-Hudaybi admits that there has been considerable controversy on the subject.
97 Compare the following references: al-Hudaybi (1977) 29 (believer who strives with hand, heart and tongue), 32 (the *shahada* is the only proof of belief), 110 (binary opposites of belief or unbelief), 157 (stages of belief).
98 For al-Hudaybi's interpretation on the necessity of the state and the Muslim's duty to engage in this construction of Islamic governance, see section 3.5.
99 al-Hudaybi (1977) 39.
100 al-Hudaybi (1977) 111–13.
101 al-Hudaybi (1977) 48–9.
102 al-Hudaybi (1977) 49–55.
103 al-Hudaybi (1977) 37–46. *Ma'asin* is the plural of *ma'siya*, which according to Wehr (1976) 618 translates as 'disobedience, insubordination, refractoriness …'.
104 al-Hudaybi (1977) 38.
105 Peters (2005) 53–65.
106 Under the most severe circumstances, Islamic legal schools might prescribe a sentence as severe as the death penalty. Nevertheless, even then, the person charged with the death penalty remains a Muslim.
107 al-Hudaybi (1977) 38–9. This issue plays into the subject of *hudud* charges. See below.
108 In fact, the Hanafi school of law does see *ridda* as a *hadd* crime.
109 For example al-Hudaybi (1977) 110–11.
110 al-Hudaybi (1977) 36–9.
111 Mir (1995) 4: 72–4 and, more extensively, Izutsu (1980) 35–56. The terms for sin used in the Qur'an are *ithm*, *dhanb* and *khatiya*. The verb *'asa*, which can be translated as 'to resist, to disobey', is also used in the Qur'an in the sense of 'to sin'. Yet, the commonly used term for sin, namely *ma'asi* (plural of *ma'siya*) is not mentioned in the Qur'an. For the semantics of *ma'siya*, which literally means disobedience, see Izutsu (1980) 39.
112 Mir (1995) 4: 72–4 and Izutsu (1980) 35–56. The passage of verse 4: 31 reads: "If you avoid the great sins (*al-kaba'ir*) which you are forbidden to do, we shall expiate from you your (minor) sins (*sayyatikum*), and admit you to a noble entrance (i.e. to paradise)." The passage of verse 42: 37 reads in translation as follows: "And those who avoid grave sins (*al-kaba'ir*), and monstrosities (*al-fawahish*), and when they are angry, forgive." It needs to be noted that the commonly used term for minor sin, *saghira* (pl. *sagha'ir*), is not mentioned in the Qur'an. Izutsu points out that the concept of venial sin is thus inferentially deduced.
113 The *Hadith* is transmitted by 'Abdallah ibn Mas'ud and quoted in Izutsu (1980) 36. The *Hadith* reads: "A certain man once asked the Apostle, 'O Apostle of God, what is the greatest sin in the eyes of God?' The Prophet replied, 'That you worship anything with God, when He alone created you.' The man then said, 'And what comes next?' The Prophet replied, 'That you should kill your child for fear of his partaking (later) of your food.' The man went on to ask, 'And what comes next?' The Prophet said, That you should commit adultery with the wife of your neighbor (sic!).'" Of relevance are also verses 6: 151–2, which contain a similar listing, but do not particularly speak of grave sin.
114 On the problematic of defining minor and grave sins Mir (1995), 4: 72–4.
115 Izutsu (1980) 1.
116 On historical and doctrinal development of the Khawarij see Watt (2002) 9–37, Hodgson (1974) 313–14 and Williams (1995b) 2:419–20; particularly on the concept of *takfir* as purported by the movement see Izutsu (1980) 1–34.
117 Watt (2002) 119–47.
118 Watt (2002) 119–28 and Izutsu (1980) 37–8, 44–7 and Shahrastani (1984) 119–24, esp.119. Al-Shahrastani (d. 1153) is the writer of a work titled *al-Milal wa al-Nihal*. This book exemplifies the classical Sunni view on sects and theological movements.

119 Shahrastani (1984), 41–71, esp. 44–5. See also Watt (2002) 126–7, 229–30 and Izutsu (1980) 38–9, 41. Izutsu and Watt point out that Hasan al-Basri, who is considered to have laid the foundation Mu'atazila thought, took the position that grave sinners have to be considered hypocrites (*munafiqun*, sing. *munafiq*). Thus, al-Basri forms a third category.

120 Mir (1995) 4: 72–4 and Ziadeh (1995) 1: 329–33. Nevertheless, the fact that a listing is not indicated in the revelation and that jurists were not able to agree on a formal or comprehensive catalogue of grave sin, is sufficient evidence for the lack of clarity on these issues.

121 For further reading on criminal law see Ziadeh (1995) 1: 329–33, El-Baradie (1983) 91–151 and Schacht (1966) 175–87.

122 El-Baradie (1983) 146–66; Ziadeh (1995) 1: 329–33 observes rightly that *ta'zir*, "because of its discretionary nature, has escaped precise definitions and detailed treatments of the elements of the crimes that it encompasses".

123 Ziadeh (1995) 1: 329–33, and El-Baradie (1983) 129–45. Schacht (1964) 181–7 uses the term *jinayat* (sg. *jinaya*; lit. offence) instead of *qisas*.

124 Ziadeh (1995) 1: 329–33, Pearl (1995) 2: 137–8, Schacht (1966) 371, 175–87 and El-Baradie (1983) 91–151.

125 Baradie points out that some juridical interpreters also include *ridda* (apostasy) and *baghy* (outrage; i.e. rebellion) to the list of *hadd* offences (El-Baradie (1983) 91–151). He adds these offences to the list, yet does not mention the dispute about them. This is thus indication of a rather orthodox stance on criminal law.

126 Ziadeh (1995) 1: 329–33 and Watt (2002) 119–47.

127 Mir (1995) 4: 72–4.

128 Mayer (1995)2: 464–72, esp. 471. The debate about criminal law is embedded in the discussion on Islam and human rights, on the one hand, and the inner Muslim discourse about *shari'a*. For further reading on the discourse on application of *shari'a* see Peters (1988) 231–59; on the dispute about human rights, see for example Dwyer (1991) 33–84 for a selection of current voices, and Mayer (1999) from a more theoretical point of view.

129 Pearl (1995) 2: 137–8.

130 Peters (1988) 3: 231–59.

131 Mayer (1995) 2: 464–72, esp. 471. It needs to be mentioned that the Egyptian constitution was revised in September 1971 and in May 1980 with the intention of appeasing the Islamist movement. For further reading see Kogelmann (1991) 87–99 and Peters (1988) 3: 231–59.

132 Esposito (1998) 225–35.

133 Examples are passages of verses 4: 59 and 26: 151. The often-mentioned extract of verse 4: 59 reads "(…) *wa man lam yahkum bi-ma 'nzala Allahu fa-'ula'ika humma 'l-kafiruna*". The verse can be translated as "whoever does not pass judgement according to what God has revealed, those are indeed the unbelievers". Similar are also passages 5: 45 and 5: 47, where, instead of the word *al-kafirun* (unbeliever) the terms *al-zalimun* (transgressors) and *al-fasiqun* (trespassers) are used.
The passage of verses 26: 151–2 states "*wa la tuti'u amra 'l-musrifina* (…) (and do not obey the command of the reckless)".

134 al-Hudaybi (1977) 36.

135 al-Hudaybi (1977) 36.

136 al-Hudaybi (1977) 37.

137 The inclusion of divine judgment in Islamic juridical though is, then, fundamentally different from secular (Western) positions of justice. At this point the question arises for secular minds as to what difference it makes to the person, who may be charged for sinful behaviour and ultimately may be subject to severe physical penalties or even lose his/her life, whether the punishment taken against him/her is a form of penalty

or repentance. Further, the idea that a person may be punished on moral and religious grounds stands obviously in contradiction to secular definitions of religious freedom as a basic tenet of human rights.

138 al-Hudaybi (1977) 35–7.
139 al-Hudaybi (1977), 37 and also al-Hudaybi (1977) 111.
140 al-Hudaybi (1977) 35–7.
141 This implies that a person must proclaim his/her non-belief to an audience of credible witnesses; there must be no threat, no psychological or physical pressure in order to force the person to decide to announce *kufr*. Further, the person must understand the possible consequences of his/her proclamation of apostasy and, therefore, must have knowledge that the punishment for this act of disclaiming belief may be death. The issue is closely related to al-Hudaybi's presentation on various excuses. See below.
142 al-Hudaybi (1977) 35–7.
143 al-Hudaybi (1977) 35–7.
144 al-Hudaybi (1977) 40–2.
145 al-Hudaybi (1977) 40–6.
146 al-Hudaybi (1977) 38–9.
147 al-Hudaybi (1977) 40–6.
148 al-Hudaybi (1977) 45–6.
149 al-Hudaybi (1977) 69–88.
150 al-Hudaybi (1977) 69–88.
151 See for example Ibn Taymiyya, who also brought forward these excuses. Ibn Taymiyya (1997) 215–20.
152 Ziadeh (1995) 1: 329–33.
153 al-Hudaybi (1977) 88.
154 al-Hudaybi (1977) 77–81 and 95–7.
155 For collective duty (*fard al-kifaya*) see the articles by Reinhard (1995b) and Juynboll (1965); for individual duty (*fard al-'ayn*) see Reinhard (1995a) and Juynboll (1965).
156 al-Hudaybi (1977) 77–81 and 95–7. In accordance with the question of intentionality, he argues that if someone principally admits the duty, but does refrain from doing so, he/she is only a sinner. Yet, if someone denies this obligation, he/she has to be considered an unbeliever. Again, this aspect plays into the question of intentionality.
157 al-Hudaybi (1977)71.
158 On *taqlid* Hallaq (1999) 121–3 and Weiss (1995) 187–9.
159 al-Hudaybi (1977)79–81 and 95–6. Regarding the common Sunni position on error in interpretation and the problem of contradictory results of legal reasoning see Hallaq (1999) 120–1.
160 al-Hudaybi (1977) 79–81.
161 al-Hudaybi (1977) 89–94.
162 al-Hudaybi (1977) 92–3 and 94–104.
163 al-Hudaybi (1977) 79.
164 On the proficiencies for juridical investigation *ijtihad* see Hallaq (1999) 117–19.
165 The fact that al-Hudaybi brings up the subject of basic formal aspects of juridical investigation can also be regarded as an implicit critique of radical stances (e.g. Qutb's analysis), since most of these interpreters do not have a classical education in the principles of Sunni jurisprudence.
166 Again, this argument can be seen as an implicit critique of grand theories as purported by radical interpretation.
167 al-Hudaybi (1977) 78–81. It is amazing, though, that al-Hudaybi associates juridical interpreters, without hesitation, as those being the holders of authority. See also below in this chapter, 3.5 for al-Hudaybi's interpretation on state and authority.
168 al-Hudaybi (1977) 79–85, also 114–17.

169 Walker (1995) 186–7.
170 al-Hudaybi (1977) 82–5.
171 al-Hudaybi (1977) 86–8.
172 al-Hudaybi (1977) 114–17.
173 al-Hudaybi (1977) 85–8. Al-Hudaybi lists murder, physical harm of a person and the impairment of someone's honour as incidences in which a person who was forced to commit these crimes cannot be excused for his deeds. The list is matched with *ta'zir* crimes.
174 Burgat (2003) 60–5.
175 For further reading on the discussion in Egypt regarding the content of *shari'a* see Peters (1988). Many descriptive works on Islamic law, legal theory and its historical development have been written. The following are merely some introductions and well-acknowledged contributions, with an emphasis on available titles in English: Schacht (1966) and Schacht (1950); Goldziher (1981); Hallaq (1999); Weiss (1998) and Coulson (1964).
176 Hooker writes in the *Encyclopaedia of Islam*: "SHARI'A (A.), derived from the root *shara'a*, having a primary range of meaning in relation to religion and religious law; also SHAR', frequently synonymous." Hooker (1965) IX: 321
177 See Qur'an verse 45: 18. Similar in meaning, the words *shir'a* and *minhaj* are used in the Qur'an. See verse 5: 48.
178 Hooker (1965) IX: 322
179 One has to consider that there are relatively few remarks in the Qur'an referring to legal issues. In the classical dispute on the legal verses of the Qur'an, interpreters differentiated between *ayat muhkamatun* and *ayat mutashabihatun*. Yet, there is no overall consensus on which verses, of all the verses of the Qur'an, fall into one or the other category; and even if there is a consensus that a particular *ayah* is referring to a legal issue, the application (particularly the form of its application) is still a possible issue of dispute.
180 For general introductions to the methodology of Islamic jurisprudence see Coulson (1964) 75–85. It should be noted, though, that the 'sound' use of *ijma'* and *qiyas* was an issue of dispute. See Hallaq (1999) 36–124, esp. 75–81 and 83–113; Weiss (1998) 66–87 and 113–44; Lambton (1981) 7–12.
181 Muhammad ibn Idris al-Shafi'i (died 204AH/820AD. al-Shafi'i's *risala* is available in translations; see al-Shafi'i (1987); regarding al-Shafi'i's legacy on legal theory consult the above-mentioned literature on Islamic law and legal theory, which covers this issue more or less extensively; further see Hallaq (1999) 21–35 and Coulson (1964) 53–61, 62–73, who critically discuss al-Shafi'i's impact on classical theory.
182 In legal theory the classification is termed *al-ahkam al-khamsa* (five qualifications); see Schacht (1965) 257 and Hooker (1965) IX: 324. For a further description of the classification see Hallaq (1999) 40–2. Norms that were characterised as required (*wajib*) are, generally speaking, considered to be duties (pl. *furud*, sing. *fard*). An exception is the Hanafi school of law, which distinguishes two categories of the obligatory, whereby *fard* describes rules with certain evidence, whereas *wajib* is established upon probable evidence. See Hallaq (1999) 40.
183 Hooker (1965) IX: 322.
184 Hallaq (1999) 207–9 and Lambton (1981) 10–12.
185 Hallaq (1999) 210. A few Muslim scholars in the late twentieth century have pointed out that a bulk of rules, which are perceived as *shari'a* laws, are in fact inferred *fiqh* regulations. Further, the relativity of *shari'a* rules is an argument of the critique against radical positions See, for Muhammad Sa'id al-'Ashmawi as a proponent of moderate Islamism, al-'Ashmawi (1989) 36–7, 45–7; the interview with al-'Ashmawi in Davis (1999) 153–65 and an analysis of his thesis by Shepard (1996) 39–58. An example of a secularist writer of is Fu'ad Zakariya; Zakariya (1992).

186 The fact that the term *islam* literally means submission is often pointed out in literature. For a study of the terms *islam* and *iman* engaging in the question of whether they are equivalent in meaning, see Izutsu (1980) 57–82.

187 This perception is common among Muslim interpreters and is often pointed out in Western scholarly work on Islam. See for example Lambton (1981) 1. Nevertheless, this thesis contains the presumption that the religious bond between God and individuals *defines* the political sphere. It is this issue, then, which is central to the secularisation and anti-secularisation debate.

188 Sonn (1995) 4:190–8. See also Moussalli's investigation on the use of the concept of *tawhid* to give emphasis to the call for an 'Islamisation' of law and for the proposal of revolutionary ideas in modern (radical) Islamism; Moussalli (1999b) 31–41.

189 Qur'an 6: 57, 12: 40 and 12: 67 contain the above-quoted passage "(...) *inna al-hukmu illa li-llah* (...) (there is no judgement except for God)."

Verse 5: 44 contains the passage "(...) *wa man lam yahkum bi-ma anzala llahu fa-'ula'ika hummu l-kafiruna'* (whoever does not pass judgement according to what God has revealed, those are indeed the unbelievers)". Similar also are passages in Qur'an 5: 45 and 5: 47, where instead of the word *al-kafirun* (unbeliever) the terms *al-zalimun* (transgressors) and *al-fasiqun* (trespassers) are used. It must be noted that the meaning of key words in these passages is still disputed; for example, there is a dispute on the meaning of derivatives of the root h-k-m. See below for al-Hudaybi's interpretation of these verses and on the meaning of words related to h-k-m; see section 3.6 in this chapter.

190 Hallaq (1999) 125–7, 153–5.

191 Hallaq (1999) 1–21, 130–4; Schacht (1966) 36–48; and Coulson (1964) 21–52.

192 Schacht (1966) 69–75 and Coulson (1964) 62–73, 75–85. Hallaq points out that it was part of theory and practice to not reconsider laws resulting from 'sound' legal hermeneutics because the assumption prevailed that the outcome was derived through an objective methodology. *Fatawa* (sing. *fatwa*) were thus considered to be an authoritative product of *ijtihad*, which then subsequently laid the foundation for positive law. With the process of recognising the authoritativeness of a bulk of legal rulings, the basis for substantive, positive law was effectively created. This move towards positive law was somewhat necessary to prevent disintegration. Hallaq (1999) 153–61, 207–9 and Hallaq (1994) 17–56.

193 Lambton (1981) 7–12. On the assumption that details of law have been explored, experts on Islamic law often put forward that the gate of legal reasoning (*bab al-ijtihad*) was closed from the 9th century onwards. See e.g. Schacht (1966) 69–75; and Coulson (1964) 73, 80–1. This understanding of legal theory entailed the perception that Islamic jurists of the subsequent centuries only followed the principle of imitation (*taqlid*), whereby they replicated the tenets of the schools of law and on that basis merely elaborated details. Hallaq, however, rightly challenges this interpretation of Islamic legal theory. Although he admits to a certain stagnation of legal rendering and law, he rightly challenges the assumption that the gate of *ijtihad* was closed, pointing out that in reality legal reasoning continued to be applied; Hallaq (1999) 143–61 and Hallaq (1984) 3–41.

194 Coulson describes that state institutions such as the court of the ruler, which was known as the court of complaints (*mazalim*), had the power to override jurists' law. Further, the judicative was not independent from the state, but judges (*qudat*; sing. *qadi*) were effectively subordinate to political authority. Thus, political decision making, i.e. the power of the leader, was in actual fact 'above' religious rules. See Coulson (1964) 120–34. Yet, classical Islamic jurisprudence did not see the dependence on state authority as being in contradiction to the concept of God's sovereignty. To even out ambiguities, classical Islamic theories of the state put emphasis on the obligation to resign to the authority of the caliph and, later, even of rulers who took power (see e.g. al-Mawardi), since these are 'God's shadow on earth'.

195 There is the question of whether proponents of Islamic revival merely reacted to questions of modernity or whether they were inspired by modernity and hence are part of it. For introductory readings on this issue see Kurzman (2002) 3–27; Muñoz (1999); Piscatori (1988); Voll (1982) and Moussalli (1999b).

196 See Adams (1933); Kerr (1966) on ʿAbduh and Rida; and Zebiri (1993) on Shaltut; further, on al-ʿAshmawi see al-ʿAshmawi (1989) 36–7, 45–7; Davis (1999) 153–65; Shepard (1996) and Krämer (1999a) 65–7. Huwaydi has not yet been recognised appropriately in secondary literature; consult Huwaydi (1982).

197 Al-Hudaybi (1978) 67–9, 73–4

198 Gomaa rightly points out that al-Hudaybi's work is continues with the quest of earlier revivalist writers such as ʿAbduh, Rida and al-Banna. Gomaa (1983) 143–58.

199 Al-Hudaybi (1978) 67–9.

200 al-Hudaybi (1977) 73.

201 al-Hudaybi (1977) 73.

202 al-Hudaybi (1977) 74.

203 al-Hudaybi (1977) 74.

204 It needs to be noted that the dispute regarding reasoning and obedience has a long tradition in Islamic thought; the origin goes back to the formative period of Islamic theology and jurisprudence. On the discussion between rationalists and traditionalists, see Abrahamov (1998). He shows that traditionalists incorporated rational arguments while discarding the rationalists' approach of using reason to explain Islamic doctrine.

205 al-Hudaybi (1977) 73–4. There is still dispute about the actual form and function of an internal council, insofar as *shura* represents to some an alternative to a parliamentary system and, hence, a central institution of democratic human decision making, whereas it is seen by others as merely a meeting of leaders in order to choose and give obedience to an authority such as a caliph. For further reading, see Krämer (1999a).

206 As mentioned above, legal theory classifies law into five categories, the so-called *al-ahkam al-khamsa* (i.e. obligatory, recommended, indifferent, reprehensible and forbidden). See Hooker (1965) IX: 321–8, esp. 324 and Schacht (1965) I: 257.

207 See Hooker (1965) IX: 321–8 and Schacht (1965) I: 257.

208 Similar to these, al-Hudaybi follows the juridical concept of *al-asl fi al-ashya' al-ibaha*, which means that what is not explicitly prohibited is legitimate. See Kerr (1966) 191 and El-Baradie (1983) 35–6, 62.

209 For the discussion on the flexible and fixed aspect of law in (modern) Islamic interpretation see Krämer (1999a) 54–8 and El-Baradie (1983) 44–6. Specifically on ʿAbduh's and Rida's categorisation see Kerr (1966) 21, 88–9, 188–90.

210 Johansen (1986) 23–5. See further Kerr (1966) 21, 188–90 on Rida's interpretation.

211 Shaltut (1987) 71–137.

212 al-Hudaybi (1977) 73.

213 Johansen (1986) 23–5.

214 Kerr (1966) 189.

215 al-Hudaybi (1977) 74.

216 al-Hudaybi (1977) 73–4.

217 As a good introduction to issues of Islamic governance and law in Islamist thought see Ayubi (1991) 1–10; see also Krämer (1999a) 43–6; Roy (1994) 4.

218 Explanations on the necessity of Islamic governance, which assures the application of *shariʿa*, largely follow the classical rationale regarding the interrelation of order and religious law. See Abou El Fadl (2001) 23–31. See below for the classical thesis as well as al-Hudaybi's modern reinterpretation.

219 Almost every Islamist writer could be quoted and referred to regarding this point. See for example al-Maududi (1968) 17–25 and Qutb (1993b) 73–8, but also Al-Hudaybi (1978) 129–42, 148.

220 For a selection of contributions see the following anthologies and edited book: Kurzman (1998) and Kurzman (2002) as well as Donohue and Esposito (1982); Muñoz (1999) and Cooper, Nettler, and Mohamed (1998). The number of relevant scholarly articles commenting on the subject is vast. As bibliographical guides, consult Haddad, Esposito, and Voll (1991) and Haddad et al. (1997). Among others, the following scholars particularly dedicated their work to the subject: Esposito, Voll, Piscatori, G. Krämer, Haddad, Ayubi and Sivan.

221 For example, see the writings of al-Banna', H. (1990); ʿAuda (1977) and ʿAuda (1986); Qutb (1978) and Qutb (1993a); Huwaydi (1982) and al-ʿAmmara (1985). See also the compilation of speeches edited by ʿAbd al-Samiʿ (1992). The book records a discourse between a number of well-known Muslim Brothers and some close to the organisation such as Muhammad al-Ghazali, Salah Shadi, Muhammad ʿAmmara, Fahmi Huwaydi, Ma'mun al-Hudaybi, etc.

222 For example, compare the strategies suggested by al-Hudaybi (1977) 88–9, 182, 186–7 and Qutb (1993b) 65–6. al-Hudaybi's motto '*Preachers not Judges*' suggests engagement with society and the propagation of Islamic belief; Qutb, however, preaches that true believers need to distance themselves from the surrounding society and from groups of zealots, which eventually overthrow the existing order through revolutionary acts.

223 Representative scholarly studies on classical theory of the state are Lambton (1981); Gibb (1955); Black (2001) and Crone and Martin (1986). Historical insights are given by Hodgson (1974); Madelung (1997) and Watt (2002). Related issues, such as the idea of resistance or the concept egalitarianism are covered by Cook (2000) and Abou El Fadl (2001) or Marlow (1997).

224 Muslim contributors consider justice (*adala*), public welfare (*maslaha*) and consultation (*shura*) to be central principles; particularly modernist interpreters see equality (*musawat*), freedom (*hurriyya*), responsibility (*mas'uliyya*) and accountability (*musa'ala*) as further principles; see Krämer (1999a) 73. For further reading on definitions of *maqasid al-shari'a* and the interconnected delineation of *maslaha*, see Hallaq (1999) 112–13, 167–9, 180–5. The concepts gained special attention in juridical theory (particularly through al-Shatibi's work) and finds reflection in modern utilitarianist perceptions of law, such as those of ʿAbduh and Rida. See Hallaq (1999) 214–31.

225 See Lambton (1981) 1–12 and Gibb (1955) 3–4

226 This forms the basis of the concept of God's *hakimiyya* (sovereignty), which is particularly emphasised by today's radical Islamists. See Ayubi (1991) 3, 15–16.

227 Sonn (1995) 4: 190–8. Summarising the use and development of the non-Qur'anic term *tawhid*, Sonn points out that classical interpretation used this fundamental dogma to explain the link between God's essence and attributes, but that it gained political significance through a reconceptualisation in the works of modern Islamic interpreters.

228 Quoted is only the last sentence of verse 5: 44. Similar also are Qur'an 5: 45 and 5: 47, where, instead of the word *al-kafirun* (unbeliever) the terms *al-zalimun* (transgressors) and *al-fasiqun* (trespassers) are used. The verse was also used to construct a right or duty of resistance following the argument that it is a moral–religious necessity to oppose unbelief and transgressions of the *shari'a*. See for example ʿAuda (1986). Yet, al-ʿAshmawi for example opposes these activist interpretations and points out that the verses apply to the Jewish community of Medina (i.e. to early Islamic history) only. See al-ʿAshmawi (1989) 140.

229 Lambton (1981) 12 and Krämer (1999b) 175. Krämer rightly emphasises that there are thus only interpretations. This point has indeed also been made by Arkoun, who applies 'post-modern' philosophy to his explanations of Islam. See for example Arkoun (1994).

230 Krämer (1999a) 107.

231 Laoust (1938) 528. The classical interpretation of this passage coincides with explanations on the necessity of the caliphate. See Gibb (1955) 4–6.

232 Examples of this extended reading can, for instance, be found in the works of al-Mawardi and al-Ghazali; see Lambton (1981) 83–129; Gibb (1955) 18–20.

233 Khalafallah (1985). Modern proponents of power-sharing and democracy often see the concept of shura as a Muslim equivalent to parliamentarism. For further reading see Krämer (1999a) passim.

234 Enayat (1982) 62; see Gaffney (1994) and Brown (1997) 359–76 on the question of why the influence and leadership of scholars declined in modern times.

235 Krämer describes this with the following words: "Von entscheidender Bedeutung, so lautet der Ausgangspunkt aller Betrachtungen zu Islam und politischer Ordnung, ist der Zweck des Staatswesens, nicht seine politische Organisation." Krämer (1999a) 73.

236 al-Hudaybi (1977) 129–37.

237 Al-Hudaybi uses both terms synonymously; al-Hudaybi (1977) 129–37.

238 al-Hudaybi (1977) 73–4.

239 Although al-Hudaybi habitually omits to reference these in his footnotes, their names or interpretations find mention in the text; al-Hudaybi (1977) 130–6.

240 al-Rayyis (1966). See also al-Hudaybi (1977) 133–6.

241 Rashid Rida's writing, for example, dismisses the idea of the caliph's lineage to the Quraysh. It was, thus, a response to the Egyptian king's attempt to claim the position of caliph, which was vacant after the abolition of the Ottoman caliphate; Rida (1988); for further reading see Kerr (1966) 153–86; Hourani (1983) 222–44 and Enayat (1982) 69–83. 'Ali 'Abd al-Raziq unleashed with his controversial book entitled *al-Islam wa Usul al-hukm* a controversy with regard to the political rather than religious nature of the caliphate. Seeing the caliphate as a purely political institution, he argued for the legitimacy of a democratic state order, which should be implemented instead. His book therefore challenged the king's claim to the caliphate. Indeed, 'Abd al-Raziq's book continues to be discussed until today, and particularly inspired the secular left; see 'Abd al-Raziq (1972); for further reading see Binder (1988) and Enayat (1982) 62–8. Muhammad Khalafallah continued 'Abd al-Raziq's argumentation for a participatory state order and speaks in favour of a parliamentary state system; Khalafallah (1984).

242 See his articles, public statements and speeches of the years 1952–54 in Al-Hudaybi (1978).

243 The insecurity over legitimacy of the state and the strategy of the Brotherhood to counter the state was also furthered by the fact that al-Hudaybi's messages of the pre-persecution period contained strong statements which emphasise the distinction between a just Islamic way and systems of unbelief. In other words, the radical position within the Brotherhood continued with and further developed ideological components which were also present in al-Hudaybi's earlier theoretical writings. See for example Al-Hudaybi (1978) 58–63 and 113–25; moreover his statement published under the title *Dusturuna*, in: Al-Hudaybi (1978).

244 Lambton remarks on the amalgamation of state and religion in classical theology: "They (i.e. jurists) did not admit the existence of the state as an institution in its own right and considered the emergence of a temporal state as a separate institution to be a usurpation due to the intrusion of elements of corruption into the community." Lambton (1981) 17.

245 Binder (1988) 1–19 and Kurzman (1998) 3–26.

246 Verse 2: 30 reads: "*wa idh qala rabbuka li-l-malakati inni ja'ilun fi 'l-ardi khalifatan* (…)" and was commonly translated as "And when your Lord said to the angels: verily, I am going to establish on earth a viceroy (…)." Verse 38: 26 reads: "*ya-Da'udu inna ja'lnaka khalifatan fi al-ardi f-ahkumu bayna 'l-nasi bi'l-haqq wa la tattabi'ui 'l-hawa* (…)". The passages translates as "O Da'ud (David), verily we placed you as a viceroy on the earth. So judge between men in truth and do not follow your desire (…)." Watt points out that both passages do not refer to the term *khalifa* as an

institution of state, but rather carry the meaning of guardian of God's rule on earth. See Watt (1961) 163–4.

247 Watt (1961) 163–4. Gibb calls the choice of the term 'fortuitous'. Yet, he maintains that its use provided jurists with Qur'anic authenticity for their theology of state; see Gibb (1955) 5. Crone and Hinds oppose this view and regard the adoption of the title *khalifat Allah* (God's caliph; i.e. rather than *khalifat rasul Allah*) as a deliberate assertion of the caliphs, which combined religious and political claims to leadership. See Crone and Hinds (1986) 1–3, 20–5.

248 Watt (1961) 163–4; Gibb (1955) 4–6 and Lambton (1981) 13–20. Again, Crone and Hinds oppose this view. While proving that caliphs of the 'Ummayyad period were referred to as *khalifat Allah*, they assume that the adoption of this title and its inherent designation as guardian of God (rather than of the prophet as in the title *khalifat rasul Allah*) stems back to as early as the period of the orthodox caliphs. They argue that the *'ulama* subsequently constructed a change in titulature to fit their own agenda; Crone and Hinds (1986) 5–11, 19–25. Although Crone and Hinds make interesting and important points regarding the usage of the title and its innate ideation, their position regarding the use of the title during the time of the orthodox caliphs is to a large extent based on assumptions rather than evidence.

249 Lambton explains that "later Sunni jurists draw a distinction between the Madinan caliphate, that of the first four caliphs, known as the *rashidun* or orthodox caliphs, and the later caliphate, which is alleged to have the character of worldly kinship (*mulk*)" Lambton (1981) 17. Nevertheless, the very same jurists upheld in their theories on the caliphate the impression of a continuously existing ideal.

250 For a detailed study of this period, see Madelung (1997).

251 The title *khalifa* (caliph) and the institution of the *khilafa* (caliphate) is derived from the verb *khalafa*, which can be translated as 'to succeed', 'to follow' or 'to take place of someone'; see Wehr (1976) 257. The various meanings led to a dispute about the actual meaning and the ideological constituent of the title *khalifa*. See e.g., Crone and Hinds, who strongly argue against the concept of succession as the source of the caliphs' legitimacy. They put forward that *khalifa* only can mean 'guardian'; Crone and Hinds (1986) 5–6; see also Watt (2002) 69, 84.

252 Hourani (1991) 22–3.

253 Watt (2002) 69, 84. See Crone and Hinds for a critique of this interpretation; Crone and Hinds (1986) 5–11, 19–25.

254 Mu'awiyya was related to the previous caliph 'Uthman and sought vengeance for his murder, accusing 'Ali's party of having been involved. Succeeding 'Ali, Mu'awiyya was later to become the first caliph of the so-called 'Umayyad-dynasty. There is a quantity of secondary literature dealing with the political history of the early caliphate; the following list is only a representative selection: Madelung (1997); Watt (2002); Hourani (1991) and Crone and Hinds (1986).

255 We will see later that the understanding of this (Qur'anic) phrase is still at the centre of claims of today's Islamists. Particularly, radical movements use the phrase as a slogan to assert their claim to political power.

256 Watt (2002) 9–37; Lambton (1981) 13–42; Gibb (1955) 4–6.

257 For the Khawarij see Crone (2000) 3–28. Regarding the Shi'a ideology of just rule, see Sachedina (1988) and Black (2001) 40–8. For the classical Sunni theology of state, see (among other previously mentioned literature) Lambton (1981) and Black (2001).

258 Sources indicate that in the *shura* (council) was practised the process of designating the orthodox caliphs. This could be seen to indicate an elective institution of control, which chooses the caliph according the idea of *primus inter pares*. However, the numbers of members of *shura* who were consulted in the election of the orthodox caliphs varied considerably and the participative powers of early the councils in the electoral process of the orthodox caliphs is in fact unknown. See Krämer (1999a) 121–3.

259 Gibb (1955) 11–13; al-Azmeh (1997) 74–9. See further Crone and Hinds (1986).
260 For historical accounts on the ʿAbbassid revolt see Watt (2002) 149–79 and Hourani (1991), 32–7.
261 See Lambton (1981) and Black (2001) as comprehensive studies of classical theories of state. The dates of the above-mentioned classical writers are: Mansur ʿAbd al-Qahir Tahir al-Baghdadi (died 1037); Abu al-Hasan ʿAli al-Mawardi (974–1058); Abu Hamid Muhammad al-Ghazali (1058–1111); Ahmad Ibn Taymiyya (1262–1328); ʿAbd al-Rahman Muhammad Ibn Khaldun (1332–1406)
262 al-Azmeh (1997) 83–92.
263 For further readings on al-Mawardi see Mikhail (1995); Lambton (1981) 83–102; Gibb (1962) 151–65; Laoust (1968) and Black (2001) 85–90.
264 al-Mawardi (n.y.); al-Mawardi's *al-Ahkam al-Sultaniyya* is translated into English by Asadullah Yate; see al-Mawardi (1996).
265 For further reading on al-Ghazali's political theory see Lambton (1981) 107–29; Gibb (1955) 19–20 and Black (2001) 96–107.
266 Al-Ghazali states: "These concessions which we make are involuntary, but necessities make allowable even what is prohibited … Who is there, I ask, who would not support this, but would argue for the voidance of the imamate in our day because of the lack of the requisite qualifications?" Al-Ghazali quoted in Gibb (1955) 19–20.
267 The term *imam*, which stands for religious leader, was in classical literature often synonymously used for *khalifa*, particularly in *fiqh*. For further literature on Ibn Khaldun see Lambton (1981) 152–77 and Black (2001).
268 Ibn Khaldun (1970). The book is also available in translation; see Ibn Khaldun (1967).
269 See Ibn Khaldun (1967) 154–5, 256–7
270 Gibb (1955) 6–16; Siegman (1964) *passim*; for a more detailed study of classical theories of the state in the context of their writing see Lambton (1981).
271 Lambton (1981) 15 and, similarly, Gibb (1955) 4–7, 11–14.
272 Al-Hudaybi (1978) 129–30.
273 Al-Hudaybi (1978) 130.
274 See for example al-Mawardi (1996) 10–36 or, more pointed, Ibn Khaldun (1967) 155.
275 There are a number of writers who put forward that an Islamic state does not necessitate the religious leaderhip of an *imam* or caliph; e.g. ʿAbd al-Raziq (1972) or Khalafallah (1984), and translations of parts of their work in Kurzman (1998) and Donohue and Esposito (1982); for further reading on ʿAbd al-Raziq see Enayat (1982) 62–8 and more extensively Binder (1988) 128–69. Moreover, Rashid Rida's exposition, which speaks largely in support of the caliphate, but recognises the problematic of establishing this order, seems to distinguish between the caliphate and the Islamic state. See Rida (1988); see further Enayat (1982) 69–83.
276 See e.g. al-ʿAshmawi, in: Davis (1999) 153–65. Although this stance also has to face the problematic of identifying the content of *shariʿa*, it seems that proponents of this position have a much broader and more liberal definition of Islamic law.
277 Proponents of this view are often influenced by secularist ideas and thus tend to argue for a separation between the religious and secular in regards to the state. See e.g. Zakariya (1992) or Fudah (1982).
278 al-Hudaybi (1977) 129–32. Saʿd al-Din Masʿud al-Taftazani (died 1390) is also mentioned, but only to a minor extent.
279 al-Rayyis (1966). See al-Hudaybi (1977) 131.
280 Al-Hudaybi (1978) 130.
281 Al-Hudaybi (1978) 130–1.
282 Al-Hudaybi (1978) 131.
283 Al-Hudaybi (1978) 132.
284 al-Hudaybi's critique may be directed against some interpretations of his time, which attempted to associate Islam with Arab socialism; see for example the head of the Syrian

branch of the Muslim Brotherhood, Mustafa al-Siba'i. The latter's work, *Ishtirakiyya al-Islam*, greatly influenced the position of leading figures of al-Azhar, which tended to support the official policies of the state (i.e since ca. 1961 Arab Socialism). See e.g. al-Hudaybi's contemporary, the Shaykh al-Azhar Mahmud Shaltut, in: Donohue and Esposito (1982) 99–102 and Shaltut (1961) 163–74. For further reading on Shaltut's conception of socialism see Zebiri (1993) 55–7; for reading on al-Azhar's support of 'Abd al-Nasir's Arab Socialism see Enayat (1982) 139–50 and further Eccel (1984).

285 Orthodox interpreters already emphasised that the failure of governance results in discord and sedition. Examples are al-Ghazali or Ibn Khaldun; (al-Ghazali particularly finds reference in al-Hudaybi's explanation on the necessity of the *khilafa*).

286 The term *fitna* is commonly used and translated as discord or sedition, but also as temptation or trial. For the various meanings of the term *fitna* and the various interpretations of the concept, refer to Williams (1995a) II: 26–8. It should be noted that the idea of *fitna* was re-evoked in modern interpretations to silence critical voices (see Williams), but also to explain the commonly sensed 'disintegration of Islam' (see e.g. writings of al-Nadwi, Qutb and many others).

287 Al-Hudaybi (1978) 132.

288 See al-Mawardi (1996) 12 or Ibn Khaldun (1967) 158–9.

289 On the requirements for *qadi* see e.g. al-Mawardi (1996) 98–100.

290 Al-Hudaybi (1978) 132–3. See al-Mawardi's description as an example for a well-known and often-used account. Indeed, the latter dismisses any doubt that the *imam* must descend from the tribe of Quraysh; see al-Mawardi (1996) 12. Admittedly, there the aspect of lineage has been disputed, as the accounts of al-Baqilani or of Ibn Khaldun show. See the relevant passage of al-Baqilani translated in Gibb (1955) 7–11; further see Ibn Khaldun (1967) 158–9.

291 The issue of lineage was a subject of fierce discussions following the abolition of the Ottoman caliphate and ill-fated attempts to revive the institution. See Enayat (1982) 52–83.

292 Gomaa (1983) 143–58 and Enayat (1982) 87 point out that Rida's thought and concept of the state had an immediate impact on the ideology of the Muslim Brotherhood. Whether his work on the caliphate was taken by al-Hudaybi as a framework for his own consideration cannot be established here.

293 Al-Hudaybi (1978) 133.

294 Al-Hudaybi (1978) 133–4.

295 Actually, only two of the four orthodox caliphs were chosen by council (*shura*) and only a small number of 'electors' was present. Furthermore, we have already seen that Abu Bakr's election was contested by other tribal leaders. See Madelung (1997).

296 Al-Hudaybi (1978) 132–3.

297 See Enayat (1982) 61–83.

298 Rida (1988); for further reading see Kerr (1966) and Laoust (1938). Another well-known contributor to the discussion was 'Ali 'Abd al-Raziq. His book *al-Islam wa Usul al-hukm* not only disputed the concept of genealogy as a prerequisite for the position of the caliph, but moreover suggested that a distinction between political leadership and religious rule needs to be made; see 'Abd al-Raziq (1972) and, further, Binder (1988) 128–69 and Hourani (1991) 184–8.

299 Al-Hudaybi (1978) 132.

300 Al-Hudaybi (1978) 130–1.

301 The passage of verse 4: 59 reads in transcription "*Ya ayyuha 'lladhina amanu atiyyu 'llaha wa atiyyu 'l-rasula wa uli 'l-amri minkum (…).*"

302 al-Hudaybi (1977) 134.

303 See for example al-Mawardi (1996) 10–36. In support of his argument he refers to a *hadith* transmitted by Ibn Hazm, which al-Hudaybi interprets, like classical writers, as confirming the legitimacy of the caliph. The *hadith* reads: "'there will be no prophet after me, but there will be successors (*khulafa'*) and they will

increase in numbers.' They asked him (Muhammad) then: what do you ask us (to do)? He said: 'Keep oath to the first (*al-awwal*) and then the first; give them their right (*haqq*). Indeed, Allah questions them on their intention'." Hadith as quoted in al-Hudaybi (1977) 134 (internal quotation-marks ('and') as printed in source).

304 al-Azmeh (1997) 172. As an example of a classic see al-Mawardi (1996) 12–16.

305 Gershoni and Jankowski (1995) 54–78 and Brown (1999) 60–80. al-Hudaybi's depiction of Muhammad is closely linked to his interpretation of history.

306 For collective duty (*fard al-kifaya*) see the articles by Reinhard (1995b) II: 2 and for individual duty (*fard al-'ayn*) see Reinhard (1995a) II: 1–2; further, see and Juynboll (1965) II: 790.

307 Al-Hudaybi (1978) 135–7.

308 Reinhard (1995b); see also Juynboll (1965) II: 790.

309 See for example Ibn Khaldun for a description of the caliph's duties (i.e. those he should ideally facilitate for); Ibn Khaldun (1967) 170–1.

310 Al-Hudaybi (1978)136. For a short description of vicarious duties see Reinhard (1995b) II: 2 and Juynboll (1965) II: 790.

311 See for example al-Mawardi (1996) 26–9 and Ibn Khaldun (1967) 154–5 and 170–1.

312 al-Hudaybi (1977) 136. Again, al-Hudaybi quotes extensively al-Rayyis (who is heavily influenced by Ibn Khaldun).

313 Note that the word '*'amm*' also carries the meaning 'communal' and that the word '*'aini*' is actually used in al-Hudaybi's statement, which adds to the conflicting reading of the passage.

314 al-Hudaybi (1977) 136.

315 al-Hudaybi (1977) 136

316 See for example al-Mawardi (1996) 12–18.

317 Al-Hudaybi (1978) 135.

318 A similar elitist argumentation is brought forward by a minority of contributors in their reading of the principle of *amr bi'l-ma'ruf wa al-nahy 'an al-munkar* (the command to do good and to avoid wrong). See Cook (2000) 17–18; for al-Hudaybi's stance on this subject see al-Hudaybi (1977) 132.

319 Al-Hudaybi (1978) 135.

320 Al-Hudaybi (1978) 135.

321 On al-Ghazali's political theory see Lambton (1981) 107–29 and Gibb (1955) 19–20.

322 Even though al-Khomeini's *welayat-e faqih* was written roughly during the same period of time, an immediate connection between both works is rather improbable.

323 This, by the way, contradicts previously made statements. In his chapters on belief and his critique of al-Maududi he denies that the belief of Muslims and hence the unifying strength of the Islamic community was ever threatened. See section 3.2 in this chapter.

324 See for example 'Auda's work on criminal law, 'Auda (1977) and 'Auda (1986), and Qutb (1993a).

325 For an insightful study of *baghy* (rebellion) in classical Islamic law see Abou El Fadl (2001). Because of apparent time restrictions, his recent work on rebellion and violence could not be appropriately incorporated into this book.

326 For a thorough study on the *amr*, its interpretation and application in the history of Islamic jurisprudence see Cook (2000).

327 Wehr suggests as possible translations for the term *hukm* the following: 'judgment, valuation, opinion; decision; (legal) judgement, verdict, sentence; condemnation; administration of justice; jurisdiction; legal consequences of the facts of a case (*Isl. Law*); regulation, rule, provision, order, ordinance, decree; judiciousness, wisdom; judgeship; command authority, control, dominion, power; government, regime …' Wehr (1976) 196. The variety of possible translations indicates the wide range of meanings the word can take in different contexts.

328 In the following, the principle of *al-amr bi'l-ma'ruf wa al-nahy 'an al-munkar* will be referred to in abbreviation as *amr*. The translation, i.e. 'commanding good and forbidding wrong' follows Cook; for an explanation see Cook (2000) 13, 563–9, 590–6. However, it needs to be noted that this translation is already an interpretation of its meaning. In fact, the idiom *'al-amr bi'l-ma'ruf wa al-nahy 'an al-munkar'* was variously translated into English, depending on the interpretation of *'al-ma'ruf'* and *'al-munkar'*. It was common to translate these terms as 'good' and 'evil'. Further, the term *'al-nahy'* allows various interpretations; hence, it can be also understood in the sense of 'abstaining from', which indeed gives the command an entirely different connotation.

329 The phrase is mentioned in the following Qur'anic verses 7: 157; 9: 69; 9: 71; 9: 112; 22: 41; 31: 17.

330 Cook (2000) 31, 590–6.

331 Therefore, theoretical and theological questions and doubts regarding the divine origin of morals also affect Islam. Although the critique of Nietzsche and those of postmodernist writers such as Foucault focus on Christianity, their claim that moral values and, ultimately, truth(s) are embedded in networks of power can also be applied to Islamic interpretation. Hence, moral codes are defined by humans, i.e. those having the power of delineating what is to be considered a religious obligation or even the truth. See for example Nietzsche (1990) and Nietzsche (1996); Foucault (1996) 379–81 and Foucault (1992).

332 Obviously, past discussions on the content of the *amr* are closely interlinked with the dispute about free will and predestination. Yet, a strong argument against the idea of predestination is that the *amr* supposes that the believer is capable of distinguishing what is good and what is wrong, otherwise the idea that he/she has of receiving divine judgement, or the prospect of being punished for transgressions against *shari'a* by worldly Islamic institutions would be void. On the controversy of free will and predestination in the discourse of early Islam, see Watt (1948)

333 Cook (2000)585–696. Cook describes this political aspect of the *amr* as the egalitarian element, which he contrasts to classical, non-political tendencies regarding the use of the concept.

334 See for example al-Mawardi's explication in his *al-Ahkam al-Sultaniyya* regarding the enforcement of *hisba* (public order); al-Mawardi (1996) 337–62.

335 As Abou El Fadl shows, his is also true for the *ahkam al-baghy*; Abou El Fadl (2001) passim.

336 Cook (2000) 505–60.

337 'Auda (1986) 1: 489–509.

338 For parts of Muhammad 'Abd al-Salam Faraj's pamphlet *al-farida al-gha'iba* (the neglected duty) and an interpretation of the ideology of the *Jihad* organisation see Jansen (1986). Regarding 'Umar 'Abd al-Rahman see Abdurrahman (1990) 49–50, 53–97 and Kogelmann (1991) 132–3 and Kepel (1985) 207.

339 Verses 26: 151–2 state *"wa la tuti'u amra 'l-musrifina; aladhina yufsiduna fi 'l-ardi wa la yuslihuna"*, which can be translated as follows: "and do not obey the command of the reckless, who are corrupt on earth and who do not do good".

340 Verse 5: 44 states: "(…) *wa man lam yahkum bi-ma 'nzala Allahu fa-'ula'ika humu 'l-kafiruna"*, and it can be translated as "whoever does not pass judgement according to what God has revealed, those are indeed the unbelievers". Similar also are passages 5: 45 and 5: 47, where instead of the word *al-kafirun* (unbeliever) the terms *al-zalimun* (transgressors) and *al-fasiqun* (trespassers) are used. Yet, some exegetes – modern as well as classical – argue that the occasions of revelation (*asbab al-nuzul*) for these passages lie in the historical conflict, of Medinan times, with the Jewish community of that time. Krämer mentions al-Tabari (died 923), Zamakhshari (died 1144) and Qurtubi (died 1258) as examples of orthodox interpreters and 'Ammara as a modern proponent of this exegesis. See Krämer (1999a) 92.

341 Qur'an 49: 9–10 states: "*Wa inna ta'ifatani mina 'lmu'minina 'qtatalu fa-aslihu bay-nahuma fa-in baghat ihdahuma 'la 'l-ukhra fa-qatilu 'llati tabgha hatta tafi'a ila amri 'llahi fa-inn fa'at fa-aslihu baynahuma bi'l-'adli wa aqsitu inna 'llah yuhibbu 'l-muqsitina. Innama 'l-mu'minuna ikhwatun fa-aslihubayna akhawaykumu wa 'ttaqu 'llaha la'allakum turhamuna.*" The verse can be translated as "If two parties among the believers fight each other, then make peace between them. But if one of them transgresses against the other, then fight, all of you, against the one that transgresses until it complies with the command of God. But if it complies, then make peace with the two parties with justice and be fair, for God loves those who are fair and just. The believers are but a single brotherhood. So reconcile your two brothers, and bear God so that you will receive His mercy."

Qur'an 5: 33–4 states: "*Innama jaza'u 'lladhina yuharibuna 'llah wa rasululahu wa yas'amuna fi 'l-ardi fasadan an yuqattalu aw yusallabu aw tuqatta'a aydihim wa arju-luhum min khilafin aw yunfa'u mina 'l-ardi dhalika lahum khizyun fi 'd-dunya wa lahum fi 'l-akhirati 'adhabun 'azimun. Illa 'lladhina tabu min qabli an taqdiru 'alayhim fa-'lamu anna 'llaha ghafurun rahimun.*" The verse translates as: "The punishment of those who wage war against God and his prophet, and strive to cause corruption on earth is that they be killed or crucified or have a hand and foot cut off from opposite ends or be exiled from the land. That is their disgrace in this world and they will receive a heavy punishment in the Hereafter. Except for those who repent before you are able to capture them. In that case, know that God is most-forgiving and merciful."

342 Qur'an 4: 59 states "*Ya ayyuha 'lladhina amanu ati'u 'llaha wa ati'u'al-rasula wa uli 'l-amri minkum (…)*", which can be translated as "O you who believe! Obey Allah and obey the Messenger, and those of you who are in authority (…)". Yet, this verse has also been reinterpreted in modern times by liberal Islamists who argue that leaders are bound to the community in a democratic way. See Krämer (1999a) 92–3.

343 Steppat (1965) 319–332. From the many traditions which imply that the command of a transgressor must be resented, the following sayings find regular mention: "there is no (duty of) obedience in sin" and "do not obey a creature against his Creator". The *Hadith* passages are quoted in Lambton (1981) 14.

344 Krämer (1993) 115. The *Hadith* is based on the authority of Abu Saʿid al-Khudri and states: "I heard the Messenger of Allah (…) say: Whoever of you sees an evil action, let him change it with his hand; and if he is not able to do so, then with his tongue; and if he is not able to do so, then with his heart – and that is the weakest of faith." Quoted in al-Nawawi (1977) 110.

345 Regarding the concept of *fitna* and its various meanings see Williams (1995a) II: 26–8.

346 al-Mawardi (1996) 29–35.

347 For further reading on the subject consult Cook (2000); Lambton (1981); Gibb (1955); Siegman (1964) and Watt (1948).

348 Gibb (1955) 14.

349 See Gibb (1955) 14–15. Critical about this view is Abou El Fadl (2001) 8–31, 37–47, 234–94.

350 Black (2001) 38, 82–5.

351 ʿAuda (1986) I: 489–509

352 al-Hudaybi (1977) 137.

353 al-Hudaybi (1977) 137–9.

354 The verse states in full: "*Ya ayyuha 'lladhina amanu atiyy'u 'llaha wa atiyy'u 'l-rasula wa uli 'l-amri minkum. fa-inna tanaza'tum fi sha'y fa-rudduhu ila Allah wa al-rasul in kuntum tu'minuna bi-Allah wa al-yaum al-akhir dhalika khayr wa ahsan ta'wilan.* (O you who believe! Obey God and obey the prophet and those of you who are in authority. So if you differ in anything amongst yourselves, refer it to Allah and his messenger, if you believe in Allah and in the Last Day. That is better and more suitable for final determination.)"

355 See verse 4: 59.
356 The *Hadith* passages al-Hudaybi quotes are: "there is no obedience to a human being, if he is sinful to God"; "who transgressed and left the community dies a *jahiliyya* death"; "listening and obedience is the virtue of the individual Muslim (*'ala al-mar' al-Muslim*) whether he loves or hates it unless disobedience was commanded; then, if he is commanded to disobedience, then there is no listening and no obedience"; "listening and obedience is right unless it was commanded to commit disobedience. If he commanded disobedience, then there is no listening and no obedience." Al-Hudaybi quotes herein al-Muslim vol. 9: 361 and Abu Da'ud vol. 9: 361.
357 Al-Hudaybi refers in the quote to Qur'an 49: 9, which jurists refer to as *aya al-baghy* (the verse of rebellion); see Abou El Fadl (2001) 37–47.
358 Abou El Fadl is dedicated to showing that the discourse about rebellion is complex. Hence, one can only speak about a tendency in classical writing; Abou El Fadl (2001) *passim*.
359 See also Al-Hudaybi (1978) 141, where he outlines that one needs to show patience before engaging in forceful opposition.
360 See section 3.3 on possible excuses in this chapter.
361 The juridical principle of *la darar wa la dirar* suggests that although punishment for criminal offences is divinely ordained, its application must not inflict more (public) disruption than it would be of assistance. See Kamali (1991) 245–82, esp. 269 for juridical theory, but also Kerr (1966)101 in regards to modern interpretation.
362 al-Hudaybi (1977) 140.
363 Krämer (1999a) 97–9.
364 al-Hudaybi (1977) 140.
365 al-Hudaybi (1977) 140.
366 al-Hudaybi (1977) 140.
367 al-Hudaybi (1977) 140. For further reading and for a description of the dispute about the interpretation of *aya al-baghy* (verses 49: 9–10) and *aya al-hiraba* (verses 5: 33–4) in early Islamic history see Abou El Fadl (2001) 34–61.
368 al-Hudaybi (1977) 140.
369 al-Hudaybi (1977) 141.
370 al-Hudaybi (1977) 141–2.
371 al-Hudaybi (1977) 140, 142. Al-Hudaybi also goes against interpretations which link illegitimate rule to the crime of thieving; al-Hudaybi (1977) 143. The connection between thieving and illegitimate rule can be made in reference to the so-called *hiraba*-verse (i.e. verse 5: 33–4), which has been linked to stealing and highway robbery. The verse states: "The recompense of those who wage war against Allah and his prophet and strive to cause corruption on the earth is that they be killed or crucified or have a hand and foot cut off from opposite ends or be exiled from the land. That is their disgrace in this world and they will receive a heavy punishment in the Hereafter. Except for those who repent before you are able to capture then. In this case, know that God is most-forgiving and merciful." On the application of the verse to thieving and highway robbery in classical interpretation, see Abou El Fadl (2001) 47–61
372 al-Hudaybi (1977)141.
373 al-Hudaybi (1977)141.
374 al-Hudaybi (1977) 142.The word *al-qital* is the verbal noun of the third root of q-t-l, i.e. *qatala, yuqatilu*. Since the basic first root '*qatala; yaqtilu*' means 'to kill', the derivative word *al-qital* has indeed a connotation which indicates the attempt to kill an opponent during fighting.
375 al-Hudaybi (1977) 141–3.
376 Kamali (1991) 149–67 and Hallaq (1999) 68–74.
377 Kamali (1991) 149–67. Hence, there are a number of options to qualify and classify the abrogated texts (i.e. explicit or implicit abrogation, partial of full abrogation etc.). When focusing on the abrogating source, one can further apply the following

sub-categories: 1. the Qur'an abrogates the Qur'an (*Qur'an yansikh Qur'an*); 2. Qur'an abrogates sunna (*Qur'an yansikh sunna*); 3. sunna abrogates Qur'an (*sunna tansikh Qur'an*); 4. sunna abrogates sunna (*sunna tansikh sunna*). Obviously, the abrogation of Quranic verses through sunna is the most controversially disputed; see Kamali (1991) 158–60 and Hallaq (1999) 72–4.

378   Hallaq (1999) 68.

379   As indicated before, it is because of the complex composition, content and style of the Qur'an as well as because of the lack of historical data that the historical moments of the actual disclosure of verses are not entirely agreed upon. Subsequently, an 'exact' chronological order of verses is not established; an example are the various scholarly attempts such as by Theodor Nöldeke or Richard Bell.

380   al-Hudaybi (1977) 144–59.

381   The verse states: "*fa-la wa rabbika la yu'minuna hatta yuhakkimunka fima sajara baynahum thumma la yajidu fi anfusihim harajan mimma qadayta wa yusallimu tasliman*". See also al-Hudaybi (1977) 143–5.

382   al-Hudaybi (1977) 143–51

383   al-Hudaybi (1977) 143, 145–8, 149, 151.

384   *Tahkim* is the verbal substantive to the second root of h-k-m, i.e. *hakkama, yuhakkimu*. The verb is used in the above-mentioned verse 4: 65 and in classical Arabic carries the meaning of 'to make (someone) the judge'. It also developed the meaning 'to appoint (someone) as ruler'. See Wehr (1976) 196

385   al-Hudaybi (1977) 148.

386   al-Hudaybi (1977) 148.

387   al-Hudaybi (1977) 149–53.

388   al-Hudaybi (1977) 151, 156.

Bibliography

Books and articles

ʿAbd al-Halim, Mahmud. 1979. *al-Ikhwan al-Muslimun. Ahdath Sanaʿat al-Tarikh. Ruʾiyya min al-Dakhil*. Alexandria: Dar al-Daʿwa.

ʿAbd al-Halim, Mahmud. 1981. *al-Ikhwan al-Muslimun. Ahdath Sanaʿat al-Tarikh. Ruʾiyya min al-Dakhil*. Alexandria: Dar al-Daʿwa.

ʿAbd al-Halim, Mahmud. 1986. *al-Ikhwan al-Muslimun. Ahdath Sanaʿat al-Tarikh. Ruʾiyya min al-Dakhil*. Alexandria: Dar al-Daʿwa.

ʿAbd al-Khaliq, Farid. 1987. *al-Ikhwan al-Muslimun fi Mizan al-Haqq*. Cairo: Dar al-Sahwa.

ʿAbd al-Majid, Ahmad. 1991. *al-Ikhwan wa ʿAbd al-Nasir. al-Qissa al-Kamila li-Tanzim 1965*. Cairo: al-Zahra li-l-Aʿlam al-ʿArabi.

ʿAbd al-Rahman, ʿUmar. n.y. *Kalimat al-Haqq. Murafaʿa al-Duktur ʿUmar ʿAbd a-Rahman fi Qidhayya al-Jihad*. Shubra: Dar al-Iʿtisam.

ʿAbd al-Raziq, ʿAli. 1972. *al-Islam wa Usul al-Hukm*. Beirut: al-Muʾassassat al-ʿArabiyya liʾl-Dirasat wa al-Nashr.

ʿAbd al-Samiʿ, ʿAmaru, ed. 1992. *al-Islamiyyun. Hiwarat haula al-Mustaqbal*. Cairo: Maktaba al-Turath al-Islami.

ʿAbd Rabbih, Nabih. 1987. *Hasan al-Hudaybi. al-Murshid al-Thani liʾl-Ikhwan al-Muslimin*. Amman: Dar al-Diyaʾliʾl-Nashr wa al-Tawziʿ.

Abdalla, Ahmad. 1985. *The Student Movement and National Poltics in Egypt*. London: Al Saqi Books.

Abdel-Malek, Anouar. 1968. *Egypt. Military Society. The Army Regime, the Left, and Social Change under Nasser*. New York: Random House.

Abdel Nasser, Hoda Gamal. 1994. *Britain and the Egyptian Nationalist Movement 1936–52*. Reading: Ithaka.

Abdelnasser, Walid M. 1994. *The Islamic Movement in Egypt. Perceptions of International Relations, 1967–81*. London, New York: Kegan Paul International.

Abdurrahman, Omar Ahmad Ali. 1990. *The Present Rulers and Islam. Are they Muslims or not?* London: Al Firdous.

Abed-Kotob, Sana. 1995. "The Accomodationists Speak: Goals and Strategies of the Muslim Brotherhood of Egypt." *International Journal of Middle East Studies* 27: 321–39.

Abou El Fadl, Khaled. 2001. *Rebellion and Violence in Islamic Law*. Cambridge: Cambridge University Press.

Abrahamov, Binyamin. 1998. *Islamic Theology. Traditionalism and Rationalism*. Edinburgh: Edinburgh University Press.

ʿAbu al-Nasr, Muhammad Hamid. 1987. *Haqiqat al-Khilaf bayna "al-Ikhwan al-Muslimun" wa ʿAbd al-Nasir*. Cairo: International Press.

Abu Rabiʿ, Ibrahim. 1984. "Sayyid Qutb: From Religious Realism to Radical Social Criticism." *Islamic Quarterly* 28: 103–26.

Abu Rabiʿ, Ibrahim M. 1996. *Intellectual Origins of Islamic Resurgence in the Modern Arab World*. New York: State University of New York Press.

Abu Rabiʿ, Ibrahim M. 2004. *Contemporary Arab Thought. Studies in Post-1967 Arab Intellectual History*. London: Pluto Press.

Adams, Charles C. 1933. *Islam and Modernism in Egypt. A Study of the Modern Reform Movement Inaugurated by Muhammad ʿAbduh*. London: Oxford University Press.

Adams, Charles J. 1983. "Mawdudi and the Islamic State." In *Voices of Resurgent Islam*, ed. John L. Esposito. New York, Oxford: Oxford University Press.

Ahmad, Khurshid and Zafar Ishaq Ansari. 1979. "Mauwlana Sayyid Abul Aʿla al-Mawdudi. An Introduction to his Vision of Islam and Islamic Revival." In *Islamic perspectives. Studies in honour of Mawlana Sayyid Abul Aʿla Mawdudi*, eds Khurshid Ahmad and Zafar Ishaq Ansari. London, Jeddah: Islamic Foundation U.K. in association with Saudi Publishing House.

Ahmad, Sayyid Asʿad. 1977. "Hasan al-Hudaybi." In *al-Islam wa al-Daʿiyya*, ed. Hasan al-Hudaybi. Cairo: Dar al-Ansar.

al-ʿAllam, Fuʾad. 1996. *al-Ikhwan ... wa Ana. Min al-Manshiyya ila al-Minassa*. Cairo: al-Maktab al-Misri al-Hadith liʾl-Tabaʿa wa al-Nashr.

al-ʿAmmara, Muhammad. 1985. *al-Sahwat al-Islamiyya wa al-Tahaddi al-Hadara*. Beirut: Dar al-Shuruq.

al-ʿAmmara, Muhammad. 1988. *al-Daula al-Islamiyya bayna al-ʿAlmaniyya wa al-Sulta al-Diniyya*. Cairo and Beirut: Dar a-Shuruq.

Arkoun, Mohammad. 1994. *Rethinking Islam: Common Questions, Uncommon Answers*. Boulder, CO: Westview Press.

Asad, Talal. 1973 *Anthology of Colonial Encounter*. London: Ithaka.

ʿAsal, Fahmi. n.y. "al-Ikhwan al-Muslimun bayna ʿAhadiyya." Cairo: unpublished document (copy with the author).

Ashcroft, Bill and Pal Ahluwalia. 1999. *Edward Said. The Paradox of Identity*. London and New York: Routledge.

al-ʿAshmawi, Hasan. n.y. *Hasad al-Ayam aw Mudhkirat Harib*. Cairo: Dar al-Tawziʿ wa al-Nashr al-Islamiyya.

al-ʿAshmawi, Muhammad Saʿid. 1985. *al-Sahwat al-Islamiyya wa al-Tahaddi al-Hadara*. Beirut: Dar al-Shuruq.

al-ʿAshmawi, Muhammad Saʿid. 1987. *Abu Aʿla al-Maududi wa al-Sahwat al-Islamiyya*. Beirut Dar al-Shuruq.

al-ʿAshmawi, Muhammad Saʿid. 1989. *al-Islam al-Siyasi*. Cairo: Sina liʾl-Nashr.

ʿAuda, ʿAbd al-Qadir. 1977. *al-Islam wa Audaʾuna al-Qanuniyya*. Cairo.

ʿAuda, ʿAbd al-Qadir. 1986. *al-Tashriʿ al-Jinaʾi al-Islami. Muqaranan biʾl-Qanun al-ʿWadiʿi*. Beirut: Muʾassasa al-Risala.

Ayubi, Nazih N. 1991. *Political Islam. Religion and Politics in the Arab World*. London, New York: Routledge.

Ayubi, Nazih N. M. 1980. "The Political Revival of Islam: the Case of Egypt." *International Journal of Middle East Studies* 12: 481–99.

al-Azmeh, Aziz. 1997. *Muslim Kingship. Power and the Sacred in Muslim, Christian and Pagan Politics*. London and New York: I. B. Tauris.

Baker, Raymond. 1990. *Sadat and After: Struggle for Egypt's Political Soul*. London: I. B. Tauris.

Baker, Raymond William. 2003. *Islam without Fear. Egypt and the New Islamists*. Cambridge, MA: Harvard University Press.

al-Banna, Hasan. 1982. *Memoirs of Hasan Al Banna Shaheed*. Karachi: International Islamic Publishers.

al-Banna', Hasan. 1990. *Majmu'at Rasa'il al-Imam al-Shahid Hasan al-Banna*. Beirut: Dar al-Da'wa.

al-Banna', Hasan. n.y. *Mudhakkirat al-Da'wa wa al-Da'iyya li'l-Imam al-Shahid Hasan al-Banna*. Cairo: Dar al-Da'wa.

al-Banna', Jamal, ed. 1990. *Khitabat Hasan al-Banna al-Sha'b ila Abihi*. Cairo: Dar al-Fikr al-Islami.

al-Banna', Jamal. 1988. *al-Islam Huwa al-Hall. Dirasa fi al-Taghayyir al-Ijtima'i wa Ifsad al-Fikr al-Misr wa Tariqa al-Khilas min al-Ma'azziq*. Cairo: Dar al-Tabi' al-Jadida.

Bassiouni, M. Cherif, ed. 1981. *The Islamic Criminal System*. London; New York: Oceana Publications.

al-Bayyumi, Zakariyya Sulayman. 1987. *al-Ikhwan al-Muslimun bayna 'Abd al-Nasir wa al-Sadat*. Cairo: Maktaba Wahba.

al-Bazz, Na'am. 1977. al-Baquri. *Tha'ir Taht al-'Ammama*. Cairo: al-Hayy'a al-Misriyya al-'Amma li'l-Kitab.

Beattie, Kirk J. 1994. *Egypt during the Nasser Years. Ideology, Politics, and Civil Society*. Boulder, CO: Westview Press.

Beattie, Kirk J. 2000. *Egypt during the Sadat Years*. New York: Palgrave.

Berger, Maurits S. 2003. "Apostasy and Public Policy in Contemporary Egypt: An Evaluation of Recent Cases from Egypt's Highest Courts." *Human Rights Quarterly* 25: 720–40.

Berger, Morroe. 1970. *Islam in Egypt Today. Social and Political Aspect of Popular Religion*. Cambridge: Cambridge University Press.

Binder, Leonard. 1988. *Islamic Liberalism: A Critique of Development Ideologies*. Chicago, London: University of Chicago Press.

Black, Anthony. 2001. *The History of Islamic Political Thought. From the Prophet to the Present*. Edinburgh: Edinburgh University Press.

Bonney, Richard. 2004. *Jihad. From Qur'an to bin Laden*. New York: Palgrave Macmillan.

Brown, Daniel. 1999. *Rethinking Tradition in Modern Islamic Thought*. Cambridge: Cambridge University Press.

Brown, Nathan J. 1997. "Shari'a and State in the Modern Muslim Middle East." *Journal of Middle East Studies* 29: 359–76.

Burgat, Francois. 2003. *Face to Face with Political Islam*. London: I. B. Tauris.

Carré, Olivier. 1995. "Banna, Hasan al- (1906–49)." In *The Oxford Encyclopaedia of the Modern Islamic World*, ed. John L. Esposito. New York and Oxford.

Carré, Olivier. 2003. *Mysticism and Politics: A Critical Reading of Fi Zilal al-Qur'an by Sayyid Qutb (1906–66)*. Leiden: Brill.

Carré, Olivier and Gérard Michaud. 1983. *Les Frères Musulmans. Egypte et Syrie (1928–82)*. Paris: Gallimard Julliard.

Choueiri, Youssef. 1990. *Islamic Fundamentalism*. London: Pinter Publishers.

Clarke, Janine A. 2004. *Islam, Charity and Activism. Middle-Class Networks and Social Welfare in Egypt, Jordan and Yemen*. Bloomington, IN: Indiana University Press.

Clarke, Lynda. 1995. "Shahada." In *The Oxford Encyclopaedia of the Modern Islamic World*, ed. John L. Esposito. New York and Oxford: Oxford University Press.

Commins, David. 1994. "Hasan al-Banna (1906–49)." In *Pioneers of Islamic Revival*, ed. Ali Rahnema. London: Zed Books.

Cook, David. 2005. *Understanding Jihad*. Berkeley, Los Angeles, London: University of California Press.

Cook, Michael. 2000. *Commanding Right and Forbidding Wrong in Islamic Thought*. Cambridge: Cambridge University Press.

Cooke, Miriam. 1994. "Zaynab al-Ghazali: Saint or Subversive?" *Die Welt des Islam* 34: 1–19.

Cooper, John, Ronald L. Nettler and Mahmoud Mohamed, eds. 1998. *Islam and Modernity. Muslim Intellectuals Respond*. New York: I. B. Tauris.

Coulson, Noel J. 1964. *A History of Islamic Law*. Edinburgh: Edinburgh University Press.

Crecelius, Daniel. 1989. "Al-Azhar in the Revolution." *Middle East Journal* 20: 304–15.

Crone, Patricia. 2000. "Ninth-Century Anarchists." *Past and Present* 176(3): 28.

Crone, Patricia. 2004. *Medieval Islamic Political Thought*. Edinburgh: Edinburgh University Press.

Crone, Patricia and Martin Hinds. 1986. *God's Caliph. Religious Authority in the First Centuries of Islam*. Cambridge: Cambridge University Press.

Davies, Eric. 1984. "Ideology, Social Class and Islamic Radicalism in Modern Egypt." In *From Nationalism to Revolutionary Islam*, ed. S. A. Arjomand. London: Macmillan in association with St Anthony's College.

Davis, Joyce M. 1999. *Between Jihad and Salaam. Profiles in Islam*. New York: St. Martin's Griffin.

Deeb, Marius. 1979. *Party Politics in Egypt. The Wafd and its Rival, 1919–39*. London: Ithaka Press in association with the Middle East Centre, St Antony's College Oxford.

Dekmejian, R. Hrair. 1971. *Egypt under Nasser: A Study of Political Dynamics*. Albany: State University Press of New York.

Diyab, Muhammad Hafiz. 1987. *Sayyid Qutb. al-Khitab wa al-Idiyulujiyya*. Cairo: Dar al-Thaqafa al-Jadida.

Donohue, John J. and John L. Esposito, eds. 1982. *Islam in Transition. Muslim Perspectives*. New York and Oxford: Oxford University Press.

Doumato, Eleanor Abdella, ed. 1995. *Jahiliyah*. New York and Oxford: Oxford University Press.

Duh, Hasan. 1989. *25 al-Amm wa Amal 'ala Tariq al-Ikhwan al-Muslimin*. Cairo: Dar al-I'tisam.

Dwyer, Kevin. 1991. *Arab Voices: The Human Rights Debate in the Middle East*. London: Routledge.

Eccel, Chris A. 1984. *Egypt, Islam and Social Change: al-Azhar in Conflict and Accomodation*. Berlin: Klaus Schwarz.

Eickelman, Dale F. and James Piscatori. 1996. *Muslim Politics*. Princeton: Princeton University Press..

El-Awaisi, Abd al-Fattah Muhammad. 1998. *The Muslim Brothers and the Palestine Question 1928–47*. London: Tauris Academic Studies.

El-Baradie, Adel. 1983. *Gottes-Recht und Menschen-Recht. Grundlagenprobleme der Islamischen Strafrechtslehre*. Baden-Baden: Nomos.

El-Ghobashy, Mona. 2005. "The Metamorphosis of the Egyptian Muslim Brothers." *International Journal of Middle East Studies* 37: 375–95.

El-Sadat, Anwar. 1957. *Revolt of the Nile*. London: Allan Wingate.

El-Sadat, Anwar. 1978. *In Search of Identity*. London: Collins.

Enayat, Hamid. 1982. *Modern Islamic Political Thought. The Response of Shi'i and Sunni Muslims to the Twentieth Century*. London: Macmillan.

Esposito, John L. 1991. *The Islamic Threat: Myth or Reality?* New York and Oxford: Oxford University Press.

Esposito, John L. 1998. *Islam. The Straight Path*. New York and Oxford: Oxford University Press.

Esposito, John L., ed. 1983. *Voices of Resurgent Islam*. New York and Oxford: Oxford University Press.

Fahmi, Ninette S. 2002. *The Politics of Egypt. State–Society Relationship*. London: Routledge Curzon.

Firestone, Reuven. 1999. *Jihad. The Origin of Holy War in Islam*. Oxford Oxford University Press.

Forstner, Martin. 1988. "Auf Legalem Weg zur Politischen Macht? Zur Politischen Entwicklung der Muslimbruderschaft Ägyptens." *Orient* 29: 386–422.

Foucault, Michel. 1992. *The History of Sexuality. Vol.II: The Use of Pleasure*. London: Penguin Books.

Foucault, Michel. 1996. "Truth and Power." In *From Modernism to Postmodernism: an Anthology,* ed. Lawrence E. Cahoone. Oxford: Oxford University Press.

Fudah, Faraj. 1982. "al-Janib al-ʿAlmani." In *Misr bayna al-Daula al-Diniyya wa al-Madaniyya. Al-Munazira al-Shahira allati aqimat fi Maʿrad al-Qahira al-Daulili'l-Kutub*, ed. S. Sarhan. Cairo: Dar al-Misriyyali'l-Nashr wa al-Tawziʿ.

Gadamer, Hans-Georg. 1981. *Truth and Method*. London: Sheed and Ward.

Gaffney, Patrick D. 1994. *The Prophet's Pulpit: Islamic Preaching in Contemporary Egypt*. Berkeley, Los Angeles and London: University of California Press.

Gershoni, I. and James P. Jankowski. 1995. *Redefining the Egyptian Nation, 1930–45*. Cambridge: Cambridge University Press.

al-Ghazali, Zainab. 1974. *Return of the Pharao. Memoir in Nasir's Prison*. Leicester: The Islamic Foundation.

al-Ghazali, Zaynab. 1987. *Ayyam min Hayati*. Cairo: al-Matbaʿa al-Adabiyya.

Gibb, Hamilton A. R. 1955. "Constitutional Organisation." In *Origin and Development of Islamic Law*, eds M. Khadduri and H. J. Liebesny. Washington: Middle East Institute.

Gibb, Hamilton A. R. 1962. "Al-Mawardi's Theory of the Caliphate." In *Studies on the Civilization of Islam*, eds W. R. Polk and S. J. Shaw. Boston, MA: Beacon Press.

Goldschmidt, Arthur. 1990. *Modern Egypt. The Formation of a Nation-State*. Cairo: American University Press.

Goldziher, Ignaz. 1981. *Introduction to Islamic Theology and Law*. Princeton: Princeton University Press.

Gomaa, Ahmad M. 1983. "Islamic Fundamentalism during the 1930s and 1970s. Comparative notes." In *Islam, Nationalism and Radicalism in Egypt and the Sudan*, eds Gabriel R. Warburg and Uri M. Kupferschmidt. New York: Praeger.

Gordon, Joel. 1992. *Nasser's Blessed Movement. Egypt's Free Officers and the July Revolution*. New York and Oxford: Oxford University Press.

Gorman, Anthony. 2003. *Historians, State and Politics in Twentieth Century Egypt. Contesting the Nation*. London and New York: Routledge Curzon.

Haddad, Yvonne. 1983. "Sayyid Qutb: Ideologue of Islamic Revival." In *Voices of Resurgent Islam*, ed. John L. Esposito. New York and Oxford: Oxford University Press.

Haddad, Yvonne Y., John L. Esposito and John O. Voll, eds. 1991. *The Contemporary Islamic Revival: A Critical Survey and Bibliography*. New York and London: Greenwood Press.

Hafez, Mohammed M. and Quintan Wiktorowicz. 2004. "Violence as Contention in the Egyptian Islamic Movement." In *Islamic Activism. A Social Movement Theory Approach*, ed. Quintan Wiktorowicz. Bloomington, IN: Indiana University Press.

Hail, J.A. 1996. *Britain's Foreign Policy in Egypt and Sudan 1947–56*. Reading: Ithaka.

Hallaq, Wael B. 1984. "Was the Gate of Ijtihad Closed?" *International Journal of Middle East Studies* 16: 3–41.

Hallaq, Wael B. 1994. "From Fatwas to Furu': Growth and Change in Islamic Substantive Law." *Islamic Law and Society* 1: 17–56.

Hallaq, Wael B. 1997. *A History of Islamic Legal Theories: An Introduction to Sunni Usul al-Fiqh*. Cambridge: Cambridge University Press.

Hallaq, Wael B. 1999. *A History of Islamic Legal Theories. An Introduction to Sunni Usul al-Fiqh*. Cambridge: Cambridge University Press.

Hallaq, Wael B. 2005. *The Origins and Evolution of Islamic Law*. Cambridge: Cambridge University Press.

Halliday, Fred. 1995. *Islam and the Myth of Confrontation: Religion and Politics in the Middle East*. London and New York: I. B. Tauris.

Halliday, Fred. 2005. *The Middle East in International Relations: Power, Politics and Ideology*. Cambridge: Cambridge University Press.

Halpern, Manfred. 1965. *The Politics of Social Change in the Middle East and North Africa*. Princeton, NJ: Princeton University Press.

Hamuda, 'Adil. 1996. *Sayyid Qutb min al-Quriyya ila al-Mashnaqa. Sira al-Adab al-Ruhi li'Jama'at al-'Unf*. Cairo: Dar al-Khayyal.

Hanafi, Hasan. 1989. *al-Din wa al-Thaura fi Misr, 1952–81*. Cairo: Maktaba Madbuli.

Harris, Christina Phelps. 1964. *Nationalism and the Revolution in Egypt. The Role of the Muslim Brotherhood*. The Hague: Mouton.

Hartung, Jan-Peter. 2004. *Viele Wege und ein Ziel. Leben und Wirken von Sayyid Abu l-Hasan 'Ali al-Hasani Nadwi (1914–99)*. Wurzburg: Ergon.

Heyworth-Dunne, James. 1950. *Religious and Political Trends in Modern Egypt*. Washington: McGregor Werner.

Hodgson, Marshall G. S. 1974. *The Venture of Islam. Conscience and History in a World Civilization: The classical age of Islam*. Chicago: University of Chicago Press.

Hooker, M. B. 1965. "Shari'a." In *Encyclopaedia of Islam*. Leiden: Brill.

Hourani, Albert. 1983. *Arabic Thought in the Liberal Age. 1798–1939*. Cambridge: Cambridge University Press.

Hourani, Albert. 1991. *A History of the Arab Peoples*. London: Faber and Faber.

al-Hudaybi, Hasan. 1977. *Du'at ... la Qudat*. Cairo: Dar al-Taba'a wa al-Nashr al-Islamiyya.

al-Hudaybi, Hasan. 1978. *al-Islam wa al-Da'iyya. Majallat – Bayanat-Nasharat – Rasa'il – Madha'at*. Cairo: Dar al-Ansar.

Hurewitz, Jacob C. 1979. *The Middle East and North Africa in World Politics. A Documentary Record; vol 2: British-French Supremacy, 1914–45*. New Haven and London: Yale University Press.

Husaini, Ishaq Musa. n.y. *The Moslem Brethren. The Greatest of the Modern Islamic Movements*. Beirut: Khayat's College Book Cooperative.

Huwaydi, Fahmi. 1982. *al-Qur'an wa al-Sultan. Humum Islamiyya Mu'asira*. Beirut: Dar al-Shuruq.

Ibn Khaldun, 'Abd al-Rahman Muhammad. 1967. *An Introduction to History: The Muqaddimah*. London: Routledge and Kegan Paul in association with Secker and Warburg.

Ibn Khaldun, 'Abd al-Rahman Muhammad. 1970. *al-Muqaddima*. Beirut: Maktab Lubnan.

Ibn Taymiyya, Ahmad Ibn 'Abd al-Halim. 1997. *Kitab al-Iman*. Beirut: Dar al-Tadamun.

Ibrahim, Saad Eddin. 1980. "Anatomy of Egypt's Militant Islamic Groups." *International Journal of Middle East Studies* 12(4): 423–53.

Izutsu, Toshihiko. 1964. *God and Man in the Koran: Studies of the Koranic Weltanschauung*. Tokyo: Keio Institute of Cultural and Linguistic Studies.

Izutsu, Toshihiko. 1980. *The Concept of Belief in Islamic Theology*. New York: Books for Libraries.

Izutsu, Toshihiko. 2002. *Ethico-Religious Concepts in the Qur'an*. Montreal, Ithaca, NY: McGill-Queen's University Press.

Jansen, Johannes J. G. 1986. *The Neglected Duty: The Creed of Sadat's Assassins and Islamic Resurgence in the Middle East*. New York: Macmillan.

Jansen, Johannes J. G. 1992. "Hasan al-Banna's Earliest Pamphlet." *Die Welt des Islams* 32: 254–8.

Jansen, Johannes J. G. 1997. *The Dual Nature of Islamic Fundamentalism*. Ithaca, NY: Cornell University Press.

Jarisha, 'Ali. 1988. *Fi al-Zinzana*. Al-Mansura: Dar al-Wafa' li'l-Taba'a wa al-Nashr wa al-Tauzi'.

Johansen, Baber. 1986. "Staat, Recht und Religion im Sunnitischen Islam – Konnen Muslime einen religionsneutralen Staat akzeptieren?" *Essener Gesprache zum Thema Staat und Kirche* 20: 16–20.

Juynboll, Th. W. 1965. "Fard." In *Encyclopaedia of Islam*. Leiden: Brill.

Kamal, Ahmad 'Adil. 1989. *al-Nuqat fauqa al-Huruf. al-Ikhwan al-Muslimun wa al-Nizam al-Khass*. Cairo: al-Sahra' li-l-I'lam al-'Arabi.

Kamali, Mohammad Hashim. 1991. *Principles of Islamic Jurisprudence*. Cambridge: Cambridge University Press.

Karawan, Ibrahim A. 1995. "Takfir." In *The Oxford Encyclopaedia of the Modern Islamic World*, ed. John L. Esposito. New York and Oxford: Oxford University Press.

Kepel, Gilles. 1985. *Muslim Extremism in Egypt. The Prophet and the Pharaoh*. London: Al Saqi Books.

Kepel, Gilles. 2004. *Jihad: The Trail of Political Islam*. London: I. B. Tauris.

Kerr, Malcom H. 1966. *Islamic Reform. The Political and Legal Theories of Muhammad 'Abduh and Rashid Rida*. Berkeley and Los Angeles: University of California Press.

al-Khabbas, 'Abdallah 'Auad 'Abdallah. 1983. *Sayyid Qutb. al-Adib al-Naqid*. al-Zarqa': n.p.

Khalafallah, Muhammad Ahmad. 1984. *Mafahim Qur'aniyya*. Kuwait: 'Amr li'l-Ma'arifa.

Khatab, Sayed. 2001. "Al Hudaybi's Influence on the Development of Islamist Movements in Egypt." *The Muslim World* 91(3–4): 451–80.

Khatab, Sayed. 2002. "Hakimiyya and Jahiliyya in the Thought of Sayyid Qutb." *Middle Eastern Studies* 38(3): 145–70.

Khatab, Sayed. 2006. *The Political Thought of Sayyid Qutb: The Theory of Jahiliyya*. London: Routledge.

Kogelmann, Franz. 1991. *Die Islamisten Ägyptens in der Regierungszeit Anwar as-Sadat (1970–81)*. Bayreuth: K. Schwarz.

Krämer, Gudrun. 1994. "Die Korrektur der Irrtümer: Innerislamische Debatte um Theorie und Praxis der islamischen Bewegungen." *Zeitschrift der Deutschen Morgenländischen Gesellschaft*. Suppl. XXV 10: 183–91.

Krämer, Gudrun. 1999a. *Gottes Staat als Republik. Reflexionen Zeitgenössischer Muslime zu Islam, Menschenrechten und Demokratie*. Baden-Baden: Nomos Verlagsgesellschaft.

Krämer, Gudrun. 1999b. "Techniques and Values: Contemporary Muslim Debates on Islam and Democracy." In *Islam, Modernism and the West. Cultural and Political Relations at the End of the Millenium*, ed. G. M. Muñoz. London and New York: I. B. Tauris.

Kurzman, Charles ed. 1998. *Liberal Islam. A Sourcebook*. New York and Oxford: Oxford University Press.

Kurzman, Charles ed. 2002. *Modern Islam, 1840–1940. A Sourcebook*. Oxford and New York: Oxford University Press.

Lambton, Ann K. S. 1981. *State and Government in Medieval Islam. An Introduction to the Study of Islamic Political Theory*. Oxford: Oxford University Press.

Laoust, Henri. 1938. *Le Caliphat dans la doctrine de Rashid Rida. Traduction annotée d'al-Khilafa au al-Imama al-'Uzma (Le Califat ou l-'Imama Supreme)*. Beirut: n.p.

Laoust, Henri. 1968. *La Penseé et l'Action Politique de al-Mawardi (364–450/ 974–1058)*. Paris: Librairie Orientaliste Paul Geuthner.

Leiken, Robert S. and Steven Brooke. 2007. "The Moderate Muslim Brotherhood." *Foreign Affairs* 86(2): 107–21.

Lewis, Bernard. 2003. *The Crisis of Islam: Holy War and Unholy Terror*. New York: Modern Library.

Lia, Brynjar. 1998. *The Society of the Muslim Brothers in Egypt: the rise of an Islamic Mass Movement, 1928–1942*. Reading: Ithaka Press.

Lia, Brynjar. 2006. *Society of the Muslim Brothers in Egypt: The Rise of an Islamic Mass Movement, 1928–42*. 1st paperback edn. Reading, England: Ithaca Press.

Madelung, Wilfried. 1997. *The Succession of Muhammad: A Study of the Early Caliphate*. Cambridge: Cambridge University Press.

Mahfuz, Muhammad. 1988. *Aladhina Zulimu. al-Tanzimat al-Islamiyya fi Misr*. London: Riad El-Rayyes Books.

Mansfield, Laura. 2006. *His Own Words. A Translation of the Writings of Dr. Ayman al Zawahiri*. n.p.: TLG Publications.

Marlow, Louise. 1997. *Hierarchy and Egalitarianism in Islamic Thought*. Cambridge: Cambridge University Press.

Marmura, Michael E. 1995. "Sunni Islam." In *The Oxford Encyclopaedia of the Modern Islamic World*, ed. John L. Esposito. Oxford and New York: Oxford University Press.

Marsot, al-Sayyid Afaf Lutfi. 1977. *Egypt's Liberal Experiment: 1922–36*. Berkeley, London et al: University of California Press.

Marsot, al-Sayyid Afaf Lutfi. 1985. *A Short History of Modern Egypt*. Cambridge: Cambridge University Press.

Martin, Richard C., Mark R. Woodward and Dwi S. Atmaja. 2003. *Defenders of Reason in Islam. Mu'tazimilsm from Medieval Schools to Modern Symbol*. Oxford: Oneworld.

al-Maududi, Abu A'la. 1968. *First Principles of the Islamic State*. Lahore: Islamic Publications Limited.

al-Maududi, Abu A'la. 1993. *al-Mustalahat al-Arba'a fi al-Qur'an*. Kuwait: n.p.

al-Mawardi, Abu al-Hasan 'Ali ibn Muhammad ibn Habib al-Basrial-Baghdadi. n.y. *al-Ahkam al-Sultaniyya wa al-Walaya al-Diniyya*. Beirut: Dar al-Kuttub al-'Alamiyya.

al-Mawardi, Abu al-Hasan. 1996. *al-Ahkam al-Sultaniyya. The Laws of Islamic Governance*. London: Ta-Ha.

Mayer, Ann Elizabeth. 1995. "Law: Modern Legal Reform." In *The Oxford Encyclopaedia of the Modern Islamic World*, ed. John L. Esposito. Oxford and New York: Oxford University Press.

Mayer, Ann Elizabeth. 1999. *Islam and Human Rights. Tradition and Politics*. Boulder, CO: Westview Press.

Mikhail, Hanna. 1995. *Politics and Revelation. Mawardi and After*. Edinburgh: Edinburgh University Press.

Mir, Mustansir. 1995. "Sin." In *The Oxford Encyclopaedia of the Modern Islamic World*, ed. John L. Esposito. Oxford and New York: Oxford University Press.

Mitchell, Richard Paul. 1993. *The Society of the Muslim Brothers*. New York and Oxford: Oxford University Press.

Mitchell, Timothy. 1990. "L'Experience de l'Emprisonment dans le Discourse Islamiste." In *Intellectuels et Militans de l'Islam Contemporain*, eds Gilles Kepel and Yann Richard. Paris: Seuil.

Mohi El Din, Khaled. 1995. *Memoirs of a Revolution*. Cairo: American University Press.

Moussalli, Ahmad. 1992. *Radical Islamic Fundamentalism. The Ideological and Political Discourse of Sayyid Qutb*. Beirut: American University of Beirut.

Moussalli, Ahmad S. 1999a. Historical Dictionary of Islamist Fundamentalist Movements in the Arab World, Iran and Turkey. Lanham and London: Scarecrow.

Moussalli, Ahmad S. 1999b. *Moderate and Radical Islamic Fundamentalism. The Quest for Modernity, Legitimacy, and the Islamic State*. Gainesville, FL: University of Florida.

Muhammad, Mahfuz. 1988. *Alladhina Zulimu. al-Tanzimat al-Islamiyya fi Misr*. London: Riad El-Rayyes Books.

Muñoz, Gema Martin. 1999. *Islam, Modernism and the West. Cultural and Political Relations at the End of the Millenium*. London, New York: I.B. Tauris.

al-Nadwi, Abu al-Hasan 'Ali al-Hasani. 1980. *Madha Khasira al-'Alam bi'Inhitat al-Muslimin*. Kuwait: Dar al-Qalam.

Nafi, Basheer M. 1998. *Arabism, Islamism and the Palestine Question, 1908–41. A Political History*. Reading: Ithaka.

Nafi, Basheer M. 2004. "The Rise of Islamic Reformist Thought and its Challenge to Traditional Islam." In *Islamic Thought in the Twentieth Century*, eds Suha Taji-Farouki and Nafi M. Basheer. New York: St. Martin's Press.

al-Nawawi, Jahya ibn Sharaf al-Din. 1977. *al-Arb'in al-Nawawiyya. al-Nawawi's Forty Hadith*. Stuttgart: Ernst Klett.

Nietzsche, Friedrich. 1990. *Beyond Good and Evil*. London: Penguin Books.

Nietzsche, Friedrich. 1996. *On the Genealogy of Morals*. Oxford: Oxford University Press.

Pearl, David Stephen. 1995. "Hudud." In *The Oxford Encyclopaedia of the Modern Islamic World,* ed. John L. Esposito. Oxford: Oxford University Press

Peters, Rudolph. 1988. "Divine Law or Man-Made Law?" *Arab Law Quarterly* 3(3): 231–59.

Peters, Rudolph. 2004. *The Jihad in Classical and Modern Islam: A Reader*. Princeton, NJ: Markus Wiener Publishers.

Peters, Rudolph. 2005. *Crime and Punishment in Islamic Law: Theory and Practice from the Sixteenth to the Twenty-first Century*. Cambridge: Cambridge University Press.

Piscatori, John. 1988. *Islam in a World of Nation States*. Cambridge: Cambridge University Press.

al-Qaradawi, Yusuf. 1985. *al-Zahirat al-Ghulu fi al-Takfir*. Kuwait: n.p.

al-Qaradawi, Yusuf. 1987. *Islamic Awakening. Between Rejection and Extremism*. London: Zain International.

Qutb, Muhammad 'Ali. 1974. *Sayyid Qutb: al-Shahid al-A'zal*. Cairo: n.p.

Qutb, Sayyid. 1949. *al-'Adala al-Ijtima'iyya fi al-Islam*. Cairo: n.p.

Qutb, Sayyid. 1974. *al-'Adala al-Ijtima'iyya fi al-Islam*. Cairo, Beirut: Dar al-Shuruq.

Qutb, Sayyid. 1978. *Khasa'is al-Tasawwur al-Islami wa Muqawimatihi*. Beirut and Damascus: Dar al-Shuruq.

Qutb, Sayyid. 1979. *Fi Zilal al-Qur'an*. Cairo and Beirut: Dar al-Shuruq.

Qutb, Sayyid. 1991. *The Islamic Concept and its Charateristics*. Indianapolis: American Trust Publications.

Qutb, Sayyid. 1992. *Dirasat al-Islamiyya*. Cairo: Dar al-Shuruq.

Qutb, Sayyid. 1993a. *Ma'alim fi al-Tariq*. Beirut: Dar al-Shuruq.

Qutb, Sayyid. 1993b. *Milestones*. Indianapolis: American Trust Publication.

Qutb, Sayyid. 1996. *Sayyid Qutb and Islamic Activism: a Translation and Critical Analysis of Social Justice in Islam*. Leiden: Brill.

Qutb, Sayyid. n.y. *Li'Madha A'damuni?* Jiddah: al-Sharika al-Sa'udiyya li'l-Abhath wa al-Taswiq.

Rahman, Fazlur. 2002. *Islam*. London and Chicago: University of Chicago Press.

Rahnema, Ali, ed. 1994. *Pioneers of Islamic Revival*. London: Zed Books.

Ra'if, Ahmad. 1986. *al-Bawwaba al-Sauda'. Safahat min al-Tarikh al-Ikhwan al-Muslimin*. Cairo: al-Zahra' li'l-I'lam al-'Arabi.

Ramadan, 'Abd al-'Azim. 1982. *al-Ikhwan al-Muslimun wa al-Tanzim al-Sirri*. Cairo: Maktab Madbuli.

Ramadan, Abdel Azim. 1993. "Fundamentalist Influence in Egypt. The Strategies of the Muslim Brotherhood and the Takfir Groups." In *Fundamentalism and the State. Remaking Polities, Economy and Militance*, eds Martin E. Marty and R. Scott Appelby. Chicago: University of Chicago Press.

Ramadan, Tariq. 2004. *Western Muslims and the Future of Islam*. Oxford, New York: Oxford University Press.

al-Rayyis, Muhammad Diya' al-Din. 1966. *al-Nazariyya li'l-Siyasa al-Islamiyya*. Cairo: Dar al-Ma'aruf.

Reid, Donald M. 1990. *Cairo University and the Making of Modern Egypt*. Cambridge: Cambridge University Press.

Reinhard, Kevin A. 1995a. "Fard Al-'Ayn." In *The Oxford Encyclopaedia of the Modern Islamic World*, ed. John L. Esposito. New York and Oxford: Oxford University Press.

Reinhard, Kevin A. 1995b. "Fard al-Kifaya." In *The Oxford Encyclopaedia of the Modern Islamic World*, ed. John L. Esposito. Oxford and New York: Oxford University Press.

Rida, Muhammad Rashid. 1988. *al-Khilafa aw al-Imama al-'Uzma'. Mabahith Shari'a*. Cairo: al-Zahra li'l-I'lam al-'Arabi.

Rippin, Andrew. 1999. *Muslims: Their Religious Beliefs and Practices*. London: Routledge.

Rizq, Jabir. 1977. *Madhabih al-Ikhwan fi Sujun Nasir*. Cairo: Dar al-I'tisam.

Rizq, Jabir. 1991. *Hasan al-Hudaybi. al-Imam al-Mumtahan*. Cairo: Dar al-Liwa' li' l-Tiba'a wa al-Nashr wa al-Tawzi'.

Robinson, Chase F. 2003. *Islamic Historiography*. Cambridge, New York: Cambridge University Press.

Roy, Olivier. 1994. *The Failure of Political Islam*. Cambridge, MA: Harvard University Press.

Roy, Olivier. 2004. *Globalized Islam. The Search for a New Ummah*. New York: Columbia University Press.

Rubin, Barry. 1990. *Islamic Fundamentalism in Egyptian Politics*. Basingstoke: Macmillan.

Sachedina, Abdulaziz Abdulhussein. 1988. *The Just Ruler in Shi'ite Islam. The Comprehensive Authority of the Jurist in Imamite Jurisprudence*. New York: Oxford University Press.

al-Sadat, Anwar. 1954. *Safahat Majhula*. Cairo: n.p.

al-Sadat, Anwar. 1956. *Qissa al-Thaura al-Kamila*. Cairo: n.p.

Saeed, Abdullah. 2006. *Islamic Thought: An Introduction*. London: Routledge.

Saeed, Abdullah and Hassan Saeed, eds. 2004. *Freedom of Religion, Apostasy and Islam*. Aldershot: Ashgate.

Said, Edward. 1995. *Orientalism: Western Conceptions of the Orient*. London: Penguin.

Sandowski, Yahya. 1993. "The New Orientalism and the Democracy Debate." *Middle East Report* 184: 14–21.

al-Sayyid, Yusuf. 1994. *al-Ikhwan al-Muslimun: hal Hiyya Sahwa Islamiyya?* Ma'adi: Markaz al-Mahrusa li'l-Nashr wa al-Khidmat al-Sahafiyya wa al-Ma'lumat.

Schacht, Joseph. 1950. *The Origins of Muhammadan Jurisprudence*. Oxford: Clarendon Press.

Schacht, Joseph. 1964. *An Introduction to Islamic Law*. Oxford: Clarendon Press.

Schacht, Joseph. 1965. "Ahkam." In *Encyclopaedia of Islam*. Leiden: Brill.

Schacht, Joseph. 1966. *Introduction to Islamic Law*. Oxford: Oxford University Press.

Schulze, Reinhard. 1990. *Islamischer Internationalismus im 20. Jahrhundert. Untersuchungen zur Geschichte der Islamischen Weltliga*. Leiden: Brill.

Schulze, Reinhard. 2000. *A Modern History of the Islamic World*. London: I. B. Tauris.

Seyyid Vali, Reza Nasr. 1994a. "Mawdudi and the Jama'at-i Islami: The Origins, Theory and Practice of Islamic Revivalism." In *Pioneers of Islamic Revival*, ed. Ali Rahnema. London Zed Books.

Seyyid Vali, Reza Nasr. 1994b. *The Vanguard of Islamic Revolution. The Jam'at-i Islami of Pakistan*. Berkeley and Los Angeles: University of California Press.

Seyyid Vali, Reza Nasr. 1996. *Maududi and the Making of Islamic Revivalism*. New York and Oxford: Oxford University Press.

Shadi, Salah. 1981. *Safahat min al-Tarikh. Hasad al-'Umr*. Kuwait: Sharika al-Shu'a' li' l-Nashr.

al-Shafi'i, Muhammad ibn Idris. 1987. *al-Risala fi Usul al-Fiqh. Treatise on the Foundations of Islamic Jurisprudence*. Cambridge: Islamic Texts Society.

Shahrastani, Muhammad ibn 'Abd al-Karim. 1984. *Muslim Sects and Divisions. The Section on Muslim Sects in Kitab al-Milal wa 'l-Nihal*. London et al: Paul Kegan International.

Shaltut, Mahmud. 1961. "Le Socialism de Orient." *Orient* 20(5): 163–74.

Shaltut, Mahmud. 1987. *al-Islam. 'Aqida wa Shari'a*. Cairo and Beirut: Dar al-Shuruq.

Shepard, William. 1989. "Islam as a System in Later Writings of Sayyid Qutb." *Middle Eastern Studies* 25: 31–50.

Shepard, William E. 1996. "Muhammad Sa'id al-'Ashmawi and the Application of the Shar'ia in Egypt." *International Journal of Middle East Studies* 28: 39–58.

Shepard, William E. 2002. "Ignorance." In *Encyclopaedia of the Qur'an*, ed. J. D. McAuliffe. Leiden and Boston: Brill.

Siegman, H. 1964. "The State and the Individual in Sunni Islam." *The Muslim World* 64: 1.

al-Sisi, 'Abbas. 1987a. *Fi Qafilat al-Ikhwan al-Muslimin*, vol. 1. Alexandria: Dar al-Qubs li'l-Nashr wa al-Tawzi'.

al-Sisi, 'Abbas. 1987b. *Fi Qafilat al-Ikhwan al-Muslimin*, vol. 2. Alexandria: Dar al-Qubs li'l-Nashr wa al-Tawzi'.

al-Sisi, 'Abbas. 1989. *Fi Qafilat al-Ikhwan al-Muslimin*, vol. 3. Alexandria: Dar al-Qubs li'l-Nashr wa al-Tawzi'.

Sivan, Emmanuel. 1989. "Sunni Radicalism in the Middle East and the Iranian Revolution." *International Journal of Middle East Studies* 21: 1–30.

Sivan, Emmanuel. 1990. *Radical Islam. Medieval Theology and Modern Politics*. 2nd edn. New Haven and London: Yale University Press.

Skovgaard-Petersen, Jakob. 1997. *Defining Islam for the Egyptian State: Muftis and Fatwas of the Dar al-Ifta*. Leiden, New York and Koln: Brill.

Sonn, Tamara. 1995. "Tawhid." In *The Oxford Encyclopaedia of the Modern Islamic World*, ed. John L. Esposito. Oxford and New York: Oxford University Press.

Steppat, Fritz. 1965. "Der Muslim und die Obrigkeit." *Zeitschrift für Politik* 12(4): 319–32.

Taji-Farouki, Suha. 1996a. *The Fundamental Quest. Hizb al-Tahrir and the Search for the Islamic Caliphate*. London: Grey Seal.

Taji-Farouki, Suha. 1996b. "Islamic State Theories and Comtemporary Realities." In *Islamic Fundamentalism*, eds A. S. Sidahmed and A. Ehteshami. Boulder, CO and Oxford: Westview Press.

Thielmann, Jörn. 2003. *Nasr Hamid Abu Zaid und die wiedererfundene Hisba. Shari'a und Qanun im heutigen Ägypten*. Würzburg: Ergon.

Tibi, Bassam. 1995. "Authority and Legitimation" In *The Oxford Encyclopaedia of the Modern Islamic World*, ed. John L. Esposito. New York and Oxford: Oxford University Press.

Tibi, Bassam. 1998. *The Challenge of Fundametalism, Political Islam and the New World Disorder*. Berkeley, CA: University of California Press.

Tripp, Charles. 1994. "Sayyid Qutb: The Political Vision." In *Pioneers of Islamic Revival*, ed. Ali Rahnema. London: Zed Books.

van Ess, Joseph. 1992. *Theologie and Gesellschaft im 2. und 3. Jahrhundert Hidschra. Eine Geschichte des relgiösen Denkens im Frühen Islam*, vol.1. Berlin and New York: Walter de Gryter.

Voll, John O. 1982. *Islam, Continuity and Change in the Modern World*. Westview: Longman.

Waldman, Marilyn Robinson. 1968. "The Development of the Concept of Kufr in the Qur'an." *Journal of the American Oriental Society* 88(3): 442–55.

Walker, Paul E. 1995. "Taqiya." In *The Oxford Encyclopaedia of the Modern Islamic World*, ed. John L. Esposito. Oxford and New York: Oxford University Press.

Watt, W. Montgomery. 1948. *Free Will and Predestination in Early Islam*. London: Luzac.

Watt, W. Montgomery. 1961. *Islam and the Integration of Society*. London: Routledge and K.Paul.

Watt, W. Montgomery. 1985. *Islamic Philosophy and Theology*. Edinburgh: Edinburgh University Press.

Watt, W. Montgomery. 2002. *The Formative Period of Islamic Thought*. Oxford: Oneworld.

Wehr, Hans. 1976. *A Dictionary of Modern Written Arabic*. Beirut and London: Librairie du Liban.

Weiss, Bernard. 1995. "Taqlid." In *The Oxford Encyclopaedia of the Modern Islamic World*, ed. John L. Esposito. Oxford and New York: Oxford University Press.

Weiss, Bernard. 1998. *The Spirit of Islamic Law*. Athens: University of Georgia Press.

Wickham, Carrie Rosefsky. 2002. *Mobilizing Islam. Religion, Activism, and Political Change in Egypt*. New York: Columbia University Press.

Wiktorowicz, Quintan. 2004. *Islamic Activism: a Social Movement Theory Approach*. Bloomington, IN: Indiana University Press.

Wiktorowicz, Quintan. 2005. *Radical Islam Rising: Muslim Extremism in the West*. Oxford: Rowman and Littlefield Publishers.

Williams, John Alden. 1995a. "Khawarij." In *The Oxford Encyclopaedia of the Modern Islamic World*, ed. John L. Esposito. Oxford and New York: Oxford University Press.

Williams, John Alden. 1995b. "Fitnah." In *The Oxford Encyclopaedia of the Modern Islamic World*, ed. John L. Esposito. Oxford and New York: Oxford University Press.

Ya-Sin, Muhammad Naim. 2000. *Book of Emaan. According to the Classical Works of Shaikhul-Islam Ibn Taymiyah [d.728H – rahimahullaah]*. London: Firdous Ltd.

Zahmul, Ibrahim. 1985. *al-Ikhwan al-Muslimun*. Auraq Tarikhiyya. Cairo: n.p.

Zakariya, Foad. 1992. "Die Historizität von Shari'a – Interpretationen. Methodische Grundlagen fur ein sakuläres Verständnis des Islam." In *Gesichter des Islam*, ed. Haus der Kulturen der Welt. Berlin: Das Arabische Buch.

Zaki, Muhammad Shauqi. 1954. *al-Ikhwan al-Muslimun wa al-Mujtama' al-Misri*. Cairo: Dar al-Ansar.

Zaman. 1995. "Bid'ah." In *The Oxford Encyclopaedia of the Modern Islamic World*, ed. John L. Esposito. Oxford and New York: Oxford University Press.

Zebiri, Kate. 1993. *Mahmud Shaltut and Islamic Modernism*. Oxford: Clarendon Press.

Ziadeh, Farhat J. 1995. "Criminal Law." In *The Oxford Encyclopaedia of the Modern Islamic World*, ed. John L. Esposito. Oxford and New York: Oxford University Press.

Zollner, Barbara. 2007. "Prison Talk: The Muslim Brotherhood's Internal Struggle During Gamal Abdel Nasser's Persecution, 1954 to 1971." *International Journal of Middle East Studies* 39: 411–33.

Zubaida, Sami. 1993. *Islam, the People and the State. Political Ideas and Movements in the Middle East*. London and New York: I.B. Tauris.

Newspapers

28 August 1952. In *al-Misri*. Cairo.

15 January 1954a. In *al-Ahram*. Cairo.

15 January 1954b. In *al-Jumhuriyya*. Cairo.

1 March 1954. In *The Times*. London.

5 March 1954. In *The Times*. London.

7 March 1954. In *The Times*. London.

9 March 1954. In *The Times*. London.

6 April 1954. In *The Times*. London.

18 April 1954. In *The Times*. London.

27 July 1954. In *The Times*. London.

28 March 1954. In *The Times*. London.

28 July 1954. In *The Times*. London.

28 August 1954. In *al-Jumhuriyya*. Cairo.

16 September 1954. In *al-Jumhuriyya*. Cairo.

19 October 1954a. In *The Times*. London.

19 October 1954b. In *al-Jumhuriyya*. Cairo.

14 November 1954a. In *al-Jumhuriyya*. Cairo.

14 November 1954b. In *The Times*. London.

17 November 1954. In *al-Jumhuriyya*. Cairo.

14 May 1984. In *Ruz al-Yusuf*. Cairo.

5 July 1984. In *al-Wafd*. Cairo.

Websites

Bangash, Zafar. 1999. "Remembering Sayyid Qutb, an Islamic intellectual and leader of rare insight and integrity." www.muslimedia.com/archives/features99/qutb.htm.

Hafez, Sabry. 2002. "Torture, Imprisonment, and Political Assassination in the Arab Novel." http://leb.net/~aljadid/features/0838hafez.html.

al-Ikhwan al-Muslimun. "al-Banna' wa al-Ikhwan." www.ikhwanonline.com/Section. asp?ID=111.

al-Ikhwan al-Muslimun. "al-Mustashar Hasan al-Hudaybi." www.ikhwanonline.com/ Article.asp?ArtID=147&SecID=453.

al-Ikhwan al-Muslimun. "al-Safaha al-Ra'isiyya." www.ikhwanonline.com.

Kupferschmidt, Uri. 2005. "Literacy, illiteracy and censorship in the tradition of the Muslim Brotherhood." http://pagesperso-orange.fr/colloque.imprimes.mo/pdf/UKT0.pdf.

Muslim Brotherhood. "About MB. MB History." www.ikhwanweb.com/SectionsPage. asp?SectionID=115.

Muslim Brotherhood. "Chairman Message." www.ikhwanweb.com/SectionsPage. asp?SectionID=74.

Muslim Brotherhood. "Official English Website." www.ikhwanweb.com/.

Index

WeBuy Books

Order Date: 03/01/2019

Marketplace Order #: 532001732
Marketplace: Abebooks
Customer Name: Muhammed Kamrul Hasan

Order Number: 10092298

Items:

The Muslim Brotherhood (Routledge Studies in Political Islam)
Zollner, Barbara

1   SKU: mon00009297533   W6-1-14-001-001-2318   Good   £7.94
     ISBN: 9780415664172 - Books
     Notes: Ex   library   copy   with   usual
     stamps/stickers

                                                              Subtotal: £7.94
                                                              Shipping: £0.00
Notes: Total: £7.94

Thanks for your order!

We value our customer feedback and we want to make sure you're happy. If you're pleased with your order and the service we provided, can we ask you to leave positive feedback on the marketplace? If you are unhappy for any reason at all, please contact us at sales@webuybooks.co.uk and give us the opportunity to put it right for you. We can't fix it if we don't know about it.

Thanks again for your order and we hope to see your custom again at WeBuyBooks.

WeBuyBooks

sales@webuybooks.co.uk   www.webuybooks.co.uk

Unit 11 Hugh Business Park, Bacup Road, Waterfoot, Lancashire, BB4 7BT, UK

Margin scheme second-hand goods VAT Number GB 901 5786 27

Lightning Source UK Ltd
Milton Keynes UK
UKOW06f1259280815

257701UK00005B/77/P